FOR DERRIDA

or Derrida

J. HILLIS MILLER

FORDHAM UNIVERSITY PRESS

New York *2009*

Fordham University Press has no responsibility for the
persistence or accuracy of URLs for external or third-party
Internet websites referred to in this publication and does not
guarantee that any content on such websites is, or will
remain, accurate or appropriate.

Library of Congress Cataloging-in-Publication Data

Miller, J. Hillis (Joseph Hillis), 1928–
For Derrida / J. Hillis Miller.
     p.   cm.
Includes bibliographical references and index.
ISBN 978–0-8232–3033–4 (cloth : alk. paper)
ISBN 978–0-8232–3034–1 (pbk. : alk. paper)
1. Derrida, Jacques—Criticism and interpretation.
I. Title.
B2430.D484M49   2009
194—dc22
2009003248

Printed in the United States of America
11 10 09 5 4 3 2 1
First edition

CONTENTS

ABBREVIATIONS OF WORKS
BY JACQUES DERRIDA

In the abbreviations, "e" means English, "f" means French. Alphabetization of the abbreviations below does not take these indications into account.

Ae   *Aporias*. Trans. Thomas Dutoit. Stanford, Calif.: Stanford University Press, 1993.

Af   *Apories*. Paris: Galilée, 1996.

AA   "Abraham, l'autre." In *Judéités: Questions pour Jacques Derrida*, ed. Joseph Cohen and Raphael Zagury-Orly, 11–44. Paris: Galilée, 2003.

AC   *L'autre cap, suivi de La démocratie ajournée*. Paris: Minuit, 1991.

AELe   *Adieu to Emmanuel Levinas*. Trans. Pascale-Anne Brault and Michael Naas. Stanford, Calif.: Stanford University Press, 1999.

AELf   *Adieu à Emmanuel Levinas*. Paris: Galilée, 1997.

AF   *Archive Fever: A Freudian Impression*. Trans. Eric Prenowitz. Chicago: University of Chicago Press, 1996.

AL   *Acts of Literature*. Ed. Derek Attridge. New York: Routledge, 1992.

AO   "Abraham, the Other." Trans. Gil Anidjar. In *Judeities: Questions for Jacques Derrida*, trans. Bettina Bergo and Michael B. Smith, ed. Bettina Bergo, Joseph Cohen, and Raphael Zagury-Orly, 1–35. New York: Fordham University Press, 2007.

AR   *Acts of Religion*. Ed. Gil Anidjar. New York: Routledge, 2002.

AT   "Of an Apocalyptic Tone Recently Adopted in Philosophy." Trans. John P. Leavey, Jr. *The Oxford Literary Review* 6, no. 2 (1984): 3–37.

AV   *Apprendre à vivre enfin*. Paris: Galilée, 2005.

B   *Béliers: Le dialogue ininterrompu: entre deux infinis, le poème*. Paris: Galilée, 2003.

BL   "Before the Law." Trans. Avital Ronell and Christine Roulston. In Jacques Derrida, *Acts of Literature*, ed. Derek Attridge, 181–220. New York: Routledge, 1992.

BS   "La bête et le souverain (deuxième année)." Private computer files, 2002–3. Since these are computer files, able to be manipulated in font and point size, I cannot give fixed page numbers. I have, however, indicated the number of the seminar from which a given citation is made. I thank Marguerite Derrida, Peggy Kamuf, and Geoff Bennington for granting me permission to cite these as yet unpublished seminars.

C   *Cinders*. Trans. Ned Lukacher. Bilingual edition. Lincoln: University of Nebraska Press, 1991.

Ce   "Circumfession." Trans. Geoffrey Bennington. In Geoffrey Bennington and Jacques Derrida, *Jacques Derrida*, 3–315. Chicago: University of Chicago Press, 1993.

Cf   "Circonfession." In Geoffrey Bennington and Jacques Derrida, *Jacques Derrida*, 7–291. Paris: Seuil, 1991.

CFU   *Chaque fois unique, la fin du monde*. Ed. Pascale-Anne Brault and Michael Naas. Paris: Galilée, 2003.

CP   *La carte postale: De Socrate à Freud et au-delà*. Paris: Flammarion, 1980.

C11S   *Le 'concept' du 11 septembre: Dialogues à New York (octobre-décembre 2001)*. With Jürgen Habermas and Giovanna Borradori. Paris: Galilée, 2004.

De   *Dissemination*. Trans. Barbara Johnson. Chicago: University of Chicago Press, 1981.

Df   *La Dissémination*. Paris: Seuil, 1972.

DDP   *Du droit à la philosophie*. Paris: Galilée, 1990.

DE   *De l'esprit: Heidegger et la question*. Paris: Galilée, 1987.

DG   *De la grammatologie*. Paris: Minuit, 1967.

Deme   "Demeure: Fiction and Testimony," In *The Instant of My Death / Demeure: Fiction and Testimony*, Maurice Blanchot / Jacques Derrida, trans. Elizabeth Rottenberg, 15–103. Stanford, Calif.: Stanford University Press, 2000.

Demf   *Demeure: Maurice Blanchot*. Paris: Galilée, 1998.

DL   "Préjugés: Devant la loi." In Jacques Derrida et. al., *La faculté de juger*, 87–139. Paris: Minuit, 1985.

DM   *Donner la mort*. Paris: Galilée, 1999.

DT   *Donner le temps: 1. La fausse monnaie*. Paris: Galilée, 1991.

ED   *L'écriture et la différence*. Paris: Seuil, 1967.

ETe   *Echographies of Television: Filmed Interviews.* With Bernard Stiegler. Trans. Jennifer Bajorek. Cambridge: Polity Press, 2002.

ETf   *Échographies: De la television—entretiens filmés.* With Bernard Stiegler. Paris: Galilée/Institut national de l'audiovisuel, 1996.

Fe   "Fors: The Anglish Words of Nicolas Abraham and Maria Torok." Trans. Barbara Johnson. In Nicolas Abraham and Maria Torok, *The Wolf Man's Magic Word: A Cryptonomy,* trans. Nicholas Rand, 7–73. Minneapolis: University of Minnesota Press, 1986.

Ff   "Fors: Les mots angles de Nicolas Abraham et Maria Torok." In Nicolas Abraham and Maria Torok, *Cryptonymie: Le verbier de l'Homme aux Loups,* 7–82. Paris: Aubier Flammarion, 1976.

FC   *feu la cendre.* Paris: des femmes, 1987.

FK   "Faith and Knowledge: The Two Sources of 'Religion' at the Limits of Reason Alone." Trans. Samuel Weber. In *Acts of Religion,* ed. Gil Anidjar, 42–101. New York: Routledge, 2002.

FLe   "Force of Law: The 'Mystical Foundation of Authority.'" Trans. Mary Quaintance. In *Deconstruction and the Possibility of Justice,* ed. Drucilla Cornell, Michel Rosenfeld, and David Gray Carlson, 3–67. New York: Routledge, 1992.

FLf   *Force de loi: Le "Fondement mystique de l'autorité."* Paris: Galilée, 1994.

FS   "Foi et savoir: Les deux sources de la 'religion' aux limites de la simple raison." In *La religion,* ed. Jacques Derrida and Gianni Vattimo, 9–86. Paris: Seuil, 1996.

Ge   *Glas.* Trans. John P. Leavey, Jr., and Richard Rand. Lincoln: University of Nebraska Press, 1986.

Gf   *Glas.* Paris: Galilée, 1974.

GII   "*Geschlecht* II: Heidegger's Hand." Trans. John P. Leavey, Jr. In *Deconstruction and Philosophy: The Texts of Jacques Derrida,* ed. John Sallis, 161–96. Chicago: University of Chicago Press, 1987.

GD   *The Gift of Death.* Trans. David Wills. Chicago: University of Chicago Press, 1995.

GS   *Il gusto del segreto.* With Maurizio Ferraris. Rome: Gius, Laterza and Figli Spa, 1997.

GT   *Given Time: 1. Counterfeit Money.* Trans. Peggy Kamuf. Chicago: University of Chicago Press, 1994.

H   *De l'hospitalité*. With Anne Dufourmantelle. Paris: Calmann-Levy, 1977.

IS   *Inconditionalité ou souveraineté: L'Université aux frontières de l'Europe*. Bilingual edition in French and Greek. Commentary by Dimitris Dimiroulis and Georges Veltsos. Notes by Vanghelis Bitsoris. Athens: Éditions Patakis, 2001.

JD   *Jacques Derrida*. Ed. Marie-Louise Mallet and Ginette Michaud. Paris: Éditions de l'Herne, 2004.

LIe   *Limited Inc*. Trans. Jeffrey Mehlman and Samuel Weber. Evanston, Ill.: Northwestern University Press, 1988.

LIf   *Limited Inc*. Ed. and trans. Elisabeth Weber. Paris: Galilée, 1990.

LLF   *Learning to Live Finally: An Interview with Jean Birnbaum*. Trans. Pascale-Anne Brault and Michael Naas. Hoboken, N.J.: Melville House Publishing, 2007.

LO/BL   "Living On / Border Lines." Trans. James Hulbert. In Harold Bloom, Paul de Man, Jacques Derrida, Geoffrey Hartman, and J. Hillis Miller, *Deconstruction and Criticism*, 75–176. New York: The Seabury Press, 1979.

LS   "Literature in Secret: An Impossible Filiation." Trans. David Wills. In *The Gift of Death*, 2d ed., and *Literature in Secret*, trans. David Wills, 119–58. Chicago: University of Chicago Press, 2008.

LT   *Le toucher, Jean-Luc Nancy*. Paris: Galilée, 2000.

Me   *Margins of Philosophy*. Trans. Alan Bass. Chicago: University of Chicago Press, 1986.

Mf   *Marges: de la philosophie*. Paris: Minuit, 1972.

MA   *Mémoires d'aveugle: L'autoportrait et autre ruines*. Paris: Éditions de la Réunion des musées nationaux, 1990.

MAPO   *Le monolinguisme de l'autre; ou, La prosthèse d'origine*. Paris: Galilée, 1996.

MB   *Memoirs of the Blind: The Self-Portrait and Other Ruins*. Trans. Pascale-Anne Brault and Michael Naas. Chicago: University of Chicago Press, 1993.

MC   "Mes chances: Au rendez-vous de quelques stéréophonies épicuriennes." *Cahiers Confrontation* 19 (1988): 19–45.

MCe   "My Chances / *Mes Chances*: A Rendezvous with Some Epicurean Stereophonies." In *Taking Chances: Derrida, Psychoanalysis, and Literature*, ed. Joseph H. Smith and William Kerrigan, 1–32. Baltimore: Johns Hopkins University Press, 1984.

MdA   *Mal d'archive*. Paris: Galilée, 1995.

MO   *Monolingualism of the Other; or, The Prosthesis of Origin*. Trans. Patrick Mensah. Stanford, Calif.: Stanford University Press, 1998.

MPdMe   *Memoires for Paul de Man*. Trans. Cecile Lindsay, Jonathan Culler, and Eduardo Cadava. New York: Columbia University Press, 1986.

MPdMf   *Mémoires pour Paul de Man*. Paris: Galilée, 1988.

OG   *Of Grammatology*. Trans. Gayatri Chakravorty Spivak. Corrected Edition. Baltimore: The Johns Hopkins University Press, 1998.

OH   *The Other Heading: Reflections on Today's Europe*. Trans. Pascale-Anne Brault and Michael Naas. Bloomington: Indiana University Press, 1992.

OS   *Of Spirit: Heidegger and the Question*. Trans. Geoffrey Bennington and Rachel Bowlby. Chicago: University of Chicago Press, 1989.

OT   *On Touching—Jean-Luc Nancy*. Trans. Christine Irizarry. Stanford, Calif.: Stanford University Press, 2005.

P   *Parages*. Paris: Galilée, 1986.

Pe   *Psyche: Inventions of the Other, Volume I*. Ed. Peggy Kamuf and Elizabeth Rottenberg. Stanford, Calif.: Stanford University Press, 2007.

Pf   *Psyché: Inventions de l'autre*. Paris: Galilée, 1987.

PIIe   *Psyche: Inventions of the Other, Volume II*. Ed. Peggy Kamuf and Elizabeth Rottenberg. Stanford, Calif.: Stanford University Press, 2008.

PIIf   *Psyché: Inventions de l'autre: II*. New augmented edition. Paris: Galilée, 2003.

PA   *Politiques de l'amitié*. Paris: Galilée, 1994.

PC   *The Post Card: From Socrates to Freud and Beyond*. Trans. Alan Bass. Chicago: University of Chicago Press, 1987.

PF   *Politics of Friendship*. Trans. George Collins. London: Verso, 1997.

PI   *Points . . . : Interviews, 1974–1994*. Trans. Peggy Kamuf and others. Stanford, Calif.: Stanford University Press, 1995.

PMe   *Paper Machine*. Trans. Rachel Bowlby. Stanford, Calif.: Stanford University Press, 2005.

PMf   *Papier Machine*. Paris: Galilée, 2001.

POOe   "Passions: 'An Oblique Offering.'" Trans. David Wood. In *On the Name*, ed. Thomas Dutoit, 3–31. Stanford, Calif.: Stanford University Press, 1995.

POOf   *Passions: "L'offrande oblique."* Paris: Galilée, 1993.

PS   *Points de suspension: Entretiens.* Ed. Elisabeth Weber. Paris: Galilée, 1992.

PTT   *Philosophy in a Time of Terror: Dialogues with Jürgen Habermas and Jacques Derrida.* With Jürgen Habermas and Giovanna Borradori. Chicago: University of Chicago Press, 2003.

R   "Rams: Uninterrupted Dialogue—Between Two Infinities, the Poem." Trans. Thomas Dutoit and Philippe Romanski. In *Sovereignties in Question: The Poetics of Paul Celan*, ed. Thomas Dutoit and Outi Pasanen, 135–63. New York: Fordham University Press, 2005.

Rog   *Rogues: Two Essays on Reason.* Trans. Pascale-Anne Brault and Michael Naas. Stanford, Calif.: Stanford University Press, 2005.

S   *Spurs: Nietzsche's Styles / Éperons: Les styles de Nietzsche.* Trans. Barbara Harlow. Introd. Stefano Agosti. Bilingual edition. Chicago: University of Chicago Press, 1979.

Sch   "Schibboleth: For Paul Celan." Trans. Joshua Wilner, with Thomas Dutoit. In *Sovereignties in Question: The Poetics of Paul Celan*, ed. Thomas Dutoit and Outi Pasanen, 1–64. New York: Fordham University Press, 2005.

SMe   *Specters of Marx: The State of the Debt, the Work of Mourning, and the New International.* Trans. Peggy Kamuf. New York: Routledge, 1994.

SMf   *Spectres de Marx: L'état de la dette, le travail du deuil, et la nouvelle Internationale.* Paris: Galilée, 1993.

SP   *Speech and Phenomena and Other Essays on Husserl's Theory of Signs.* Trans. David B. Allison. Evanston, Ill.: Northwestern University Press, 1973.

SPPC   *Schibboleth: Pour Paul Celan.* Paris: Galilée, 1986.

SSP   "Structure, Sign, and Play in the Discourse of the Human Sciences." In *The Structuralist Controversy: The Languages of Criticism and the Sciences of Man*, ed. Richard Macksey and Eugenio Donato, 247–72. Baltimore: The Johns Hopkins Press, 1970.

TA   *D'un ton apocalyptique adopté naguère en philosophie.* Paris: Galilée, 1983.

TP   *The Truth in Painting*. Trans. Geoff Bennington and Ian McLeod. Chicago: University of Chicago Press, 1987.

TR   "Typewriter Ribbon: Limited Ink (2) ('within such limits')." Trans. Peggy Kamuf. In *Material Events: Paul de Man and the Afterlife of Theory*, ed. Tom Cohen et al., 277–360. Minneapolis: University of Minnesota Press, 2001.

TS   *A Taste for the Secret*. With Maurizio Ferraris. Trans. Giacomo Donis. Ed. Giacomo Donis and David Webb. Cambridge: Polity, 2001.

TT   "The Time of a Thesis: Punctuations." Trans. Kevin McLaughlin. In *Philosophy in France Today*, ed. Alan Montefiore, 34–50. Cambridge: Cambridge University Press, 1983.

UCe   "The University Without Condition." Trans. Peggy Kamuf. In *Without Alibi*, ed. and trans. Peggy Kamuf, 202–37. Stanford, Calif.: Stanford University Press, 2002.

UCf   *L'Université sans condition*. Paris: Galilée, 2001.

UGe   "Ulysses Gramophone: Hear Say Yes in Joyce." Trans. Tina Kendall, rev. Shari Benstock and Derek Attridge. In *Acts of Literature*, ed. Derek Attridge, 253–309. New York: Routledge, 1992.

UGf   *Ulysse gramophone: Deux mots pour Joyce*. Paris: Galilée, 1987.

WA   *Without Alibi*. Ed. and trans. Peggy Kamuf. Stanford, Calif.: Stanford University Press, 2002.

WAP   *Who's Afraid of Philosophy: Right to Philosophy 1*. Trans. Jan Plug. Stanford, Calif.: Stanford University Press, 2002.

WD   *Writing and Difference*. Trans. Alan Bass. Chicago: University of Chicago Press, 1978.

WM   *The Work of Mourning*. Ed. Pascale-Anne Brault and Michael Naas. Chicago: University of Chicago Press, 2001.

Vf   *Voyous: Deux essays sur la raison*. Paris: Galilée, 2003.

VP1f   *La voix et le phénomène*. Paris: Presses Universitaires de France, 1967.

VP2   *La Vérité en peinture*. Paris: Flammarion, 1978.

Methode ist Umweg [Method is detour].

—WALTER BENJAMIN

All these chapters but the first have been written in the years since Derrida died. All were "commissioned" for some special issue of a journal, for some book on Derrida, or for some conference on his work. Though considerable reference is made to Derrida's earlier work, this is primarily a book about his later books and essays. It only gradually dawned on me that they might be revised and gathered together as a book "for Derrida." The chapters are organized here primarily in the order of their composition as occasional essays. My revision of them has involved regularizing modes of reference, cutting repetition, making links between chapters explicit, adding new material here and there, and other forms of reshaping. I have done much rereading of Derrida for these revisions.

Nevertheless, the chapters do not progress forward to tell a sequential story. They are, rather, a series of perspectives on the heterogeneity of Derrida's work or forays into that heterogeneity. They do this by way of different key Derridean words or themes, a different one in each essay, "irresponsibilization" for one, "touching" for another, *destinerrance* for another, "remains [*restes*]" for another, and so on. Each use of these words, however, reaches out rapidly to include, in a singular way each time, not only a local cluster or configuration of related Derridean words or concepts but also, with dismaying rapidity, the whole enormous "database" of Derrida's writings, published and unpublished.

I have no doubt that my procedures in these chapters have been unconsciously influenced by new ways of research made possible by the "electronic revolution." These are changes in ways of reading facilitated by what might be called, in modification of Walter Benjamin's famous title, "the work of reading and writing in the age of digital reproduction."[1] I have followed recurrences of the word *reste* ("remainder") or the word *deuil* ("mourning") in Derrida's work as though I were "searching it" in an electronic database of the sort that does not yet exist for Derrida's writings. Perhaps some day it will. Of course, when you find something that way, you still need to interpret it. Those who google will know what I mean. A conspicuous feature of the World Wide Web or of individual databases, such as all Derrida's works hypothetically on a site in the Web, is that every item is present simultaneously, both infinitely near, a mouse-click away from wherever your computer happens to be, and infinitely distant, by virtue of having become "virtual," impalpable, intangible, so many bits and bytes flying around in Cyberspace, potentially everywhere at once. This ubiquity means that Cyberspace is not a space that can be mapped by any visible geometry. The figures we use for it only tame its strangeness by beguiling us into thinking of it as a three-dimensional Euclidian space.

Geoffrey Bennington, already in 1991, when the Internet was in its infancy, calls his comprehensive essay on Derrida's works up to that point "Derridabase." His goal, he says, is, with information theory as his model, to "systematize" Derrida's work to the point where he can make of it "an interactive program [*un logiciel interactif*] which, in spite of its difficulty, would in principle be accessible to any user."[2] Bennington, at that time, could produce only a simulacrum of such an electronic Derridabase, that is, he wrote a text that offers itself to be read in linear sequence within a printed book. Derrida himself has, well after Bennington's work, reflected at length on the changes effected on writing and reading by the electronic revolution. See *Paper Machine* (*Papier machine*). (*Papier machine*, by the way, means "typing paper.") We could now have on the Web, in all the actuality of its virtuality, what Bennington could only dream of, and simulate, in 1991.

Much earlier in the twentieth century, Marcel Proust, in his preface to a translation into French of John Ruskin's *The Bible at Amiens*, spoke of his essay as providing for the reader an "improvised" or, as we would say today, "virtual" memory of other passages in Ruskin that echo a given passage in *The Bible of Amiens*.[3] Georges Poulet, following Proust, developed a sophisticated thematic criticism drawing together passages from everywhere in a given author's works, including letters and other "extra-literary" texts, that express versions of a certain theme. Both Ruskin and Poulet imply that an ideal reader should have total recall of all a writer's works, so that a given word or phrase will make her or him think instantly of all the other examples of that detail. Criticism is a prosthetic substitute for that total memory. A fully searchable CD-ROM is now available that contains all thirty-nine volumes of the comprehensive Cook and Wedde-rburn edition of Ruskin's writings, illustrations and all. You no longer have to remember anything, with Proustian extravagance. The computer RAM, or "random access memory," harnessed to that CD, will remember for you. Many works by Ruskin are of course available online, for example at Project Guttenberg (http://www.gutenberg.org/browse/authors/r#a359), including *The Bible of Amiens* (http://www.gutenberg.org/files/24428/24428-8.txt). By no means all Ruskin's works have been digitized, how-ever, and they are not collectively searchable online. In addition, as I have said, you still must read and interpret what the computer finds for you. We do not yet even have a Cook and Wedderburn–like edition of all Der-rida's works, much less a searchable CD-ROM. Critics, like me, for in-stance, are still, happily or unhappily, left on their own, at the mercy of their own fallible memories. I have no grandiose goal of all-inclusiveness in the essays in this book. My primary desire is to encourage people to read Derrida for themselves, with the same "micrological" care he bestowed on Hegel, on Freud, on Celan, on Nancy, and on so many other writers.

Each chapter of this book can be read separately, as a "stand alone." Each chapter has its own integrity, in spite of cross-references to other chapters. The book as a whole is more like a collection of songs by the same performer downloaded on iTunes than like a consecutive opera, a work that tells a sequential story, with a beginning, middle, and end. My figure of iTunes songs indicates the way this book is a product of digital technology. It depends in various ways, as I have suggested, on having been written on a computer connected to the Internet. What I have writ-ten has been open, for example, to more or less interminable on-screen revision and interpolation, such as this sentence. Each chapter could be called a "gloss" on a given Derridean word or theme. "Gloss," as Leland de la Durantaye reminds me, is derived from Latin *glossa*, from a Greek word meaning "tongue."[4] A "gloss" originally named a hard word requir-ing commentary, as though it were an enigmatic term in a given tongue that sticks on the tongue. The meaning of "gloss" then transferred by metonymic drifting from the word to the commentary itself. Together, the twelve chapters here make, to borrow a formulation from Derrida's *Le toucher*, "the closure of a combinatory play around a vacant center [*la clô-ture d'une combinatoire au centre vacant*]" (OT, 16, trans. modified; LT, 28). That vacant center Derrida calls *le tout autre*, the wholly other.

Although I read almost all of Derrida's books and essays originally in French, I have cited the existing translations where they are available.

Though I have minimized citation of words and phrases in French, Derrida, after all, wrote in that language. I have put in bits of French where something idiomatic and hard to translate exists in the French. In most cases I have indicated the page numbers in the French original, so that those who wish to do so may look up the French. Those who "ignore French," to borrow Paul de Man's quaint Gallicism for his ignorance of Russian,[5] may ignore my French interpolations in citations. Problems of translation abound in Derrida's work, though Derrida was lucky in having gifted translators. David Wills, for example, in *The Gift of Death* (GD, 82), translates Derrida's *tout autre est tout autre* as "every other (one) is every (bit) other," whereas Peggy Kamuf renders the second part of the phrase as "altogether other" (UCe, 235). I have preferred "every other is wholly other." Derrida spends several pages in *The Gift of Death* (*Donner la mort*) teasing out different possible meanings of this sentence (GD, 82–88; DM, 114–22). My guiding assumption in all the chapters has been that Derrida should be read in terms of such specificities, taking each more or less as far as it will go, rather than by way of an attempt at global generalizations.

My chief goal has been, to borrow a phrase from Wallace Stevens, "plainly to propound" what Derrida says.[6] I want, above all, to render Derrida's writings justice. It should be remembered, however, that, according to Derrida himself, every rendering of justice is also a transformative interpretation. A collection of essays like this book is not a substitute for reading Derrida for oneself. I hope this gathering will encourage my readers to do just that. This book is for Derrida in the double sense of "in memory of Derrida, dedicated to Derrida," and "on behalf of Derrida."

Reworking these essays to be gathered in that portentous thing, "a book," I have been struck by how partial they are. I mean "partial" in two senses. They are "partial to Derrida," on his side, taking his part, gratefully submitting themselves to the demand made by Derrida's writings to be read, slowly, carefully, faithfully, with close attention to semantic detail. Only occasionally does there appear in my glosses the latent smile of an irony, or an expression of amazement at how counter-intuitive, how much against the millennial Western tradition of common sense and reason, what Derrida says is. It would be a mistake to underestimate how difficult it is to be, without reservation, "partial to Derrida."

These essays also now strike me as "partial" also in the sense that they are only incomplete sketches of what might have been said on their topics. The work seems all to do over, in an interminable reading and rereading, writing and rewriting. Nevertheless, I have greatly enjoyed writing these essays. I dare to hope that some of that pleasure will carry over to my readers.

In substantially revising, reworking, and augmenting these "occasional" essays to make them more or less fit together within the covers of a book, I have recognized that, though they deal with many different topics in Derrida's work, as was dictated by the topics of the conferences or journal issues they were destined for—Derrida's legacy, his politics, his characteristic styles, his notions about decision or responsibility, and so on—nevertheless, whatever the ostensible topic, what I have written for Derrida has been, more or less unconsciously, oriented by two main concerns.

1. Derrida's special way of "being toward death," which includes his resolutely saying "Yes" to life, as he says in his last interview, in *Le Monde*: "Everything I say—at least from 'Pas' (in *Parages* [P, 19–116]) on—about survival as a complication of the opposition life/death proceeds in me from an unconditional affirmation of life. This surviving is life beyond life, life more than life, and my discourse is not a discourse of death, but, on the contrary, the affirmation of a living being who prefers living and thus surviving to death, because survival is not simply that which remains but the most intense life possible" (LLF, 51–52).

2. Derrida's wavering between a resolute quasi-solipsism and a conviction that some "wholly other" or other may nevertheless break through those monadic walls and "call" or "command" us. My belated recognition of the latter theme is expressed in an interpolation added as late as February 4, 2008, in Chapter 3, apropos of an extraordinary passage in "Telepathy" about the way each one of us has, must have, but cannot have, a strange sort of internal television receiver (Derrida's figure) allowing us to receive messages from the hidden hearts and thoughts of other people. My book could perhaps be seen as an attempt on my part to activate such a magic TV.

I am grateful to all those who have allowed me to reuse these essays in revised form in the present book. I also thank Helen Tartar for encouraging me to get on with it and for her enormously valuable help at the copyediting stage. This book, like a number of my previous books, owes an unrepayable debt to her for instigating revisions made in the light of her thoughtful reading, comments, and suggestions.

Sedgwick, Maine
February 28, 2008;
December 24, 2008

ACKNOWLEDGMENTS

Chapter 1, in an earlier version, was originally published in a French translation by Patrick Di Mascio, as "Une profession de foi," in a special number of *L'Herne*, no. 83 of essays in homage to Derrida and by Derrida, entitled *Jacques Derrida*, ed. Marie-Louise Mallet and Ginette Michaud (Paris: Éditions de l'Herne, 2004), 307–11. I thank the translator and I thank also Marie-Louise Mallet for inviting me to contribute to this volume.

Chapter 2, in its initial form, was prepared for the conference Rhetoric, Politics, Ethics at the University of Ghent on April 21–23, 2005. I thank Gert Buelens, Ortwin De Graef, and Sigi Jottkandt for inviting me to participate in this event. Papers from the conference are scheduled to be published by Palgrave-Macmillan in a volume entitled *The Catastrophic Imperative: Time, Subjectivity and Memory in Contemporary Thought*, ed. Dominiek Hoens, Sigi Jöttkandt and Gert Buelens..

Chapter 3 was published, in an initial form, as "Derrida's *Destinerrance*" in a special Derrida memorial issue of *Modern Language Notes* 121 (2006), 893–910. I am grateful to Professor Lawrence D. Kritzman, of Dartmouth College, for inviting me to contribute an essay to this collection. I also thank The Johns Hopkins University Press. Julian Wolfreys and John P. Leavey, Jr., helped me to track down, in their wandering appearance and reappearance, examples of the word *destinerrance* in Derrida's work.

Chapter 4 was given in an earlier form as a lecture on May 6, 2005, in a lecture series on Derrida at the Humanities Institute at Birkbeck College, University of London. This lecture has now been published as "The Late Derrida," in *Adieu Derrida*, ed. Costas Douzinas (London: Palgrave-Macmillan, 2007), 134–52. I thank Costas Douzinas and Slavoj Žižek for inviting me to participate in this series.

Chapter 5, in an earlier form, appeared in *After Derrida*, a special issue of *Mosaic* 39, no. 3 (September 2006): 97–211. I thank Dawne McCance, the editor of *Mosaic*, for inviting me to participate in this issue and for permitting me to reuse it in revised form.

Chapter 6 appeared, in an earlier form, in *The Late Derrida*, ed. W. J. T. Mitchell and Arnold I. Davidson, a special issue of *Critical Inquiry* 33, no. 2 (Winter 2007): 248. I am, grateful to W. J. T. Mitchell for inviting me to contribute to this issue and to him and the editorial board of *Critical Inquiry* for a number of helpful suggestions for revision of the original essay.

Chapter 7 was originally prepared, in a much shorter form, as an exercise in "disambiguation," for the conference Performativity in Music and Literature at the University of Oslo, on May 3–5, 2006. I am grateful to Professor Christian Refsum for giving me an opportunity to think through these issues. The lecture was subsequently published, in a form somewhat different from the chapter here, as "Performativity as Performance / Performativity as Speech Act: Derrida's Special Theory of Performativity," in *Late Derrida*, ed. Ian Balfour, a special issue of *The South Atlantic Quarterly* 106, no. 2 (Spring 2007): 219–35. I thank Ian Balfour for inviting me to participate in this issue and thank him and Duke University Press for allowing me to reuse this material in a considerably revised and extended form. The section of this chapter on *Daniel Deronda* was presented, in an earlier form, at a conference held June 25, 26, 2007 at the University of Bergen, Norway, sponsored by the research group TAS (Text, Action, and Space). I am grateful to Lars Saetre for encouraging me to think further about the two performativities as they are dramatized in *Daniel Deronda*.

The original version of Chapter 8 was prepared for a lecture at the conference Thinking Institutions at the University of Portsmouth. It was subsequently published as "'Don't Count Me In': Derrida's Refraining," in *Thinking Institutions*, ed. Simon Morgan Wortham, a special issue of *Textual Practice* 21, no. 2 (2007): 279–94, and then, under the same title, in *Encountering Derrida: Legacies and Futures of Deconstruction*, ed. Allison Weiner and Simon Morgan Wortham (London: Continuum, 2007), 45–57

Chapter 9 was originally prepared as a lecture for the conference Irresponsibility at the Nanyang Technological University in Singapore on September 28–30, 2006. I thank Brendan Quigley for inviting me to participate in this conference. The lecture, an earlier form of my Chapter 9, will appear in *Literature and Ethics: Questions of Responsibility in Literary Studies*, eds. D. Jernigan, N. Murphy, B. Quigley, and T. Wagner (Amherst: Cambria Press, 2009). A section of this chapter in an earlier form was presented as a lecture entitled "Literature and Scripture: An Impossible Filiation" at Calvin College on October 18 , 2007.

Chapter 10 was originally prepared in an earlier form for a conference on Derrida's work organized by Dragan Kujundzic at the University of

Florida in Gainesville, on October 8–11, 2006. I thank Professor Kujundzic for inviting me to participate in this conference. My essay will also appear in a journal issue and volume edited by Professor Kujundzic.

Chapter 11 was initially prepared for a conference on Jacques Derrida and Jean-Luc Nancy held at Leeds University on March 8–9, 2007. In my absence, Tom Cohen presented orally an earlier and shorter version of the chapter's middle section, "Touching Derrida Touching Nancy: The Main Traits of Derrida's Hand." This has appeared in *Derrida Today* 1, no. 2, 145–66, published by Edinburgh University Press. I thank Martin McQuillan for inviting me to this conference and Tom Cohen for, so I have heard, admirably ventiloquizing me. The original version has been elaborately revised for this book. I thank John Barton for providing me with the epigraph from Sir Philip Sydney.

Chapter 12 was prepared for the conference Mourning and Its Hospitalities (after . . .), held at the University of Queensland, in Brisbane, Australia, on July 19–20, 2007. I thank Judith Seaboyer and Tony Thwaites for organizing this conference and for inviting me to present a paper. Some of the conference papers, including mine, will probably eventually appear as a book. My original paper has been substantially extended and revised for this book.

FOR DERRIDA

CHAPTER I

A Profession of Faith

My first encounter with Jacques Derrida was a decisive moment in my life.[1] I met him at the famous Johns Hopkins University international colloquium The Languages of Criticism and the Sciences of Man, in October 1966. I missed his lecture "Structure, Sign, and Play in the Discourse of the Human Sciences" ("La structure, le signe et le jeu dans le discours des sciences humaines") (SSP, also in WD, 278–93; ED, 409–18). I could not go because I had a class to teach at that hour. I did hear, however, Derrida's interventions in the discussions of other papers. I also read later, in the translated and published papers and discussions from the conference, his shocking (to me then) assertion, after his paper, in response to a challenge from a phenomenologist, Serge Doubrovsky, that "I don't believe that anything like perception exists. . . . I don't believe that there is any perception" (SSP, 272).

I met my colleague and friend Georges Poulet in the Hopkins quadrangle just after Derrida's lecture. Poulet told me that Derrida's lecture was opposed to everything to which his own work (that is, Poulet's) was committed. Poulet at that time was writing on circles and centers, whereas Derrida's talk was about decentering. Nevertheless, said Poulet, it was the most important lecture of the conference by far, even though Jacques Lacan, Roland Barthes, and many other distinguished intellectuals were

also giving papers. I have always remembered Poulet's insight and generosity in saying that. He was right. Derrida's lecture marked the moment
of the entry of so-called deconstruction into U.S. intellectual life. I had
already, however, begun to read Derrida, on Eugenio Donato's recommendation: the long, two-part essay published in *Critique* in December
1965 and January 1966 that was developed into the first part of *Of Grammatology* (*De la grammatologie*).

When Derrida came a couple of years later as a visiting professor to
Hopkins, I went to his first seminar. I went just to see whether I could
understand his spoken French. It was the seminar contrasting Plato on
mimesis and Mallarmé's "Mimique," part of "The Double Session" ("La
double séance") (De, 175–285; Df, 201–317). I thought, and still think, it
was an absolutely brilliant seminar. I still have somewhere the sheet he
passed out juxtaposing "Mimique" and a passage from Plato's *Philebus*. I
faithfully attended Derrida's seminars thereafter, first at Hopkins, then at
Yale, then at the University of California at Irvine. We began to have
lunch together at Hopkins and continued that practice for over forty years
of unclouded friendship. Derrida and his writings have been major intellectual influences on me.

One of the strongest Derridean influences on my thinking has been his
notion of the "wholly other." This became a more and more salient motif
in Derrida's work. Just what he means by "the wholly other," *le tout autre*,
is not all that easy to grasp. For many people, it is even more difficult to
accept or to endorse with a profession of faith or a pledge of allegiance.
One way to approach the Derridean wholly other is by way of his distinction between sovereignty and unconditionality. Unconditionality is, for
Derrida, a name for the research university's hypothetical freedom from
outside interference. Derrida defines the university's unconditionality as
the privilege without penalty to put everything in question, even to put in
question the right to put everything in question.

In the interview with Derek Attridge that forms the first essay in the
volume of Derrida's essays on literature Attridge gathered in English
translation and called *Acts of Literature* (AL, 33–75), Derrida defines literature in much the same way as he defines the university in more recent
lectures, for example, in "The University Without Condition" (*L'Université sans condition*), originally a Presidential Lecture at Stanford, and in a
related essay, the speech he gave on receiving an honorary degree from
the University of Pantion in Athens in 1999. That essay is entitled "Inconditionalité ou souveraineté: L'Université aux frontiers de l'Europe" (IS,
14–67).

Both lectures are based on a fundamental distinction between sovereignty and what Derrida calls (the word is a neologism in English) "unconditionality." What is the difference? Sovereignty, says Derrida, is a theologically based "phantasm." It is something that looks like it is there, but is not there. Sovereignty has three features. (1) The sovereign is above the law. He or she is free to subvert the law, as in the act of pardon. (2) The concept of sovereignty cannot be dissociated from the idea of the nation-state. (3) The sovereign is God's vicar, appointed by God, authorized by God. Even in a country like the United States, a country that was founded on the principle of the separation of church and state, the Pledge of Allegiance to the flag defines the United States as "one nation, under God." All U.S. citizens were exhorted to sing "God Bless America" after the World Trade Center destruction of 9/11. George W. Bush apparently thinks of himself as appointed by God to preserve the United States from the "threat of terrorism." Such assumptions are a "phantasm," a ghost in broad daylight, since no verifiable data exists on which to base an assumption that God is on the United States' side, any more than any data exists supporting the "terrorists'" assumption that Allah was on their side when they blew up the World Trade Center towers, or when they kill another American soldier in Iraq. Being told that sovereignty is a phantasm by no means cures one of faith in it. Far from it. The ghost of sovereignty always returns, as a "revenant."

Unconditionality has, apparently, no such suspect theological basis. Literature is dependent in its modern form on the rise of constitutional democracies in the West from the seventeenth century on, and on the unconditional democratic freedom to say anything, to put everything in question. Such a democracy is, of course, never wholly established in fact. It is always "to come":

> "What is literature?" [asks Derrida]; literature as historical institution with its conventions, rules, etc., but also this institution of fiction which gives *in principle* the power to say everything, to break free of the rules, to displace them, and thereby to institute, to invent and even to suspect the traditional difference between nature and institution, nature and conventional law, nature and history. Here we should ask juridical and political questions. The institution of literature in the West, in its relatively modern form, is linked to an authorization to say everything, and doubtless too to the coming about of the modern idea of democracy. Not that it depends on a democracy in place, but it seems inseparable to me from what calls forth a democracy, in the most open (and doubtless itself to come) sense of democracy. (AL, 37)

Such a definition of literature allows us to understand better the role of the *comme si* or "as if" in "The University Without Condition." Literature, or what Derrida here calls "fiction," can always respond (or refuse to respond) by saying: that was not I speaking as myself, but as an imaginary personage speaking in a work of fiction, by way of a *comme si*. You cannot hold me responsible for my "as ifs." Derrida says just this in passages that follow the one just quoted:

> What we call literature (not belles-lettres or poetry) implies that license is given to the writer to say everything he wants or everything he can, while remaining shielded, safe from all censorship, be it religious or political. . . . This duty of irresponsibility, of refusing to reply for one's thought or writing to constituted powers, is perhaps the highest form of responsibility. To whom, to what? That's the whole question of the future or the event promised by or to such an experience, what I was just calling the democracy to come. Not the democracy of tomorrow, not a future democracy which will be present tomorrow but one whose concept is linked to the to-come [*à-venir*, cf. *avenir*, "future" (Attridge's note)], to the experience of a promise engaged, that is always an endless promise. (AL, 37, 38)

Crucial in the passage just cited is the "To whom, to what?" How can a refusal to take responsibility, a refusal addressed to sovereign state powers, be defined as "perhaps the highest form of responsibility"? To whom or to what else can it have a higher obligation? I shall discuss these questions further in Chapters 2 and 9. I say now, however, that Derrida's answer to this question goes by way of the new concept of performative language he proposes in "Psyche: Invention of the Other" ("Psyché: Invention de l'autre"; Pe, 46; Pf, 61), and again as the climax of "The University Without Condition." It might seem that literature, conceived by Derrida as an "as if," as a free, unconditioned fiction, would correspond to a concept of literature as ungrounded performative speech acts, speech acts based neither on previously existing institutionalized sanctions nor on the authority of the "I" who utters the speech act. The title of the honorary degree lecture in Athens is "*Inconditionalité ou souveraineté*," "Unconditionality *or* Sovereignty" (my emphasis). "The University Without Condition" distinguishes sharply between the phantasm of theologically based state sovereignty and the unfettered, "unconditioned" liberty to put everything in question in the ideal university, the university without condition. Such a university, like a truly democratic state, is always "to come." Derrida seems to pledge allegiance to, or, to use his own expression, make a "profession of faith in," a stark either/or. His word *profession* alludes, of course, to the academic title of "professor." A professor professes faith in the validity of what he or she teaches or writes. The *ou* or "or" in Derrida's title opposes always-illegitimate sovereignty to unconditional freedom.

This unconditionality, it might seem, is especially manifested in literary study. Literature, as institutionalized in the West in the last three centuries, is, according to Derrida, itself unconditioned, irresponsible, free to say anything. Literature is an extreme expression of the right to free speech. To study literature is to profess faith in literature's unconditionality.

Matters, however, are not quite so simple. In the last section of "The University Without Condition," in the seventh summarizing proposition, Derrida makes one further move that undoes all he has said so far about the university's unconditionality. He poses a "hypothesis" that he admits may not be "intelligible" (UCe, 236; UCf, 79) to his Stanford audience. Derrida admits, in a quite unusual confession, that what he asserts is not easy to understand. It is. What he says is based on a hypothesis that is prima facie highly unlikely, "extremely difficult, and almost im-probable, inaccessible to proof [*extrêmement difficile et presque im-probable, inaccessible à une preuve*]" (UCe, 235; UCf, 76). What he proposes, that is, is contrary to a true scientific hypothesis. A bona fide hypothesis can be proved to be false, if it is false.

What is this strange hypothesis? It is the presupposition that the unconditional independence of thinking in the university depends on a strange and anomalous speech act that brings about what Derrida calls an "event" or "the eventual [*l'éventuel*]" (UCe, 235; UCf, 76). Such a speech act is anomalous both because it does not depend upon pre-existing rules, authorities, and contexts, as a felicitous Austinian speech act does, and also because it does not posit freely, autonomously, lawlessly, outside all such pre-existing contexts, as, for example, de Manian speech acts might seem to do, or as judges do in Austin's surprising and even scandalous formula: "As official acts, the judge's ruling makes law."[2]

No, the performative speech act Derrida has in mind is a response to the call of what Derrida calls *le tout autre*, the wholly other. Such a response is to some degree passive or submissive. It obeys a call or command. All we can do is profess faith in the call or pledge allegiance to it. Only such a speech act constitutes a genuine "event" that breaks the predetermined course of history. Such an event is "impossible." It is always an uncertain matter of what, Derrida recalls, Nietzsche calls "the dangerous modality of the 'perhaps' [*peut-être*]" (UCe, 234; UCf, 75). Nevertheless, says Derrida, "only the impossible *can* arrive" (UCe, 234; UCf, 74). That is why Derrida speaks of "the possible event of the impossible unconditional, the altogether other [*le possible événement de l'inconditionnel impossible, le tout autre*]" (UCe, 235; UCf, 76). Derrida is playing here on the root sense of *event* as something that comes, that arrives. It appears of its own accord and in its own good time. We can only say, "yes" or, perhaps, "no," to it. We cannot call it. It calls us.

What is "the wholly other"? Derrida works out in detail, in "Psyche: Invention of the Other," what he means by "invention" as discovery, as uncovering rather than making up, and what he means by "the wholly other." For my purposes here, however, the crucial text is *The Gift of Death*. In that book Derrida makes spectacular readings of the story of Abraham and Isaac in Genesis, of Kierkegaard's *Fear and Trembling*, and of Melville's "Bartleby the Scrivener." Derrida defines the wholly other, at least at a moment when he is paraphrasing St. Paul, in ways that identify it with a certain conception of God, a deity "absent, hidden and silent, separate, secret, at the moment he has to be obeyed" (GD, 57; DM, 83). The wholly other is identified by Derrida with the secret in general, and with death, the gift of death, death as always my own solitary death, and as wholly other to my knowledge. Derrida says:

> Without knowing from whence the thing comes and what awaits us, we are given over to absolute solitude. No one can speak with us and no one can speak for us; we must take it upon ourselves, each of us must take it upon himself [*prendre sur soi*] (*auf sich nehmen* as Heidegger says concerning death, our death, concerning what is always "my death," and which no one can take on [*se charger*] in place of me). (GD, 57; DM, 83)

The wholly other is also manifested, without manifesting itself, in the total inaccessibility of the secrets in the hearts of other people: "*Every other (one) is every (bit) other* [*tout autre est tout autre*; Derrida's emphasis], every one else is completely or wholly other. The simple concepts of alterity and of singularity constitute the concept of duty as much as that of responsibility. As a result, the concepts of responsibility, of decision, or of duty, are condemned a priori to paradox, scandal, and aporia" (GD, 68; DM, 98). I shall return in Chapters 2 and 9 to more extended investigations of this paradox, scandal, and aporia.

Included in this concept of the wholly other is literature. Literature too hides impenetrable secrets. A work of literature too is a response to a wholly other that strongly recalls the relation of literature to death in Blanchot's "Literature and the Right to Death."[3] This is made explicit in Derrida's reading of Melville's "Bartleby the Scrivener" in *The Gift of Death*, but also in an essay added to *Donner la mort* when it was published in book form in French, now included in the second English edition. In this essay, entitled "Literature in Secret: An Impossible Filiation" ("La literature au secret: Une filiation impossible"), further discussing Abraham and Isaac, Kierkegaard, and Kafka, Derrida reaches the surprising conclusions not only that literature hides secrets that cannot be revealed but also that literature is both irresponsible and at the same time works by "increasing in inverse proportion, to infinity, responsibility for the singular event constituted by every work (a void and infinite responsibility, like that of Abraham)" (LS 156; DM, 206). Literature, so defined, is the unfaithful inheritor of a theological legacy without which it could not exist:

> literature surely inherits from a holy history within which the Abrahamic moment remains the essential secret (and who would deny that literature remains a remainder [*reste un reste*] of religion, a link to and relay for what is sacrosanct in a society without God?), while at the same time denying that history, that belonging, that heritage. It denies that filiation. It betrays it in the double sense of the word: it is unfaithful to it, breaking with it at the very moment when it reveals its "truth" and uncovers its secret. Namely that of its own filiation: impossible possibility. (LS 157; DM, 208, trans. modified)

It is only necessary to add, to what Derrida says here, that literary study, as institutionalized in the university, is especially the place where the responsible/irresponsibility of literature, its unconditionality, is received or "professed" by professors and passed on to students. One small example: the dissident notions of state sovereignty in E. M. Forster's *Howards End*.[4]

I have now professed, in the sense of specifying and transmitting, Derrida's notions of sovereignty and unconditionality. I have done this, however, apparently at the cost of blurring the distinction between theologically based state sovereignty and the unconditional freedom of the university and of literary study within the university. Both, in the end, seem to be theological or quasi-theological concepts. What is the difference?

That difference is easy to see, but perhaps not all that easy to accept. The distinction is "im-probable" and "not provable," though it is essential to Derrida's thinking. For Derrida, and for me too, all claims by earthly sovereigns, such as those made implicitly by George W. Bush, to wield power by mandate from God are phantasms. They claim to see and to respond to something that is not there. A work of literature, on the other hand, and therefore the teaching of that work in a "university without condition," if there ever were to be such a thing, are responses to a call or command from the wholly other that is both impossible and yet may perhaps arrive. Each literary work is entirely singular, "counter, original, spare, strange," as Gerard Manley Hopkins puts it.[5] Each work is as different from every other work as each person differs from all others, or as each leaf differs from all others. When I as reader or teacher respond to the wholly other as embodied in a literary work and try to mediate it to my students or to readers of what I write, I am, perhaps, just "perhaps," fulfilling my professional duty to put everything in question and to help make or keep my university "without condition."

Whether or not I have "got Derrida right" in my profession of faith in what he says I must leave to Derrida himself to tell me. Probably, however, he will not tell me one way or the other. According to Derrida's own testimony and according to his profession of faith, I will be left on my own, as professors always are, to respond as best I can to the demand made on me by his notion of the wholly other.

CHAPTER 2

Who or What Decides, for Derrida: A Catastrophic Theory of Decision

Who? Who? Who? What?
A summer evening?

—WILLIAM CARLOS WILLIAMS, *Paterson*

The previous chapter attempts to identify Derrida's answer to an urgent question he raises in his work on the university without condition. "To whom, to what," he asks, am I responsible when I refuse to "reply for my thought or writing" to "constituted powers," that is, powers of state or institutional powers, such as my university? What justifies my saying "No; I won't do what you ask"? Derrida's answer, as I have shown, is that I have a higher obligation to *le tout autre*, "the wholly other," whatever, exactly, that may mean. In this chapter I raise a different question. For Derrida, who or what decides? How, for Derrida, does a bona fide decision take place?[1] Decision is analyzed in many places in Derrida's work, particularly in the late work. It is one of his "big deals." Rather than follow the word or concept of *decision* around from work to work, however, as I have done for *destinerrance* in Chapter 3, and for *reste* in Chapter 5, I have decided to focus "micrologically" on what seems to me Derrida's fullest and most elaborate expression of what he means by "decision." This is an intricate sequence in "Force of Law" (*Force de loi*).

I begin with an apparently peripheral subquestion. Can a decision be a catastrophe? If so, in what sense? In everyday language we speak of a catastrophic decision, as when we discuss "Isabel Archer's catastrophic decision to marry Gilbert Osmond" (in Henry James's *The Portrait of a Lady*),

9

or George W. Bush's "catastrophic decision to invade Iraq." I claim, however, that Jacques Derrida's theory of decision is catastrophic in a more
precise sense. This sense is related to what is called, in mathematics and
climatology, "catastrophe theory." This is the theory that a tiny change in
one part of a dynamic system, for example, in a famous version, the flapping of a butterfly's wings in Guatemala, can, through a series of relays,
produce a sudden wholesale rupture, a gigantic and "catastrophic" change
in the whole system. The butterfly's wingflap triggers a hurricane in the
Gulf of Mexico that devastates the U.S. Gulf Coast. The butterfly's wing-
flapping tips the balance, as we say, in a system that is precariously poised.
Mathematicians have mapped the way this happens.

The online encyclopedia, *Wikipedia*, defines a catastrophe as a disaster
and as the solution of the plot in a Greek tragedy. The word *catastrophe*
means, etymologically, "to turn downward," from Greek *kata*, "down,"
and *strephein*, "turn" (http://en.wikipedia.org/wiki/Catastrophe). *The
American Heritage Dictionary* stresses the suddenness of a catastrophe by
defining it as "a great and sudden calamity; disaster" and as "a sudden
violent change in the earth's surface; cataclysm." An example, I suppose,
would be an earthquake or a volcanic eruption. How can a decision be like
an earthquake, like a volcanic eruption, or like that hurricane brought
about by a butterfly?

The reader will see the equivocations in my title. It may be read three
ways. (1) In Derrida's view, "for Derrida," who or what decides? (2) This
essay is for Derrida, dedicated to his memory. (3) Who or what, one might
ask, decides in favor of Derrida, swears allegiance to him, as I hereby decide to do. But Derrida, "who, he?" Or perhaps I should say, "what, he"?

A decision seems a straightforward, even paradigmatic, speech act. I say
"I decide so and so" or a judge issues a judicial decision. Such an utterance
acts to bring about the decision by making it enter the circumambient
social realm. The utterance involves the first person singular pronoun and
a present tense indicative verb. The "who" is the "I" who speaks. That I
is a self-conscious ego or subject in full possession of his or her faculties.
This "who" is embedded in a social situation and within established institutions that give him or her the responsibility for deciding in this particular case. The "what" enters into a decision as a name for the contingent
factors that make me decide in a certain way.

Like all paradigmatic speech acts, however, a decision has its peculiarities. For one thing, people do not usually, in ordinary language, say "I
decide." They say "I have decided." That suggests that the decision is
taken as an inward and spiritual act of conscience. This is then reported

later on, constatively, by saying, in effect, "I want you all to know that I have decided." J. L. Austin criticizes such a claim as a high-minded, but false, spiritualizing. "Accuracy and morality alike," he says, "are on the side of the plain saying that *our word is our bond.*"[2] A decision, like a promise, Austin, I take it, would want to argue, takes place when the decision is put into public words.

Matters are not quite so simple with decisions, however, as examples of life-determining decisions dramatized in literature indicate. One such example is Anthony Trollope's report, in *Phineas Finn*, of how Marie Goesler decided to refuse the Duke of Omnium's offer of marriage. A woman's decision to accept or refuse a proposal was perhaps the crucial form of decision, for women at least, in Victorian middle- and upper-class society as represented by its novelists. The reader looks in vain for a moment when Madame Goesler says, or could say, "I decide." What Trollope's narrator gives is, rather, several days of agonized indecision marked by a painful awareness that nothing on earth or beyond it can help her decide. This is then followed by the report of a time when she has already decided and needs only to write her letter of refusal to the Duke. Trollope's narrator says, "she did make her resolution," but he does not recount that moment directly. It seems to be unrepresentable as a present event reported from the interiority of a consciousness:

> But she had given herself to the next morning, and she would not make up her mind that night. She would sleep once more with the coronet of a duchess within her reach. She did do so; and woke in the morning with her mind absolutely in doubt. When she walked down to breakfast, all doubt was at an end. The time had come when it was necessary that she should resolve, and while her maid was brushing her hair for her she did make her resolution.[3]

What does Jacques Derrida have to say about the moment of decision? Does he confirm or put in question Trollope's view of decision? Derrida's discussion of the aporias of decision comes in the context of a distinction he makes between law (*droit*) and justice. This is expressed most eloquently in the long preparatory introduction to his reading of Benjamin's "Critique of Violence" ("Zur Kritik der Gewalt") in "Force of Law." This section is entitled, in the French version, "Du droit à la justice" ("From Law to Justice"; FLe, 3–29; FLf, 13–63). On the one hand, what Derrida says seems straightforward enough. On the other hand, some features of it are more than a little obscure. They are perhaps also hard to accept, when you have figured them out. My goal is to read what Derrida has written as accurately as possible, that is, to do it justice. I want also to identify the presuppositions that lead him to say what he says.

The distinction between law and justice that is Derrida's starting point seems fairly sensible. Law is the institutionalized body of regulations within a specific culture. Though laws are particular, in the sense of being instituted within a given history and culture, they are universal in the sense that "everyone is equal before the law" and in the sense that laws are general rather than specific. They do not take into account the singularity of each special case. Laws are immanent, this-worldly. Justice, however, is transcendent and ineffable. Just to apply the laws is by no means necessarily to be just.

Isabel Archer, in Henry James's *The Portrait of a Lady*, at one point soon after she has inherited a large fortune, says to Ralph Touchett that she doesn't want to be "liked too much" by everybody, as Ralph says is the case. She says, "I want to be treated with justice; I want nothing but that."[4] She wants a lot. In fact, she wants almost too much. How would you know you were treating another person with justice? Do we ever treat other people with justice? Certainly, if we ever do, it is not by applying mechanically to them a general law, moral or legal. Each person makes a particular demand on me for justice that no appeal to rules or laws will help me much to fulfill. It is all very well to say I should love my neighbor as myself, but just how do I do that and know that I am doing it in a particular case? How can I, as a reader of *The Portrait of a Lady*, render justice to Isabel Archer? That's all she asks, but it may be an infinite request, one impossible to fulfill.

In the context of his distinction between law and justice, Derrida turns to what he calls three "aporias" of decision. An aporia is, etymologically, a blind alley, an impasse, a no-thoroughfare, in a sequence of logical thinking. You follow through a perfectly rational line of argument, one depending on clear and self-evident distinctions and definitions. Suddenly (or gradually) you hit the wall and can proceed no further. There seems no way out. Derrida, however, as he explains in one of the interviews in *Paper Machine*, as well as in *Aporias*, uses the term in a fundamentally different way. "The aporia I say so much about," says Derrida in the interview "Others Are Secret Because They Are Other" ("Autrui est secret parce qu'il est autre"), "is not, despite its borrowed name, simply a momentary paralysis in the face of the impasse. It is the testing out of the undecidable [*l'epreuve de l'indécidable*]; only in this testing can a decision come about [*advenir*]" (PMe, 154; PMf, 389). Just what Derrida means by this assertion, the rest of this chapter will try to explain. That Derrida's concept of the aporia has something to do with the coming of the other seems evident already, since the undecidable is a result of the otherness of the other, as the context of the citation I have just made demonstrates and as what follows in this chapter will confirm.

The first aporia Derrida calls "*épokhē* of the rule [*l'épokhē de la règle*]" (FLf, 50–2; FLe, 22–4). *Epokhē* is a Greek word meaning "suspension." In particular, it is a Husserlian word naming the suspension of epistemological questions about "what is really out there." This suspension is performed in order to describe with minute accuracy just what consciousness is conscious of, without reference to the objective existence or nonexistence of those referents of consciousness. That is the "phenomenological suspension." In Derrida's use of the word, *épokhē* names the necessary suspension of rules in the application of justice, while at the same time the one who does the suspending must recognize the necessity of rules. This is the first aporia. Throughout this part of his argument, Derrida applies his three aporias to the situation of someone making a decision, whether it is an ethical decision in relation to another person, a legal decision (e.g., one made by a judge in a criminal case), or a legislative decision, such as a decision to vote for or against a proposed law.

No one would deny that a just decision would need to be made freely, not by someone who is coerced. "We would not say," says Derrida, "of a being without freedom, or at least one without freedom in a given act, that its decision is just or unjust" (FLe, 22–23; FLf, 50). If, on the one hand, the decision, of whatever kind, is made by mechanically following preexisting rules or laws, it is preprogrammed. Therefore, it is neither free nor just, though it may be "legal," that is, lawful. On the other hand, justice requires that the decision conform to rules, that it not be wildly willful and arbitrary. That is the impasse, the aporia.

Here is part of Derrida's expression of this aporia, in Mary Quaintance's very just translation. Is a translation, however, ever wholly just or justified? Is it not always to some degree a free and unjustified interpretation of the original, not fully justified, that is, by the original? "But this freedom or this decision of the just, if it is one [*pour être et être dite telle, être reconnue comme telle*]," says Derrida, according to Quaintance,

> must follow a law or prescription, a rule. In this sense, in its very autonomy, in its freedom to follow or to give itself laws [*la loi*], it must have the power to be of the calculable or programmable order, for example, as an act of fairness [*équité*]. But if the act simply consists in applying a rule, in enacting a program or effecting a calculation, we might say that it is legal, that it

conforms to law, and perhaps, by metaphor, that it is just, but we would be wrong to say that the *decision* was just. (FLe, 23, trans. modified; FLf, 50)

When a logician encounters an aporia in his or her train of thinking, he or she has been taught to assume that there must be something wrong with the primary definitions or presuppositions. The theorems or positings that make the whole train of logical thinking possible must be askew. We ought not to be taken in too easily by an aporia or too easily enchanted by the claim that an ineluctable one has been found. Could it be that there is something wrong with Derrida's presuppositions? Perhaps following out a logical application of the law is not a loss of freedom, just as we do not feel unfree when we follow a line of mathematical reasoning. Is Derrida barking up a wrong tree or inventing a problem, an aporia, which does not really exist? Is there not, finally, something a little fuzzy about the meaning of "just" when Derrida says "we would be wrong to say the *decision* was just"? Why is it not just to decide to mete out justice rigorously, according to a strict application of the law? How else would you, or could you, or should you do it?

In what follows Derrida makes more plausible, or perhaps even irresistible, what he wants to say by appealing to two additional factors. One is the claim that no formulation of the law is wholly transparent. All laws require an act of interpretation. An example would be the endless minutiae of controversies over constitutional law in the United States. There is the United States Constitution. It was intended to be wholly unambiguous. It was carefully framed to allow no misunderstandings. Nevertheless, it has given rise to a special field among lawyers and law professors, with conflicting schools of thought and different traditions of interpretation about just what a given phrase in the Constitution ought to be taken to mean.

Every decision made by a judge requires not just a blind or mechanical application of the law but what Derrida, following Stanley Fish, calls a "fresh judgment" (FLe, 23; FLf, 51). The judge must not just follow the law but "must also assume it, approve it, confirm its value, by a reinstituting act of interpretation, as if ultimately nothing previously existed of the law, as if the judge himself invented the law in every case" (FLe, 23; FLf, 50–51). Here is a good example of Derrida's penchant for hyperbole. Into the tiny crack of a logical problem he inserts a tool of hyperbole that widens that crack immeasurably. He goes within a few phrases and by way of an "as if" to the claim that the judge in all cases of decision invents the law. This, however, is just what the more temperate and ironic J. L. Austin says in a passage already cited in Chapter 1: "As official acts, a judge's ruling makes law."[5] The judge does this by a speech act that declares some law or other applies in this particular case. "I sentence you to six months in jail" or "I sentence you to be hanged by the neck until dead." Derrida says:

> The "fresh judgment" [*La fraîcheur nouvelle, l'initialité de ce jugement inaugural*] can very well—*must* very well—conform to a preexisting law, but the reinstituting, reinventive and freely decisive interpretation, the responsible interpretation of the judge requires that his "justice" not just consist in conformity, in the conservative and reproductive activity of judgment. In short, for a decision to be just and responsible, it must, in its proper moment if there is one, be both regulated and without regulation: it must conserve the law and also destroy it or suspend it enough [this is the *épokhē*] to have to reinvent it in each case, rejustify it, at least reinvent it in the reaffirmation and the new and free confirmation of its principle. (FLe, 23; FLf, 51)

The first additional factor stressed by Derrida, then, is this ever-renewed need for an act of interpretation that may by a hyperbolic sleight of hand be defined as making the law. This is reinforced elsewhere in Derrida, for example, in *Specters of Marx*, where he stresses the inaugural and therefore in a sense unjustified feature of every act of reading, for instance, his reading of Marx. Every reading is truly inaugural:

> This dimension of performative interpretation, that is, of an interpretation that transforms the very thing it interprets, will play an indispensable role in what I would like to say this evening. "An interpretation that transforms what it interprets" [*une interprétation qui transforme cela même qu'elle interprète*] is a definition of the performative as unorthodox with regard to speech act theory as it is in regard to the 11th Thesis on Feuerbach ("The philosophers have only *interpreted* the world in various ways; the point, however, is to *change* it [*le* transformer]. [*Die Philosophen haben die Welt nur verschieden interpretiert; es kömmt aber drauf an, sie zu verändern*]"). (SMe, 51; SMf, 89)

The other newly stressed feature is the claim that every case is "other," that is, other to all other cases. Each case is singular, unique. If that is so, then it would follow that no general law (and all laws must be general in order to be laws) fits perfectly any particular case. There are always special or mitigating circumstances. The law is like a shoe that is supposed to fit every foot. Obviously such a presumption is absurd, because "Each case is

other, each decision is different and requires an absolutely unique interpretation, which no existing, coded rule can or ought to guarantee absolutely"(FLe, 23; FLf, 51).

Law, lawyers, and judges, the whole institution of the law, have invented a clever way around this aporia between the singular case and the
general law. Or at least they have devised a way to sidestep it or to shift
the incompatibility between the conceptually general law and the specific
case to a somewhat different aporia. Derrida does not mention this expedi-
ent. It is the use of precedent, as in the use of Roe vs. Wade to re-establish
a woman's right to choose. If a new case can be shown to be analogous to
the precedent that has been, always more or less arbitrarily or accidentally,
chosen as the proper one to cite, then the law or the court decision that
derived from the precedent can be applied. The problem, it is easy to see,
is that this has done no more than redefine the impasse, not only because
the choice of a precedent is always to some degree arbitrary, therefore in
a sense unjustified, but also because no new case, if every case is "other,"
is really "like," or analogous to, the case taken as precedent. The claimed
"analogy" is really a legal fiction turning a metaphorical similarity into a
quasi-identity.

Derrida makes two final moves in the two paragraphs that expound the
first aporia. One move is prepared for in the ominous phrase that speaks
of the "proper moment if there is one" of a just decision. Derrida always
uses this formulation when he wants to indicate that something is radically
unknowable or undecidable, as when he says, in *Given Time* (*Donner le
temps*), "*the gift maybe, if there is any* [le don peut être, s'il y en a]" (GT,
35, Derrida's italics; DT, 53). Every decision is made in a moment, as is
indicated in a phrase I have used elsewhere: "moments of decision," but
whether that moment of genuine or just decision does or does not exist
cannot be told or decided. It may exist, or it may not. The moment of just
decision is undecidable.

Derrida in these paragraphs comes back by a circuitous route to the
suspension or *épokhē* of the Heideggerian presentness of the present that
has been from the beginning the basis for his critique of Heidegger. It is
also the basis of his development of an alternative notion of human temporality. This happens by way of the concept of *différance*. *Différance* differs
from the "ecstasies" of temporality that are the basis of Heidegger's notion of decision. In Derrida's case, the justice or not of a given moment of
decision can never be known. "It follows from this paradox," he says, "that
there is never a moment that we can say *in the present* that a decision *is* just
[*juste, purement juste*] (that is, free and responsible), or that someone *is* a

just man—even less, '*I* am just'" (FLe, 23; FLf, 52). Justice is not a matter of "is" or of presence or of the present. "Instead of 'just,' we could say legal or legitimate, in conformity with a law, with the rules and conventions that authorize calculations but with a law whose founding origin only defers the problem of justice" (ibid., trans. modified).

A consequence of this nonpresence of decision is that, as the subsequent two aporias make clear, the moment of decision is, paradoxically, unpresentable and unrepresentable. James's *The Portrait of a Lady* gives striking examples of what this means in practical terms for the representation of moments of decision in literature, whether ethical, juridical, or political. None of Isabel's crucial moments of decision is directly represented in the novel, only what comes before and after each of them. The reader sees Isabel before she has decided. The reader sees her after she has decided. James does not show her actual instants of decision.

A reference to "founding origin" is the final move in these tightly knit two paragraphs. To take the founding origin of the law as a solid ground, says Derrida, is a mistake. The act of founding a law, for example, by the "framers" of the United States Constitution, was just as arbitrary, capricious, and subject to this first aporia as is any attempt to apply the law in a moment of decision once it has been laid down. "Here the best paradigm," says Derrida, in concluding this first aporia, "is the founding of the nation-states or the institutive act of a constitution that establishes what one calls in French *l'état de droit*" (FLe, 23–24; FLf, 52). On what is that "state of law" founded? On nothing but the ungrounded say-so of those who establish the law, as in the transition from British law to U.S. law when the United States was founded.

The second aporia is named, in English, "the ghost of the undecidable," in French *la hantise de l'indécidable*, which more properly means "the haunting of the undecidable" (FLe, 24–26; FLf, 52–57). Moments of decision are always haunted by the undecidable. Decision is "based on," that is, abyssally undermined, by the undecidable. The undecidable is here called a ghost that haunts decision and that may not be exorcised. A ghost is neither here nor there, neither present nor nonpresent, neither material nor immaterial, neither bodily nor disembodied. Derrida's notions about ghosts may be seen in *Specters of Marx*, which presents itself as a "hauntology," a theory of ghosts or of haunting.

The undecidable, Derrida says, is usually taken to be a feature of so-called deconstruction. The undecidable is taken to mean "the oscillation between two significations or two contradictory and very determinate rules, each equally imperative (for example respect for equity and universal right but also for the always heterogeneous and unique singularity of the unsubsumable example)" (FLe, 24; FLf, 53). This has been the topic of the first aporia. The judge or the maker of a moral decision must respect the rules, (e.g., "Honor thy father and thy mother," one of the Ten Commandments; Exodus 20:12), but at the same time he or she must respect the singularity of a situation that never fits the rules: "And every one that hath forsaken houses, or brethren, or sisters, or father, or mother, or wife, or children, or lands, for my name's sake, shall receive an hundredfold, and shall inherit everlasting life" (Matthew 19:29)," said Jesus. It is impossible to decide between these two equally compelling obligations. The conflict is undecidable, though in a given situation one *must* decide.

Derrida, however, in a characteristic gesture of upping the ante, says that this is not all that he means in this case by "undecidable." What he does mean takes the reader into a realm that is essential to Derrida's theory of decision. At the same time it is both difficult to understand and difficult, for many, to accept, in its scandalous rigor and even irrationality, its madness, its *folie*. What Derrida means by the undecidable as a feature of true decision, he says, "is the experience of that which, though heterogeneous, foreign to the order of the calculable and the rule, is still *obliged*—it is of *obligation* [devoir] that we must speak—to give itself up to the impossible decision, while still taking account of law and rules. A decision that didn't go through the ordeal of the undecidable would not be a free decision, it would only be the programmable application or unfolding of a calculable process. It might perhaps be legal; it would not be just" (FLe, 24, trans. modified; FLf, 53).

Just what in the world does this mean? It means that justice is "something" that makes an implacable demand on us to decide, obliges us to decide, while being so foreign, so wholly other, so alien to existing law and its rational calculations, that it does not give clear directions for just what we should decide, even though it obliges us to decide. That's what Derrida means by "the impossible decision." I am obliged to decide, by an irresistible call, something like Heidegger's "call of conscience" or Jehovah's command to Abraham, discussed in Chapter 9, below. Nevertheless, I don't have any clear or rational grounds for decision. Derrida calls this the "undecidable," something very different from the undecidable oscillation between two significations in the interpretation of a text. If you happen to think what Derrida says is just irrational hooey, if you have never heard that demand, obligation, or call, then your ideas about moments of ethical or political decision will be very different from Derrida's. Whether or not any literary texts say anything like what Derrida says would require further careful investigation. I have attempted to do that for Toni Morrison's *Beloved*, in an essay planned for a book on communities in literature.

Derrida is in this second aporia affirming that, for him, "justice" is another name for the *tout autre*, the wholly other, that is a central motif of *The Gift of Death* and "Psyche: Invention of the Other." In the latter, "invention," as the previous chapter shows, means "find," or even "be invoked by," more than "make up" or "concoct." We do that finding in response to a call from the wholly other. In addition, the structure of our relation to justice can be said to be like the structure of the gift as Derrida has analyzed it in *Given Time*. Language that echoes those works appears a little later in "Force of Law," in the further development of this second aporia. Derrida says "the deconstruction of all presumption of a determinant certitude of a present justice itself operates on the basis of an infinite 'idea of justice,' infinite because it is irreducible, irreducible because owed to the other, owed to the other, before any contract, because it has come, the other's coming as the singularity that is always other [*la venue de l'autre comme singularité toujours autre*]" (FLe, 25; FLf, 55).

In a further development of this idea of justice as something that comes as an implacable demand from the "wholly other," Derrida is led rapidly to the idea that justice is mad, *une folie*, or that it makes those subject to it mad, insane. "This 'idea of justice,'" says Derrida, "seems to be irreducible in its affirmative character, in its demand of gift without exchange, without circulation, without recognition or gratitude, without economic circularity, without calculation and without rules, without reason and without theoretical rationality. And so we can recognize in it, indeed accuse, identify a madness. And perhaps another sort of mystique. [This is a reference to Montaigne's phrase about "the mystical foundation of authority," cited earlier in Derrida's essay, and in the subtitle of the book.] And deconstruction is mad [*folle*] about this kind of justice. Mad about this desire for justice" (FLe, 25; FLf, 55–56).

This notion of a justice that is wholly other explains why Derrida, a little earlier in this section, develops further the idea that the moment of decision is not present. You can follow what leads up to it. You can know afterward that the decision has been made and what the decision was, but you can never know or be present at the moment of decision itself. "But in the moment of suspense of the undecidable, it is not just either, for only a decision is just (in order to maintain the proposition 'only a decision is just,' one need not refer decision to a structure of a subject or to the propositional form of a judgment)" (FLe, 24; FLf, 53). Just what this means and what the stakes of saying this are I shall explain in a moment. Derrida continues with his hollowing out or making ghostly of the present moment of decision:

> And once the ordeal of the undecidable is past (if that is possible) [*si cela est possible mais cette possibilité n'est pas pure, ce n'est jamais une possibilité comme une autre: la mémoire de l'indécidabilité doit garder une trace vivante qui marque à jamais une decision comme telle.* The additional phrases were probably not in the initial manuscript Mary Quaintance translated. They mean: "but that possibility is not pure, it is never a possibility like another: the memory of the undecidability must harbor a living trace that forever marks a decision as such."], the decision has again followed a rule or given itself a rule, invented it or reinvented, reaffirmed it, it is no longer *presently* just, fully just. There is apparently no moment in which a decision can be called presently and fully just: either it has not yet been made according to a rule, and nothing allows us to call it just, or it has already followed a rule—whether received, confirmed, conserved or reinvented—which in its turn is not absolutely guaranteed by anything; and, moreover, if it were guaranteed, the decision would be reduced to calculation and we couldn't call it just. (FLe, 24; FLf, 54)

This is really weird, if you think about it. You can identify or experience the time right up to the decision, and all the time after it has been made. The moment of decision itself, however, vanishes from direct experience. It does not exist as a moment of which consciousness can be conscious. "The rule is, jam to-morrow and jam yesterday—but never jam *to-day*," to borrow a formulation from Lewis Carroll's *Through the Looking-Glass.*[6] Derrida calls this the "ordeal of the undecidable." It is a "ghostliness" that inhabits the act of decision before, during, and after. Because apparently no moment exists in which a decision can be called presently and fully just, and because the moment of decision is not experienced as a present moment in which I say "I decide so and so," therefore "the ordeal of the undecidable that I just said must be gone through by any decision worthy of the name is never past or passed [*passée ou dépassée*], it is not a surmounted or sublated (*aufgehoben*) moment in the decision" (FLe, 24; FLf, 54).

The undecidable that presides over the nonphenomenal moment of decision is a kind of ghost, neither present nor not present, neither embodied nor wholly disembodied. It haunts and undermines the whole temporal process of decision. The result is that one can never speak of a decision as an "event." A decision never takes place or can never certainly be said to have taken place: "The undecidable remains caught, lodged, at least as a ghost [*fantôme*]—but an essential ghost—in every decision, in every event of decision. Its ghostliness deconstructs from within any assurance of presence, any certitude or any supposed criteriology that would assure us of the justice of a decision, in truth of the very event of a decision. Who will ever be able to assure us that a decision as such has taken place?" (FLe, 24–25; FLf, 54).

It follows from this impossibility to experience decision in the presence of the present that it is no longer possible to think of a decision as the act of an I, ego, or subjectivity. In a passage added for the French version of *Force de loi*, but not present in the English, Derrida asserts, with proper care, this shocking detachment of decision from the deciding subject: "In a certain way, one could even say, at the risk of shocking, that a subject can never decide anything: a subject is even that to *which* a decision cannot happen except as a peripheral accident which does not affect the essential identity and the substantial presence to itself that make a subject a subject—if the choice of this word is not arbitrary, at least, and if one has faith in what is in effect always required, in our culture, of a subject" (FLf, 53–54, my trans.). If decision makes a cut, a division between before and after, it goes strikingly against received opinion to say this is not because someone, being of sound mind and with authority to do so, utters a performative statement that effects the decision but rather because the decision happens to someone, from the outside, as the coming of the other. It is a coming, moreover, that does not make any change in the presence to itself of the ego.

Derrida spells out one result of this. It puts in question the axiomatic of responsibility that is used in the courts, by medical authorities, and so forth to determine responsibility or premeditation. If a decision is not something that I "take," in sovereign freedom, but something that happens to me, something that is "owed to the other, before any contract," then the conventional legal rules for determining malice prepense, for example, premeditated murder as opposed to accidental manslaughter, are seriously flawed. "The whole subjectal axiomatic of responsibility," says Derrida, "of conscience or consciousness, of intentionality, of property [*propriété*: "properness," that is, the proper act of the person who commits some putative crime] that governs today's dominant juridical discourse and the category of decision right down to its appeals to medical expertise is so theoretically weak and crude that I need not emphasize it here" (FLe, 25, trans. modified; FLf, 55).

Derrida makes it sound as if this conclusion is so obvious that it goes without saying, but a lot is at stake at this point in Derrida's exposition of his theory of decision. If he is right, then, for example, J. L. Austin's attempt to use speech act theory to maintain law and order by holding people to performatives they have uttered is destined to fail. Law and order, it may be, can only be secured by unjustified force, by *Gewalt* or violence, as Walter Benjamin's "Critique of Violence" ("Kritik der Gewalt"), discussed at length later on in "Force of Law," affirms. Law and order, as both Benjamin and Derrida, though in different ways, affirm, are fundamentally opposed to justice.

Finally, as a transition to the third aporia, Derrida says that he resists relating this "idea of justice" to a Kantian regulatory idea or to any sort of messianism. Why does he resist this? It would seem that his idea of an "infinite justice" that implacably commands decision, so that decision is more something that happens to a self than a choice made by that self, is without question a form of a transcendental, something either like a Kantian regulatory idea that irresistibly presides from on high or like the many forms of messianism that dominate from the future as a horizon of hope toward which decision is oriented. The third and last aporia, "the urgency that obstructs the horizon of knowledge [*l'urgence qui barre l'horizon du savoir*]" (FLe, 26–29; FLf, 57–63) shows that this is not the case.

It is difficult to present a "reading" of this third aporia of decision, since, though it is only four paragraphs (in the English translation), every sentence counts. A number of remarkable moves are economically made. They are, moreover, to some degree not all that easy to grasp and accept, just as the notion of an infinite idea of justice that is never present but that is irresistibly commanding is hard to grasp and accept.

Derrida begins by explaining that he resists associating the infinite idea of justice that demands decision with the horizons of the Kantian regulative idea or with the messianic advent (in whatever religious tradition: Jewish, Christian, or Islamic) precisely because these are horizons, "far-off divine events," in Tennyson's phrase, that are supposed to govern present action and judgment as their goal. This happens in a species of prolonged waiting or anticipation, as Christians are still waiting for the Second Coming.

Decision, however, does not wait. It is urgent, precipitous. I must decide now, or sooner or later, usually sooner. The deadline comes, and I must decide one way or the other. In James's *The Portrait of a Lady*, Caspar Goodwood, Lord Warburton, and Gilbert Osmond at different times, sometimes more than once, propose to Isabel Archer. In each case, she must decide whether or not to accept the proposal. She must say yes or no, and she must answer more or less right away. She does not have the luxury of indefinitely postponing her decision. You never have time enough to get all the facts, or even if you did have "world enough and time,"

> the moment of *decision, as such* [en tant que tel, *ce qui doit être juste*; "that which must be just," not in the English translation], *must* always remain a finite moment of urgency and precipitation, since it must not be the consequence or the effect of this theoretical or historical knowledge, of this reflection or this deliberation, since it always marks the interruption of the juridico- or ethico- or politico-cognitive deliberation that precedes it, that *must* precede it. (FLe, 26, trans. modified; FLf, 58)

You have an obligation to think it out as best you can, but, when the moment comes, all that thinking does not really help, and you must rush blindly into a decision. The relation between decision and cognition is consonant with what Trollope says about Madame Goesler's decision to reject the Duke's proposal, but it is not quite the same as what James says of Isabel's decisions in *The Portrait of a Lady*, as a detailed reading would show.[7] James "motivates" Isabel's decisions by having the narrator show them to be results of her quintessentially American desire for freedom. In all three of Isabel's decisions to say no or yes, however, the process is not that of a careful thinking out that leads to a reasoned decision, such as we have been taught to believe characterizes a good decision. Isabel's decisions are spontaneous. She tells her friends and relatives that she can give them no explanation for them.

This incongruity between knowledge and decision leads Derrida to remember what Kierkegaard says about decision: "The moment of decision is a madness, says Kierkegaard. This is particularly true of the *just* decision that must also rend time and defy dialectics. It is a madness [*folie*]" (FLe, 26). The French version adds two sentences in explanation of why the moment of decision is a madness: "A madness because such a decision is at once super-active and submissive, it retains something of passivity, even of the unconscious, as if the decider were not free to allow himself or herself to be affected by his or her own decision and as if that decision came to it from the other. The consequences of such heteronomy appear redoubtable, but it would be unjust to elude the necessity" (FLf, 58, my trans.).

The madness of decision derives from the fact that it is not the result of a conscious deliberation on the part of the decider. It is something that just happens to him or her, something he or she passively endures, as though the decision were made somewhere else, as though it came from the other. The decider is, as it were, not free to decide but is "affected" from the outside by his or her decision, just as an insane person is not in control of what he or she thinks, does, or decides. We are all mad when it comes to making decisions.

Derrida goes on to relate this "decision of urgency and precipitation, acting in the night of non-knowledge and non-rule" (FLe, 26; FLf, 58), to the opposition between constative and performative utterances in standard speech act theory. Derrida makes it clear, as have his earlier writings on speech act theory, that he cannot accept at face value the opposition between constative and performative enunciations as Austin develops it. Nevertheless, Derrida goes on to use this opposition in order to set the madness of decision, which he correctly sees as in one way or another a performative, against the presumed rationality and truth-value, or at any rate testability, of constative statements. You can, at least so it seems, find out whether or not it is raining and so verify or disqualify the constative statement "It is raining." (I note in passing that matters are not quite so simple. Marcel, in Proust's *À la recherche du temps perdu*, is never able to get a satisfactory answer to what looks like a question that ought to be answerable by a verifiable constative statement: "Is or is not Albertine lesbian? Yes or no?")

If constative statements are at least in principle verifiable, this is not the case with performative utterances, like "I promise" or "I bet." Such statements are neither true nor false. They are, rather, either felicitous or infelicitous. They either succeed in making something happen or they do not succeed. The problem is that it is exceedingly difficult, perhaps impossible, to find out whether a given performative has worked or, if it has worked, just what it has made to happen. Performative utterances are not of the order of the cognizable. They belong to the night of nonknowledge. Here is Derrida's way of putting this congruence between decision and performatives in general:

> If we were to trust in a massive and decisive distinction between performa-
> tive and constative—a problem I can't get involved in here—we would have
> to attribute this irreducibility of precipitate urgency, at bottom this irre-
> ducibility of thoughtlessness and unconsciousness, however intelligent it
> may be [an amazing characterization of decision: thoughtless, unconscious,
> however intelligent!], to the performative structure of speech acts and acts
> in general as acts of justice or law [Derrida means, I think, that the judge,

to borrow an example from Austin, does not have to speak to condemn a
man to death, but just to appear with a black hood], whether they be performatives that institute something or derived performatives supposing anterior performatives. [The French version adds a sentence here that may
be translated as follows: "And it is true that every standard (*courant*) performative presupposes, in order to be efficacious, an anterior convention."]
A constative can be *juste* (right), in the sense of *justesse* [in the sense, that is,
that a margin is "justified" when it matches a straight line], never in the
sense of justice. But as a performative cannot be just, in the sense of justice,
except by founding itself on conventions and so on other anterior performatives, buried or not, it always maintains within itself some irruptive violence, it no longer responds to the demands of theoretical rationality. (FLe,
26–27; FLf, 58–59)

In the beginning was the performative, and it's more performatives all
along the line. Even the most banal and easily testable constative statement, such as "It is raining," presupposes a prior performative: "I swear
that I believe it is raining." Derrida's expression of this is characteristically
exuberant and hyperbolic:

> "I tell you that, I speak to you [*Je te dis que je te parle*; Derrida uses the
> familiar second person singular], I address myself to you to tell you that
> this is true, that things are like this, I promise you or renew my promise to
> you to make a sentence and to sign what I say when I say that I tell you, or
> try to tell you the truth," and so forth. (FLe, 27, trans. modified; FLf, 59)

Derrida goes on to express this through appropriation or misappropriation of a sentence from Levinas: "Truth supposes justice [*La verité suppose
la justice*]." (FLe, 27; FLf, 60). Justice comes before truth and guarantees,
or supports, or underlies it as its presupposition. Derrida transforms this
into his own extravagant manipulation of French idiom, "dangerously par-
odying the French idiom," as he puts it (ibid.). The sentence is cited incor-
rectly (unjustly!) in the English version, as "La justice, y a qu'ça de vrai,"
or at least Derrida changed it for the final book version in French. In the
latter it is, "La justice, il n'y a que ça de vrai" (FLf, 60). "Justice: there is
nothing of truth but that," or "Nothing but justice is truth."

Two additional important moves are made in the two final paragraphs.
In the first, Derrida asserts that it is, paradoxically, just because decision
is a species of performative utterance characterized by excessive urgency,
haste, and precipitation, just because it cannot be characterized as having
a regulative or messianic horizon, that it, perhaps (since justice is always a

matter of perhaps, never of certainty), has a future or, rather, acts to bring about an unforeseen future, perhaps a future that is more just:

> Justice remains, is yet, to come, *à venir*, it has an, it is *à-venir*, it deploys the very dimension of events irreducibly to come. It will always have it, this *à-venir*, and always has. . . . There is an *avenir* for justice and there is no justice except to the degree that some event is possible which, as event, exceeds calculation, rules, programs, anticipations, and so forth. Justice as the experience of absolute alterity is unpresentable, but it is the chance of the event and the condition of history. (FLe: 27; FLf, 60, 61)

The final paragraph is of great importance as a counter to claims some- times made by his critics that Derrida is a political quietist, lost in the abstractions of speculations about "infinite justice" and detached from ev- eryday politics. In the clearest way Derrida asserts here the contrary: "That justice exceeds law and calculation, that the unpresentable exceeds the determinable cannot and should not serve as an alibi for staying out of juridico-political battles, within an institution or a state or between institu- tions or states and others" (FLe, 28; FLf, 61). Derrida ends this first sec- tion of "Force of Law" by listing a whole series of specific responsibilities where the adjudication between justice and law, which belongs to neither domain because it exceeds each in the direction of the other, is urgently necessary: "laws on the teaching and practice of languages, the legitimiza- tion of canons, the military use of scientific research, abortion, euthanasia, problems of organ transplant, extra-uterine conception, bio-engineering, medical experimentation, the social treatment of AIDS, the macro- or micro-politics of drugs, the homeless, and so on, without forgetting, of course, the treatment of what we call animal life, the enormous question of so-called animality" (FLe, 28–29, trans. modified; FLf, 63). Derrida might today add the "enormous questions" of cloning, stem-cell research, and gene altering to this list.

Prior to saying this, however, Derrida had, early in this last paragraph, made an extremely important admission. Left to itself, the appeal to an unpresentable justice, however necessary and legitimate it may be, puts one in danger of the bad or the worst: "Left to itself, the incalculable and giving [*donatrice*] idea of justice is always very close to the bad, even to the worst for it can always be re-appropriated by the most perverse calcula- tion" (FLe, 28; FLf, 61). He means that a bad person can always say, "I was called by God to decide to do that," for example, invade Iraq. It is for this reason that we must always enter into the realms of politics, of legisla- tion, of activism, and "calculate" in the most radical way possible as we negotiate between law and justice:

Not only *must* we calculate, negotiate the relation between the calculable and the incalculable, and negotiate without the sort of rule that wouldn't have to be reinvented there where we are cast [*jetés*: an oblique echo of Heidegger's *Geworfenheit*], there where we find ourselves; but we *must* take it as far as possible, beyond the place we find ourselves and beyond the already identifiable zones of morality or politics or law, beyond the distinction between national and international, public and private, and so on. (FLe, 28; FLf, 62)

Far from being a political quietism, Derrida's idea of justice in its relation to law demands the most strenuous, difficult, innovative, and responsible engagement and activism. Fulfilling this demand is a neat trick if you can do it, but we (professors) are required every day to face up to this demand in one way or another, even in the most everyday acts of teaching, or in our relations to students, family, and friends.

Derrida always emphasizes the "madness" of decision, the irruptive violence of decision, the way a genuine decision is always a "decision of urgency and precipitation, acting in the night of non-knowledge and non-rule," the way a decision is irresponsible and at the same time exigently responsible, the way a decision is an anomalous kind of performative speech act, the way a decision has unpredictable and incalculable consequences. A decision is a decisive break in the continuity of things. It cannot be explained by what came before it. Nor are the results of a decision commensurate with the decision itself. Nothing but her "misreading" of Gilbert Osmond justified Isabel Archer's disastrous decision to marry him, just as nothing in the intelligence reports, far from it, justified George W. Bush's decision to invade Iraq. The results of these catastrophic decisions, however, were far-reaching and not what either decider anticipated or intended.

All these features of Derrida's notion of decision mean that it can be defined, in a more or less technical sense modeled on climatological theory, as a "catastrophic theory of decision." The butterfly's wing "causes" the hurricane. Isabel's decision brings her (and Osmond) lifelong misery. Bush's decision has "caused," so far, the deaths of over four thousand Americans, with tens of thousands maimed for life or suffering post-traumatic stress syndrome, the deaths of as many as five hundred thousand Iraqis, or more, with more still dying every day, and civil war in Iraq. The longer-term effects are still hidden in the future, the *à-venir*, the to come.

CHAPTER 3

Derrida's *Destinerrance*

a letter does *not always* arrive at its destination, and from the moment
that this possibility belongs to its structure one can say that it never
truly arrives.

—DERRIDA, "Le facteur de la vérité"

What is destined to happen to the corpus of Derrida's works? What fate
will befall them? As I will show in Chapter 5, Derrida was anxious about
what would happen after his death to his "remains," in the double sense
of his dead body and of the body of his writings, his "corpus." This anxiety
is expressed both in *A Taste for the Secret* and in the long, amazing reflection on death, apropos of Robinson Crusoe's fear of it, carried on from
seminar to seminar in his last seminars, "The Beast and the Sovereign
(Two)" ("La bête et le souverain [deux]"), in 2002–3. This in turn echoes
the prolonged reflection on being toward death in *Aporias*. Derrida elsewhere put his reasons for worrying about what would happen to his legacy
after his death under the aegis of a striking neologism: *destinerrance* ("destinerring"). The word is a concocted present participle used as a noun. I
shall primarily use the French word throughout, partly because its basic
meaning is clear enough, partly to retain its not easily translatable strangeness. The word implies "wandering" as well as "erring." Like the word
deconstruction, *destinerrance* combines a positive and a negative in the same
word: "destiny" and "wandering."

What is *destinerrance*? Discussing it fully would be a virtually endless
task. It is a concept, or better, motif, or better still, spatiotemporal figure,
that connects intimately with the other salient spatiotemporal figures in

Derrida's work. I call *destinerrance* spatiotemporal because, like many of Derrida's key terms, it is a spatial figure for time. It names a fatal possibility of erring, by not reaching a predefined temporal goal, in terms of wandering away from a predefined spatial goal. *Destinerrance* is like a loose thread in a tangled skein that turns out to lead to the whole ball of yarn. It could therefore generate a potentially endless commentary. *Destinerrance* is connected to *différance*, that is, to a temporality of differing and deferring, without present or presence, without ascertainable origin or goal; to trace, iterability, signature, event, context, play (*jeu*, in the sense that one says "There is play in this machine"); to Derrida's anomalous concept of speech acts; to the future (*l'avenir*) or the "to come" (*l'à venir*); to the democracy to come in that *avenir* to come; to decision, obligation, responsibility, and, in another of Derrida's neologisms, "irresponsibilization [*irresponsabilisation*]" (GD, 61ff.; DM, 89 ff.; this is the subject of Chapter 9); to interruption, dissemination, the wholly other; to "exappropriation," *adestination*, justice, law, right, the gift, the secret, hospitality, testimony, sendings or dispatches (*envois*); to the messianic without messianism, as developed in *Specters of Marx* and elsewhere; to the specter, singularity, the apocalyptic, the apotropaic or, in John Leavey's coinage, the "apotropocalyptic,"[1] *clandestination*; finally, always and everywhere, to "the impossible possibility of . . . death" (SMe, 114; SMf,187). Each of these motifs is connected in one way or another to *destinerrance*, in fulfillment of Derrida's claim, in *A Taste for the Secret*, that his works are not a heterogeneous collection of occasional essays but that portentous thing, an oeuvre, an organic "corpus" (TS, 14–15).

The word or the notion of *destinerrance* appears in a large number of Derrida's works, early and late. It appears in the contexts of quite different topics. The word, or sometimes the concept without the word, appears in: "Le facteur de la vérité," in *The Post Card* (*La carte postale*; PC, 413–96, the English translation uses the French title; CP, 441–524); in "Envois," also from *The Post Card* (PC, 1–256; CP, 7–273); in "Telepathy" ("Télépathie"; Pe, 226–61; Pf, 237–70); in "Of an Apocalyptic Tone Recently Adopted in Philosophy" (*D'un ton apocalyptique adopté naguère en philosophie*); in "No Apocalypse, Not Now: Full Speed Ahead, Seven Missiles, Seven Missives" ("No apocalypse, not now [*à toute vitesse, sept missiles, sept missives*]") (Pe, 387–409, trans. Catherine Porter and Philip Lewis; Pf, 363–86); in "My Chances / *Mes chances*: A Rendezvous with Some Epicurean Stereophonies" ("Mes chances: Au rendez-vous de quelques stéréophonies épicuriennes") (Pe, 344–76, trans. Irene Harvey and Avital

Ronell; MC); and in *The Other Heading: Reflections on Today's Europe* (*L'autre cap*). These uses, the reader will note, include psychoanalytic and political contexts, as well as the question of letters in the epistolary sense and the question of the subject or ego in its relation to others. No doubt *destinerrance* appears in other places too that I have not identified. Chapter 10 invokes some of the more explicitly political uses of the word (or the concept) of *destinerrance*.

One final example of the word occurs in the last segment of "Circumfession." It is the fifty-ninth section because that was Derrida's age when he wrote it. Here several threads of this strange text come together without coming together. If they were to be tied up into a neat knot, then Atropos, the third of the Fates, or Moirae, might be able to cut Derrida's thread of life and so end it. The tangled and diversifying threads include: Derrida's mourning for his mother; the theme of circumcision (as castration and resurrection) and Derrida's complex relation of affirmation of and refraining from his Jewishness; analogies with St. Augustine's *Confessions*; the aleatory and therefore unpredictable "perversity" of the P.C., that is, Derrida's computer "system, MacWrite Macintosh SE Apple of PaRDeS," from which he downloads and "archives" what he has written, where *Pardes* is the word for Derrida's family garden back in El-Biar, Algiers, the apple of the Garden of Paradise (get it?), but also the famous apples or pears that Augustine and Rousseau stole and then confessed to having stolen in their *Confessions*; the orientation of what Derrida writes to an unwritable secret; the off-course course, without predefined destination, of Derrida's life, his "Moira" or fate, his "life will have been so short [*la vie aura été si courte*],[2] the voyage short, scarcely organized, by you with no lighthouse and no book"; and, finally, Derrida's desire, by what he writes in "Circumfession," to "throw G's [that is, Geoffrey Bennington's] theologic program [*le théologiciel*: a portmanteau word; *logiciel* means "computer program" in French] off course"—Bennington's attempt, that is, to create in his section of the book the simulacrum of a computerized digital "Derridabase" that would allow any reader full command over all Derrida has written. All these themes come together in the word *destinerrancy* (*destinerrance*). Destinerrancy is both the catastrophe of a permanent scattering, the failure of the threads ever to come neatly together or to be combed out and Derrida's good luck or "fate," since that coming together would be death. Derrida remains alive only so long as he "destinerrs":

> resurrection [after circumcision] will be for you "*more than ever the address, the stabilized relation of a destination, the game of a-destination finally sorted out* [réglé], *for beyond what happens in the P.C., it is now the work to dispatch it*

[pour destiner] *that must win out, toward the secret that demanded, like a breath, the "perversity" of the P.C., not to be finished with a destinerrancy* [destinerrance] *which was never my doing, nor to my taste, but with a still complacent and therefore defensive account of that Moira"* (7–6-81 [the date at which he wrote the section in italics]), too late, you are less, you, less than yourself. (Ce, 311–15, trans. modified; Cf, 288–91)

Happily, it is always too late to dispatch a full and unambiguous account of his life, attested to by responsible witnesses, to Bennington or to anyone else.

The Post Card is a novel in letters about the way those exposed letters called postcards deconstruct (if I may dare to use that word) sender, message, and addressee, all three, divide them from within and scatter them. In *The Post Card* Derrida uses the alternative neologism *adestination* (PC, 29; CP, 35). The notion of *destinerrance* was already present in Derrida's putdown of Lacan in "Le facteur de la vérité." It appears in the powerful investigation of telepathy as *destinerrance* in "Telepathy." *Destinerrance* underwrites the discussion of Greek atomism and Freud's notion of chance and the aleatory in "My Chances." Speaking there of the *clinamen* or unpredictable deflection of atoms falling in the void in the atomism of Democritus, Epicurus, and Lucretius, Derrida says: "Only this deviation can change the course of [*détourner*] an imperturbable destination and an inflexible order. Such erring (I have called it elsewhere 'destinerring' [*destinerrance*]) can contravene the laws of destiny, conventions or contracts, agreements of *fatum* (*fatum foedera* [Lucretius, *De natura rerum*, 2:254])" (Pe, 351; MC, 24). I shall return to this essay, after some wandering.

A peculiarity of many places where the word or the concept, if it can be called that, of *destinerrance* appears is that they tend to say, in an act of *différance*, something like: "as I have elsewhere explained, with examples." I have not yet found, in the labyrinth of Derrida's writings, what might be called the "mother lode," the place where the word appears for the first time, with full explanation, though the concept without the word is perhaps first developed in the essay on Lacan, "Le Facteur de la vérité." Perhaps no such origin for the word exists. Perhaps the word itself is the consequence of a *destinerrance*, a wandering from locus to locus that to some degree takes for granted its meaning as something always already established somewhere else.

Each of the essays or books I have mentioned is characteristically intricate. Each is a brilliantly innovative argumentation. Each calls for an extended commentary. To avoid an interminable accounting, I must necessarily be brief, whatever injustice to the tangled skein (with its virtu-ally innumerable crossings and knots) that leads me to commit. I want to look with a sharp eye at a number of the passages where the word or the concept appears, in order to see if I can identify just what Derrida is say-ing. I want then to speculate on just what *destinerrance* might mean for the destiny of Derrida's own writings, now that he is dead.

The logic, if it can be called that, of *destinerrance* seems straightfor-ward enough. It is a small bomb that is one of the chief weapons in some of Derrida's most exuberant acts of deconstruction. In calling it a bomb, I am thinking of Derrida's fantasy, expressed in *A Taste for the Secret*, of blowing up a railway during the Resistance and of his connection of that fantasy with deconstruction. This confessional passage is strange enough and disquieting enough to justify citing it here. It is particularly disquiet-ing when juxtaposed to today's roadside bombs set by "insurgents" in Iraq. What right-minded person, however, could be against the terrorist acts performed by the French Resistance during the Nazi occupation? Make what you will of this passage, dear reader, as it makes its way to you by *destinerrance* and by what Derrida calls, in another neologism, *exappropriation*:

> Naturally my heroic phantasms . . . usually have to do with the period of the Resistance, which I did not experience firsthand; I wasn't old enough, and I wasn't in France. When I was very young—and until quite re-cently—I used to project a film in my mind of someone who, by night, plants bombs on the railway: blowing up the enemy structure, planting the delayed-action device and then watching the explosion or at least hearing it from a distance. I see very well that this image, which translates a deep phantasmic compulsion, could be illustrated by deconstructive operations, which consist in planting discreetly, with a delayed-action mechanism, de-vices that all of a sudden put a transit route out of commission, making the enemy's movements more hazardous. But the friend, too, will have to live and think differently, know where he is going, tread lightly. (TS, 51–52)

I take that last sentence as a warning. It warns friends of deconstruction, such as me, that deconstruction is dangerous for them, too. We too must tread lightly, or we may set off an improvised explosive device placed dis-creetly by Derrida, for example, in the passages about *destinerrance* I am reading in this essay. Our transit routes too, such as mine here from cita-tion to citation leading to a conclusion, might be put out of commission.

Destinerrance arises from the feature of iterability, which Derrida associ-ates with any sign, trace, or mark, even prelinguistic marks. *Destinerrance* is, however, especially a feature of performative utterances or of the performative dimension of any utterance. Iterability is explained most elaborately in "Signature Event Context" ("Signature événement contexte"; LIe, 1–23; LIf, 15–51), originally published in French in 1972, in *Marges* (M, 367–93). That essay is Derrida's initial challenge to orthodox speech act theory. Careful explanations recur, however, for example, in "My Chances" (Pe, 360–61; MC, 31). Iterability means that the same sign, set of signs, mark or marks, trace or traces, can function in radically different contexts. This means, as Derrida puts it in "Signature Event Context," that the context is "never . . . entirely certain or saturated [*jamais assurée ou saturée*]" (LIe, 3; LIf, 20). The context of a given utterance cannot be certainly identified or exhaustively delimited. "To function," in this case, means both to have meaning and to have felicitous performative force, that is, to make something happen by way of the words or other signs employed in a given case. This limitless multifunctionality means, to put it simply, that any utterance or writing I make may escape my intentions both as to what it should mean (for others) and as to the destination it is supposed to reach. It may be destined to err and to wander, even though it may sometimes, by a happy accident, reach the destination I intended for it. "I" and "intended," as I blithely use them here, are of course extremely problematic notions for Derrida, and for me too.

Derrida expresses succinctly this tendency to wander in "Le facteur de la vérité." He does this apropos of Lacan's logocentric claim, in the last sentence of the first part of his seminar on Poe's "The Purloined Letter," that "a letter always arrives at its destination."[3] Derrida replies that, for him, a letter may always fail to reach its destination. This means that it never really reaches its destination. Here is Derrida's careful formulation of the letter's destiny to wander and to err:

> The divisibility of the letter . . . is what chances [*hasarde*] and sets off course [*égare*], without guarantee of return, the remaining [*restance*] of anything whatsoever: a letter does *not always* arrive at its destination, and from the moment that this possibility belongs to its structure one can say that it never truly arrives, that when it does arrive its capacity not to arrive torments it with an internal drifting. (PC, 489; CP, 517)

He goes on to add that the divisibility of the letter, taking "letter" in the double sense of alphabetic letter and epistle, means "the divisibility of the signifier to which it gives rise" (PC, 489; CP, 517). "Signifier" here means a collection of letters turned into a meaningful word or sentence. The divisibility of the signifier gives rise, in turn, to a divisibility of the "subjects," "characters," or "positions" (e.g., sender, receiver, or witness, in whatever places they may be) that are subjected to that signifier. I shall return to this pluralizing of the sender and receiver.

Just what does Derrida mean by the divisibility of any letter or mark? In "My Chances" and in "Le facteur de la vérité," he defines it in terms of his resistance to what he calls "l'atomystique de la lettre" (CP, 517). This phrase has been dropped in the translation. *Atomystique* is Derrida's coinage, defining the mystified belief that a letter or other mark is an indivisible atom, like those in Epicurus referred to by Poe in "The Murders in the Rue Morgue." On the contrary, says Derrida in "My Chances," because these "atoms," that is, letters, numbers, or proper names, are without significance in themselves, they are multiplied and divided internally by their consequent capacity to be used differently in innumerable contexts: for example, innumerable singular persons can be named "Pierre." *Pierre*, without the capital, is also the general name for any stone whatsoever:

> The ideal iterability that forms the structure of every mark is doubtless what allows it to withdraw from a context, to free itself from any determined bond to its origin, its meaning, or its referent, to emigrate in order to play elsewhere, in whole or in part, another role. I say "in whole or in part" because by reason of this essential insignificance, the ideality or ideal identity of each mark (which is only a differential function without an ontological basis) can continue to divide itself and give rise to a proliferation of other ideal identities. This iterability is thus what causes a mark to be valid more than once. It is more than one. It multiplies and divides itself internally. This imprints a power of diversion on its very movement. It is, in the destination (*Bestimmung*), a principle of indetermination, chance, randomness [*hasard*], or destinerring [*destinerrance*]. No destination is assured precisely because there is mark and proper name, in other words, insignificance. (Pe, 360; MC, 31)

"My Chances" gives me a chance to identify another conspicuous feature of Derrida's procedure in all these essays about *destinerrance*. They mime the thing they talk about. This may be seen in both large-scale and small-scale features of style. Derrida's seminars remained focused on the topic at hand—hospitality, or cannibalism ("eating the other"), or capital punishment, or sovereignty, or the animal, or whatever—but they tended conspicuously to wander from author to author as exemplifications of his theme. As you listened to one of his seminars, if you turned your attention away for a moment and then returned to listening you were likely to find that he was no longer talking about Carl Schmitt but about, say, St. Augustine, in a dizzying aleatory whirl. The one thing you could be sure of was that sooner or later, usually sooner rather than later, you would find him talking about Heidegger. Heidegger was, more than Kant, Hegel, Freud, or any other author, Derrida's King Charles's Head,[4] Heidegger was destined to come up whatever the ostensible topic.

This wandering is a feature of Derrida's published essays, too. "My Chances" is about the chances, good and bad, that befall the thinker or lecturer, Derrida in this case. The essay-lecture itself wanders from a beginning with—guess who?—Heidegger, to Democritus, Epicurus, and Lucretius, to Heidegger again, to Lacan on Poe, to Derrida's own essay on Lacan on Poe, to Epicurus again, as referred to by Poe, to Baudelaire's translations and essays on Poe, and finally to Freud, who was presumably meant to be the center of this lecture on psychoanalysis and literature.[5]

Wandering is also a conspicuous feature of Derrida's local style. Often a sentence will contain a long list of words or phrases in apposition. Sometimes these appear to be just different ways to say "the same thing" (as if Derrida were perhaps striving, not altogether successfully, to find just the right word or even to avoid saying the right word). Sometimes, however, the series names quite different things that are related metonymically, at best. An example is an amazing sequence in Derrida's last seminars in which he postpones, for obvious reasons, uttering the word *mort* ("dead"). The word falls, with a clang like a funeral bell or *glas*, at the end of the sequence. I allow myself the luxury of citing the whole passage, partly for the sake of passing on to my readers Derrida's moving and resonant French, since these seminars have not yet been published, in either French or English: "quand je serai passé, quand j'aurai passé, quand je serai parti, décédé, éloigné, disparu, absolument sans défense, désarmé, entre leurs mains, c'est-à-dire, comme on dit, pour ainsi dire, mort [when I will have passed, when I have passed, when I will have departed, deceased, gone away, disappeared, absolutely without defense, disarmed, in their hands, as one says, so to speak, dead]" (my trans.; BS, 5th seminar).[6] In "My Chances," Derrida says to his audience: "The 'things' I throw, project [*jette, projette*], or cast in your direction, toward your encounter, fall often and well enough upon you, at least upon certain of those among you" (Pe, 346; MC, 21). A few pages later he asserts, in a waterfall of words playing on several roots that mean "fall, befall, chance," that "the sense of the fall in general (symptom, lapsus, incident, accidentality, cadence, coincidence, expiration date [*échéance*], luck [*chance*], good luck, bad luck [*méchance*]) is thinkable solely in the situation, the places, or space of finitude, within the multiple relation to the multiplicity of elements, letters, or seeds" (Pe,

352; MC, 25). Innumerable examples of such sentences could be adduced from Derrida's writings. The effect of such sentences is to suggest a bristling multiplicity of etymological connections, synonyms, homonyms, metaphors, and metonymies that forbids the writing of simple declarative sentences with a single word in each syntactical place. At this point the reader may happen to fall on the reflection, highlighted by Derrida, that in French *mes chances* ("my chances, my strokes of luck") and *méchance* ("bad luck") are pronounced the same. Derrida's title contains a "destinerring" pun dividing the signifier from within and deflecting any straight line to a single meaning. Derrida's chances or strokes of luck (that Freud, for example, mentions Democritus) are at the same time the bad luck of a perpetual drifting, wandering, or erring away from any straight path toward any predetermined goal.

In other examples of such a series in "My Chances," the words or phrases form a chain leading from one to another by an apparently random set of links or by the accidental filiation of a strange family heritage. Derrida cites the passage in Poe's "The Murders in the Rue Morgue" in which Dupin explains to the narrator how he guessed that the word the narrator muttered to himself was the Epicurean word *stereotomy*. The word defines an intricate cutting of something, for example, a paving stone, so that it will fit: "The larger links in the chain run thus—Chantilly, Orion, Dr. Nichols, Epicurus, Stereotomy, the street stones, the fruiterer" (cited in Pe, 356; MC, 28). The phrase "larger links" suggests that there were a lot of smaller links that Dupin does not think it necessary to mention. The "chain" of associations is almost limitlessly intricate. A few pages later Derrida gives the reader another such "destinerring" series apropos of a passage in Freud's *The Psychopathology of Everyday Life*, this time leading backward from Freud to "Democritus, and so on":

> In this textual abyss, there are thus only analysts, that is, analysands, all of them more engendered, generated, indebted, affiliated, subjected, than the others [note the series effect again], all descended or fallen from a series of proto-analysts in an eminently indivisible chain of proper names and singularities: Freud, Stross, Sterne, the son and the father in *Tristram Shandy*, Protagoras, Democritus, and so on. Each of them has interpreted and reduced, with the same blow, a random series. Each of them has given it [the chain] to be read by the other—before the other. This chain is heterogeneous: there are only proper names, the texts and situations being different each time, yet all the subjects are inscribed and implicated in the scene that they claim to interpret. (Pe, 364, trans. modified; MC, 34)

Derrida, I conclude, does not just name *destinerrance* as an objective fact. Nor does he just exemplify it in the local style and overall structure of his essays. He is also himself the joyfully willing victim, as one might call it, of *destinerrance*. A playful exuberance, or joyful wisdom, *eine fröhliche Wissenschaft*, to borrow Nietzsche's title, is an evident feature of Derrida's writings. However hard he tries to stick to the point, he is destined to wander. That is his *chance* or his *méchance*, his good or bad luck.

The consequences of destinerred iterability for everyday life are considerable, to say the least. I write a postcard and send it to my beloved. The postcard means to tell her how much I love her. On it I write *Je t'aime* ("I love you") and other endearments. The postcard sends my beloved kisses indicated by a row of Xs at the bottom of the message area. A postcard, however, is open to all those under whose eyes it happens to fall. Anyone who intercepts it and reads it can take it as addressed to him or to her. Anyone can interrupt its passage to its intended destination. Anyone can short-circuit that passage. Anyone can make my postcard have a meaning I in no way intended. My intimate postcard can function perfectly well in all kinds of situations. My intention and the address I put on the postcard fail to limit its functioning. One distressing result of this is that I cease to be as single, pre-existing "I." I double, triple, quadruple myself in the act of writing that postcard. I become legion. "You are right," says Derrida in *The Post Card*, "doubtless we are several"(PC 6, CP, 10). In the copy of *La carte postale* that Derrida gave me at the time of its publication, with "à Hillis, à Dorothy" added in blue ink after "Envois," he has put "Jacques" (also in blue ink) after the last sentence of the preamble, which ends with "I am signing them [the envois] here in my proper name, Jacques Derrida" (PC, 6; CP, 10). It looks like Derrida's handwriting. The footnote to this sentence, however, invites the recipient of this direct address to be suspicious of the authenticity of the signature because "you are right, doubtless we are several." Many years later, in 1997, in a response to a questionnaire from the journal *Lignes* about the nature and responsibility of "intellectuals" in these latter days Derrida expresses his quasi-refusal to speak as a public intellectual

> because there are several of us, as you know, and "I" will begin by positively claiming this plurality, close to dizzying heights [*au bord des vertiges*], especially juridically and politically, which are already turning my head "within me." Can I form a community with myself, and what's more, yet another thing, a *civic* community in a court of innermost justice that doesn't end up being closed in on itself? Being self-identified? Avoiding betraying or perjuring itself? So someone, within me apart from me [*en moi à part moi*],

gives himself permission not to respond or correspond to this "function" of the "intellectual" or to its usual definition. (PMe, 34; PMf, 230–31)

Iterability also means that the recipient, however fortuitously he or she may come upon that postcard, for example, me as a reader of "Envois," is transformed into someone else, put beside himself or herself, dislocated, by reading it. I become the person to whom those words seem to be addressed, their fitting recipient.

When Derrida gave at Irvine, in improvised English translation, a spectacular two-hour seminar on the phrase *Je t'aime*, "I love you," his claim that he was only "mentioning" this phrase, not "using" it did not keep it from functioning, when he said *Je t'aime* over and over again, as a felicitous performative utterance. That utterance seemed to be addressed individually to each one of us in the large auditorium full of students and faculty of both sexes. It was received as such, consciously or not, received, that is, as a declaration of love addressed to each auditor uniquely and individually. These are the figurative presuppositions that underlie one of Derrida's wildest and most exuberant works, the philosophical *roman à clef* in letters he called *La carte postale*. I read *The Post Card* at first with the assumption that I was intercepting, so to speak, letters, postcards, Derrida wrote to some beloved woman or other, since he calls the addressee, repeatedly, in English, oddly enough, "my sweet darling girl" (PC, 239), or something like that, and because he uses the familiar *tu*. At a certain point, however, an uneasy and anxiety-making change takes place. The reader, male or female, straight or gay, feels as if he or she were the *tu* to whom the discourse is being addressed. After all, "I" am reading these (fake) postcards, and they are in any case far too long to be inscribed on a postcard.

I always associate those presuppositions, in a short circuit, interruption, or *destinerrance* of my own, with a moving passage in Franz Kafka's *Letters to Milena*. I have discussed this letter, as well as its connection to Derrida's "Telepathy," in my "Thomas Hardy, Jacques Derrida, and the 'Dislocation of Souls.'"[7] My essay, by the way, generated some, no doubt justified, strong resistance in some readers:

> The easy possibility of letter-writing must—seen theoretically—have
> brought into the world a terrible dislocation [*Zerrüttung*] of souls. It is, in
> fact, an intercourse with ghosts, and not only with the ghost of the recipient
> but also with one's own ghost which develops between the lines of the
> letter one is writing and even more so in a series of letters where one letter
> corroborates the other and can refer to it as a witness. How on earth did

anyone get the idea that people can communicate with one another by letter! Of a distant person one can think, and of a person who is near one can catch hold—all else goes beyond human strength. Writing letters, however, means to denude oneself before the ghosts, something for which they greedily wait. Written kisses don't reach their destination, rather they are drunk on the way by the ghosts. It is on this ample nourishment that they multiply so enormously. . . . The ghosts won't starve, but we will perish.[8]

The ghosts in question here are the distorted phantoms of the sender and receiver of the letter. These phantoms are generated by the words of the letter. The letter is an invocation of ghosts, but these are not to be identified with the sender and receiver of the letter as such. The letter itself deflects the letter, along with the written kisses it contains, away from its intended message and away from its goal, its destination. The letter is deflected toward the ghosts of sender and recipient that the letter itself raises, by a powerful incantation or conjuration. For Kafka too, as for Derrida and against Lacan, the letter never reaches its destination, or, if it does, it has lost its precious gift of kisses along the way. Message and kisses never reach their destination, according to Kafka's version of the law of *destinerrance*. To write a letter, in Kafka's strange metaphor, is to make oneself naked before the hungry, hovering specters the letter generates. To write a letter is to denude oneself and therefore to put oneself at the mercy of the ghosts the letter conjures up. The ghosts greedily drink the kisses meant for the beloved. This spectral act associates drinking and kissing with a quasi-obscene denuding, a making public of what ought to remain private.

By a strange happenstance or serendipity, Derrida had fallen upon the same Kafka letter to Milena in the "Envois" of *The Post Card*, a year or two before I wrote my essay for the volume that contained the initial publication (it first appeared in English) of Derrida's "My Chances" (MCe, 1–32). Was this really an accident, or did I come upon Kafka's letter by way of the "Envois"? I do not think so, but I no longer remember. This is the excuse, I am aware, offered by witnesses when they want to cover up something incriminating. I swear I no longer remember where I encountered Kafka's letter. I think I would have cited the reference in "Envois" if I had then been aware of it when I was writing my essay. Perhaps both of us were led to the *Letters to Milena* by Blanchot's remarkable essay of 1954, "L'échec de Milena,"[9] though Blanchot, it is true, does not cite that particular letter. In any case, my citation and Derrida's reference come together, like two atoms falling in the Democritean, Epicurean, or Lucretian void. They bump against one another by a fortuitous *clinamen*. Juxtaposed, in a happy rendezvous, the two references to Kafka's letter form a stereophonic echo generating a solid surround sound.

Here is Derrida's notation: "Spirits [*Des fantômes*], why are spirits always called upon in letter writing? One lets them come, one comprises them rather, and one writes for them, one lends them one's hand, but why? You [*Tu*] had me read that letter to Milena where he more or less said that, something like speculating with spirits, denuding oneself before them" (PC, 34–5; CP, 40). The referent of *tu*, singular "you," here, as Derrida's initial note to the "Envois" says explicitly about all the pronouns in this work, is entirely unidentifiable. Even Derrida, according to his solemn declaration, does not know to whom his dispatches (the meaning of "envois") are addressed or who speaks them (PC, 5; CP, 9).

As I did not fully understand, in my earlier essay on Kafka, Hardy, and Derrida, what Kafka says is not quite what Derrida means by *destinerrance* as it applies to any sending (*envoi*), missive, missile, performative utterance, or just plain letter, in the sense of "epistle." "Telepathy" is an essay that was mysteriously displaced, destinerred, one might say, among Derrida's papers. He calls it a *restant*, a remains or a remainder, something left over (Pe, 423; Tf, 5). I explore Derrida's words *reste*, *restant*, and *restance* in Chapter 5 of this book. Since "Telepathy" was buried alive, so to speak, it was left out by mistake from *The Post Card*. Or was it really a mistake? Did Derrida forget it "accidentally on purpose," perhaps because it too explicitly "blew the gaff" on the project of "Envois," perhaps because Derrida was embarrassed by his interest in telepathy, as one might be anxious about either saying "I believe in ghosts" or "Of course I don't believe in ghosts"? Can there have been some denial there, some denegation or, in Freud's language, *Verneinung*? Derrida, as usual, has already been there. His initial footnote to "Telepathy" anticipates that "there will perhaps be talk of omission through 'resistance' and other such things. Certainly, but resistance to what? To whom? Dictated by whom, to whom, how, according to what routes [*voies*]?" (Pe, 423; Pf, 237). Well, I have suggested a couple of possibilities. Derrida then disinterred "Telepathy" again, to publish it separately, or rather, according to him, he just fell upon it again, by accident, by a happy chance or *méchance*.[10]

In a remarkable couple of pages in "Telepathy," Derrida imagines a letter that has no intended receiver and no fixed message. It just somehow gets written. Someone, male or female, comes upon it by accident and says, quite without any authority or textual evidence, "This letter is addressed to me. It is meant for me." This decision creates a sender, a receiver, and a content that did not exist before the letter followed its errant trajectory. It may bind the newly created sender and receiver together in a life-long liaison. As opposed to Kafka, who sets the real sender and receiver against the ghosts the letter generates, Derrida imagines a transaction by letter that involves nothing but the ghosts it invokes. I must cite a lengthy extract, with omissions, in which Derrida develops this idea:

> I am not putting forward the hypothesis of a letter that would be the external occasion, in some sense, of an encounter between two identifiable subjects—and who would be already determined. No, but of a letter that after the event seems to have been launched toward some unknown addressee at the moment of its writing, an addressee unknown to himself or herself, if one can say that, and who is determined, as you [*tu*] very well know how to be, on receipt of the letter; this is then quite another thing than the transfer of a message. Its content and its end no longer precede it. . . . So you say: it is I, uniquely I, who am able to receive this letter, not that it has been reserved for me, on the contrary, but I receive as a present the chance to which this card delivers itself. It falls to me. [*Elle m'échoit.*] And I choose that it should choose me by chance, I wish to cross its path [*son trajet*], I want to be there, I can and I want—its path or its transfer. In short you say "It was me," with a gentle and terrible decision, altogether otherwise: no comparison here with identifying with the hero of a novel. . . . Others would conclude: a letter thus *finds* its addressee, him or her. No, one cannot say of the addressee that s/he exists before the letter [*avant la lettre*]. (Pe, 229; Pf, 240)

It is perhaps a little too easy to accept at face value and without challenge what Derrida says. It is expressed so winningly and so persuasively! One is tempted simply to paraphrase it and pass on. After all, Derrida was a great and highly influential theorist. He presumably knew what he was saying. He presumably meant what he said. What he says, however, I am tempted to assume, is not likely to change all that much the assumptions on the basis of which I carry on my daily life. Too much is at stake to take Derrida seriously, a small internal voice whispers to me. Anyway, everybody knows how "playful" he is. What Derrida says is just "theoretical," "nonserious," after all. It may even be no more than a fictive "as if," *als ob*, or *comme si*, such as those he discusses as a fundamental feature of professing the humanities in "The University Without Condition," discussed here in Chapter 1.

Think for a moment, seriously, of what Derrida asserts in the passage I have just cited. When I write a letter I think of myself, my pre-existing and perdurable self, as its author. I think of myself as in control of what I say. Though of course I may be misunderstood, I know what I mean to say and what I intend to mean. I try my best to get this down on paper. I try to turn it into words that are as clear and unequivocal as possible. I also write this letter to a specific person. I address it to him or her as someone just as pre-existing and perdurable as I am. The letter will communicate something, but it will not change either of us fundamentally. Of course the letter may go astray. It may never reach its intended destination. It may end up in the dead letter office. It may be intercepted along the way and read by someone for whom it is not intended. That would be an unhappy accident, but it would not disturb my assumptions about the stable selfhoods of me as sender and of my intended recipient as receiver. The meaning of my letter, moreover, also remains stable, even though it may of course be misunderstood. When I spoke of myself a moment ago as the "I" who has just cited the passage from Derrida, I took for granted that I know who "I" am, just as my use of the proper name *Derrida* makes the blithe assumption that this cognomen refers to a single, stable person. Of course, I assume, "Derrida" continued to be the same individual through time from his earliest writings until he died! How can we get on with it if I do not take all this for granted and do not try to put it in question?

An enormous number of everyday transactions depend on the set of assumptions "I" have just listed, for example, my ability to make promises and to keep them or to be held responsible for a breach of promise if I do not; my ability to commit myself to a contract and to be held responsible for fulfilling its conditions; my liability to be hailed by subpoena before the law and interrogated, forced to give my name and to answer questions truthfully, on pain of punishment for perjury (unless I plead the Fifth Amendment, which protects me against incriminating myself); my responsibility to answer for things I wrote and published years ago, to say "Yes, I wrote that"; my ability to sign all sorts of documents—checks, letters, credit-card receipts, publication agreements—on the presumption that I know who I am and that I go on being the same person from day to day and year to year.

Since what Derrida says firmly contradicts and negates the assumptions underlying all the everyday performatives I have just listed, a lot that is not "just theoretical" is at stake in what Derrida says. What he says goes well beyond the disquieting implications of Kafka's letter to Milena. After all, we assume, "Kafka" wrote this letter, and it did reach "Milena," two circumscribed and unitary persons. All Kafka does is lament the way a letter generates fictive senders and receivers that interfere with the transmission of the message (and the kisses) the letter is intended to send from the real, extra-literary or extra-letteral Kafka to the real, extra-literary Milena. What Kafka fears is bad enough, but what Derrida holds is much more devastating. He hypothesizes a letter that is not the external occasion of a communication between two pre-existing and identifiable subjects, let us say, "Kafka" and "Milena." No, he hypothesizes a letter that seems, after the fact, to have been thrown out (*lancée*), at the moment it was written, toward an unknown receiver. The sender, male or female, does not know ahead of time the recipient. The recipient's "who" is determined at the moment of reception.

It would follow that the letter does not have a predetermined content. It does not simply communicate a message. Its content and its goal do not precede it. Someone or other chances upon the letter and says, "It falls to me. And I choose that it should choose me by chance. . . . [I] say, 'It was me [*c'etait moi*].'" That might seem to imply that the letter has found its intended recipient. No, the recipient did not exist before receiving the letter. The letter creates the recipient, unpredictably, incalculably, by chance or even by error. The letter reaches that recipient by *destinerrance*. If what Derrida says is true, if Derrida is right, then the whole structure of everyday assumptions "I" outlined above falls to the ground, like a fragile house of cards. I, we, you (whomever these pronouns designate) find ourselves at the mercy of whatever piece of language comes upon us. That language falls upon us by chance. Nor would this apply only to epistolary letters. My reading of "Telepathy," for example, creates or re-creates me. I, you, we, they, would do well to think twice or three times before giving credence to what Derrida says. That saying truly *is* a delayed-action improvised explosive device.

All he has said implies, as Derrida asserts just after the passage I have been discussing, a new, anomalous, unconventional theory of performative utterances. "Anomalous" should be given here its strong meaning of "lawless." A standard performative depends on a pre-existing self or *ego* who utters it and on a pre-existing authorized recipient of the utterance. I say to someone, for example, "I bet you a nickel it will snow tomorrow." That utterance binds me according to certain social laws and conventions. These too are assumed to be solidly in place beforehand. Derrida, correctly, in my view, imagines that the speech act he is discussing and, perhaps, disquietingly, every performative utterance of whatever sort creates the self of the one who speaks. It also creates the recipient, unpredictably, turning him or her into the one who is interpellated by the speech act, bound by it. The person to whom I say "I bet you a nickel it is going to snow" is bound by my utterance in the sense that he or she must either say "Done! I accept your bet" or "No thanks. Snow is 100 percent predicted." I am changed by the performative utterance that is directed toward me, and who knows just how I will respond to the violence that is done to me by words? "If there is something performative in a letter," says Derrida, "how is it that it can produce all kinds of events, foreseeable and unforeseeable, and even including its addressee [*destinataire*]? . . . the unforeseeable should not be able to form part of a performative structure *stricto sensu*, and yet . . ." (Pe, 230; Pf, 241).

Another version of Derrida's resistance to the idea of a pre-existing self, ego, or subject appears in "'Eating Well,' or the Calculation of the Subject" ("'Il faut bien manger' ou le calcul du sujet") (PI, 255–87, trans. Peter Conner and Avital Ronell; PS, 269–301). The word *destinerrance* appears five times in this interview with Jean-Luc Nancy, like a recurrent leitmotif. Derrida's chief gesture in this interview is to register the inevitable survival of the subject, the "who," even after it has apparently been deconstructed or "liquidated" for good by radical modern thought. At the same time, Derrida argues that the notion of the independent, perdurable subject is the product of an act of "throwing" or "jetting." This throw both generates the illusion of the subject and undermines it, pulls the rug out from under it, so to speak. Though each of the five appearances of the word calls for commentary, the most important, for my purposes, is the following:

> In the text or in writing, such as I have tried to analyze them at least, there is, I wouldn't say a place (and this is the whole question, the topology of a certain locatable non-place, at once necessary and undiscoverable) but an instance (without stance, a "without" without negativity) for some "who," a "who" besieged by the problematic of the trace and of differance [*différance*], of affirmation, of the signature and of the so-called proper name, of the *je[c]t* [with a play on *je* "I," on *jet*, and on the stem *ject*, *jet* in French] (before all subject, object, project [*sujet, objet, projet*]), as *destinerring* [*destinerrance*] of missives [*des envois*]. I have tried to elaborate this problematic around numerous examples. (PI, 260, trans. modified; PS, 275)

This passage was improvised as an answer to a question posed by Jean-Luc Nancy, "Can you be more precise?" ("Peux-tu préciser?") It is a good example of the complex rhetoric of Derrida's style. In the act of being more precise, he takes away with one hand what he offers with the other. He says that a "who," that is, a subject, a *qui*, has what he would call not a place but a sort of assignable nonplace, both necessary and impossible to find. Well, he would not, after all, call it a place, but an *instance*. An *instance*, in French, is something that stands in, inserts itself, or insists, such as an authoritative legal court (with an overtone of the German or Heideggerian *Instanz*, that is, a higher authority that imposes itself). The *qui*, however, is an *instance* without a *stance*, that is, without a ground to stand on. This "without," nevertheless, is without negativity, in an echo of the Blanchotian trademark phrases that say "*X* without *X*." The reader will note the series of key words that corresponds to part of the list I gave earlier of Derrida's most salient motifs: trace, *différance*, affirmation, signature, proper name. Derrida calls this *qui*, or "who," a *jet* without subject, object, or project. He cuts off all the usual prefixes. The who as *jet* is just something thrown out, *jeté*, with another Heideggerian echo, this time of *Geworfenheit*, throwness. *Dasein*, for Heidegger, is "thrown," *geworfen*, jetted forth into the world. The word *destinerrance* appears at the end of Derrida's remarkably twisted sequence. It appears as a definition of what the *qui* casts forth or jets, namely, dispatches (*envois*) that are, perhaps, destined to err and to wander without ever reaching their goal. "There is a goal," says Kafka in one of his aphorisms, "but no way; what we call the way is only wavering [*Es gibt ein Ziel, aber keinen Weg; was wir Weg nennen, ist Zögern*]."[11]

Derrida's *qui* is no more than a baseless *lieu de passage* between a mysterious source that throws out or instantiates the who and an unpredictable goal that the who throws itself out toward, in a crucial modification of Heidegger's definition of human time in *Being and Time*. In the last sentence in the passage cited above, Derrida tells the reader that if you do not get what he is saying, he has elaborated all this elsewhere, with numerous examples, and you might want to go there, though he does not exactly say where. The sentences mime what they talk about, wandering from term to term until finally landing, with a thud, on the word *destinerrance*, before gesturing toward other unidentified places where that word is used and explained more fully.

A quite late example of the idea of predestined wandering, though without the word *destinerrance*, appears in Derrida's last seminars, "The Beast and the Sovereign (Two)." There Derrida applies to Heidegger's use of the word *Weg* ("way") the same forceful repudiation he had applied to Lacan's touching belief that the letter always reaches its destination. The figure of *destinerrance* in the second session of these last seminars appears in the context of a long and intricate discussion of Heidegger's use of the figure of the path or *Weg* in *The Fundamental Concepts of Metaphysics: World,*

Finitude, Solitude (1929). "It is all very well," says Derrida, "often to mock those who seek the security of a safe-conduct, a passport [*sauf-conduit*], or a foundation, a foundational ground and a sure road, he himself does not wish to lose himself, he is a thinker of erring and wandering [*errance*] who does not want to err when he philosophizes, when he thinks, writes, and especially when he teaches (for this is a seminar [which I, Derrida, have been citing and analyzing]), and he wants not only order and a map, but the way out, the escape route [*la sortie, l'issue*] (*Ausweg*). He wants a good orientation and a good direction in order to escape from enclosure in insular circularity" (BS, 2d seminar). [12] The allusion at the end is to Robinson Crusoe's imprisonment on his circular island, the subject of lengthy discussion elsewhere in Derrida's final seminars. The discreet implication of Derrida's reading of Heidegger, in this case, as always, presented ever so gently and indirectly, is that Heidegger too is destined to err, to wander. This will happen however hard he tries to become correctly oriented, however much he believes he is aided by some magical metaphysical Global Positioning Satellite device implanted in his *Dasein*, orienting him toward Being with a capital *B*. That virtual GPS, Heidegger wants to believe, tells him just where he is, where the goal is, and how to get there. "No," says Derrida in effect, no such grafted prosthetic device exists.

As time went on, Derrida inflected or deflected, in an unpredictable wandering, the figure of *destinerrance* away from his thinking of iterability's consequences for the sending of a message. He redirected it toward a claim that each valid piece of writing or any utterance is not an autonomous speech act. It is, rather, a response to the demand made on the writer or speaker by the wholly other, which changes radically the direction in which he is headed. All we can do is to say "Come!" and "Yes" ("Oui, Oui") to the demand made on us by the wholly other. This leads, in "Psyche: The Invention of the Other" to an even more radically revisionary concept of the performative than the one proposed in "Limited Inc a b c . . ." : "The very movement of this fabulous repetition can, through a crossing of chance and necessity, produce the new of an event. Not only with the singular invention of a performative, since every performative presupposes conventions and institutional rules—but by bending these rules with respect for the rules themselves in order to allow the other to come or to announce its coming in the opening of this dehiscence. That is perhaps what is called deconstruction" (Pe, 44; Pf, 58–59). "Dehiscence" is a name for an opening up along a line or slit, as in the spontaneous cracking open of a seed pod. Deconstruction is defined here as a way to capitalize on *destinerrance* by saying yes to whatever call from the wholly other comes our way. That call commands us to deflect our course and to begin again anew from a new starting point to move in a new direction, destinerred again.

Every valid promise, wager, or decision, such the one Derrida proferred, as he says in *A Taste for the Secret*, to make what he called "deconstruction" serve as the ground without ground of his oeuvre or corpus, is now seen as a response to the wholly other. Such a decision is something like Abraham's obedience to God's command that he sacrifice Isaac or, in a perhaps better analogy, one suggested by Derrida himself for his relation to his unforeseen readers, like "the place left vacant [at the dinner table in Jewish tradition] for who is to come [*pour qui va venir*], for the *arrivant*— maybe Elijah, maybe anyone at all" (TS, 31). This means that every performative decision, such as the decision to write such and such an essay or book, usually, for Derrida, in response to some request or commission, is a radical break with what came before. It also has an unpredictable future or to come, *avenir* or *à venir*. Only such an invention or intervention, breaking with before and after, only such a happening or advent, merits the name "event."

Who knows when such an event will come or what is to come of such an event when it does come? As Derrida explains in an interview with Maurizio Ferraris in *A Taste for the Secret*, the wager he made, a bet that was materialized in all those essays and books he wrote, is a hazardous throw of the dice. It is a wager that his works will continue to function in the future, but in ways that are impossible to predict, except that he can be sure they are perhaps destined to *errance*, to erring and to wandering (TS, 12–34). Fragments of what Derrida wrote have, for example, wandered into the essay you are reading at this moment.

This shift from *destinerrance* as a name for the way a letter may never reach its destination, therefore never really does, to using it as a name for the unpredictable inflection of my route when I receive a call from the wholly other is more than a simple "course correction." It is not, as perhaps one might think, a response to a signal from Derrida's internal GPS getting him back on track. This shift is a major reorientation of Derrida's thought. The moment of this reorientation is, I am tempted to think, signaled in yet one more appearance of the word *destinerrance*, this one, once more, in "Telepathy." That essay (if you can call it that) is quite amazing in its complexity and in the unpredictable twists and turns of its trajectory. Too many to follow here. At one moment in that wandering, Derrida, or at any rate one of the Derridas, one of the multiple voices that speak in *The Post Card* and in its lost child, "Telepathy," draws himself up and says that he finds himself more and more believing in telepathy and such magic, "occult" things. Perhaps in this case Derrida is speaking as and for Freud, as Freud's "medium," bringing the old man back from the dead. The context suggests that possibility. The speaker has become, he says, "a surface more and more open to all the phenomena formerly rejected (in the name of a certain discourse of science), to the phenomena of 'magic,' of 'clairvoyance' [*voyance*], of 'fate' [*sort*], of communications at a distance, to the things said to be occult" (Pe, 236; Pf, 247).

What is the significance of this change? "Derrida" goes on to say that it is the only thing that has allowed him to move forward in his thinking about, you guessed it, *destinerrance*: "and we," says whoever is writing this, whichever of the Derridas (since he says "we"), "we would not have moved a step forward in this treatment of the dispatch [*envoi*] (adestination, destinerrance, clandestination) if among all these tele-things [*télé-choses*] we did not get in touch with Telepathy in person. Or rather if we didn't allow ourselves to be touched by her. Yes, touch, I sometimes think that thought . . ." (Pe, 236; Pf, 247). The sequence, as is characteristic of *The Post Card* and "Telepathy," just stops in mid-sentence, stalls, to borrow a term that appears more than once in "Telepathy": "I'm stalled [*je cale*]" (Pe, 230; Pf, 242). Derrida relates *cale* to the first syllable of *calculation* and to *callus* (*cal* in French), as in Flaubert's remark, in a letter to his beloved Louise Colet, that he has a callus in his heart (Pe, 235; Pf, 246). *Cal* is part of the set of fragmentary permutated syllables (*lac, cla, alc, cal, acl, gla*) that are woven pervasively into the "Envois," "Telepathy," and *Glas*. The passage cited above goes on to anticipate *Le toucher*, written so many years later. That whole enormous book, discussed here in Chapters 11 and 12, might be defined as a filling in of the blanks left by Derrida's three periods of ellipsis at the end of the citation. Derrida in "Telepathy" defines telepathy as essentially touching at a distance. It is a kind of extension of hearing and seeing. Seeing and hearing were already defined by Aristotle as forms of telepathy, in the sense of being long-distance touching, as in "Reach out and touch someone," in the old AT&T advertisement: "before 'seeing' or 'hearing,' touch, put your paws on it [*y met les pattes*], or that seeing and hearing come back to touch at a distance—a very old thought, but it takes some archaic to get to the archaic" (Pe, 236; Pf, 247).

Well, why is telepathy such a big deal at this moment, breaking a stalemate, a stall, and allowing some more carefully calculated "steps forward"? The answer is that telepathy is another name for the communication at a distance that Derrida came to call the call or demand of the wholly other.

This notion, as other chapters in this book show in detail, is crucial to Derrida's later thinking and writing. I claim that the basic impetus of Derrida's spectacularly productive thinking and writing is an irreconcilable "aporia" between two convictions. On the one hand, Derrida steadfastly believed Husserl was right to deny that we have any direct access to the mind of another person, only indirect "analogical apperception." On the other hand, Derrida felt, like Husserl, that this quasi-solipsism, this windowless monadism without God, is intolerable. Some way out must exist. Chapter 6 of this book, "Derrida Enisled," shows that Derrida's quasi-solipsism and his resistance to it persisted hyperbolically even into his last seminars. The way off Crusoe's island was Derrida's concomitant belief in my (your, his, her, everybody's) susceptibility to a call, almost like a telephone call or a cell-phone call, from the wholly other. What in "Telepathy" is Derrida's unexpected quasi-commitment to telepathy became later on his fully developed commitment to the wholly other, as developed, for example, in *The Gift of Death*. That book is discussed at length in Chapter 9. One brief notation toward the end of "Telepathy" puts these two penchants succinctly against one another by way of a doubleness Derrida finds in the word *telepathy*, as it echoes the disjunction in Freud's famous "*Fort/Da*,"[13] which means "away/there [in the sense of there in front of me]": "*Fort: Da*, *tele*pathy against tele*pathy*, distance against menacing immediacy, but also the opposite. Feeling (always close to oneself, it is thought), against the suffering of distancing that would also be called telepathy" (Pe, 259; Pf, 268).

I do not think these contradictory commitments, to a quasi-solipsism and to each person's telepathic exposure to the wholly other, can by any means be reconciled. Irreconcilable convictions of this sort fuel most highly productive thinking or writing, whether in philosophy or in literature. The impossible attempt to "get it straight" at last, to borrow a phrase from Wallace Stevens,[14] to bring these two ineradicable convictions into harmony, was what kept Derrida writing and thinking, with such fantastic productivity, urgency, and inventiveness, until the end. If he had been able to work it out, he could have stopped writing. The moment in "Telepathy" that is dated July 10, 1979, and from which I have been citing records an important crossroads in Derrida's *destinerrance*. It is a place where these two penchants in Derrida's thought collide, like Oedipus encountering his father Laius "where three roads meet," like Shelley's Magus Zoroaster meeting his own image in the garden,[15] or like the encounter with one's double that is one of Freud's examples of "the uncanny" in "Das Unheimliche." Is not Oedipus Laius's double, the son doubling the father and

taking the father's place in mother-wife Jocasta's bed? The various Derridas are all doubles of one another, encountering one another in uncanny
meetings. I shall return to Derrida's interest in doubles in the next chapter.
"Telepathy" has much to say about doubles, about, for example, Freud's
belief that he had a double. It presents, in indirect discourse, like a novel,
whichever Derrida is writing at the moment as the double of Freud, Freud
revenant, just as, come to think of it, I am speaking "for Derrida" in this
book.

The passage I cited above culminates, if you can call it that, in a quite
extraordinary leaning of a "part" of Derrida toward belief that we are not
enisled after all. Here is already an example of what Derrida, in *Le toucher*,
following Jean-Luc Nancy, came to call "ecotechnicity." This is the indistinguishable mélange of the organic and the prosthetic machinal in human
bodily and psychic life. Here Derrida proposes that each of us is a trans-
mitter of thought signals and also a powerful television set that can pick
up signals, sent out inadvertently, telepathically, by some other or other:

> The truth, what I always have difficulty getting used to [*du mal à me faire*]:
> that nontelepathy is possible. Always difficult to imagine that one can think
> something to oneself [*à part soi*], deep down inside, without being surprised
> by the other, without the other being immediately informed, as easily as if
> he or she had a giant screen inside, at the time of the talkies [*au temps du
> parlant*], with remote control [*télécommande*] for changing channels and
> fiddling with the colors, the speech dubbed with large letters in order to
> avoid any misunderstanding. For foreigners and deaf-mutes. This puerile
> belief on my part, of a part in me, can only refer to this ground—OK, the
> unconscious, if you like—from which there arose objectivist certainty, this
> (provisional) system of science, the discourse linked to a state of science
> that has made us keep telepathy at bay [*tenir en respect*]. Difficult to imagine
> a theory of what they still call the unconscious without a theory of telepa-
> thy. They can be neither confused nor dissociated. (Pe, 237; Pf, 247–48)

This passage, however, as the reader can see, is full of reservations and
waverings. On the one hand, the possibility of nontelepathy is "the truth"
and whichever Derrida is speaking here knows that, even though he cannot bring himself to believe it. His spontaneous and ineradicable belief in
telepathy, on the other hand, is "puerile." It is a belief held, moreover,
however tenaciously, by only "part" of Derrida. He can never give himself
wholly to either of his two penchants or allow that path to take him where
it would lead him, and so he is destined to wander and err. As Kafka said,
what we call the way is only wandering.

Sure enough, a few pages later the writer, whether it is a ventriloquized Freud or some other one of the many Derridas, says, "telepathy, you won't know [*vous saurez pas*], and I tell you that I don't know myself whether I believe in it" (Pe, 243; Pf, 253–54). A little earlier, at the end of the section dated July 10, 1979, Derrida expresses in so many words the paradox or aporia, crucial to his thought, that I have been trying to pin down. Telepathy, he says, far from guaranteeing that my message always reaches its destination, far from ensuring that your internal television set can always tune in on my secret thoughts and feelings, is the ground without ground of *destinerrance*:

> For here is my latest paradox, which you alone will understand clearly: it is because there would be telepathy that a postcard can always not arrive at its destination. The ultimate naïveté would be to allow oneself to think that Telepathy guarantees a destination that "posts and telecommunications" fail to assure. On the contrary, everything I said about the postcarded structure of the mark (interference [*brouillage*], parasiting, divisibility, iterability, and so on ["and so on" is in English in the original]) is found in the network. This goes for any tele-system—whatever its content, form, or medium. (Pe, 239; Pf, 249–50)

Does anything Derrida wrote or said many years later, with Bernard Stiegler in *Echographies of Television* (*Échographies: de la television*) or in *Paper Machine*, about the displacement of the printed book by the new telecommunications media, about the Internet, about electronic databases, about "terror" as a function of the new media, about the way the virtual reality, the "artefactuality," of television images and sound is neither present nor not present, about the word processor as a prosthetic device that is a strange sort of external unconscious or even superego, sternly correcting my spelling and style and making its own decisions about what I can be allowed to put up on the screen (as is happening to me at this very moment as I write these words)—does any of what Derrida wrote about all that contradict what he says in "Telepathy"? Would the Internet, the World Wide Web, personal Web sites, cell phones, iPods, iPhones, e-mail, instant messaging, blogs, FaceBook, MySpace, Google, and Wikipedia, none of which existed in 1979, disqualify "Telepathy" by giving so many examples of messages that apparently reach their destinations instantly? I do not think so, though it would require another essay, about Derrida on prosthetic technologies, to show this in detail. Derrida, by the way, always refused to use email. He evidently wanted his little Mac laptop to be as much like a typewriter as possible, though he was still frightened by his sense that something inside the machine was watching him, "surveying us like the eye of the Other," and by his awareness that he did not really know how the thing worked, what was happening inside it (PMe, 25, 23; PMf, 158,155–56). Connection of the little Mac to email and the Internet would have added immeasurably to Derrida's fear of the machine.

Exploring all that would be a long, digressive road to follow, in *destinerrance*, a big *Umweg*. It must suffice to note here that, as Derrida also notes, the telephone was already, long before the Internet, a prosthetic device that fulfills the dream of telepathy. I note also that Derrida, in 1979, was already talking about primitive versions of telecommunication devices we have today. He was fascinated (because of the famous postcard of the medieval miniature in the Bodleian showing Plato dictating to Socrates that instigated *The Post Card*[16]) to discover that the names "Socrates" and "Plato" had recently been used as names for what we would now think of as extremely primitive networking software and computer servers:

> with the telepathic transfer, one could not be sure of being able to cut (no need now to say *hold on* [in English in the original], *don't cut*, it is connected day and night, can't you just picture us?) or to be able to isolate the lines. All love would be capitalized and dispatched by a central computer like the Plato terminal produced by Control Data: one day I spoke to you about the Honeywell-Bull software called Socrates, well, I've just discovered Plato. (I'm not making anything up, it's in America, Plato.) (Pe, 242, trans. modified; Pf, 253)

"Telepathy," you can see, already foretells the later teletechnological developments that have put us where we are today, wirelessly "wired" in all directions and by manifold telepathic devices, subject to illegal and unconstitutional "electronic surveillance," wiretapping, and wireless eavesdropping. Now we don't say "I plugged in my ear-buds" but, as I saw on television recently: "My daughter was plugged into her iPod. She did not hear a thing I said, or see anything around her." My ears, body, nervous system, and brain have now become prosthetic devices plugged into some quasi-organic "World Wide Web" outside of me, into music files downloaded into the iPod, or into the monster body of the Internet, which continues its quasi-conscious life independently of me and of everyone else. Who knows what it is thinking, or even what my computer is thinking about what I write with its somewhat grudging help? It appears often to disapprove, since it puts red or green lines under a good bit of what I write. Derrida foresaw all that.

What is sauce for the goose is sauce for the gander. Derrida must expect others to do unto him as he has done unto them. What he did to them is exemplified in all those exemplary essays and books he wrote about his friends and colleagues after they died, books on de Man and Levinas, along with essays on many others collected in *The Work of Mourning* (*Chaque fois unique, la fin du monde*). I discuss these eulogies in my final two chapters. If all locutions, performative utterances, writings, messages, letters, postcards, marks, traces, or philosophical essays are destined, perhaps, to deviate from their destined goal and be deflected off on a detour, if they will, perhaps, never reach their intended destination, this must apply as much to Derrida's writings as to any others. Derrida knows this, and this knowledge makes him anxious. He also knows, however, that this inevitable *destinerrance* is also his chance. What, he asks, will happen to my remains after I am, so to speak, dead?

On the one hand, Derrida carefully tries to control the meaning and reception of his work by explaining, with patient generosity, over and over, just what he means. In this he is like a person writing a will who tries to control absolutely what will happen to his body and to his other remains, his legacy, after he is dead. Nevertheless, as Derrida knows, after his death his body and his works, his *corpus* in both senses, will be at the mercy of others, to do with what they like. Plato had already, in the *Phaedrus*, proclaimed that the trouble with written documents is that they are like orphans wandering the world with no father to protect them. When you ask them what they mean, they can do nothing but repeat again the words on their pages. They do not answer our urgent interrogation, "Stand and unfold! Tell us what you mean,"[17] whereas a living speaker, such as Derrida in all those brilliantly loquacious interviews he gave, can try to explain what he meant when he wrote or said so and so. Derrida's "Plato's Pharmacy" ("La pharmacie de Platon") (in De, 61–171; Df, 69–197), one of his earliest acts of deconstruction, brilliantly analyzes and dismantles Plato's distinction between writing and speaking. Nevertheless, a latent acceptance of what Plato says seems to underlie Derrida's anxiety about what will happen to his writings after he is gone. It may have motivated his willingness to explain himself orally in interviews, patiently, over and over.

On the other hand, Derrida's wager, as he explains in a passage already referred to in *A Taste for the Secret*, is that, since his works form a systematic/asystematic oeuvre, a corpus, they will be capable of functioning decades and centuries later in radically different contexts. They will function, that is, to enter those contexts and performatively change them, in new events of reading. The worst thing that could happen after Derrida's death, from his perspective when he was still living, would be that his works would simply be forgotten, would gather dust on the shelves. Better than that is to welcome all the misreadings and misappropriations, along with the more productive exappropriations, that are almost certain to occur, according to the law of *destinerrance*.

Just what will happen to Derrida's writings in the future, the "to come," is impossible to foresee, since that future, we know, and that is all we know for sure, will be discontinuous with the past, partly through the interruptions caused by readings of Derrida's work. These interruptions will repeat with a difference the original performative force of what he wrote. His writings were, according to him, interruptive events brought about by his response to the demand made on him by the wholly other. Those events are echoed by the happenings now of exappropriative readings of his work by others, such as by me in this essay. I read Derrida's works as if they were addressed to me. They have chosen me, by a happy *destinerrance*, and I choose to be chosen. I can be sure only that Derrida's corpus is probably destined to err and to wander, like a specter, revenant, or ghost come back from the dead. That is the price of its survival, its "living on," after Derrida's "passing," when he will have "departed, deceased, gone away, disappeared, absolutely without defense, disarmed, in their hands, as one says, so to speak, dead," and when he and his writings are, as a result, "exposed or delivered without any possible defense, once totally disarmed, to the other, to the others" (BS, 5th seminar, my trans.).

CHAPTER 4

The Late Derrida

Derrida is always late, *en retard*, the late Derrida. This is not because he was habitually late for appointments, lunch engagements, or seminars. Far from it. He was even compulsively ahead of time, always a few minutes early. Nevertheless, Derrida was always late, always behind time, until the end. A good thing too. I promise sooner or later to show why.

"I Could Never Tell a Story"

Derrida more than once said that he could never tell a story (MPdMe, 3; MPdMf, 27). I suppose he meant that something in him resisted organizing things neatly in a narrative, with a beginning, middle, and end, such as Aristotle said all good plots (*muthoi*) should have. Derrida's *The Post Card* can, however, be seen as a novel, even, by certain definitions, as a brilliantly innovative "postmodern" or at least "modernist" novel. It tells, or appears to tell, with exorbitant obliqueness, a love story, or several simultaneous love stories. A resistance to telling a story in straightforward chronological order is, however, a feature of twentieth-century Western fiction from Conrad and Faulkner on. This resistance crosses the boundaries from modernist to postmodernist, and of course it is present in earlier

55

fictions, too. It is even present already in Cervantes, for example, in "The Dogs' Colloquy," one of the *Exemplary Stories*. It is also one primary organizing (or disorganizing) feature of Laurence Sterne's *Tristram Shandy*, along with its concomitant, digression, *destinerrance*.

In Derrida's last set of seminars, "The Beast and the Sovereign (Two)," he once again tells a story. It is the story of me running toward death as death runs toward me. The immediate "context" of the citations I shall make from the second of these second ten seminars is, of course, the other seminars, in their tangled complexity, as they move back and forth from Defoe's *Robinson Crusoe* to Heidegger's seminar of 1929–30, *The Fundamental Concepts of Metaphysics* (*Die Grundbegriffe der Metaphysik*). Though Derrida was concerned with the question of death from his early work about Husserl on to the end, the next wider context of the concern with death in these last seminars is the abundant discussion of that grim topic in Derrida's late work, from "Circumfession" and the "exordium" ("Exorde") to *Specters of Marx* (SMe, xvii–xx ; SMf, 13–18), through *Aporias*, *Demeure*, on down to the interview in *Le Monde*, published a few weeks before Derrida's death, now published as *Learning to Live Finally* (*Apprendre à vivre enfim*). Behind all these are still earlier books, *The Gift of Death*, of course, then behind that *Cinders* (*Feu la Cendre*) and, behind once more, the works referred to in that strange and wonderful text "Envois," in *The Post Card*, "Telepathy," *Glas*, going all the way back to *Dissemination* and *Speech and Phenomena*, the latter with its epigraph from Poe's "The Facts in the Case of M. Valdemar," "*I am dead* [Je suis mort]" (SP, 1; VP1f, [i]). According to Derrida, this sentence is one that the "I," or conscious ego, can never utter. Once I am, so to speak, dead, "no more event to come from me [*plus d'événement à venir de moi*]," to exappropriate a phrase from "Circumfession" that has a different context, (Ce, 30; Cf, 30). All these works I have listed, one behind the other, are like the ghostly hands Thomas Hardy sees hovering over old furniture that has been used for generations: "Hands behind hands, growing paler and paler, / As in a mirror a candle-flame / Shows images of itself, each frailer / As it recedes."[1] The context I have invoked includes in the end all of Derrida's published work, not to speak of the unpublished seminars. To quote Percy Bysshe Shelley, "Death is here and death is there, / Death is busy everywhere,"[2] in Derrida's writings. The "determination" of context may, however, not be "saturated [*saturée*]," to borrow the strange word Derrida uses in his put-down, in "Signature Event Context," of the claim by Austin and Searle that an identifiable context determines the "felicity" or "infelicity" of a speech act (LIe, 3; LIf, 20). The context of a given statement or performative enunciation about death by Derrida is not easy to map, and that context is without identifiable borders. This presupposition about context is iterated in *Aporias*, with a modification that makes it more comprehensible: "we will dogmatically begin with the axiom according to which no context is absolutely saturable or saturating [*saturable ou saturant*]. No context can determine meaning to the point of exhaustiveness. There the context neither produces nor guarantees impassible borders, thresholds that no step could pass [*trespasser*], *trespass* [in English in the original]" (Ae, 9; Af, 26–27). *Saturate* comes from Latin *satura*, meaning "filled, stuffed." It is related to Latin *satis* ("enough") and English *satire* and *satisfaction*. If the context were to fill to saturation the text that dwells within it, that context would determine the text's meaning completely. Some people in "cultural studies" may sometimes be tempted to believe this. It would make research so much simpler and so much more satisfying. Derrida, however, "dogmatically" and "axiomatically" asserts that this is never the case. The text always exceeds its context. It must therefore be read for itself, micrologically, no doubt with the contexts, immediate and more distant, extending out to borderless indetermination, always in mind.

Analysis of these texts, even if it were limited to Derrida's late works on death, would be a lengthy matter, a *processus infini* (B, 38). This must be postponed for now, in order to focus on what "The Beast and the Sovereign (Two)" says about death. Several recurrent and salient motifs, however, may be identified in the work mentioning death not discussed in detail here. Derrida always speaks of death, my death, as possible impossible. He insists that death cannot be a matter of firsthand experience, of what the German phenomenological tradition calls *Erlebnis*. You can experience everything up to the moment of death, the "edge of life," but not death itself. Derrida, moreover, remains to the end unreconciled to his own death. He says he has neither learned to live nor learned how to die, which Montaigne and the Greek philosophers said was the same thing. When asked by Jean Birnbaum, the interviewer for *Le Monde*, whether he has "learned to live at last," he answers, after some evasions, "In fact not at all! . . . I have never learned to accept it, to accept death, that is [*Mais alors, pas de tout! . . . Je n'ai pas appris à l'accepter, la mort*]" (LLF, 24; AV, 24). Derrida iterates resolutely, contra Crusoe and contra what we know of Defoe, his disbelief in any life after death, in any redemption or resurrection. Derrida claims, in the last interview, that "I have the feeling that two weeks or a month after my death, *there will be nothing left [quinze jours ou un mois après ma mort, il ne restera plus rien]*" (LLF, 34; AV, 35). About the remains that remain when nothing remains, I shall have more to say in Chapter 5. Derrida, finally, always connects death with the wholly other and with a new concept of the performative utterance as saying "Yes" to a demand that comes from that wholly other.

Well, if you cannot experience death and therefore cannot speak referentially about it, you can tell fictitious stories about it.

The story about death in Derrida's last seminars is a story apropos of another famous story, Robinson Crusoe's response when he encounters the print of a naked foot in the sand. Derrida's improvisation on this episode and on what Defoe tells the reader went on in Crusoe's mind after he saw the footprint is wild and exuberant in a way characteristic of "the late Derrida," or indeed of Derrida's writings in general. What Derrida writes about *Robinson Crusoe* is a story about a story about a story, three stories nested within one another. Derrida's discourse digresses suddenly from his improvisations on Crusoe's fear of that footprint to tell another story, this one inspired by a passage from John Donne that, says Derrida, suddenly comes into his mind apropos of Crusoe's fear of that naked footprint. In addition, no one can doubt, Derrida is obliquely telling his own story. He is expressing his own fear of death. He is even, in later seminars in the series, making a frightening story of his fear, apropos of a few phrases in *Robinson Crusoe*, of being buried alive or eaten alive, as well as of the aporia, as he sees it, between being cremated or interred. The latter undecidability takes up an entire two-hour seminar! The sequence in the novel proper, from Crusoe's discovery of "the Print of a Man's naked Foot on the Shore" to Crusoe's actual encounter with Friday, takes a good many pages.[3] Derrida is especially interested, however, in Crusoe's initial reaction of abject terror and, within that, in the moment when Crusoe imagines that the footprint he has seen may be his own, so that he may be chasing and being chased by himself:

> In the middle of these Cogitations, Apprehensions and Reflections, it came into my Thought one Day, that all this might be a meer Chimera of my own; and that this Foot might be the Print of my own Foot, when I came on Shore from my Boat. This chear'd me up a little too, and I began to persuade my self it was all a Delusion; that it was nothing else but my own Foot, and why might not I come that way from the Boat, as well as going that way to the Boat, again, I consider'd also that I could by no Means tell for certain where I had trod, and where I had not; and that if at last this was only the Print of my own Foot, I had play'd the Part of those Fools, who strive to make stories of Spectres, and Apparitions; and then are frighted at them more than any body.[4]

Ghost stories, Crusoe here says, raise the fearful ghosts they appear only to describe. Here is a part of the improvisation that Derrida develops, in ornate arabesque, on the theme that Defoe has established of the possibility that Crusoe has seen his own footprint and is frightened by the trace of his own uncanny double or *revenant*. Derrida makes quite a story of it, placing himself, as a good storyteller or narrator does, within the mind and feelings of his protagonist. Derrida speaks eloquently for that imaginary, terrorized subjectivity, first in free indirect discourse and then in the intimacy of an interior monologue. A fairly lengthy extract must be cited, since the wordplay, exuberant hyperbole, and constantly self-topping inventiveness, like a great Charlie Parker riff or a Bach fugue, are fundamental features of what is going on here in Derrida's language. I shall return later to the jazz/Bach analogy and its implications.

> *Finally*, now that he has put down his Bible and has comforted himself with prayer, now he asks himself where he is, in what place and what will have been his path. He asks himself with even more anxiety if that print of a naked foot is not that of his own foot? Of his own foot on a path he has already traversed. At bottom, he never comes to decide if that trace is or is not his own, a trace left on a path about which he doesn't really know whether he has already impressed it, marked it out, or passed there or not. He doesn't know anything at all about it; he knows that he knows nothing about it. [*Il n'en sait trop rien.*] Is it I? [*Est-ce moi?*] Is it my track? Is it the specter of my print, the print of my specter? Am I in the process of returning? Am I or am I not a ghost, a *revenant?* a *revenant* of myself which I cross on my path as the trace of the other, on a path which is already a path of return and of coming back, etc.? I know too much nothing at all about it, or I know too well that I know nothing at all [*J'en sais trop rien, ou je n'en sais trop rien*] about the possibility of this *uncanny* [in English in the original], *unheimlich* double.
>
> He makes himself afraid. He becomes the fear that he is and that he causes himself to have. And all these pages, among the most extraordinary in the book, those that show him, where he shows himself in the process of meditating, in terror, about the trace of a naked foot, these pages should be read step by step [*pas à pas*], and, for example, in parallel with Freud's *Gradiva*, with all the *phantasmata*, that is to say, the phantasms and the phantoms who return on the imprint of a step, or of a naked foot, *the print of a naked foot* [in English in the original]. (BS, 2d seminar, my trans.)[5]

The reader will see how far Derrida goes beyond Defoe's words, while still responding responsibly to them. Defoe's ascription of fear to Crusoe is the product of a rationalist and empiricist early eighteenth century. To this has been added a peculiar Defoesque form of slightly ironic English Protestant sensibility, along with a superstitious streak, which, as Crusoe says in one place, means he is not sure whether or not he believes in ghosts. I say "ironic Protestant sensibility" because Defoe is not Crusoe. Though only Crusoe speaks in *Robinson Crusoe*, nevertheless a slightly amused and condescending Defoe may be glimpsed behind the terror Defoe ascribes to Crusoe at the "meer" sight of a footprint in the sand. Derrida's words about Defoe's words, however, could only have been written by Derrida, and only by a Derrida concerned to make a certain reading of Heidegger (the other topic of these seminars, though the passage just cited makes allusion also to Freud's essay on Jensen's *Gradiva*), as well as to appropriate *Robinson Crusoe* for his own ends. One might almost dare to say that Derrida turns *Robinson Crusoe* into a postmodern narrative, though just what that might mean is not all that easy to specify. Derrida also makes Heidegger into a kind of Crusoe, a "Heidegger-Robinson" (BS, 2d seminar), in his isolation and in his determination to find out his own path for himself.

Derrida's Crusoe is imagined to ask himself where he is, in what place, and by what pathway he got there, as though he were just waking from sleep or suddenly waking into existence, like those Cartesian and post-Cartesian wakers that so fascinated Georges Poulet in *Études sur le temps humain*.[6] For Crusoe to ask about his pathway or *chemin* is, like Descartes again, or like Heidegger after him, in Derrida's reading of Heidegger in these seminars, to seek a method, a way forward. *Method* comes, etymologically, from Greek *meta* ("after") plus *hodos* ("road or journey"). A good method follows after a track implicitly already laid out as a sure way to get where you want to go, that is, to a goal that is already there, waiting for you to get there.

The previous chapter has shown how Derrida's concept of *destinerrance* casts doubt on whether we can ever know where we are going or how we can be sure we are on the way, methodically, to a predetermined and preexistent goal. Derrida's Crusoe, however, is anxious less about the way forward, or even about the way he has got where he finds himself, than about the question of whether he has been there before. It could be that he has no more than inadvertently retraced his steps. He has, it may be, traveled in a circle without intending to do so. He may have come back to meet up with his own footprint in the sand. To have done that would be uncanny, *unheimlich*. It would have the particular form of uncanniness Freud associated with encountering one's own ghostly double. Shelley's

Zoroaster, to cite again a passage cited in the previous chapter, "met his own image walking in the garden."[7] To meet oneself would be even more terrifying than meeting the ghost of another. "We have met the enemy, and he is us," says Walt Kelly's Pogo.

Revenant: the word means something that has come back. It is the return, it may be, of a repressed or forgotten trauma. It might be better, for my mental health, that I should successfully repress or forget such a trauma. Toni Morrison's *Beloved* suggests that this might be the case with slavery in the United States. It might be better not to remember it, even though the goal of *Beloved* is to make all its readers remember it, in what she calls "rememory." If Crusoe has traveled this path before, it was, Derrida says, without knowing it. This is expressed in a characteristic Derridean wordplay. Crusoe may have been "describing" a trajectory without knowing it. But to describe, says Derrida, is also *parcourir*, to run through. To describe a journey is to make that journey. Crusoe does not know whether he decided to take this path once before and so is now haunted, so to speak, by himself or whether he is himself now haunting his other self. He cannot decide whether this is his own footprint or not. Derrida stresses this absolute nonknowledge and this absolute inability to decide, whereas in *Robinson Crusoe* Crusoe comes back some time later and discovers by careful measurement that a foot much bigger than his own made the footprint. It cannot be his own footprint. No such Enlightenment science for Derrida.

Derrida's Crusoe expresses, on the contrary, a hyperbolic nonknowledge. This happens just at the moment when Derrida shifts from the third person to the first person, in a more or less untranslatable French idiom: *J'en sais trop rien* or *Je n'en sais trop rien*, one of which means, literally, "I know too much nothing of it," the other, "I don't know too much nothing of it." Either locution could be translated, I suppose, as "I know nothing whatsoever about it" or "I know too well that I know nothing about it." "Is it me? Is it my trace? Is it my track? Is it the specter or my footprint, the imprint of my specter . . . Am I or am I not a revenant? . . . I know nothing at all about it . . . Who has decided what? and to go where?" and so on, in an amazing, inexhaustible, circling repetition of the same words or almost the same words.

I have compared this repetition with variation to Bach or to jazz. Such repetition is an essential feature of Derrida's late style. Here the stylistic repetition mimes the experience of being haunted by oneself, of obsessively retracing a path already traversed and coming back incessantly to confront oneself either as the haunter or the haunted, or rather, as both.

This doubling of the solitary self within itself empties out the self or overfills it, so that it is no longer unified, fixed, and self-contained. This destruction of the unitary self is the goal toward which the whole passage moves. I am alone, completely alone. At the same time, I am accompanied by the other me, the other in me. My specular phantom or uncanny double puts me in the situation of not knowing whether I am myself, whether, if I look into the mirror, I shall see my own image there or some stranger: "the other man as me, me as another, I who am another" (BS, 2d seminar). (This is an echo of Arthur Rimbaud's *Je est un autre*, "I is an other.") *J'en sait trop rien*. I know damn all about it.

The result is abject terror. This terror is generated by nothing more than seeing "the Print of a Man's naked Foot on the Shore." Derrida makes the circular island, with its path around the perimeter, a figure for Crusoe's self-duplicating solitude. At the climax of this sequence, Derrida identifies *fear* as the chief feature of Crusoe's reaction to seeing the naked footprint. It is both generalized terror, the worst kind, and at the same time fear of himself. He becomes the fear that he is and that he has made himself into: "He makes himself afraid. He becomes the fear that he is and that he has made for himself [or, has himself made; *Il se fait peur. Il devient la peur qu'il est et qu'il se fait*]" (BS, 2d seminar).

What Derrida says has drifted pretty far away from Defoe's words. It has turned into a marvelous descant on their implications. Derrida ends, however, with an exhortation to read again the words Defoe wrote, "step by step," but in parallel with a reading of Freud's *Gradiva* essay ("Delusions and Dreams in Jensen's *Gradiva*"). To do that would be yet another digression or deviation from the straight path. But perhaps the proper methodological way can here proceed only by such sideways juxtapositions or detours, by *destinerrance*. *Methode ist Unweg*, as Walter Benjamin said.

The reader will note that Derrida's reading of *Robinson Crusoe* has one important peculiarity. This feature distinguishes what Derrida says from most recent scholarship. He focuses primarily, though not exclusively, on Crusoe's solitary experiences, his relations, one might say, to himself, whereas much current scholarship of the "cultural studies" sort has been more concerned with Crusoe's enslavement of Friday, with his ownership of slaves on his plantation in Brazil, with his imperial sovereignty over his island as an example of European racist colonization, or with Crusoe's role as an exemplary Protestant capitalist and *homo economicus*. All that is relatively less interesting to Derrida than Crusoe's exemplification of the solitude of *Dasein* in the world. "Solitude" (*Einsamkeit*) is, after all, one of the fundamental themes of Heidegger's *The Fundamental Concepts of*

Metaphysics, the work that Derrida reads in tandem with *Crusoe*. Derrida, as I have said, weaves or wanders back and forth from one path to the other, from Heidegger to Defoe and back again, throughout the whole set of ten seminars.

What, exactly, motivates Derrida's repetitive style in these late seminars? Is it no more than a way of filling up enough pages to make a two-hour seminar? Or is it a pedagogical device, saying everything over a number of times to make sure that his auditors "get it"? Or is it a product of Derrida's inexhaustible, fantastic, linguistic inventiveness? He can always think of a thousand different ways to say almost the same thing. Or is it an attempt, by varying the phrasing, to get it right at last, to utter the "open sesame" that will lead to a direct confrontation with the "wholly other"? Or is there some even deeper motivation? The pages that follow the ones I have cited from the second seminar may give a clue. After all he has said about Crusoe's fear that it may be his own footprint, Derrida is not yet finished. He draws breath, and, perhaps inspired by Defoe, perhaps inspired by his own train of thought generated by Defoe's words, in response to them, he suddenly remembers two lines from a poem by John Donne. They come from who knows where into his mind. That sets him off again on another extraordinary, circular improvisation.

Running Toward Death, While Death Runs Toward Me

The improvisation is inspired (in the etymological sense of "breathed in") by his reading aloud of the lines by Defoe I began by quoting. In Derrida's seminar the citation comes after the commentary, preposterously, one might say, or metaleptically, the cart before the horse, whereas I have quoted it first. Citing Defoe leads Derrida to remember that Crusoe's fear leads him to retreat into his "castle" and immure himself there in abject terror. Derrida's Crusoe feels, as we have seen, as if himself as revenant were pursuing him, but that other self is really death. Time reverses, in a brilliantly succinct formulation in which the death toward which Crusoe runs, toward the future, is really running after him, from the past, or from the future anterior. It is as if he were already dead and as if everything that happens to him were happening not for the first time but as repetition, as *revenance*. Tomorrow is really yesterday, in a perpetual déjà vu. The future is something already past. Perhaps. He really does not know anything at all about it. It is not something open to cognition:

He feels himself followed by a trace [*une trace*], in short, chased or tracked by a trace. That is to say, by his own trace. Perhaps persecuted by himself and by his own return. As if he lived entirely in the past of his own passing as a terrifying future. He believes that he is about to die, that he runs after his death, or that life runs after him, that life will have been so short, and therefore, as if he were already dead, because of this speed race with his ghostly return [*sa revenance*], everything that happens to him happens not as novel, new, or to come, but as (perhaps; he doesn't know anything at all about it) already past, already seen [*déjà vu*], to come as yesterday and not as tomorrow. (BS, 2d seminar)[8]

This frightening reflection reminds Derrida suddenly of two verses by Donne that just pop into his mind: he says the quotation "comes from I don't know where into my memory (blackboard) [*revient de je ne sais plus où à ma mémoire (tableau)*]." I thought at first that *tableau* was a reference to Hamlet's phrase about "the tablets of my memory," but then I saw that it must be a note to himself to write the lines on the blackboard (*tableau*) for his auditors to see, to have before their eyes as he goes on talking. Derrida puts the lines in italics in his computer file:

I run to Death, and Death meets me as fast,
And all my Pleasures are like Yesterday.[9]

The passage from Derrida I cited a moment ago anticipates the essential points of what Derrida gets out of these two lines from Donne. That does not keep him, however, from writing an amazing commentary that goes on for six extraordinary pages more, too many to quote in toto here. I can only hope that all ten of these last seminars will soon be published, as is promised, or made available online or in a Derrida archive. They are a work of great genius, comparable, in their strange combination of repetitive abstraction and a kind of eerie ethereal passion, to Wallace Stevens's late poems or to Beethoven's late quartets. Here, as a sample, are just the first two paragraphs of the improvisation on the two lines from Donne. The passage repeats over and over, like a dominant note in a musical development, the word *hier*, "yesterday." *Hier, hier, hier*, "yesterday, yesterday, yesterday," until the word almost loses all meaning and becomes a mere sound:

I run toward death, I precipitate myself toward death, and death comes to meet me just as fast. (I run straight toward death, I run to death (*I run to Death* [in English in the original]) and death comes toward me, the encounter with death [*mort de rencontre*] seizes me, captures me or recaptures me just as fast, recaptures me at the same speed, just as soon.)

And all my pleasures are like yesterday, *like Yesterday* [in English in the original], like the yesterday, as if come from yesterday, my pleasures are already from yesterday, my pleasures are yesterday itself, they are dated in advance—and from yesterday. In advance they have passed, they are passed, already passed over, passed beyond [*passés dépassé*], already memories of lost pleasure [*jouissance*] or of returns of pleasure, ghosts [*revenances*] of pleasure. My present pleasures *are* [in English in the original] in the present yesterday's presents, they are yesterday. Not at all: they have been or they were yesterday, but they are presently yesterday. Their present is yesterday, the yesterday. (BS, 2d seminar)[10]

And so on. *Und so weiter.* One is tempted to go on and on, quoting the whole six pages. It is hard to find a place to stop. What Derrida writes is so eloquent, so passionate, so clearly inspired by a superb oratorical inspiration such as only the greatest speakers or writers possess, that one wants to have it go on and on. Nor does Derrida just repeat himself. The six pages turn this way and that the two lines by Donne in a spectacular tour de force that attempts, never quite completely, to exhaust their implications. The sequence ends with the following sentences. These return, once more, to the theme of doubling, to that echoing *hier* ("yesterday"), here repeated eight times in as many lines, to the fear of being haunted by oneself, or of encountering oneself as the wholly other, like meeting over and over that inescapable *hier*, or one's own image walking in the garden:

Not only what I enjoy is yesterday but perhaps, it is perhaps *my* yesterday or perhaps the yesterday, already, today, of *another*, and in every way of another, even if it is already, even if it were already another me myself. My pleasure is from yesterday, altered by yesterday, come from the other, the coming of the other [*venu de l'autre, la venue de l'autre*].

And the other would say to me, or I would say to the other: since I always run for dear life [*à mort*] after yesterday, yesterday will always be to come; not tomorrow, in the future, but to come, from in front, there in front, before yesterday [*au-devant, là devant, avant hier*]. (BS, 2d seminar)[11]

What can one say of the whole sequence, Derrida's spectacular verbal invention initiated by the passage about the "print of a naked foot"? Though one resists taking Derrida's reflections on death, which run through all ten of the last seminars, as disguised autobiography, it is hard not to see them as premonition of his own death, or as inspired by his fear of death. They were written, it happens, in the months and weeks just before his mortal disease was diagnosed and less than two years before his death. He seems to have known that "life will have been so short [*aura été*

si courte]," as he says, echoing Seneca's *De brevitate vitae* (Ae, 2; Af, 16).
He knew that he was speeding with ever-increasing rapidity toward death
or that death was rushing toward him. In an encounter I refer to more
than once in these chapters, an encounter that sticks in my mind as somehow decisive, I once, a few years before Derrida's death, said to him that
I was beginning to think, now and then, about death. With great earnest-
ness, he answered, "I think about it *every* day." All philosophy, Nietzsche
averred, is disguised autobiography. These seminars are the expression of
Derrida's unique version of Heidegger's definition of man (or *Dasein*) as
"being toward death" (*Sein zum Tode*).

Derrida emphasizes, perhaps even more than Heidegger, the terrifying
solitude of one's encounter with death. Only I can die my own death,
both Heidegger and Derrida affirm, but Heidegger asserts this relatively
dispassionately, as a universal feature of every *Dasein*, whereas Derrida
conveys to the reader, as affective passion, by way of what he says about
Crusoe, the solitude of being surrounded by death, pursued by death, pursuing death, having death as an immediate tomorrow that is a perpetual
yesterday, so that, dying, one is as if always already dead, or an example of
the "living dead" (*mort vivant*). That last phrase Derrida uses repeatedly
later, in the fifth and sixth of his last seminars. Both seminars are long
meditations on facing death. For both Heidegger and Derrida, death is
always already interior to *Dasein*. Being toward death is an essential component of my existence as a human being. Nevertheless, for Derrida, death
is experienced, at least in part, as not so much inside me as outside, in the
form of a quasi-personified being that is rushing toward me to devour me
or to bury me alive. Heidegger's phrase "being toward death" suggests
that death is always future, something toward which I move, as toward a
goal, whereas for Derrida death is before, behind, below, above, exterior
to me and within me, in whatever temporal or inside/outside direction I
look. Derrida, finally, is respectfully dubious about Heidegger's claim that
animals cannot die, that only human beings (*Daseins*) can die. "Only man
dies," says Heidegger. "The animal comes to an end. [*Nur der Mensch
stirbt. Das Tier verendet.*]" (Cited in BS, 5th seminar).[12] Derrida is not so
sure about that.

Why All That Repetition?

I have spoken so far as if Derrida's reflections on Crusoe's fear of death
were purely constative, wholly descriptive, no more than a truthful report

of the implications of what Defoe wrote. This is not the case. I shall turn now to an account of how Derrida's words are a peculiar kind of speech act or performative. I have asked what the function is in these seminars of inexhaustible repetition with a difference. I have compared this linguistic feature to jazz or to Bach. Derrida's lectures were notorious for giving their auditors their money's worth, so to speak. His lectures at the various Cerisy Décades devoted to his work went on for six hours, with a break for dinner after three hours. His plenary lectures at a Celan symposium in Seattle and at the Joyce symposium at Frankfort went on for two hours or more and were eventually published as short books. His "Rams" (*Béliers*) was written at the same time as the seminars on Defoe and Heidegger. It is a whole book devoted primarily to the reading of just one line from a poem by Paul Celan: "The world is gone, I must carry you [*Die Welt ist fort, ich muss dich tragen*]." This little book is a splendid example of Derrida's repetitive late style. The Celan line is cited and commented on more than once in the Defoe/Heidegger seminars, as if he could not get it out of his mind, just as this line from Celan appears more than once in this book's chapters, approached from a different perspective each time.

How can Derrida go on for so long? Why does he do it? I suggest that Derrida writes in this way in order to avoid coming to an end or, so to speak, "dying," in more ways than one.

The musical parallel may help to understand this. Derrida's rhetoric of repetition with a difference is like an aria accompanied by orchestra in Bach's *Christmas Oratorio*. An example is the heartbreakingly beautiful alto aria, near the beginning, "Prepare thyself, Zion" ("Bereite dich, Zion"), in which the same melody is repeated over and over, as if it could never end, until, finally, it leads to the triumphant chorale, "How Shall I Receive Thee?" ("Wie soll ich dich empfangen?"). Or, since Derrida was a jazz buff, one might say that his rhetoric is like a jazz structure, which repeats the motif and its development with a different instrument or in wilder and wilder variations, for example, a Charlie Parker solo. Just when you think such music must be at an end it starts again, inexhaustibly, with a patience that can be defined as a resistance to coming to the end. If I can just improvise something slightly different, I can go on even longer! In Bach's case, the inexhaustible repetition works as a form of prayer. I must pray incessantly, in the hope that sooner or later God will hear me and answer my prayer, and that I shall then have prepared myself and be fit to receive Him.

Neither a Charlie Parker solo nor a Derrida improvisation is exactly prayer, though they are not exactly not prayer either. The question of prayer comes up explicitly and is discussed at length later in the eighth seminar of "The Beast and the Sovereign (Two)" Derrida's meditation on prayer begins with the characteristic repeated questions with which these seminars often start. Early in the first seminar, for example, Derrida asks: "What exactly is an island? What is an island? [*Qu'est-ce qu'une île? Qu'est une île?*]." The pun on *île, il,* "island," "he," is explicit. Now, in the eighth seminar, he begins by asking:

> What is praying? How to pray? How not to pray? More precisely, if pray-ing consists in doing something, in a gesture of the body or a movement of the soul, what does one do when one prays? Does one do something? (to allow oneself or to make oneself pray, to develop)?
>
> Qu'est-ce que prier? Comment prier? Comment ne pas prier? Plus précisé-ment, si prier consiste à faire quelque chose, en un geste du corps ou un mouvement de l'âme, que fait-on quand on prie? Fait-on quelque chose? (se laisser et se faire prier, développer)" (BS, 8th seminar; my trans.)

You will have noticed Derrida's note to himself at the end that promises an even further development in the spoken seminar. What he sketches out here is to be developed, as a jazz riff develops a motif, perhaps in the oral presentation of the seminar. A lot more remains to say about praying or not praying. This, I suppose, would have been a discussion of the differ-ence between letting oneself pray and making oneself pray. Derrida's questioning initiatory style, the reader can see, is yet another way to avoid getting on with it, or perhaps it is the only way to get on with it, to keep oneself open to the other and to avoid coming to an end. Bach, Parker, and Derrida are all anxious, in the full sense of the word, to avoid doing that—coming to an end.

The first part of the sentence in Celan that Derrida quotes so often, *Die Welt ist fort,* is one of Derrida's basic presuppositions in these seminars. It is a quite different starting place from Nancy's or Husserl's or Heideg-ger's. All three of the latter, in different ways, see being with others, to-getherness, *Mitsein, Mitdasein, Miteinandersein, être avec,* as a primordial feature of *Dasein.* That means we all in one way or another share a single world. Heidegger may seem to contradict this claim when he celebrates the way *Dasein* in isolation forms its own world, forms the world, is *Welt-bilden,* world fashioning. That world, my world for me, however, for Hei-degger always primordially involves my own particular way of being with others, *Mitsein.* Each *Dasein* is a *Mitsein* ("being with"), a *Mitdasein* ("being there with"), a *Miteinandersein* ("being with one another"). All three words are used by Heidegger in *Being and Time*.[13] I investigate this Heideggerian assumption further in Chapter 6. For Derrida, on the contrary, each of us is primordially and forever denied sharing in a collective world. Each "I" turns in a circle within its isolated self. This turning is a chasing of death and being chased by it. Here is part of what Derrida has to say about Celan's *Die Welt ist fort*:

> "Die Welt ist fort": the world has gone, already, the world has left us, the world is no more, the world is far off [*au loin*], the world is lost, the world is lost from sight, the world is out of sight, the world has departed, farewell to the world, the world has died [*décédé*], and so on.
>
> But what world? What is *the* world? And, sooner or later: what is *this* world? So many inevitable and far-reaching questions. (R, 149; B, 46–47)

The long passage discussed earlier, descanting on Donne's two lines about his relation to death, does not simply paraphrase the lines. It does what it talks about, performatively, that is, it enacts a chasing of death that is a fleeing from death. It does this through words. Derrida's tacit presupposition is that as long as he can go on talking, he is not yet dead.

Derrida has so much to say, and he wants to say it all before it is too late. So he goes on talking, keeping time, in time, "against time." Talking, giving seminars, writing philosophy, writing criticism, writing poetry, are different forms of the postponement of death. At the same time, of course, such talking is the incorporation of death within oneself. The words spoken against death, out of mortal fear of death, speak of death, speak death. They anticipate a death that has already come, that is already belated, a thing of the past, a yesterday. I am already living a posthumous life/death. "I live my death in writing," said Derrida in that last interview (LLF, 33) and, in "Circumfession," "I posthume as I breathe" (Ce, 26; Cf, 28). Derrida always already speaks, writes, and breathes as the late Derrida. He spends his whole life running for dear life (*à mort*) to catch up with death and to escape death.

In these last seminars, the late Derrida makes constant digressions from his announced topics, Defoe and Heidegger. He brings in Donne, Rousseau, Blanchot, Freud, Celan, and so on, in a kind of constant evasion or putting off of coming to the point. *Digression* means getting off the path, getting on a detour, an *Umweg* ("detour") or a *Holzweg* ("forest path that leads nowhere"), to remember terms Heidegger uses. The question of finding the right path, of choosing the right path, is an essential theme of Derrida's last seminars. The theme is drawn from passages early in the Heidegger seminar of 1929–30, that is, *The Fundamental Concepts of Metaphysics*, but also from Crusoe's meditations on which path to choose on his island. All ten of the seminars are a digression from their announced theme, "The Beast and the Sovereign." Not all that much is said about either in these seminars.

On the one hand, Derrida affirms, no doubt truthfully, that he could make a whole year of seminars on this or that passage he cites, that he will talk of it later, cannot talk of it now, or has talked about it elsewhere, in a complex rhetoric of evasion, temporizing, and postponement. On the other hand, he keeps inserting new material from other authors that prevents him from moving forward on the path he begins by saying he has chosen. He calls this path, in the file name of each computer file: "Hei Foe." The sudden insertion of two lines from Donne, lines that, he says, appeared out of nowhere in his memory, is one such digression.

Derrida's discourse of digression turns in a round of constant rhetorical iteration, saying the same thing over and over in slightly different ways, often within the same sentence. It might be called an inexhaustible rhetoric of apposition, since it often advances, and does not advance, through a series of phrases in apposition. Here is a small-scale example, a cascade of phrases for being dead that I have had, and will have, occasion to cite from different perspectives more than once in these chapters: "when I will have passed, when I have passed, when I will have departed, deceased, gone away, disappeared, absolutely without defense, disarmed, in their hands, as one says, to put it that way, dead [*quand je serai passé, quand j'aurai passé, quand je serai parti, décédé, éloigné, disparu, absolument sans défense, désarmé, entre leurs mains, c'est-à-dire, comme on dit, pour ainsi dire, mort*]" (BS, 5th seminar; my trans.). This could go on interminably, since there is no reason not to add yet another phrase in apposition, though the passage as written ends with the dead clunk or clank of the word *mort*, death, as if Derrida had finally brought himself, reluctantly, to avoid euphemism. "Ask not for whom the bell tolls," said John Donne. "It tolls for thee."

The passage cited above about Celan's *Die Welt ist fort* is a good example of Derrida's rhetoric of apposition. Derrida proceeds without proceeding, in a constant process of capping what he has just said with a still deeper insight, as if he were saying: "You think that is all I can find to say about this passage I have cited, but you ain't seen nothing yet." He then proceeds to another higher, even less obvious or less predictable insight, like Charlie Parker transposing a melody to a yet higher harmonic.

Though I do not find this boring, quite the opposite, nevertheless Derrida's linguistic strategy is something like the temporal structure of profound boredom as Heidegger describes it in his example of waiting four hours for the next train in a provincial railroad station or as when we say

"I'm bored to death." Derrida has relatively little to say about the theme of boredom, *Langweile*, in Heidegger's seminars, though the discussion takes up over a hundred pages in *The Fundamental Concepts of Metaphysics*. We want the train to come, and we do not want the train to come, since profound boredom, like the fear of death, or like mourning or melancholy, puts us, Heidegger argues, in tune (*Stimmung*) with our authentic *Dasein*, the deepest levels of our being. An analysis of profound boredom will lead us to find the right path for an understanding of "World, Finitude, Solitude [*Welt—Endlichkeit—Einsamkeit*]," as they are named in the subtitle of Heidegger's seminars. All ten of Derrida's last seminars, as I have said, are governed by the running away from death that is a running toward death. That movement in place has a temporal structure not unlike that of profound boredom as Heidegger describes it.

Derrida's latest seminars constitute an energetic resistance to becoming the late Derrida. This just makes him later than ever, further and further away from his announced goal, like the white rabbit in *Alice in Wonderland*. "Oh dear! Oh dear! I shall be too late!" says the rabbit, after taking a watch out of its waistcoat pocket.[14] All of us will ultimately be late, really late. To reach the goal, to be on time, would be to be dead, so Derrida keeps talking, not to reach the goal, but to avoid reaching the goal. He must keep being late in order to avoid being late.[15] The later he is the better, until finally he is, alas, on time. The train comes to the lonely station, and he becomes the late Derrida. At that point, nothing remains but his remains.

CHAPTER 5

Derrida's Remains

Literature remains a remainder [*reste un reste*] of religion.

—DERRIDA, *The Gift of Death*

For although the people be as the sand of the sea,
yet a remnant of them shall be saved.

—Isaiah 10:22

And all the rest is literature.

—PAUL VERLAINE

to be dead, before meaning something completely different, signifies,
for me, to be delivered, in what remains of me [*dans ce qui reste de moi*],
as in all my remains [*comme dans tous mes restes*], to be exposed or
delivered without any possible defense, once totally disarmed, to the
other, to the others.

—JACQUES DERRIDA, "The Beast and the Sovereign (Two)"

In a remarkable passage I have cited in part as an epigraph, Derrida
gives, in the fifth of his last seminars, one more definition of *l'autre*, the
other. The concept of the other, as I have partly shown in Chapter 1, plays
a crucial role in Derrida's later writings on ethics, responsibility, politics,
friendship, decision, religion, sacrifice, death, and other topics. An example is the long meditation on the phrase *tout autre est tout autre*, "every
other is wholly other," in *The Gift of Death* (GD, 82–115; DM, 114–57).
In the last seminars, in a passage already cited in earlier chapters, Derrida
defines the others as those who will survive my death, "after the distancing
step of trespass [*après le pas d'éloignement du trépas*], after this passage, when
I will have passed, when I have passed, when I will have departed, deceased, gone away, disappeared, absolutely without defense, disarmed, in
their hands, as one says, to put it that way, dead" (BS, 5th seminar, my
trans.). To be dead, Derrida says in my epigraph, in a characteristically
hyperbolic or emphatic way, is to have ones remains, not just one's body,
but everything one leaves behind, totally at the mercy of others, to be
exposed, in what remains of him, in all his remains, to be delivered over
to the others, without any possible defense, to be at once totally disarmed.

72

What will happen, or should happen, to Derrida's remains, now that he is, so to speak, dead, and therefore at the mercy of us others? Who should have responsibility for deciding about that? What is the destiny of Derrida's legacy? Will Derrida's work continue to be read or will it be rapidly forgotten? Will what Derrida wrote and said, that is, his "remains," be understood and appropriated correctly, or will they be misunderstood and misappropriated? What does that mean, "appropriated correctly"? How would one, with the best will in the world, "apply Derrida" accurately? How should his work be used productively, now that he is dead? How would we (or I) wish it to be used?

"Understanding Derrida" implies a constative or cognitive operation. I either understand correctly what Derrida wrote or I do not. "Appropriating Derrida," however, is a double performative event. It assumes, first, that Derrida's work is not simply the object of cognitive understanding or misunderstanding but that it works performatively to make something happen in the reader when it is read. Reading Derrida is a way of letting something be done to me with words by responding responsibly to the demand Derrida's works make on me to read them. Second, reading Derrida obliges me to do something with words in my turn, to intervene productively, performatively, in my own situation or context, on the basis of my response to the demand to be read Derrida's works have made on me.

My context or "life situation" may be, almost certainly is, radically different from Derrida's own context when he wrote whatever it is that I am now reading by him. Derrida is a "world writer," that is, his works are read all over the world, perhaps most often, as is the case with Freud, in English. Derrida is a world writer in English. This means that people of all sorts read Derrida in translation, as part of the extremely problematic global hegemony of English. Derrida's readers are in radically diverse cultural and personal situations. What in the world do all these readers in China, in India, in Brazil, in Norway, in Africa, in Russia, in Canada, not to speak of the United States, make of Derrida? What *should* they make of him? How should they all use his work? Surely in different ways in each case. But should they all even read him at all? That does not go without saying, certainly not for all people.

If it is in general good to read Derrida, nevertheless it is possible to imagine a situation in which it might be bad for a given person to read Derrida, just as the "as if" or hallucination of the hegemonic nation-state is in many cases a bad thing but may aid liberation in certain situations, or just as the "essentialism" of some aspects of feminism may be politically useful and do good in some cases, even though that essentialism is theoretically suspect. Certainly those people who claim Derrida is saying "It's all language" or "A text has no meaning; you can make it mean anything you like" or "Deconstruction is out to destroy Western civilization" would perhaps do better either to keep silent or actually to read Derrida, with care, instead of just repeating what they have read in the newspapers. Quite a lot of such people exist, for example, the ignorant and malicious author of the *New York Times* Derrida obituary.

I conclude that the "destiny" of Derrida's legacy, now that he is dead, is uncertain and problematic. It is difficult to tell what will happen to that work and even more difficult, perhaps, to tell what *ought* to happen.

Derrida, it happens, had a lot to say over the years about legacies. He was even, one might say, obsessed with the question of inheritance. Conspicuous examples are *Archive Fever* and *Specters of Marx*. Derrida was anxiously concerned, more narrowly, with the question of what would happen to his own work after he was dead. It is impossible, for me at least, to read the magnificent, prolonged meditation, in Derrida's last seminars, on the fear of death, as it is expressed in Defoe's *Robinson Crusoe*, without thinking that this meditation expresses Derrida's attempt to confront his own death. That death occurred less than two years later. To put it mildly, Derrida did not exactly, in Dylan Thomas's phrase, "go gently into that good night."[1] He spends a good part of an exuberant seminar, the sixth of those last seminars, asking whether it is better to be cremated or interred. He asks this question apropos of Robinson Crusoe's fear that he may be buried alive and in a global context of different religions and cultures. He concludes that thinking about this choice leads to a genuine aporia, an undecidable either/or. If I am interred, I may not yet be dead. I may be buried alive, a horrible thought. If I am cremated, my ashes may be scattered to the winds, disseminated, destinerred, disinterred. I will then have no *place* to mark the fact that I once lived. Derrida obviously worried quite a bit about these alternatives. He was, in the event, interred, not cremated.

It is not possible, in my view, to read the passage I have cited in my epigraph without seeing it not only as a hyperbolic expression of Derrida's frightening idea that after he is dead those who survive him can do anything they like with his body but also as the expression of an anxiety about what will happen after his death to his *restes*, his remains, in the secondary sense of all those pages he wrote, published and unpublished. To be dead, says Derrida, means, for him, to be delivered over, in what remains of him, as in all his remains, to the others and to be completely disarmed before those others. The phrase *tous mes restes*, "all my remains," plays on the double meaning of "remains" as my dead body and as the writings I leave behind me.

That double meaning, however, is more evident in English than in French, so you might call my play on "remains" a violence I am doing to Derrida's *restes. Reste* in French is more likely to be used, for example, to name what is left over after a collective meal, the remains of a feast, as in Hamlet's "funeral baked meats" that "did coldly furnish forth the marriage tables" (*Hamlet,* 1.2.180–81). "Remains" in the sense of writings left after the writer's death are often called, in an ominous Latinate term, the writer's "corpus," for example, when I say "I have read the entire corpus of Derrida's writings." The second and third meanings of *remains* in the *American Heritage Dictionary of the English Language* are "a corpse" and "the unpublished writings of a deceased author." Note the limitation in the word *unpublished.* This restriction is not entirely pertinent in Derrida's case, since most of his unpublished manuscripts have already been made public as orally delivered seminars, often taped by auditors. In any case, I am daring to use the word *remains* to refer to all Derrida's writings and speakings, published and unpublished, including recorded oral presentations.

The first dictionary meaning of r*emains* is "all that is left after other parts have been taken away, used up, or destroyed," and the fourth meaning is "ancient ruins or fossils." What Derrida left behind in the form of the twenty thousand or more pages of unpublished writings, mostly seminars given over the years, are, one might say, "ancient ruins or fossils." Derrida used to talk, somewhat wistfully, of his hope that in his old age he might find time to revise and rewrite these for publication. I have been told that he left instructions that they not be published as he left them, as his remains. In a similar way, he refused to have official tapes made of the wonderfully eloquent improvised translations he made into English of his last fifteen years of seminars when he presented them at the University of California at Irvine. My English is not good enough, he said. It was a big mistake not to tape those seminars, in spite of his prohibition, surreptitiously, since they often contained wonderful, arabesque commentaries, asides not in the French texts he was translating. Derrida never stopped students who were making tapes of their own, so some remains of these impressive performances must exist, floating around somewhere out there in the universal teletechnical archive or database. Happily, all Derrida's "remains," in the sense of his unpublished manuscripts and computer files, will be published, so we are promised, in French and in English, over the next decades. This will be done by Galilée in France and by the University of Chicago Press in the United States.

Both columns of Derrida's *Glas* begin with a complex play on the French words *reste* ("remains, detritus") and *rester* ("remain"). On the right-hand, Genet side, the text begins with a citation from Genet. This presents the scandalous image of someone flushing the neatly torn-up pieces, that is, the *restes*, of a Rembrandt down the toilet: "'*what remained* [ce qui est resté] *of a Rembrandt torn into small, very regular squares and rammed down the shithole*' is divided in two" (Ge, 1b; Gf, 7b). So much for the great European aesthetico-mimetic tradition, represented here by Rembrandt! It is divided in two from within, like everything else. On the left hand, Hegel, side, the speaker/narrator begins by asking, ("what, after all, of the remain[s] [*quoi du reste*], today, for us, here, now, of a Hegel?") (Ge, 1a.; Gf, 7a). The French makes a pun on *aigle* (eagle) and Hegel, both pronounced more or less the same in that language: "His name is so strange. From the eagle [*aigle*] it draws imperial or historic power" (ibid.; ibid.). The eagle, symbol of German nationalist and imperialist aims, is merged, in a pun, with the Hegelian view of history as a preordained destiny. "What remains of that double legacy today?" Derrida, or his spokesperson, asks.

Many salient examples of the words *reste*, *rester*, or *restance* may be found scattered throughout Derrida's works, like the ashes of a holocaust victim or of a more benign cremation, if there is such a thing. *Reste* and its cognates were important words for him. I shall cite and discuss three more salient cases, each referring by a silent relay to the others, in a way that is characteristic of Derrida's writing. This abyssal cross-reference makes any example of the word *reste* or its cognates the ghost, trace, or cinder of all the others, or they hover as specters behind it, with never a solid, bodily, substantial example that can be said to be the founding "source" for the others.

The word *remains* appears insistently at one place in the interview with Derek Attridge that opens *Acts of Literature*. It comes up apropos of Derrida's claim that literature is an institution in the West allowing in principle the right to say everything, to put everything in question. "What is it?" asks Derrida. "What 'remains' when desire has just inscribed something which 'remains' there, like an object at the disposal of others, one that can be repeated? What does 'remaining' mean?" (AL, 37). The words in quotation marks in the original French were presumably *reste*, *reste*, and *restance*. "Remaining," in this passage, remains a question. The question is related to the strange fact that a literary work is at once an "object,"

something that remains after an act of inscription, and something repeatable, something ghostly, which is detachable from its material substratum,
something that would remain, at least "virtually," even if every copy were
destroyed, as Derrida affirms in "The Time of a Thesis" ("Ponctuations:
Le temps d'un thèse") (TT, 37 ; DDP, 443).[2]

The most important exegesis of what "remains" might mean that I have
found in Derrida's writing appears in *Paper Machine*. Here Derrida makes
explicit what he means by saying that "remains" are not just something
physical, like a corpse, or like we tend to assume Derrida's manuscripts
are in the two archives that house them. The passage is lengthy, but it
makes a sequential argument. That argument is crucial to understanding
my topic in this chapter. In this interview with Antoine Spire for *Le monde
de l'éducation* (September 2000), Derrida connects his thinking about *reste*
to his more familiar concept of the trace. Since Spire was having some
difficulty understanding what Derrida was saying and since what Derrida
means by *reste* is counter-intuitive in any case, Derrida spells out his meaning with particular care:

> A trace is never present, fully present, by definition; it inscribes in itself the
> reference to the specter of something else. The remainder [*Le reste*] is not
> present either, any more than the trace as such. And that is why I have been
> much taken up with the question of the remainder, often under this very
> name or more rigorously under that of *restance* or remaining. [I suppose
> *restance* is more rigorous because what is in question with *reste* is not a fait
> accompli but a continuous process, not a remainder but an act of remain-
> ing. A present participle names that better.] The remaining of the remain-
> der [*La restance du reste*] is not reducible to an actual residue, or to what is
> left after a subtraction, either. The remainder *is* not, it is not a being *[un
> étant]*, not a modification of that which is. Like the trace, the remaining
> offers itself for thought before or beyond being. [Oblique references to
> Heidegger and Levinas here.] It is inaccessible to a straightforward intu-
> itive perception (since it refers to something wholly other [*du tout autre*], it
> inscribes in itself something of the infinitely other), and it escapes all forms
> of prehension [A phenomenological term for a grasping by consciousness
> of something other than itself, a grasping that is not comprehension or
> apprehension, but just "prehension"], all forms of monumentalization, and
> all forms of archivation. Often, like the trace, I associate it with ashes [*à la
> cendre*]: remains without a substantial remainder [*reste sans reste substantiel*],
> essentially, but which have to be taken account of and without which there
> would be neither accounting nor calculation, nor a principle of reason able
> to give an account or a rationale (*reddere rationem*), nor a being [*étant*] as

such. That is why there are *remainder effects* [effets de reste], in the sense of
a result or a present, idealizable, ideally iterable residue. What we are saying at the moment is not reducible to the notes you are taking, the record-
ing we are making, or the words I am uttering—to what will remain
[*restera*] of it in the world. The remains of what remains cannot be calculated in this way. But there will also be remainder effects, sentences fixed
on paper, more or less readable and reproducible. These remainder effects
will thereby have presence effects—differently in one place or another, and
in an extremely uneven way according to the contexts and the subjects that
will get attached to it. A dispersion of the remainder effects, different interpretations, but nowhere the substance of a remainder that is present and
identical with itself. (PMe, 151–52; PMf, 385–86)

This is, I must say, even for Derrida, a bizarre paragraph, remarkable
in its intransigent negativity. A remainder or *reste*, he is saying, must not
be thought of as any kind of material residue, such as all those Derrida
manuscripts, printed books and essays, all those tapes and digital record-
ings, that remain after his death, stored or archived here and there. A
remainder is not the leftover part of something larger, the product of an
act of subtraction. A remainder is not in any way ever present, nor is it any
kind of being. It is not present. It is nothing substantial. It is not what it
is, or what it seems to be—as, for example, the pages of manuscript in
the Critical Theory Archive at the University of California at Irvine seem
examples of Derrida's "remains." A *reste*, in the sense Derrida meant that
word, is not amenable to reason or to any form of calculation, such as the
arithmetic of subtraction I mentioned a moment ago.

Well, then, what in the world *is* it, a *reste*? Derrida gives various hints
in the passage. For one thing, he asserts that a *reste* is not amenable to the
rational logic of the "is," the copula. It is not what it is. A remainder,
moreover, is like a trace. According to Derrida, as we know, a trace is not
what it is because it is a sign referring to something ghostly, something
other than itself and prior to itself or posterior to itself, "a movement in
which the distinction between space and time has not yet come about"
(PMe, 150; PMf, 384). A trace is subject to the law of what Derrida called,
notoriously, *différance*, differing and deferring at once. As I shall show
below, Derrida warns us against thinking of the trace on the model of
a track left by an animal that may be followed again from pawprint to
pawprint.

If a remainder is like a trace (though the extent of this likeness is not
entirely clear), then it is a sign of the same peculiar sort that a trace is.

The word "iterable" in the passage connects Derrida's thought of the remainder with all he says about performative language in *Limited Inc.* A remainder is the trace of an iterable set of signs. That means that it can be detached from any single material base and from any "saturable" context. It can function differently in many different contexts and with many different material substrates. The phrase "idealizable, ideally iterable residue" connects what Derrida is saying here with his way of reading Husserl and with his claim, in "The Time of a Thesis," mentioned already, that he planned at one time a dissertation on literature as an ideal object, that is, as an object free or able to be freed from any material base, though it is "bound" to a particular language, whereas the ideal triangle does not depend on the existence of any material triangle, such as those printed on the paper of geometry books, nor is a triangle language-bound (TT, 37; DDP, 443).

That is part of what Derrida means by saying that, though a remainder is not a material residue, there are "remainder effects" in the sense that a given embodiment of a *reste*, "sentences fixed on paper," can have effects, can give rise in many different contexts, unpredictably, through "dispersion," to different "interpretations," such as the interpretation of Derrida's *reste* I am at this moment proferring.

The claim that "since [a remainder] refers to something wholly other, it inscribes in itself something of the infinitely other" is a precious clue to what Derrida means by *reste*. It authorizes us to think of a remainder as insubstantial, immaterial, nonpresent, a specter, because it comes from the wholly other, is invoked by the wholly other, and therefore has something of the wholly other inscribed within it. Derrida may have put pen to paper or fingers to computer keyboard and written such and such a set of words, leaving the manuscript or printout behind, but actually it was the wholly other speaking through him, commanding his "invention," that inscribed itself in those words. That source defines the nature of Derrida's remains. They are inscriptions of the *tout autre*, and therefore anything but substantial.

If remains are as fragile and immaterial as Derrida says, then we would be wrong to think of those two archives of Derrida's manuscripts, the one at Irvine and the one at IMEC (L'Institut Mémoires de l'Édition Contemporaine) near Caen, plus what remains in his home in Ris-Orangis, as safely preserving what Derrida wrote. Derrida's remains are still in danger, even though the originals now at Irvine were carefully photocopied in Ris-Orangis before being sent to California, so the duplicates could be stored at IMEC, far from the danger of nuclear holocaust in Paris. This is like having a double backup for computer files. Derrida compulsively made more than one backup of things he was writing on the computer. But all that was for naught, or practically for naught.

Why? As Derrida forcefully argues in *Archive Fever*, any archive functions doubly. Archivization works not just to preserve someone's writings, safe and sound, but also to aid in their forgetting and destruction. This happens by way of the Freudian death drive or destruction drive, by what Derrida here names with the Greek word *hypomnēma*, that is, weak, partial, or incomplete memory, brought about by the very effort of trying to preserve memory. This penchant toward making unsafe in the very act of trying to make safe was later on to be called by Derrida the self-destructive "logic of autoimmunity": "right on that which permits and conditions archivization, we will never find anything other than that which exposes to destruction, and in truth menaces with destruction, introducing, *a priori*, forgetfulness and the archiviolithic into the heart of the monument. Into the 'by heart' [*par coeur*] itself. [As when we say, "He knows Derrida's works by heart."] The archive always works, and *a priori*, against itself" (AF, 12; MdA, 26–27). We think Derrida's manuscripts are safe and sound in the Irvine Critical Theory Archive and at IMEC, but just putting them there tends to lead to their forgetting, just as Derrida expressed in his last interview his fear that two months after his death his work would be completely forgotten, even though his books would remain in libraries. *"There will be nothing left,"* he said (LLF, 34; AV, 35). Precious little use, so far, has been made of either archive, though with at least one notable exception (the admirable work of Jason Smith on the manuscript antecedents of *Specters of Marx*). A big project is being carried out to transcribe and publish all Derrida's seminars, in both French and English. But will they be read, even then? Most people tend to rejoice that Derrida's manuscripts have been saved, but to postpone reading them, much less memorizing them "by heart." Just because they are safely stored, we can safely forget them. When Derrida saw his catalogued manuscripts in the Irvine library, neatly and professionally stored in long rows of gray cardboard file boxes, he said, "They look like so many tombstones!"

My readers may think the digital revolution has changed all this fragility of the paper archive. This vulnerability makes Derrida's remains still like papyrus rolls in the famous library of Alexandria. That library's burning destroyed many precious remains of Greek civilization. Now, with scanning, hard drives and servers that are terabytes in capacity, distributed databases, multiple backups, and all the other wonders of prestidigitalization, archives, you might think, can be made absolutely safe. Not so, says Derrida.

Derrida recognizes and brilliantly identifies the revolutionary changes digitization and new telecommunications devices have made in people's lives, as well as in institutions such as psychoanalysis or the university. Derrida argues that not just the external means of archiving have been changed. Internal perception and memory systems that generate "material" to be archived have been radically altered too in the change from handwriting to the typewriter to the computer to the iPhone. Derrida singles out e-mail as of special importance:

> electronic mail today, even more than the fax, is on the way to transforming the entire public and private space of humanity, and first of all the limit between the private, the secret (private or public), and the public or the phenomenal. It is not only a technique, in the ordinary and limited sense of the term: at an unprecedented rhythm, in quasi-instantaneous fashion, this instrumental possibility of production, of printing, of conservation, and of destruction of the archive must inevitably be accompanied by juridical and thus political transformations. These affect nothing less than property rights, publishing and reproduction rights. (AF, 17; MdA, 35)

Psychoanalysis, during Freud's lifetime, depended on handwritten letters and notes, and on the postal system, that is, on what today we, in our impatience, call "snail mail." Psychoanalysis would have been altogether different, both theoretically and practically, says Derrida, if Freud and his associates had had email. Derrida says he would have liked to have devoted his whole lecture to the "retrospective science fiction" project of imagining psychoanalysis "if . . . Freud, his contemporaries, collaborators, and immediate disciples, instead of writing thousands of letters by hand, had had access to MCI or AT&T telephonic credit cards, portable tape recorders, computers, printers, faxes, televisions, teleconferences, and above all E-mail" (AF, 16; MdA, 33). Why would psychoanalysis have been radically different if Freud had possessed email? Because, says Derrida in striking (and counter-intuitive) formulations, the technical mode of archiving alters what it stores not just when it stories it, but in its coming into existence: "the archive, as printing, writing, prosthesis, or hypomnesic technique in general, is not only the place for stocking [*stockage*] and for conserving an archivable content *of the past* which would exist in any case, such as, without the archive, one still believes it was or will have been. No, the technical structure of the *archiving* archive also determines the structure of the *archivable* content even in its very coming into existence and in its relationship to the future. The archivization produces as much as it records the event. This is also our political experience of the so-called news media" (AF, 16–17; MdA, 34).

As H. Marshall McLuhan long ago said: "The medium is the message."

The pages in *Archive Fever* that take note of these revolutionary psychic, institutional, and political changes in the way we live now, changes brought about by new prosthetic devices externalizing memory, could be supplemented by more elaborate analyses by Derrida in *Echographies, Paper Machine*, "Faith and Knowledge," *Rogues, Le toucher*, and elsewhere. The import of these technological changes is one of the big topics in Derrida's late writings. It deserves a chapter to itself. Despite Derrida's acute recognition of "these radical and interminable turbulences" (AF, 18; MdA, 35–36), however, he argues that the destruction drive operates, if anything, even more powerfully and more inevitably with archived digital databases than with paper archives. The "archive drive" is still as much as ever divided between "archive desire," the desire to save and store everything, written and graphic alike, and "archive fever," or *mal d'archive*, which cannot exist "without the threat of this death drive, this aggression and destruction drive" (AF, 19; MdA 38).

"Bugs" always remain in software. Hard drives sooner or later fail. An inadvertent wrong command can erase a hard drive. Hackers are, one might say, the destructive drive built into the World Wide Web. Though hackers may in some cases think they are politically motivated, they often appear to act on the basis of sheer anarchic, technophiliac desire to see what can be done to destroy "archives" stored in hard drives and available by way of Web sites. They do this by sending out viruses and worms, or through "bots," that is, surreptitiously and undetectably commandeered private computers all over the world, made into unwitting "robots" or "zombies." These zombies then send out millions of commands to selected Web sites. This overload will tie up thousands of hard drives and servers, bringing a whole national Internet system, government, banks, and commercial companies alike, to a standstill. Even a country's security may be threatened, as in the case of Russian hackers of the Estonian computer system in 2007.[3]

Hackers are in this remarkably like the antibodies of the human immune system. I am borrowing the figure Derrida later used for what he calls in *Archive Fever*, following Freud, the destruction (*Destruktion*) drive, the aggression drive, or the death drive (AF, 10, 11; MdA, 24, 26). This drive is instinctive and irresistible. Most hackers are highly trained programmers, often professionally employed by banks, companies, or government agencies, including military ones, to enhance the security and secrecy of their computer systems, to set up "firewalls" and the like. My

Mac receives frequently from Apple or Microsoft an invitation to download an enhancement to the security program of the Apple operating system or of Microsoft Word, the word-processing program I am using at this moment. I just downloaded today (February 20, 2008) from Microsoft a Security Update to protect my Word program from a "malicious" invader, as their update message calls it, that would erase my hard disk. Needless to say, I hastened to install the update. Soon new invasions will be devised, however, in the endless internecine battle of the Internet against itself. As soon as I have an "Internet connection" I am, willy-nilly, part of this system.

These "security updates" are no doubt prepared by highly trained programmers at Apple or Microsoft. Something, however, often goes wrong with some of those trained programmers, by an apparently inevitable mutation. Benign computer nerds become hackers. These programmers are prosthetic appendages to the system, with great power over its workings. Nevertheless, a certain number of these specialists turn against the system itself. This is analogous to the behavior of antibodies in autoimmune reactions. The function of antibodies is to protect the body against "antigens" that come from outside the body, such as viruses. Nevertheless, in certain catastrophic cases, these antibodies turn against the body's own organs and tissues, destroying them.

It not an accident that we call the destructive programs hackers insert into computers by way of the Internet "viruses." Computer viruses function in relation to the Internet in the same way as organic viruses function in the human body. Both kinds of viruses replicate themselves endlessly and destroy what they inhabit. The figure of the "computer virus" encourages us to think of the World Wide Web as a living organism, which in a sense it almost is, or of the body as a computer system, which in a sense it almost is. The bottom line, as Derrida says, is that "remains," in the multiple sense of paper remains, digitized files, and human bodies, are subject to a cruel law that says: "The archive always works, and *a priori*, against itself" (AF, 12; MdA, 27).

Putting all Derrida's remains online, though it would make them, happily, more easily available, would not protect them from the destruction drive or from the disaster of autoimmune self-destruction, just as Derrida was, ironically, killed by a cancer that some medical scientists think is the result of an autoimmune response. I say "ironically" because he had, years before his death, so brilliantly identified the way autoimmunity works in the archive and in any given political community. I discuss Derrida's extended concept of autoimmunity in Chapter 6. Derrida's final interview, with *Le Monde*, was called, citing him, "I Am at War with Myself." This was a covert allusion, among other things, to his mortal illness. In a similar way, the World Wide Web is at war with itself. To translate *Mal d'archive* as *Archive Fever* is accurate enough, since in French one says *Je suis mal* for "I am sick," but the translation misses the way *mal* also means "bad" or "evil," as in Baudelaire's title for his collected poems: *Fleurs du mal*. Derrida makes that overtone explicit when he says, in the last sentence of his "exergue" on the destruction drive as it inhabits the archive: "There is not one archive fever, one limit or one suffering of memory among others: enlisting the in-finite, archive fever verges on radical evil [*le mal d'archive touche au mal radical*]" (AF, 20; MdA, 38–39).

A final, extremely helpful clue to what Derrida meant by "remains" is his assertion, in the long passage cited above, that "Often, like the trace, I associate it [i.e., *reste*] with ashes [*à la cendre*]: remains without a substantial remainder [*reste sans reste substantiel*]." Why is that association helpful? The word *reste* occurs at a crucial moment in Derrida's *Cinders*. This is the last of my three salient occurrences of the word *reste*, dispersed like scattered ashes here and there in Derrida's work. A cinder is, at least in English, not quite the same thing as ashes. A cinder may, to my sense, still have fire latent in it, as in Derrida's title *Feu la cendre*, while ashes are what remains of a completely burnt-out cinder. We rarely speak of "an ash." The habitual plural in "ashes" suggests that we English speakers tend to think of ashes as multitudinous, pulverized, light as air, almost insubstantial, whereas a cinder, in English, at least to my ear, retains some cohesiveness in maintaining, to some degree, the skeletal shape of what was burned to make it.

Derrida plays on that nuance of a distinction. The passage in *Cinders* I shall cite explicitly associates cinders or ashes with remains. As the context makes clear, the Holocaust, in which so many millions of Jews were turned to ashes, hovers in the background throughout *Cinders*. The Holocaust reference is sometimes made explicit, as in the passage that follows. *Cinders*, like "Envois" in *The Post Card*, is a strange polylogue, in which various imaginary persons speak. The passage in question, like all of *Cinders*, is a commentary or a developmental variation on a single motif, the untranslatable phrase, strange even in French, "il y a là cendre." This strange verbal cinder, Derrida says, just came into his mind. The phrase is translated, plausibly enough, by Ned Lukacher as "cinder there is." By the weird idiomaticity of French, however, it means literally something like "it there has there cinder," since both *y* and *là* are ways of saying "there." As whoever is speaking says, about some "he," perhaps "Derrida himself," this phrase is "gray dusty words [*poussière grise de mots*]," "something material—visible but scarcely readable" (C, 41, 43). It is scarcely readable because it "refers only to itself," that is, to its self-reflexive working as words, not to any referent outside itself, as meaningful words are supposed to do. Here is the passage:

> At present, here and now, there is something material—visible but scarcely readable—that, referring only to itself, no longer makes a trace, unless it traces only by losing the trace it scarcely leaves.
>
> —that it just barely remains [—*qu'elle reste pour peu*]
>
> —but that is just what he calls the trace, this effacement. I have the impression now that the best paradigm for the trace, for him, is not, as some have believed, and he as well, perhaps, the trail of the hunt [*la piste du chasse*], the fraying [*le frayage*], the furrow in the sand, the wake in the sea, the love of the step for its imprint, but the cinder (what remains without remaining [*ce qui reste sans rester*] from the holocaust, from the all-burning [*du brûle-tout*], from the incineration the incense)
>
> —That it remains [*Qu'elle reste*] for very few people, and, however slightly one touches it, it falls, it does not fall into cinders, it gets lost down to the cinder of its cinders. In writing this way, he burns one more time, he burns what he still adores although he has already burned it, he is intent on it (C, 42)

"The cinder of its cinders" would, perhaps, be the grey dust of ashes. Traces, cinders, ashes, remains, all are alike in being the locus of one of those Blanchotian formulations, "*X* without *X*," that are so important for Derrida, for example, when he speaks in *Aporias* of the possible impossibility of death. In this case, *le reste*, the remainder, such as Derrida's archived manuscripts, is what "remains without remaining," and that is pretty much all you can say about it, though I have been trying, proleptically and at some length, to gloss that formulation.

Well, what remains without remaining, here and now, of Derrida's legacy? What is destined to happen to his remains, in all the obscurity and aporetic complexity of what Derrida meant by this word? It is best to answer this question in Derrida's own terms, as a way of taking possession, by exappropriation, of Derrida's legacy and then casting it forth again, as in this essay you are reading right now. Derrida's investigation of this issue takes three forms. I shall analyze the first two of these in this essay. The third is the focus of Chapter 3 of this book. These forms are: (1) Derrida's reflections on his own legacy; (2) his reflections on the legacies of others;

(3) his general reflections on how events that take place in the nonpresent "now," especially those registered in the performative aspect of writings or speech, will inflect the future, the *avenir*, the "to come." This will happen in the unpredictable and adventitious ways that Derrida called *destinerrance*. That portmanteau word or its "concept" appears frequently, as I have shown, in many works by Derrida over the years.

Derrida was too modest to have had anything much to say about his own legacy or, it might perhaps be better to say, too scrupulously polite not to cover up his lack of modesty. He did not often openly confront the question of his works' future or destiny after he was dead, though a passage in *A Taste for the Secret* and some remarks in the last interview, *Learning to Live Finally*, are exceptions. After his death, his works would be, like his dead body, totally disarmed, totally at the mercy of others, without any chance, any longer, for him to set the record straight. Derrida, or his remains, are, my readers will not have failed to note, entirely at my mercy at this moment. He is not around to tell me I have misunderstood him. While he was alive, Derrida did often try to set the record straight, especially in the many interviews he granted, but also in seminars and in published essays and books. He was always kind, perhaps even a little ominously kind, in what he said about things I wrote on his writings over the years before his death.

One of the relatively rare places where Derrida discusses what will happen to his remains, in the sense of his works, after his death is in the first of the interviews he granted Maurizio Ferraris and Gianni Vattimo in Paris, at his home in Ris-Orangis, and then in Turin, on different occasions from 1993 to 1995, published as *A Taste for the Secret*. In the passage I shall cite, from the first interview, with Ferraris (Paris, July 16, 1993), Derrida has been defining deconstruction in its relation to the great canonical, putatively systematic Western philosophers. Each such philosopher has left what may be called an oeuvre, that is, something capable of being signed (in all the ambiguity of "signature") with a single name: "Plato," "Heidegger," or whatever. These systematic texts have, Derrida says, most occupied him in his philosophical teaching and writing. He lists Plato, Kant, Hegel, and Husserl (TS, 4). Derrida then makes once more a patient attempt to define deconstruction and to correct a common misunderstanding of it. The definition is expressed this time in relation to deconstruction's approach to systematic philosophers and in relation to what he has just been saying about the way time is always "out of joint," in Hamlet's phrase; *aus den Fugen*, in Heidegger's formulation. (The fullest Derridean exploration of this figure for time is in *Specters of Marx*.) That time is out of joint, disarticulated, means that it resists being thought about by way of a present now or of the contemporaneous. Here is Derrida's definition of deconstruction:

> Deconstruction is not a method for discovering that which resists the system; it consists, rather, in remarking, in the reading and interpretation of texts, that what has made it possible for philosophers to effect a system is nothing other than a certain dysfunction or "disadjustment," a certain incapacity to close the system. Wherever I have followed this investigative approach, it has been a question of showing that the system does not work, and that this dysfunction not only interrupts the system but itself accounts for the desire for system, which draws its *élan* from this very disadjoinment, or disjunction. (TS, 4)

Derrida emphasizes that this strategy must be applied differently to each oeuvre. Deconstruction is not an all-purpose tool that deconstructs every system in the same way, like a recipe for cooking all fish, flesh, or fowl identically. What works for Plato does not work for Hegel. The *pharmakon* is the element that unworks Plato's system, but it does not work to unwork Kant or Hegel. It is necessary to read each oeuvre to find out what, in each case, is the element that does not fit, the element that is out of joint with the system in question but that makes the system possible/impossible. That variability in terminology and approach has sometimes confused Derrida's readers.

Well, what about Derrida's own work? Does it form a system or oeuvre? Derrida's answer is interesting and perhaps even a little surprising, given the perhaps seemingly incoherent abundance of his work. He claims that all of his work has emerged from what he calls a *pari stratégique*, a strategic wager. He says this wager is unjustified and fortuitous, in the sense that he has no right or reason to make just this commitment. It is a leap in the dark. A wager is a specific form of speech act. By definition, you may either win or lose a bet. You cannot know ahead of time, otherwise it would not be a wager at all, but an absolutely certain prediction. Derrida's bet was a decision to enter, in a specific way he calls "deconstructive," by way of his own singularity into the singular context in which he found himself. He decided to practice in a "deconstructive" way his profession of philosophical teaching and writing within the institutions that had appointed him, initially the École Normale Supérieure, then the École des Hautes Études en Sciences Sociales, plus numerous U.S. universities where he taught as a visiting professor: Johns Hopkins, Yale, the University of California at Irvine, Cornell, New York University.

It was a double wager. First, Derrida bet that he would be able to enter his immediate context and change it. Second, he bet that what he wrote on the basis of that wager would form a nonsystematic oeuvre that would hang together without hanging together, as Maurice Blanchot might say. This oeuvre would therefore be able to function in radically new and different contexts in the future, that is, when it would come to be read by all sorts of people all over the world:

> when I began to write such and such about, say, Husserl, the writing corresponded to a context that can be described: a world-wide philosophical context, and more specifically a French context at a certain moment, and, even more specifically, in a certain academic field, and so forth. But, over time, the coherence and consistency of what I have called an *oeuvre* should make it possible that—and this is the wager—twenty, thirty, forty years from now what has been said in the context might not simply be contradicted or out of date, and thus might resist—insist—to the point where the context would no longer simply be a collection of conditions circumscribing what I say, but also formed by what I have said within it. (TS, 14)

A work (oeuvre) does not simply enter into or respond to the ever-widening circles of its surrounding contexts. It enters into those contexts as a large-scale speech act to form or deform, in any case to change, those contexts. The work then makes sense and functions in that changed context. Derrida, somewhat scandalously, confesses that he has sometimes deliberately written in such a way that he hopes he will not be understood, or at any rate not understood at first, so that what he has written will strike people as strange, untimely, perhaps even a little mad. He says he does this, however, so that what he writes will change the context in such a way as to make what he has written readable, "legible." That has certainly happened.

Derrida formulates the general law that justifies his wager by saying: "What I have called *oeuvre*, making use of this somewhat suspicious or conventional term, is a manner (endogenous, to some degree) of producing the conditions of legibility of that which has been produced" (TS, 15). "Endogenous" means "produced from within." The work itself works to make itself legible. An example of this law at work in literature is the way Joyce's *Ulysses* at first seemed to a considerable degree unreadable to many people but gradually became so normal a mode of writing in modernist literature that now *Ulysses* seems to most people "a piece of cake," perhaps even a little *vieux jeu*, old hat. Derrida's bet is that the law that an oeuvre produces its own context or modifies any existing one will work with his own work, his remains, his corpus, his legacy. If that happens, if he wins his strategic wager, this will mean that his work will have changed all the different worldwide contexts enough so that his work will be performatively effective, in all its singularity and idiosyncrasy, though in unpredictable ways, in widely different contexts in the future.

If this turns out to be the case, if Derrida wins his bet, then he has no reason to be anxious about what happens to his remains after he dies. They have a secure future to come, a felicitous *avenir*, a happy destiny. This is a wonderfully cheerful and optimistic confidence. Why, then, does Derrida worry so much about what will happen to him when he is gone away, passed, deceased, departed, disappeared, and, in a manner of speaking, "dead"? If his work works, if he wins his bet, then he should have nothing to worry about. Nevertheless, he worries. He worries because, whatever he says about that wager, he knows that when he is gone he will then be totally disarmed, wholly at the mercy of others, completely unable, as a ghostly voice from "beyond the grave," to try once more to straighten people out about what deconstruction is. He will be completely unable to say: "No, you have misunderstood. You have got me wrong. Let me try to explain."

A small example of that straightening out is a somewhat surprising remark Derrida makes in one of the interviews with Ferraris. He sharply distinguishes his work from structuralism and from what is, often still today, called "the linguistic turn." His opposition to "logocentrism," he says, was an opposition to linguistics and to the form of it called "structuralism":

> The irony—painful, at times—of the story is that often, especially in the United States, because I wrote "il n'y a pas de hors-texte" [there is nothing outside the text], because I deployed a thought of the "trace," some people believed they could interpret this as a thought of language (it is exactly the opposite). Deconstruction was inscribed in the "linguistic turn," when it was in fact a protest against linguistics! (TS, 76)

As Derrida elsewhere explains, more than once, his deconstruction is not "a thought of language" because it is always, from the beginning to the end of his oeuvre, a thought of the unthinkable, that is, of what is beyond language. He calls this beyond *le tout autre*, "the wholly other." If it is really other, wholly other, beyond language, unsayable, not much more than that can be said about it. Derrida goes on in the passage just cited, in one of the few places where he explicitly (and with extreme prudence) differentiates his thought from that of Paul de Man, to say: "I do the best I can to mark the limits of the linguistic and the limits of the rhetorical—this was the crux of my profound debate with Paul de Man, who had a more 'rhetoricist' interpretation of deconstruction" (TS, 76).

Derrida's remark about de Man gives a clue as to why Derrida was right to be anxious about what would happen to his work after his death. The clue lies in what had happened at Derrida's hands, so to speak, to the helpless remains of others. This is the second of the three rubrics I listed above. Derrida wrote extraordinary essays about living contemporaries, for example, his essays about Foucault, Lacan, Levinas, Blanchot, Ricoeur, and even about my own work. These combine generosity and sharp disagreement in different mixes in each case.

The most important testimonies, for my purposes here, are the essays Derrida wrote as memorials or works of mourning for friends after their deaths. Many people (myself, for example) remain mute, speechless, inarticulate after a friend dies, perhaps in a way that is not altogether healthy. Silence may prolong the mourning and may even turn it into that forever incomplete mourning Freud called "melancholy." Derrida, it happens, challenged Freud's distinction. For him, all mourning, as he said more than once, is perhaps really interminable melancholy. (See Chapter 12 in this book.) Derrida had, in any case, a conspicuously different reaction to the death of a friend from my ineffectual stammerings. The death of a friend or associate characteristically generated in him an extraordinary outpouring of words. Derrida was one of the greatest writers of such memoirs or memorials of all time. Chapters 11 and 12 of this book discuss further the motivation for these eulogies.

To be human is to feel the need for obituaries, eulogies, or memorial celebrations of the dead, as well as for grave-markers, tombstones with inscriptions, and epitaphs. We want to locate the bodies of the dead and to give them decent burial. An example is the inordinate effort still being made to recover and identify the bones or bodies of those missing in action in the Vietnam War. Until we find those remains, we think those soldiers may still be alive somewhere. This need to memorialize the dead was conspicuously and hyperbolically present in Jacques Derrida. His response to the death of a friend was immediately, in a hurry, before it was too late, to write an essay or book about that person—Paul de Man, for example, or Emmanuel Levinas, or Maurice Blanchot, or all those others who are the subjects of Derrida's memorial portraits of the dead in *The Work of Mourning*, or, as the augmented French version is called, *Chaque fois unique, la fin du monde* (*Each Time Unique, the End of the World*). Derrida hurried into print after a friend's death, despite his frequent assertion that this death left him dumb, speechless.

An example of the latter demurer is what he said in the newspaper *Libération* just hours after receiving the news of Jean-François Lyotard's death: "I feel at such a loss, unable to find public words for what is happening to us, for what has left speechless [*coupe le soufflé de*] all those who had the good fortune to come near this great thinker" (WM, 214; CFU, 255). Being left speechless did not keep Derrida from speaking, and right away, as if there were need for haste. He speaks, publicly, in the act of saying he is speechless. Nor was he kept silent by the resolution he affirms in the earliest of these works of mourning, "The Deaths of Roland Barthes," never to yield to invitations to speak or write about friends soon after their deaths: "What I thought impossible, indecent, and unjustifiable, what long ago and more or less secretly and resolutely I had promised myself never to do . . . was to write . . . just following the death, *upon or on the occasion of the death*, at the commemorative gatherings and tributes, in the writings 'in memory' of those who while living would have been my friends" (WM, 49–50; CFU, 77). Nor was Derrida kept in silence by his full awareness, expressed frequently in his works of mourning, of the traps laid by such writings, the temptations to bad faith, to narcissistic exposure of grief, to the revelation of private facts that ought perhaps to have been kept secret, to the use of a friend's death as an occasion to score points and get even.

In defiance of all these prohibitions, Derrida wrote many such essays or books anyway. He did this in response to what seems to have been an irresistible compulsion to speak or write. Within a few days, weeks, or months of the deaths of Paul de Man and of Emmanuel Levinas, Derrida had written brilliant books on each, *Memoires for Paul de Man* and *Adieu to Emmanuel Levinas*. He interrupted the course of the last seminars "The Beast and the Sovereign (Two)" to produce, over the weekend after Maurice Blanchot died, a wonderful memorial seminar about Blanchot. This was read at Blanchot's funeral ceremony.

Derrida himself, so I am told, directed that no tributes by others be read at his interment. He asked that a short statement he himself had prepared, on his deathbed, so to speak, be read. That last wish was granted, though I am told some citations from his own work were read. Derrida clearly wanted to have the last word about himself. He did not want anyone else to play the role of graveside orator he had played for Blanchot. *Chaque fois unique* is, so far as I know, one of the last two books to be proofread by Derrida before his death, plus the sections by him in the celebratory volume of essays brought out as a big volume of *L'Herne*. The other is *Béliers* ("Rams"), an amazing little book about one line in a poem by Paul Celan—"Die Welt ist fort, ich muss dich tragen [The world is gone, I must carry you]"—in the guise of a memorial for Hans Georg Gadamer. I suppose Celan means by this sentence that now you are dead, the world has ended. I am left as survivor to bear the burden of carrying your posthumous survival. That is my situation now, in relation to Derrida. It is the situation of all us survivors, now that Derrida is dead. His final proofreading of these three books was done during his mortal illness, when he was living in the shadow of death. He told me during that time, in the fall of 2003, that he could no longer work, that is, add to his oeuvre, but that he was able to proofread work written earlier.

The death of a friend generated speech or writing in Derrida, lots of words. Why? What did he hope to accomplish with these words? They were written, always, with his own imminent death in mind. In *A Taste for the Secret*, in response to a question from Vattimo, "Do you think about a 'survival' [afterlife] or not?" Derrida answers:

> I think about nothing but death, I think about it all the time, ten seconds don't go by without the imminence of the thing being there. I never stop analyzing the phenomenon of 'survival' as the structure of surviving, it's really the only thing that interests me, but precisely insofar as I do not believe that one lives on post mortem. And at bottom it is what commands everything—what I do, what I am, what I write, what I say. (TS, 88)

Why did Derrida think about death all the time, and why did he hasten to write essays or books about dead friends? It was, I suggest, because his urgent desire to render them all justice was motivated by his own constant fear that he might die before he could do that. Elsewhere in *A Taste for the Secret*, speaking of the urgent demand for justice, the demand that justice be rendered *now*, not some time in the future, and the relation of that to the eschatological or messianic, Derrida says:

> When I say this, I know I am speaking of my death—where, to be sure, I can reappropriate nothing, where I will no longer be able to reappropriate the future. Only a mortal can speak of the future in this sense, a god could never do so. So I know very well that all this is a discourse—an experience, rather—that is made possible as a future by a certain imminence of death. The imminence here is the fact that death may arrive in any moment—Heidegger discusses this brilliantly in *Being and Time*—and the fact that death may arrive in any moment gives this justice the character of an immediate injunction. (TS, 23)

Why was Derrida's attempt to act justly in response to the death of another an outpouring of memorial words, that is, just what he was to prohibit at his own burial? I think the motive was double. On the one hand, he wanted, as I have said, to render justice to his dead friends. These memorials are, for the most part, wonderfully generous and hospitable. These say with great eloquence the best that can be said for what these dead friends wrote and for them as persons. These acts of mourning are inhabited by a sense of urgency, a desire to eulogize the dead. This he did in obedience to the adage that one should speak only good of the dead: *de mortuis nil nisi bonum dicendum est.* He needed to do that as quickly as possible, before it was too late to render that justice or before the person might be forgotten. Derrida wanted to fulfill the survivor's debt to the dead other by securing as best he could the survival of the other's remains, in this case, what he or she wrote. This he did in recompense for those writings, though they were a gift that could never be repaid. He wanted to praise his dead friends, to thank them for the gifts of their friendship and of their writings. He wanted to do this in spite of his theory that the gift, *s'il y en a*, if there is one, is a debt that can never be paid off.

Derrida also wanted to account for the dead friend's writings, to reckon them up accurately. He wanted to have the last word, so to speak. He wanted to confirm that the dead friends were really dead, as in certain cultures the skull is cracked open or the heart removed to make sure the dead person will not rise from the dead. He also wanted to be sure of the permanent location of that dead body. It was virtually located, safely enclosed, beneath or within all those eloquent words of memorial celebration, Paul de Man within *Mémoires pour Paul de Man*, Emmanuel Levinas within *Adieu to Emmanuel Levinas*, Maurice Blanchot within "To Maurice Blanchot," and so on. That even the titles of these essays sometimes contained an edge is exemplified by *Adieu to Emmanuel Levinas*. *Adieu* means "good-bye" in French, but it literally means "May you be consigned to God," just as the English word *good-bye* comes from "God be with you." As readers of Derrida's various essays on Levinas will know, his reservations about Levinas had in part to do with what Derrida saw as the latter's tendency to think of God as a person. To say "adieu" to Levinas is a way of saying that he hopes that the God in whom Levinas believed exists and will take good care of him. As for Derrida, he has his doubts.

Derrida's memorials are inhabited by a desire to put the dead friend in his or her place, to have the last word, to pay back a debt in a less benign sense. Derrida's acts of mourning characteristically contain a discreet and sometimes almost invisible desire to make evident and clearly marked Derrida's difference from what Levinas wrote, or from what de Man wrote, or even from what Blanchot wrote. Derrida spontaneously, and apparently without much reflection about what he was doing, took advantage of the fact that the other was now dead and could not answer back. He saw this as a chance to settle scores, ever so generously and covertly. Of course it would be going too far to say what I am about to say, to take advantage in my turn of Derrida's present helplessness. Nevertheless, it sometimes seems to me as if Derrida, in spite of the genuineness of his grief and his need to write something as part of his work of mourning, was waiting for these friends to die, one by one, so he could write a spectacularly brilliant essay about the work of each, now that they were departed, deceased, gone away, in short, dead, and could no longer add anything to their work, nor respond to anything he might say about that work.

Obsequies of whatever kind in whatever culture tend to have this double, aporetic motive. On the one hand, they want to make sure the dead person is really dead, that he or she will not return as a ghost to haunt the living. It is best not to take any chances. Rituals of obsequy are a way of having done with the dead, washing one's hands of him or her once and for all. On the other hand, eulogies for the dead, such as graveside orations or tombstone inscriptions, are intended to ensure that the dead will not be forgotten, that they will survive accurately in the memories of the survivors. It therefore is urgently necessary to render justice to the dead. This is the aporia of mourning.

A further step toward understanding mourning in Derrida may be taken by looking at the titles of the English and French volumes collecting Derrida's memorials for his dead friends. Pascale-Anne Brault and Michael Naas wrote a fine introduction on mourning in Derrida's work for *The Work of Mourning*. The title presumably had Derrida's blessing. It asserts that mourning is not something that just happens of its own accord and ultimately passes away, as you "get over" the death of a friend. Mourning is work. It takes an effort. You have to work hard at it. One way to work at it is to write memorial essays about dead friends, a set of works, like the essays collected in *The Work of Mourning*. Such work-essays would be, strictly speaking, speech acts, performative enunciations. They are a way of using words to make something happen. They work to bring about the working through of mourning, so that one may ultimately reach the point where one has survived grief.

If Derrida is right in what he says about the perpetual contamination of mourning by melancholy, however, reaching that point is impossible.

He says as much in many places. In *Memoires for Paul de Man*, for example, Derrida speaks of "the impossible mourning [*deuil impossible*], which, leaving the other his alterity, respecting thus his infinite remove, either refuses to take or is incapable of taking the other within oneself, as in the tomb or vault of some narcissism" (MPdMe, 6; MPdMf, 29). Mourning is like the endless labor of Sisyphus. In the afterworld, Sisyphus pushed a heavy stone uphill, only to have it roll down again, and again. Or mourning is like the endless labor of the Danaids. They were condemned to all eternity to carry water in leaky vessels. As the English idiom puts it, they were forced to "carry water in a sieve." The mourner's melancholy work is never done.

The most extravagant reason for this compulsion to render justice to dead friends is encapsulated in the title Derrida gave to the French version of *The Work of Mourning: Chaque fois unique, la fin du monde*. This book augments the English version with essays on Gérard Granel and Maurice Blanchot, who had died after the English version appeared. The title was no doubt Derrida's own. It appears to mean that the death of a friend is each time a unique event, no doubt because each person is unique, singular, irreplaceable, just as my relation to each friend differs from my relation to any other of my friends. The death of a friend is, as we say, like "the end of the world." "It would be the end of the world for me if she were to die." Or "each time unique, the end of the world," can be taken to mean that the death of my friend or of my beloved is the end of that person's unique world. That world exists only for that person, just as my world only exists for me. My friend's unique world is snuffed out in an instantaneous and catastrophic de-creation when that person dies.

No, says Derrida in the "Avant-propos" to *Chaque fois unique*, that is not at all what I mean. (This "Foreword" does not, of course, exist in *The Work of Mourning*.) I mean, says Derrida, the end of the whole world, his or hers, mine, and everyone else's. That end happens when any person (or an animal or a divinity) dies. This means that the world can come to an end and yet not come to an end, that the end of the whole world has the strange property of being repeatable. It can, and does, happen over and over. The unique world comes to an end not just for the one who dies but also for the survivor, in what Derrida calls an "impossible experience." It is impossible because the infinite totality seems to have the possibility of disappearing, once and for all, and yet to reappear, and then disappear once more, over and over, every time someone, or even an animal, dies. That is what "world" means for us mortals. It has its meaning only by way of what the French call *la mort*, "the death," death as a hypostatized or even anthropomorphized entity. Nothing can really be done about this recurrent catastrophe. If the death of another, especially of a friend or of someone I have loved, means the end of world not just for him or her, but for me too, that's that. All I can do is to register this calamity in a work of mourning that takes the form of a torrent of words that is always too many and at the same time not enough, since no work of mourning is ever complete.

The reader will note, as Derrida himself does, that the strange formulation in Derrida's title presupposes that there is no life after death, no *anastasis* ("resurrection"), such as consoles Nancy in *Noli me tangere: On the Raising of the Body*, and that presupposes the existence of some God:

> "God" means: death [*la mort*] can put an end to *a* world, it ["God"] would not know how to signify the end of *the* world. One world can always survive another world. There is more than one world. More than one possible world. That is what we would wish to believe, however little we believe or believe that we believe in "God." But "the death" ["*la mort*"], death itself, if there is such a thing, does not leave any place, not the least chance, either for the replacement or for the survival of the sole and unique world, of the "sole and unique" that makes of every living being (animal, human, or divine), a sole and unique living being. (CFU, 11, my trans.)

I suppose Derrida means that God, if God were to exist, would guarantee the continued existence of *the* world, across the successive deaths of all living beings. That is what we believe or believe that we believe, but Derrida has his doubts. It is on the basis of this intransigent resistance to the consolations of belief that Derrida glosses the meaning of his title, posing it "in the fashion of a thesis":

> the death of the other, not only but especially if one loves that other, does not announce an absence, a disappearance, the end of *this or that* life, that is to say, of the possibility for a world (always unique) to appear to *a given* living being. Death [*La mort*] declares each time *the end of the world in totality*, the end of every possible world, and *each time the end of the world as unique totality, therefore irreplaceable and therefore infinite.*
>
> As if the *repetition* of the end of an infinite whole were once more possible: the end of the world *itself*, of the only world which exists [*du seul monde qui soit*], each time. (CFU, 9, my trans.)

The italics here indicate Derrida's urgent insistence that we understand what he is saying, as well as his awareness of how counterintuitive his "thesis" is. The evident absurdity of saying that the whole world comes to an end when one person (or animal) dies should not be glossed over. What does this mean? Derrida patiently explains it in the sentences I have cited. The death of another is not just the disappearance of a singular life that was the possibility of a certain unique world that appeared to a certain living person. That death was, on the contrary, the end of the world in totality, the end of every possible world, the end of the unique and therefore irreplaceable world. Then, in a kind of daily miracle, the sole and unique world reappears again, with me remaining alive in it as a survivor of the death of my friend or beloved.

Derrida's essays about Paul de Man are a particularly salient case of his double motive for writing about a dead friend. During all those years he was a survivor after de Man's death in 1983, Derrida stoutly maintained his fidelity to what de Man had written. He kept resolutely silent about what must have, to put it mildly, somewhat annoyed him, that is, de Man's attack on him in "The Rhetoric of Blindness: Jacques Derrida's Reading of Rousseau," published in book form originally in 1971, in the first edition of *Blindness and Insight*.[4] Now, after all those years of hyperbolic praise of de Man's remains, Derrida takes his revenge. He does this, moreover, at a conference entitled "Material Events," a conference devoted to de Man's work. The conference was organized, at the instigation of Tom Cohen, on the assumption that enough time had passed since the revelation of de Man's wartime writings so that a dispassionate look at what de Man actually wrote might once again be possible. Derrida's strategy in the paper he gave at that conference, "Typewriter Ribbon: Limited Ink (2) ('within such limits')" works, in part at least, by deploying the same ploy de Man had used to defend Rousseau against Derrida. De Man, to put it somewhat crudely, had argued that the superior insight Derrida claimed to have, in *Of Grammatology*, into what Rousseau was blind to, was already present in Rousseau's writings. Rousseau knew it all already. Derrida had borrowed or stolen from Rousseau the weapons he used to attack him. One of de Man's targets is the periodization that underlies Derrida's argument. Rousseau, Derrida presupposed, belonged to the metaphysical or logocentric epoch. Therefore he could not yet have known what we twentieth-century deconstructionists know. De Man argues that Rousseau was there already. He is our contemporary.

Derrida now, decades later, returns to what Rousseau wrote, what de Man wrote, and what he himself wrote, to argue not only that de Man misread Rousseau on certain points, but that he, Derrida, had already said what de Man said in refutation of him (that is, Derrida). Andrzej Warminski, in an admirable quite recent (and so far unpublished, to my knowledge) essay, "Machinal Effects: Derrida With and Without de Man," presented at a Derrida memorial conference at Yale, uses the same strategy once more, this time to argue, with carefully presented evidence, that de Man, to put it somewhat crudely again, had already said everything Derrida claims to be putting forward as a correction to de Man's reading of Rousseau. Derrida takes from de Man what he claims to be adding to what de Man said, just as de Man claimed Derrida did with Rousseau.

Talk about the pot calling the kettle black! These fellows play hardball, indubitably, but they seem to exploit, again and again, the same rules or strategies of the game. No doubt this sequence has its comic side. It is analogous to the comedy, commented on long ago by Derrida, of the way Nietzsche claimed to be beyond philosophy, beyond metaphysics, whereas Heidegger came along and said, "No! Nietzsche is the last metaphysician. I, Martin Heidegger, am beyond metaphysics." Derrida himself, carefully, scrupulously, in (literally) ten thousand pages of seminars over many decades, puts Heidegger back in the logocentric camp. Derrida is too clever to claim that he, Derrida, is at last beyond metaphysics. No one, he says, can escape logocentrism, by whatever hyperbolic strategy. Nevertheless Derrida would define deconstruction as at least a demonstration of why it is impossible to get beyond metaphysics and why even the most rigorous and systematic expression of logocentrism contains elements that keep that system from ever closing. Plato, the father of metaphysics, was, in a sense, already beyond metaphysics as soon as he started talking about that *pharmakon*, just as Aristotle's treatment of metaphor, and, especially, of catachresis, undoes the apparently coherent, logocentric, totalizing system of the *Poetics* as an integral part of Aristotle's oeuvre.

The sequence of Derrida's essays on de Man, which includes the brilliant discussion of Henri Thomas's roman à clef about de Man in "'Le Parjure,' *Perhaps*: Storytelling and Lying ('abrupt breaches of syntax')" ("Le parjure, peut-être ['brusques sautes de syntaxe']"; WA, 161–201, JD, 577–600), is a spectacular demonstration of Derrida's combination of eulogy and scrupulous criticism in what he wrote about the legacy of others, their remains. It also, in his anxiety always to have the last word, suggests why he may have had reason to be anxious about what would happen to his own legacy after his death. This was an anxiety about what would happen "after Derrida," that is, after that particular end of the world called the death of Derrida, followed by its new beginning. "After Derrida" was the name of the special issue of *Mosaic* for which this chapter was originally written.

Derrida, in the interview in *Le Monde* published just two months before his death, expresses his anxiety about his remains in the form of double contradictory hypotheses. One uses a form of the word *reste* and has been cited already. On the one hand, Derrida feels that "one has not yet begun to read me," and that "it is later on that all this has a chance of appearing," that is, that he will perhaps be seriously read at last, that justice will be done to what he has written, but only after his death. On the other hand, he has the feeling that "two weeks or a month after my death, *there will be nothing left* [il ne restera plus rien: *nothing more will remain*]" (LLF, 34; AV, 35). He will be forgotten completely. Nothing will remain but those now unread books moldering in libraries. Happily, he was wrong about the second hypothesis. As for the first, it is certainly true that many books and essays about his work, such as this one, for example, have appeared since Derrida's death. Whether, if he were around to read them, he would feel they do justice to his remains is another question. Probably not, though he would remain discreet and secret about that.

No doubt I, by an ineluctable necessity, am repeating Derrida's double gesture toward his dead friends. I am pronouncing a eulogy for my departed friend, in a work of endless mourning that is like the end of the world, my world as well as his. My last chapter here returns to the question of mourning and to the way this book is a work of mourning, no doubt not a wholly successful one. At the same time I am trying to render justice to Derrida by putting him in his place, perhaps even, unbeknownst to me, trying to have done with him, so I can get on with it now that he is gone. The sun also rises, bringing a new world. All the many conferences and journal issues devoted to memorializing Derrida, such as the issue of *Mosaic* in which this chapter first appeared in an earlier form, conspicuously have this double force.

Derrida exploited with admirable amplitude and eloquence this double act of faithful/unfaithful taking possession of a legacy for present purposes. He did this, in relation to the always uncertain future of *destinerrance*, in *Specters of Marx*. *Destinerrance*, as I have shown in more detail in Chapter 3, means that whatever I write, whatever message I send, is, perhaps, though we can never be sure, destined to wander, to err. It is capable of functioning, but in unpredictable ways, in new contexts, by an implacable performative law. To be faithful to Marx today, for example, we must be unfaithful to him. In *Specters of Marx*, this exappropriation is explicitly formulated as a new theory of performatives and as something different from what Marx said in the *Theses on Feuerbach*:

> This dimension of performative interpretation [*de l'interprétation performative*], that is, of an interpretation that transforms the very thing it interprets,

will play an indispensable role in what I would like to say this evening. "An interpretation that transforms what it interprets" is a definition of the performative as unorthodox with regard to speech act theory ["speech act theory" is in English in the French original] as it is with regard to the 11th Thesis on Feuerbach ("The philosophers have only *interpreted* the world in various ways; the point, however, is to *change* it." [*Die Philosophen haben die Welt nur verschieden* interpretiert; *es kömmt aber drauf an, sie zu* verändern.]) (SMe, 51; SMf, 89)

Derrida's performative interpretation differs from standard speech act theory in being unauthorized either by a pre-existing self or by a pre-existing conventional context. It creates or recreates both performer and context. In this case the context is the text of Marx, which Derrida's unauthorized interpretation enters to change by a transformative interpretation. An interpretation that transforms what it interprets is a scandalous deformation of the ideal of an interpretation that strives to be as faithful as it can to what it interprets, not to go one iota beyond what the text says. It differs from Marx's eleventh thesis on Feuerbach in daring to believe that interpretation itself, interpretation as exappropriation, can be revolutionary. It can change the world as much, or better, than tearing up paving stones and mounting the barricades.

This essay is no doubt an example of what will happen, is already happening, to Derrida's corpus now that he is no longer around to defend it. I can only hope that it is more exappropriation than misappropriation. Such an exappropriation is an unauthorized, legitimate/illegitimate response to the demand made on me to read Derrida and to take possession of what he wrote, for my own purposes here and now, in a new context. That context can be called, as the best name for the place in which we now survive: "The World Recreated Once More, after Derrida."

CHAPTER 6

Derrida Enisled

Yes! in the sea of life enisled,
With echoing straits between us thrown,
Dotting the shoreless watery wild,
We mortal millions live *alone*.

—MATTHEW ARNOLD

I propose the following three hypotheses.

1. Heidegger defined the human being as *Dasein*, "being there." I suggest that the assumptions in a fiction or in a critical-theoretical-philosophical text about the nature of *Dasein* and about the mode of access each *Dasein* has to others, in what Heidegger called *Mitsein*, tends to be consonant with the concept of community each such writer has.

2. Unless you begin with the assumption that *Dasein* is in some way or another fundamentally and primordially *Mitsein* or *Mitdasein*, you cannot easily think your way out of an assumption of *Dasein*'s essential solitude to a conception of community as "being with." This is the case unless, like Nancy, you define this being with as an agglomeration of solitaries all in the same boat of solitude, that is, as all dwelling together in a what Nancy calls a *communauté désoeuvrée*, an "unworked community." Derrida expresses his reservations about this continued use of the word *community* in a forceful passage in *A Taste for the Secret*: "Why call it a community? Just to conform to what certain of our friends have attempted to do, to Blanchot's 'unavowable' community or Nancy's 'inoperative' [*désoeuvrée*] one? I have no qualms about these communities; my only question is, why call them communities?" (TS, 25).

3. Jacques Derrida is unusual, if not unique, in explicitly denying that *Dasein* is *Mitsein*. His concepts of ethics and of community are consonant with this assumption of each ego's inescapable solitude. According to Derrida, I remain alone, on my own, however much I may be open to the ethical demand each other, though "wholly other," makes on me. Each demand, moreover, as Derrida says in *The Gift of Death* (GD, 68; DM, 98), is incommensurable with the demands made at the same moment by all the other "wholly others." I discuss this aporia in detail in Chapter 9 of this book.

Most modern and postmodern philosophers or theorists, in one way or another, assume that our primordial, inalienable situation is a "being with" others who are more or less like ourselves and to whose interiority we are granted some degree of access. I want to show this in some detail for a number of writers, along with some of Derrida's commentary on what they say, before turning to show how intransigent, even scandalous, Derrida is in the context of what these philosopher-critics say.

Versions of Mitsein

My first and chronologically earliest example, from Walter Benjamin, makes explicit the often hidden linguistico-Judeo-Christian ground of the assumption that I can know what my neighbor is thinking. In an essay of 1916, "On Language as Such and on the Language of Man," not published until after his death, Benjamin spells out this grounding. Derrida explicitly "postpones" (*ajourne*) discussing this essay in "Des tours de Babel" because, as he says, of its "overly enigmatic character . . . , its wealth [*richesse*] and its overdeterminations" (Pe, 200; Pf, 211), in spite of its explicit reference to the Tower of Babel. I shall nevertheless dare to say a word about one thread in Benjamin's argument. With explicit reference to the account in Genesis of man's creation and his assigned task of giving names to all God's creatures, Benjamin says: "*It is therefore the linguistic being of man to name things. . . . he* communicates himself by naming *them.* To whom does he communicate himself?"[1] Benjamin gives an explicitly theological answer on the next page: "*in the name, the mental being of man communicates itself to God.*"[2] Well, how does that help "man" know what his fellows are thinking? Benjamin on the following page gives the answer. Because man's mental being is linguistic, by way of the names he has given, as God's surrogate, to things and because human language is universal communicability, language is the medium whereby my mental being is communicated to my fellows and their mental beings to me:

> If mental being is identical with linguistic being, then a thing, by virtue of its mental being, is a medium of communication, and what is communicated in it is—in accordance with its mediating relationship—precisely this medium (language) itself. Language is thus the mental being of things. Mental being is thus postulated at the outset as communicable, or, rather, is situated *within* the communicable, and the thesis that the linguistic being of things is identical with the mental, insofar as the latter is communicable, becomes in its "insofar" a tautology. *There is no such thing as a content of language; as communication, language communicates a mental entity—something communicable per se.*[3]

One can see why Derrida found Benjamin's formulations in this early essay enigmatic and overdetermined. I would call them utopian or millennial, and more than a little weird. Benjamin speaks as though "man" still dwelled, or could dwell, before the Fall and before the confusion of tongues in Babel. Though Benjamin does not explicitly draw this conclusion, it would follow that, if mental being is linguistic being, if the two overlap and are identical, then each separate man or woman exists bathed in a universal linguistic "medium" of communicability, based on the God-given responsibility to name things. Benjamin goes on after the passages I have quoted to write at length about "the concept of revelation" as something that follows naturally from the "equation of mental and linguistic being."[4] What is communicated in language is language, but that language is also, at the same time, mental being, apparently the same for everyone. That means that as soon as I speak (or, I suppose, write), regardless of the referential content of what I say, I am magically (Benjamin uses the word[5]) exposed to all other people because they too dwell within the same medium of communicability. This is an admirable confirmation of my hypothesis that you must begin with a notion of "being with" as primordial if you are ever to posit it plausibly at all.

Basic features of Raymond Williams's assumptions about community emerge in *The Country and the City* and in the entry "Community" in *Keywords*.[6] Williams is explicitly aware that his ideal community is Utopian, something never yet fully accomplished. One of his assumptions is the conviction that a true community is not just a relatively small group of people living together in the same place and sharing the same immemorial assumptions in kindness and mutuality. A true community must also be classless. Class structures, particularly those generated by capitalism, destroy community. A second, crucial assumption is never stated in so many

words. Nevertheless, it is fundamental to Williams's thinking about community. This is the presumption that the individual is and should be his
social placement, with no residue or leftover that is not determined by the
surrounding culture. A small freeholder is a small freeholder through and
through. I *am* my subject position. I raise wheat or Brussels sprouts, or
make shoes, or work as a carpenter, or milk cows, therefore I am. Williams's third essential assumption is that the warmth and mutuality of a
true community depend on the way I know my neighbor. My social placement exposes me entirely to other people, with no corner of private subjectivity hidden away from them. I understand my neighbor or I am
understood by him or her, in kindness and mutuality, because he or she is,
through and through, his or her social role in a small group. This happy
intersubjectivity works because all members of the group have in common
a set of traditional habits and beliefs that thoroughly determines what they
are. This makes Williams's ideal, classless rural community a true *Gemein-
schaft*. Williams's agreement with Marxist assumptions about self and community is indicated by the resonance between what Williams says and what
Marx and Engels say in a passage near the end of the first part of *The
German Ideology*: "Only in community with others has each individual the
means of cultivating his gifts in all directions; only in the community,
therefore, is personal freedom possible."[7]

Various other theories of community roughly contemporary with Williams's ideas have been developed and may be compared to his. Some
come before Williams's *The Country and the City*. Some are more recent.
It is unlikely that Williams had read all these writers, or they him. Such
theorists of community include Heidegger, Bataille, Blanchot, Nancy,
Levinas, Lacan, Agamben, Alphonso Lingis—and Derrida.[8] These writers are by no means all singing the same tune. Many subtle discriminations and careful readings would be necessary to do them justice. A full
account of what they say about community would take a big book. Nevertheless, all but Derrida—along, perhaps, with Blanchot—tend to assume,
or to want to assume, in one way or another, that *Dasein* is primordially
Mitdasein.

Husserl, in a passage in the Fifth Cartesian Meditation, to which Derrida refers a number of times, defines each ego's knowledge of other egos
as a matter of analogical apperception.[9] The phrasing escapes solipsism,
but just barely, since each word in the phrase distances the other ego from
my consciousness. It is not direct perception but indirect apperception. It
is not literal penetration of the other ego but recognition that the other
consciousness must be analogous to mine. Husserl was not satisfied with

this formulation and, so I am told, spilt much ink in his later years in attempts to persuade himself that being with others is part of each ego's constitution, as he also does in the later pages of the Fifth Meditation, for example, when he hypothesizes "*a community of men* and . . . *of man*—who, even as solitary, has the sense: member of a community."[10]

Here is Derrida's commentary on Husserl's phrase "analogical apperception." It appears in "Rams ," apropos of Derrida's own extended meditation on Celan's line "Die Welt ist fort, ich muss dich tragen." Derrida here ascribes to Husserl some of his own intransigence about my knowledge of the other ego:

> In this absolute solitude of the pure *ego*, when the world has retreated, when "Die Welt ist fort," the *alter ego* that is constituted in the *ego* is no longer accessible in an originary and purely phenomenological intuition. Husserl must concede this in his *Cartesian Meditations*. The *alter ego* is constituted only by *analogy*, by *appresentation*, indirectly, inside of me, who then carries it where there is no longer a transcendent world. I must then carry it, carry *you* [te *porter*: second person singular], there where the world gives way: that is my responsibility. Yet I can no longer carry the other or you, if *to carry* means to include in oneself, in the intuition of one's own egological consciousness. It's a question of carrying without appropriating to oneself. *To carry* now no longer has the meaning of "to comprise" [*comporter*], to include, to comprehend in the self, but rather *to carry oneself or bear oneself toward* [se porter vers] the infinite inappropriability of the other, toward the encounter with its absolute transcendence in the very inside of me, that is to say, in me outside of me [*en moi hors de moi*]. (R, 161; B, 75–76)

It would be necessary to read Husserl's Fifth Meditation carefully, word for word, to decide whether or not Derrida's commentary exceeds hermeneutical exegesis, as he claims in "Rams" all good reading does (R, 152–53; B, 54).

Heidegger, in *Being and Time* and in *The Fundamental Concepts of Metaphysics*, asserts that *Mitsein*, "being together," is a primordial feature of *Dasein*, his name for human "being there." Here is his formulation in *Being and Time*: "This 'with' is something of the character of Dasein. . . . By reason of this *with-like* [mithaften] Being-in-the-world, the world is always one that I share with Others. The world of Dasein is a *with-world* [Mitwelt]. Being-in is *Being-with* Others. Their Being-in-themselves within-the-world is *Dasein-with* [Mitdasein]."[11] Nevertheless, Heidegger notoriously condemns the discourse of everyday shared experience as *Gerede*, "idle talk," a falling away into *das Man*, "the they." He most prizes those moments when a *Dasein* becomes aware of itself in its uniqueness and finitude, its *Sein zum Tode*, its "being toward death." Such a *Dasein* may then resolutely decide to take responsibility for itself by "wanting to have a conscience (*Gewissen-haben-wollen*)."[12] What is for Williams the bad alienation of a character like Jude Fawley in Hardy's *Jude the Obscure* or Clym Yeobright in *The Return of the Native* is for Heidegger the condition of authenticity. Authenticity means taking possession, in solitude, of my "ownmost Self (*eigenste Selbst*),"[13] that is, of the possibilities special to my own *Dasein*, rather than living in submission to *das Man*.

Heidegger's valuation seems exactly the reverse of Williams's. Heidegger, it may be, is closer to the Protestant tradition of valuing private spiritual life than Williams. Williams gives short shrift to the Protestantism of his rural Welsh border villagers. He sees the local vicar as part of the oppressive class structure. He values the dissenting chapels that were a resistance to the hegemony of the Church of England,[14] but says nothing about the forms of solitary spirituality those chapels promoted, for example, private prayer. In the Marxist millennium one will not have a private subjective life. One will not *need* to have such a thing.

Heidegger, in the discussion of *Mitsein* in *Being and Time* already cited and in a remarkable passage in *The Fundamental Principles of Metaphysics*, asserts categorically that *Mitsein* is aboriginal. It makes sense, says Heidegger in the latter, to ask whether we can ever know what is going on in the "mind" of an animal, but it makes no sense to ask this about my knowledge of another human being. Why? Heidegger's answer is unequivocal:

> With respect to man and the human potential for self-transposition into another human being, it transpired that the question is superfluous because in a sense it does not know what it is asking. [*Diese Frage ist überflüssig, sie weiß gewissermaßen nicht, was sie fragt.*] For if the question is really directed toward man in his essence, it becomes redundant to the extent that being human means being transposed into the other, means being with the other [*sofern Menschsein heißt: Versetztsein in den Anderen, Mitsein mit dem Anderen*]."[15]

I suspect that Heidegger chose to assert so firmly that each *Dasein* is from the beginning *Miteinandersein*, transposed into the other, set over into the other, in order to make a pre-emptive strike against the danger of solipsism. He, it may be, wanted to avoid the perhaps insuperable difficulty of getting from an initial solitude to some kind of being together. He may have wanted to avoid getting into the pickle in which Husserl permanently found himself.

Further confirmation that Heidegger presumes *Dasein* is *Mitsein* is given in a later section of *The Fundamental Principles of Metaphysics*, read in detail by Derrida in the eighth seminar of "The Beast and the Sovereign (Two)." Heidegger argues that human beings are *Weltbilden* ("world building"), as opposed to the stone, which is *Weltlos* ("worldless"), and to the animal, which is *Weltarm* ("poor in world").[16] In spite of Heidegger's stress in these seminars on *Dasein*'s solitude (*Einsamkeit*), the process of world building, through language, by way of *Dasein*'s openness to beings in their totality and its ability to name things as such, happens through collective action, as a result of the primordial being together of all *Daseins*. Here is Derrida's succinct and elegant commentary on Heidegger's *Miteinandersein*:

> Heidegger himself is in the process of making his path, of breaking his own proper trail when, claiming to translate Aristotle's genial but confused and insufficiently explicated intuition, Heidegger explains to us, he, that words are born of this essential accord (*jener wesenhaften Übereinkunft*) of men among themselves in their *Miteinandersein*, insofar as they are together, in their *Miteinandersein*, in their being-one-for-the-other [*leur être-l'un-pour-l'autre*], ones-with-the-others [*uns-avec-les-autres*], open to being [*l'étant*], which surrounds them, to being [*l'étant*] as such. It is this transcendence shared in *Mitsein*, in the common opening to being, that is the foundation [*Grund*] of their original accord and that as a result makes discourse [*Rede*] possible. Therefore it is always *umgekehrt* (reversed): it is not convention that comes to add itself to natural sound, that is, animal sound, in order as a result to make language possible, then human society possible. On the contrary, reversed, *umgekehrt*, it is transcendence, the opening to being as such and in totality (to the world), transcendence that, originally common, shared in the *Miteinandersein*, permits accord, language, convention, etc. And one cannot separate transcendence from *Miteinandersein*. Transcendence, the movement that carries, that connects to being [*l'étant*] as such, is from the start a social movement, if you wish, a being-one-with-the-other [*un être-l'un-avec-l'autre*], a *Mitsein*. There is no transcendence without the *Miteinandersein*. Even solitude, which is one of the major themes of this seminar [Heidegger's seminar], as soon as it assumes transcendence and language, also assumes, as solitude as such, as Robinsonophilia, Robinsonocracy, Robinsonocentrism, if you wish, [solitude assumes] *Mitsein* and *Miteinandersein*. (BS, 8th seminar, my trans.)[17]

Language, I note, would be in big trouble if this original intersubjectivity were a fiction, if each human being were as alone as Derrida often claims each of us is. Wittgenstein worries a lot about this in *Philosophical*

Investigations. How am I to be sure what my boss in the work-gang build-ing the Tower of Babel means when he says, "Slab"? This is one of Witt-genstein's examples of a command in a primitive language.[18] "Slab" may be the name of that stone toward which he points, but how do I learn what pointing means and that he wants me to bring him a slab? "Slab" may also be the name of a tool, or of a sandwich, or even a proper name, the name of one of my fellow masons, or maybe, unbeknownst to me, my own name. If Derrida is right, then we did not need to wait for God's decree at the site of the Tower of Babel to have confusion of tongues. Endless possibilities of misunderstanding exist even in a single community all speaking the "same" language. There was babble before Babel. Abyssal depths of specu-lation open up, in infinite regress, deep beneath deep, as soon as you begin to think along these lines. Heidegger, wisely, avoids this abyss by positing an originary being with as the basis of human language, though why we do not all therefore speak the same language might remain a puzzle.

Various answers have been given to this puzzle. Examples would in-clude the episode of the Tower of Babel in Genesis 11:1–9; Leibniz's dream of a universal language; Noam Chomsky's idea of a more or less universal generative grammar, hard-wired into our brains and nervous sys-tems; the discipline of "comparative literature," which tends to assume that all literature can be translated into a single dominant language, En-glish, or French, or Chinese, or whatever; and Walter Benjamin's concept of *reine Sprache*, pure language. Paul de Man's " 'Conclusions': Walter Benjamin's 'The Task of the Translator' " is a brilliant analysis of Benja-min's essay.[19] For Derrida's discussion of these issues by way of an ex-tended commentary on Benjamin's essay, see "Des tours de Babel" (Pe, 191–225, the English translation, by Joseph Graham, retains the French title, presumably to keep the pun on *detours*; Pf, 203–35). Here is part of what Derrida says about Benjamin's "pure language":

> Through each language [says Derrida in exegesis, elucidation, and implicit critique of Benjamin], something is intended [*visé*] that is the same and yet that none of the languages can attain separately. They can claim, and prom-ise themselves to attain it, only by co-employing or co-deploying their in-tentional modes [*leur visées intentionnelles*], "the whole of their complementary intentional modes." This co-deployment toward the whole is a replying [*reploiement*] because what it intends to attain is "the pure language" [*die reine Sprache*], or the pure tongue [*langue*]. What is intended, then, by this co-operation of languages [*langues*] and intentional aims is not transcendent to the language; it is not a reality that they besiege from all

sides, like a tower that they are trying to surround [*comme une tour dont elles tenteraient de faire le tour*]. No, what they are aiming at intentionally, individually and together, in the translation is the language itself as Babelian event, a language that is neither the universal language in the Leibnizian sense nor is it a language that is the natural language each still remains [*reste*] on its own; it is the being-language of the language [*l'être-langue de la langue*], tongue or language *as such*, that unity without any self-identity that makes for the fact that there are *some* languages and that they are *languages* [*qu'il y a des langues, et que ce sont des langues*]. (Pe, 221–22, trans. modified; Pf, 232)

It will not have escaped my readers that I am disobeying, necessarily, the Benjaminian rule that translation of a translation is illegitimate. I am commenting in English on the English translation of Derrida's French essay (though I have also read it in French) on Benjamin's essay in German (which I have read in English translation, as well as in German, whereas Derrida refers to the French translation by Maurice de Gandillac, as well as to the German original), with the Hebrew of Genesis somewhere in the background. Paul de Man shows that in one place Gandillac resists Benjamin's rigor by making Benjamin say in French the exact opposite of what his German actually says. Benjamin says that "where the text pertains, without mediation, to the realm of truth and of dogma [*der Wahrheit oder der Lehre*], it is, without further ado [*schlechthin*], translatable."[20] Gandillac's translation says *intraduisable*, "untranslatable." Derrida, in his seminars in Paris on Benjamin's essay, de Man says he has been told, at first followed this mistake, until a student pointed out his error and Gandillac's. "I'm sure," says de Man cheerfully, "Derrida could explain that it was the same . . . and I mean that in a positive sense, it *is* the same, but still, it is not the same without some additional explanation."[21] De Man refrains from providing that additional explanation. De Man's basic language, the language that came into his mind when he was really tired, was, he once told me, Flemish, his mother tongue. Benjamin's "Die Aufgabe des Übersetzers" was a preface to Benjamin's translation into German of Baudelaire's *Tableaux parisiens*, though in the essay he leaves a particularly obscure prose passage by Mallarmé in the original French.[22] Talk about confusion of tongues! Where is the *reine Sprache* in all this babble? A word-for-word, "literal" translation, however, as opposed to a translation that exploits the possibilities of the translated language to make a creative equivalent, would be, to use a Benjaminian example, like those strange translations by Friedrich Hölderlin of Sophocles. "Hölderlin's translations from Sophocles," says Benjamin, "were his last work; in them meaning plunges from abyss to abyss until it threatens to become lost in the bottomless depths of language [*in ihnen stürtz der Sinn von Abgrund zu Abgrund, bis er droht, in bodenlosen Sprachtiefen sich zu verlieren*]."[23]

In stressing, with Derrida, Heidegger's repeated assertion that *Dasein* is *Mitsein*, I am, as Arnold Davidson reminds me in an extremely helpful response to an earlier version of this chapter, going against a strong tradition in writings about Heidegger. That tradition assumes that Heidegger's doctrine of *Mitsein* is peripheral and superficial. Each authentic *Dasein*, this tradition claims, is, for Heidegger, alone in its decision to take possession of its ownmost possibilities of being. All *Dasein* is required to do in order to fulfill its obligation to the other person is let that other person be. This ontology of solitude, as it might be called, is, it is assumed, fundamental in Heidegger's thinking. An influential paper by Levinas, dating back to 1951, "Is Ontology Fundamental?" ("L'ontologie est-elle fondamental?"), asserts just that. From his earliest important work on, Levinas wanted above all to define himself as different from Heidegger. I discuss Levinas here only briefly for two reasons. (1) It would take a lot of space to do justice to Levinas's ideas about self, other, and community. (2) The relation to the other, in my judgment, takes precedence, in Levinas's thinking, over any relation of the self to the community. The latter is my primary topic here, or rather, I want to show how the relation between two persons is related to the relation of the self to the community. The two relations are by no means identical or subject to the same problematic.

Evidence of the priority of my relation to the individual other for Levinas is the way he insisted repeatedly that the face-to-face relation that most interested him was not just my relation to my neighbor, in the sense of someone living together with me in my community and sharing my language and my assumptions, but my relation to any other person, however alien, in all his or her inability to be known as I can know an inanimate object. In this assertion, a link to Derrida's thinking may be glimpsed, though Derrida goes somewhat beyond Levinas in the extravagance of his insistence that *tout autre est tout autre*, which, in one of its meanings, can be translated as "Every other person is wholly other." When Levinas uses the word *communauté* ("community"), he tends to use it to name what is held in common by two persons in the face-to-face encounter generated by language, that is, through the other's forceful and even coercive invocation of me, or my invocation of the other.[24]

The relation between the two forms of invocation in Levinas is complex, and perhaps changed over time. Levinas uses the word *socialité* in the same way as he uses *communauté*, that is, as a name for the relation between two persons. Here are examples from "Is Ontology Fundamental?" "The point is to see the function of language not as subordinate to the *consciousness* we have of the presence of the other, or of his proximity, or of our community [*communauté*] with him, but as a condition of that conscious realization."[25] "Expression . . . consists, prior to any participation in a common content through understanding, in instituting sociality [*socialité*] through a relationship that is, consequently, irreducible to understanding."[26] One does not, ordinarily, use language to invoke a stone or a screwdriver, or feel that one is "called" by these objects, but language (called by Levinas, variously, *langage, discours, parole*), is, for him, fundamentally necessary to the other person's invocation of me in a face-to-face encounter, or to my invocation of him.

Levinas answers his question "Is Ontology Fundamental?" with a resounding "No!" Ontology is *not* fundamental, not a universal ground. Why not? It is because my face-to-face encounter with my neighbor or with the other person generally (*autrui*) is something "otherwise than being" (*autrement qu'être*), as the title of one of Levinas's important books puts it. The self-quotation on the back cover of a French edition of *Otherwise than Being or Beyond Essence* (*Autrement qu'être ou au-delà de l'essence*) expresses Levinas's position succinctly: "Ethics, here, does not come as a supplement to a preexisting existential base. . . . To be human means to live as if one were not a being among beings" (my trans.).[27]

For Heidegger, on the contrary, in Levinas's reading, *Dasein*'s solitary relation to Being in its occultation or withdrawal is fundamental. My relation to other *Daseins* is peripheral, a matter of "letting the other be."[28] As Levinas puts it in "Is Ontology Fundamental?": "To Heidegger, being-with-the-other-person—*Miteinandersein*—thus rests on the ontological relation."[29] For Levinas, being with the other, in a face-to-face responsiveness and taking of responsibility, is outside of being, not something that rests on the ontological relation.

Levinas's polemic against Heidegger in this early essay, "Is Ontology Fundamental?," is based on a series of oppositions. He opposes the "invocation" of me by the other person (*autrui*), or of him by me, to knowledge or representation of the other. The latter would imply that he is an object among other objects that could be cognized and described. Levinas opposes invocative speech to silent comprehension or objective description. Though Levinas does not use the terminology of speech act theory, one might say that his term *invocation* names a performative speech act, while his idea of knowledge or comprehension involves a constative use of language. Levinas opposes the inspection of objects, to obtain knowledge of them and of the universal "Being" they simultaneously reveal and hide, to the face-to-face "encounter" (*rencontre*) with the *visage* of the other. (Though *visage* is an English word, it hardly sounds idiomatic today as a word for "face," so I shall leave it in French.) The Levinasian encounter is not accurately defined by the word *Sein*, "Being," as in Heidegger's *Mitsein*. Such an encounter is not only ethical. It is also properly "religious," since the other person mediates the *Infini* ("Infinity") that Levinas puts in the place of Heidegger's "Being," with a capital *B*:

> The relation to the other is therefore not ontology. This bond with the other which is not reducible to the representation of the other, but to his invocation, and in which invocation is not preceded by an understanding, I call *religion*. . . . If the word *religion* is, however, to indicate that the relation between men [*avec des hommes*], irreducible to understanding [*compréhension*], is by that very fact distanced from the exercise of power, but in human faces [*visages*] joins the Infinite—I accept that ethical resonance of the word and all those Kantian reverberations.[30]

"His invocation" in this passage may be read, in my judgment, in two ways, either as naming my invocation of the other when I encounter him, as opposed to representing the other in a cognitive act, or as defining what I encounter in the other not as his representation but as his invocation of me. As the word *religion* here and its defiant Kantian justification suggest, an "invocation" is not just any kind of speech act. To invoke is to call forth, with a suggestion of magic power to raise spirits or even to raise the dead, as in Jesus' "Lazarus, come forth" (John 11:43) or in the way the narrator of Henry James's "The Aspern Papers" calls forth his idol, the dead poet Jeffrey Aspern: "I had invoked him and he had come; he hovered before me half the time; it was as if his bright ghost had returned to earth."[31] The "Invocation" at the beginning of a church service calls God to be present in the church and to assist at the service. This invocation of the other, for Levinas, is a response to the other's invocation of me.

The question about any "invocation," thought of a special form of speech act, however, is how one could ever verify what Austin calls its "felicity." How can one be sure in a given case whether what is invoked actually comes forth? Glendower, in Shakespeare's *Henry IV*, 3.1, boasts, "I can call spirits from the vasty deep," to which Hotspur replies, "Why, so can I, or so can any man; / But will they come when you do call for them?" That is the question, all right. A similar question can be asked about the call from the other, whether from my neighbor or from God. Can I ever be sure that I have really been called? Derrida asks that question in "Abraham, the Other," discussed in Chapters 7 and 11. Levinas, however, seems more or less confidently to assume that when I am face to face with the other and am invoked coercively by him or her, or invoke the other, the invocation always works and is "felicitous."

Further evidence that what is in question is an "invocation" in the religious sense is the way Levinas explicitly names the calling forth of the other, here generalized as "discourse," a form of prayer: "The essence of discourse [*discours*] is prayer."[32] What, exactly, is prayer? Derrida devoted a whole seminar, the eighth in the unpublished seminars of 2002–3, "The Beast and the Sovereign (Two)," to this question. Prayer is a performative similar to invocation. It is a curious kind of speech act that aims both to implore God and at the same time subtly to coerce Him. Prayer forces God's hand, at least in the sense of putting Him to the necessity of either answering or not answering my prayer. But how can I ever be absolutely sure that my prayers have been answered, that a felicitous outcome has been God's work and not just the way things have naturally turned out? If my invocation of the other when I confront his or her *visage*, in response to the other's invocation of me, is a form of prayer addressed through the other, through *autrui*, to the Infinite, then it is taking a lot for granted to assume that my prayer will be answered in any verifiable way. Nevertheless, Levinas assumes that the experience of what he calls "*affection*" is its own verification, a verification beyond any sort of conceptual knowledge. In "The Idea of the Infinite in Us," in *Entre Nous*, Levinas says: "In the idea of the infinite, which as such is the idea of God, the *affection* of the finite by the infinite takes place . . . . An affection which would have to be described other than as an appearing, other than as a participation in content, a conception, a comprehension. An irreversible affection of the finite by the infinite."[33] The testimony to the "infinite," God, is not anything cognitive, not an appearance, not a sharing in some content, not a conception, not a comprehension. It is just "affection," that is, the working within me of an affect. That experience of being affected, however, is altogether compelling, even persecutory, in its power over me.

A few sentences later Levinas relates this affection of me by the infinite to my limitless responsibility for my neighbor, a responsibility that extends even to my willingness to sacrifice my life for that neighbor. Since that responsibility extends to every other whatsoever, not just my neighbor in the restricted sense of someone who lives nearby, the notion of "sociality," a word near to "community," surfaces here again, this time as a name for the extension of my responsibility for a single other to my universal responsibility for all others: "It is an excellence of love, of sociality and 'fear for others' which is not my anxiety for my own death."[34] That last phrase is a negative allusion to Heidegger's solitary "being toward death." This opposition to Heidegger is made explicit in an essay about Heidegger in *Entre Nous* entitled "'Dying For . . .'" ("'Mourir pour . . .'"). In the last paragraph of this essay, Levinas distinguishes sharply his idea of death from Heidegger's: "The priority of the other over the *I* [*le* moi], by which the human *being-there* is chosen and unique, is precisely the latter's response to the nakedness of the face [*visage*] and its mortality. It is there that the concern for the other's death is realized, and that 'dying for him' 'dying his death' [*'mourir pour lui' et 'de sa mort'*] takes priority over 'authentic' death."[35] I die for the other by a species of unwilled transference. The same idea is expressed in the Preface to *Entre Nous*, as if to stress its importance up front, at the beginning of the book: "In the general economy of being in its inflection back upon itself [*sa tension sur soi*], a preoccupation with the other, even to the point of sacrifice, even to the possibility of dying for him or her; a responsibility for the other [*autrui*]. Otherwise than being! It is this shattering of indifference—even if indifference is statistically dominant—this possibility of the one-for-the-other, which is the ethical event."[36] The "idea" of community in Levinas's thought is not prior to my responsibility for a given single other, present to me, affecting me, as *visage*. *Community, sociality,* are, for Levinas, names for the extension of my responsibility from one other to all others.

Levinas sometimes uses still another word to name my use of language when I encounter another face to face, *salut*: "Man is the only being I cannot meet without my expressing this meeting itself to him. . . . In every attitude toward the human being there is a greeting [*un salut*]—even if it is the refusal of a greeting [*comme refus de saluer*]."[37] *Salut* here does not mean a military salute but a greeting, as in a "salutation" in which I wish the other good health and good fortune. "To salute" also suggests the kiss of friendly greeting or welcome, as in "He saluted her with a gallant kiss." Levinas does not overtly refer to that connotation. Nevertheless, there are suggestions, in Levinas's use of the word *salut*, of a bodily intimacy in the encounter with another. This is also implied in his emphasis on the confrontation with the naked and exposed *visage* of the other when I meet him face to face. "The nakedness of the face," says Levinas, "is not a figure of speech [*une figure de style*]—it means by itself."[38] In Romans 16:16, St. Paul, in the King James translation, exhorts the Romans to "Salute one another with an holy kiss. The churches of Christ salute you." To be kissed by a church! That would be truly an encounter.

The difference between Levinas and Derrida is perhaps no more than a nuance, but it is the nuance of a considerable gulf. Both assume the singularity and absolute alterity of the other, but Levinas believes the naked *visage* of the other, when I invoke it in prayer or greeting, in response to its invocation of me, opens itself to me and opens to me the Infinite it mediates (though Levinas would probably resist that word *mediates*). For Derrida, on the contrary, the other remains always wholly other, even though that other, as for Levinas, makes infinite demands on me. Any Derridean ethics must be based on the complete otherness of the other. Derrida, moreover, resists, not entirely successfully, any conflation of ethics with religion. I shall return to these differences later in this chapter, when I focus directly on Derrida.

I have hypothesized that a thinker's assumptions about the relation to the other, that is, the possibilities of knowing the other or of being ethically related to him or her, are consonant with that thinker's assumptions about community. Confirmation of this, in Levinas's case, is suggested by his relative lack of interest in the question of community. That relative disinterest follows from his central concern with the face-to-face ethical relation to one other person as a means of reaching toward "Infinity," in a properly religious relation. I find only one unequivocal reference to what appears to be a community, under the name of *collectivité*, in "Is Ontology Fundamental?" In the last paragraph of the essay, Levinas lists some questions that remain open for further investigation. In one of these he asks "to what extent is the relation with the other or the collectivity—which cannot be reduced to understanding—a relation with the infinite?"[39] "Collectivity" seems added here more or less as an afterthought and not to require an analysis any different from the one provided for my relation to *autrui*.

Derrida's view of the exclusiveness of the ethical relation, as passages I discuss later indicate, is not far from Levinas's view, though it is not identical. Levinas's use of the word *autrui*, for example, a word Derrida tends to avoid, as more or less a synonym for *autre*, is a subtle difference. *Autrui* tends to mean specifically another person, my neighbor, for example, and therefore begs a question Derrida wants to keep open by always saying autre, understood as *tout autre*, wholly other, that is, not certainly to be identified as another person like me. Moreover, in *The Gift of Death* Derrida stresses, in a way Levinas, in his association of *autrui* and *collectivité*, does not, the way *all* the others demand my response, incommensurably, all at once, every instant, so that to answer one call I must, inevitably, betray all the others, thereby fracturing the community. I shall discuss this in detail in Chapter 9.

To investigate in detail the relation of Levinas's thought to Heidegger's, in one direction, and to Derrida's, in the other, along with Derrida's own ceaseless dialogue with Heidegger, for example, on the question of death, not to speak of the relation of all three to Kant's thinking about ethics, would take many seminars or books and much careful adjudication of nuances. Derrida wrote three important essays, one book-length, on Levinas. References to Levinas appear at many important moments in other Derrida essays. An example is a footnote in *The Gift of Death* , discussed in Chapter 9. This note identifies the way Levinas's reading of the Abraham and Isaac story differs from Kierkegaard's and, apparently, from Derrida's own.[40] As for Derrida and Heidegger, or Derrida and Kant, Derrida wrote many thousands of pages on Heidegger in seminars over the years. He gave, moreover, a whole unpublished seminar on Kant's second critique, *The Critique of Practical Reason*. The latter contains, as the only part as yet published, the first version of the great Derrida essay on Kafka's parable "Before the Law."

I have stressed, somewhat against the grain of expert received opinion, Heidegger's insistence that "being with" goes all the way down to the ground, so to speak, and is generated by the way *Dasein* is defined as sharing language with others. I have done so in part because I think it helps understand what happened in the later Heidegger, after the famous *Kehre*, or turn. The sinister development of Heidegger's thinking about community, language, and nation, and his concomitant political commitment to National Socialism in the 1930s is made possible, though perhaps not inevitable, by the presuppositions about *Mitsein* in the works of the 1920s, *Being and Time* and *The Fundamental Principles of Metaphysics*. Raymond Williams made somewhat similar assumptions about the need for community belonging and went, as I have shown, in a quite different direction. What happened with Heidegger was not foreordained, but it happened.

Two different versions of community exist in Heidegger's thought, the bad, inauthentic one he calls *das Man*, the they, and a good one he calls *Mitsein* or *Miteinandersein*. The latter lays the ground for his concept of the German "folk" in the work of the 1930s and 1940s. A continuity between early and late Heidegger therefore exists, despite his "turn." Heidegger came to associate, in a single system of thought, "world," "spirit," the German language, and the destiny of the German people (*Volk*). Derrida has with admirable tact and care explored this complex of ideas in *Of Spirit: Heidegger and the Question* (De *l'esprit: Heidegger et la question*), as well as in many seminars on Heidegger. Germany's destiny, Heidegger thought, was to save world civilization from what he saw as a disastrous "darkening" (*Verdüsterung*). He associated that degeneration especially with the United States and with the Soviet Union. He saw both as the incarnation of *das Man* and the descent of a world darkening by way of the triumph of technology. Germany was geographically in the middle. Only Germany could save the world. In *The Introduction to Metaphysics* (*Einführung in die Metaphysik*, 1935), for example, Heidegger asserts that "asking of the question of being" "is indispensable if the peril of world darkening is to be forestalled and if our nation in the Center of the Western world is to take on its historical mission."[41] The translation elides a key word, for my purposes here, by translating *Volk* rather tamely as "nation." It is only the German people or folk, Aryans who live in Germany and speak the German language, who can speak Being or respond to Being's withdrawal. German, Heidegger held, is the only philosophically and poetically valid language, now that ancient Greek is dead. German may even be better than classical Greek, since German *Geist* is a better word than Greek *logos* for speaking Being. At the beginning of the same paragraph Heidegger quotes with approval his own notorious *Rektoratsrede* of 1933: "Spirit is a fundamental, knowing resolve [*Entschlossenheit*] toward the essence of Being."[42]

The same dangerous and at the same time absurd nationalist assumptions inhabit the *Elucidations of Hölderlin's Poetry* (*Erläuterungen zu Hölderlins Dichtung*), for example, the following passage in "Homecoming / To Kindred Ones" ("Heimkunft / An die Verwandten"): "So it [the "reserved find," *der gesparte Fund*] will remain, if those who 'have cares in the fatherland [*im Vaterlande*]' become the careful ones. Then there will be a kinship [*Verwandschaft*] with the poet. Then there will be a homecoming [*Heimkunft*]. But this homecoming is the future of the historical being of the German people [*die Zukunft des geschichtlichen Wesens der Deutschen*]."[43] As Jennifer Bajorek has demonstrated in a brilliant essay, Heidegger makes Hölderlin here say the opposite of what he really says.[44] The same cluster of ideas reappears in Heidegger's seminars at the University of Freiburg of 1942 (that is, in the middle of World War II), *Hölderlin's Hymn "The Ister"* (*Hölderlins Hymne "Der Ister"*).[45]

I have said that such notions are sinister, dangerous, and absurd. What is disquieting about them is brought into the open even more clearly, in a way that causes me a frisson of anxiety for our own historical destiny in the United States (said by George W. Bush to be "to spread democracy throughout the world"), when I remember that Newt Gingrich, then at the height of his power as a leader in the U.S. House of Representatives,

gave a speech in Iowa in which he said that the future of civilization depends on the English language. English language, German language—
take your pick. The same disquieting nationalist assumptions are expressed
in both cases, though by way of making claims for different languages.[46]

Lacan is, somewhat surprisingly, in accord with Heidegger on the question of primordial *Mitsein*, as well as on some other points. Like Heidegger, Lacan posits in his own way "being with" or "being together," or
what he calls a *complexe intersubjectif*, as an aboriginal feature of the human
condition. In the well-known section on *la politique de l'autruiche* (a characteristic Lacanian pun on the French words for "ostrich" and "Austria") in
"The Seminar on 'The Purloined Letter'" ("Le séminaire sur 'La letter
volée,'") Lacan asserts that the king, the queen, and the policeman in
Poe's story are locked in a pattern of *political* intersubjective coercion that
repeats itself in different ways with different characters: "Thus three moments, structuring three glances, borne by three subjects, incarnated each
time by different characters." [47] Where does the ostrich come in? Here's
how:

> In order to grasp in its unity the intersubjective complex thus described,
> we would willingly seek a model in the technique legendarily attributed to
> the ostrich attempting to shield itself from danger; for that technique might
> ultimately be qualified as political, divided as it here is among three part-
> ners: the second believing itself invisible because the first has its head stuck
> in the ground, and all the while letting the third calmly pluck its rear; we
> need only enrich its proverbial denomination [*la politique de l'Autriche*, a
> reference to the cumbersome and self-defeating diplomacy and politics of
> the Austrians] by a letter, producing *la politique de l'autruiche*, for the ostrich
> itself to take on forever a new meaning [*un nouveau sens pour toujours*].[48]

I suppose Lacan's cheeky boast is justified, since the passage has become
a famous one, producing something like a *Bouvard et Pécuchet* reaction in
many people. "*Autruiche*"? "Lacan's *politique de l'autruiche*," like "the Pyr-
amids"? to which the knee-jerk response is: "How did they build them?"

Lacan's complicated joke leads to his way of formulating the originary
overlapping of subjects, his version of our inescapable *être avec*:

> The plurality of subjects, of course, can be no objection for those who are
> long accustomed to the perspectives summarized by our [he means "my"]
> formula: *the unconscious is the discourse of the Other* [l'inconscient, c'est le
> discours de l'Autre]. And we will not recall now what the notion of the
> *immixture of subjects* [l'immixtion des sujets], recently introduced in our re-
> analysis of the dream of Irma's injection, adds to the discussion.[49]

For Lacan, as for Heidegger, the self is never alone and never has been alone, but is always already "being with" others. I and the others are all mixed up, immixed, all smoorged together, as Walt Kelly's Pogo puts it, by way of the language of the unconscious, which always speaks to me the discourse of the Other. This is why, for Lacan, the letter always arrives at its destination,[50] whereas for Derrida, in his critique of this essay by Lacan in "Le facteur de la verité" (literally: "The Factor [Postman] of Truth"), the letter never reaches its destination or may never reach its destination, so never really reaches its destination (PC, 489; CP, 517). Chapter 3 of this book investigates Derrida's disagreement with Lacan about the efficiency of the postal system by way of the Derridean concept of *destinerrance*.

Nancy's thinking about community, in *The Inoperative Community* (*La communauté désoeuvrée*) and *Being Singular Plural* (*Être singulier pluriel*) is complex and somewhat heterogeneous. It is not easy to summarize in a few sentences. For Nancy, each individual is at once unique, singular, and at the same time plural, "exposed," in the etymological sense of "set out- side," to others. The singular is always already plural, "being with" others. Those others remain, however, fundamentally other, alien, strangers each enclosed in his or her singularity. A community, for Nancy, is, in Donald Pease's fine phrase, a "congregation of singularities." What we most share is that we shall all die, though each singularity will die its own death. This means that each community, at all times and places, is *désoeuvrée*, "unworked," "inoperative." Nevertheless, the leitmotif of *Being Singular Plural*, a somewhat later book, is *être avec*, being with. That book argues tirelessly that the plurality of "being with" goes all the way down, so to speak, to each ego's bottom and also to the bottom of being in general. The first part of this assumption is something like Heidegger's claim that *Mitsein* is primordial but differs from Heidegger is ascribing this cleavage to Being. Being is singular in its plurality, unlike the unified Being of the ontotheological tradition or of Heidegger's thought. For Nancy, "being" is always already divided and unified by the togetherness of a plural being with:

> That Being is being-with, absolutely, this is what we must think. The *with* is the most basic feature of Being, the mark [*trait*] of the singular plurality of the origin or origins in it. . . . What is proper to community, then, is given to us in the following way: it has no other resource to appropriate except the "with" that constitutes it, the *cum* of "community," its interior- ity without an interior, and maybe even with, after its fashion, its *interior*

intimo sui. As a result, this *cum* is the *cum* of co-appearance [*com-parution*: "compearing" in English, " a legal term that is used to designate appearing before a judge together with another person"—translator's note], wherein we do nothing but appear together with one another, co-appearing before no other authority [*instance*] than this "with" itself, the meaning of which seems to us instantly to dissolve into insignificance, into exteriority, into the inorganic, empirical, and randomly contingent [*aléatoire*] inconsistency of the pure and simple "with."[51]

I give, to conclude this section, even shorter shrift to what Agamben, Blanchot, and Lingis say about "being with." Each would merit a long discussion. For Agamben, the "coming community" will be agglomerations, not necessarily malign, of "whatever [*quodlibet*] singularities," just as Lingis's title names "the community of those who have nothing in common." Lingis's book asserts that the encounter with the stranger is essential to human life today. Blanchot's *The Unavowable Community* (*La communauté inavouable*) is a small book commenting on Nancy's *The Inoperative Community*, in relation to Bataille's "acephalic" community. Blanchot describes communities that are *inavouable*, unavowable, in the sense of being secret, hidden, shameful, but also in the sense of being incompatible with "felicitous" public speech acts. Such public "avowals" found, support, and constantly renew the communities we all would like to live in or may even think we live in, but they are absent from "the unavowable community." All four of these authors are less certain than Benjamin, Husserl, Heidegger, Lacan, or Nancy that "being with" is originary, but they are less radical than Derrida is when he asserts without qualification that each of us is irremediably isolated, as if alone on a desert island.

"There Are Only Islands"

All of the authors I have mentioned, except to some degree the last four, hold, in many different ways, that *Dasein* is *Mitsein*, or at least they have a strong nostalgia, a wish to live in a community that is defined as "being with," togetherness. Derrida differs from all these in the intransigence with which he affirms, especially in his last work, each *Dasein*'s irremediable solitude. He is deeply suspicious of Heidegger's *Mitsein*, as of the validity of anything like Williams's celebration of a community of people who share the same assumptions and live in kindness and mutuality. Derrida's seminar of 2002–3 is, as earlier chapters of this book have observed, on Defoe's *Robinson Crusoe* and Heidegger's *The Fundamental Concepts of*

Metaphysics—an odd couple, as Derrida himself says. Derrida, in the first session of this seminar, expresses his rejection of *Mitsein* in a paragraph quite extraordinary for its resolute confrontation of the consequences of each human being's isolation from all others. In this paragraph, speaking apparently for himself as much as for Crusoe's experience of solitude, Derrida firmly asserts that each man or woman is marooned on his or her own island, enclosed in a singular world, with no isthmus, bridge, or other means of communication to the sealed worlds of others, or from their worlds to mine:

> neither animals of different species, nor men of different cultures, nor any individual, animal or human, inhabits the same world as another, however close and similar these living individuals may be (humans or animals), and the difference between one world and another remains forever uncrossable [*infranchissable*], the community of the world being always constructed, simulated by a group of stabilizing positings [*dispositifs*], more or less stable, therefore also never natural, language in the broad sense, codes of traces being destined, with all the living, to construct a unity of the world always deconstructible and nowhere and never given in nature. Between my world, the "my world," what I call "my world," and there is no other for me, every other world making up part of it, between my world and every other world, there is initially the space and the time of an infinite difference, of an interruption incommensurable with all the attempts at passage, of bridge, isthmus, communication, translation, trope, and transfer that the desire for a world and the sickness of the world [*mal du monde*], the being in sickness of the world [*l'être en mal de monde*] will attempt to pose, to impose, to propose, to stabilize. There is no world, there are only islands. That is one of the thousand directions toward which I would interpret the last line of a short and great poem by Celan: "Die Welt ist fort, ich muss dich tragen," poem of mourning or of birth. (BS, lst seminar, my trans.)[52]

An amazing passage! Since "the difference between one world and another remains forever uncrossable," any community is both constructed, primarily by language, and therefore always, like any collective code, "deconstructible," and in no way a natural given. This claim is shocking in its remorseless rigor, in its refusal of any of the copouts that almost everyone else from Husserl to Nancy rushes to embrace. It is also, as Arnold Davidson has reminded me, an amazing passage because it goes against what one might assume Derrida believed, on the basis of his somewhat earlier work on hospitality, on friendship, or on the concept of Europe. One might take for granted that Derrida believes some kind of togetherness in a community is a fundamental aspect of human existence, for example, in ethical decision. Careful reading of that earlier work, however, shows that Derrida tends to oppose quite sharply my relation to the other person and my relation to any community. The seminars on hospitality focus on my absolute, unconditional obligation to give hospitality to anyone who knocks on my door. This includes any stranger, someone from another community, someone speaking another language, or someone coming from another culture. Derrida's work on the politics of friendship focuses on the I/other relation named "friendship," "if there is such a thing," as one of the repeated leitmotifs of *The Politics of Friendship* has it. The other repeated leitmotif is the chilling phrase, cited by Montaigne and attributed to Aristotle, "O my friends, there is no friend." Even the earlier seminars on nation and nationalism aimed to put in question the notions that I am defined by my nationality or that a nation is a unified community. *The Other Heading* has as its goal the deconstruction of any presumption that Europe is a unified community:

> it is necessary [*il faut*] to make ourselves the guardians of an idea of Europe, of a difference of Europe, *but* of a Europe that consists precisely in not closing itself off in its own identity and in advancing itself in an exemplary way toward what it is not, toward the other heading or the heading of the other [*le cap de l'autre*], indeed—and this is perhaps something else altogether—toward the other *of* the heading [*l'autre du cap*], which would be the beyond of this modern tradition, another border structure, another shore. (OH, 29; AC, 33)

One further consequence of Derrida's assumption that each of us is enisled is the following: not only am I isolated from others, with no isthmus across to them, but they are also isolated from me, radically impenetrable and secret. This is said in an eloquent passage in *The Gift of Death*: "each of us, everyone else, each other is infinitely other in its absolute singularity, inaccessible, solitary, transcendent, nonmanifest, originally nonpresent to my *ego* (as Husserl would say of the *alter ego* that can never be originarily present to my consciousness and that I can apprehend only through what he calls 'appresentation' and analogy [*que de façon apprésentative et analogique*])" (GD, 78; DM, 110). Derrida's assertion here of the radical inaccessibility of the other person is an important difference from Levinas. Levinas assumes that when I invoke the other, in something that can be called "prayer," he or she responds, however infinitely other are both the other person and the God I invoke through my prayer to the other. The open, nude face of the other gives me access to that other, singular though he or she is, and through that access further access to the "Infinite" behind or within him or her, however problematic that access may be. As Derrida puts this in *The Gift of Death*:

> Even in its critique of Kierkegaard concerning ethics and generality Levi-nas's thinking stays within the game—the play of difference and analogy—between the face [*visage*] of God and the face of my neighbor, between the infinitely other as God and the infinitely other as another human being. . . . But for his part, in taking into account absolute singularity, that is, the absolute alterity obtaining in relations between one human being and an-other, Levinas is no longer able to distinguish between the infinite alterity of God and that of every human. His ethics is already a religion. In the two cases [Kierkegaard and Levinas] the border between the ethical and the religious becomes more than problematic, as do all attendant discourses. (GD, 83–84, trans. modified; DM, 116–17)

Derrida's concept of ethics, on the contrary, as expressed, for example, in *The Gift of Death*, follows from the assumption that the limitless call on me made by the other, by every other, incommensurably, comes, in each case, from someone who is "wholly other," *tout autre*, and therefore from something never directly, or even indirectly, accessible, not even in such a way as the nude *visage* of the other, for Levinas, gives me mediated access to the two infinites, the other person and God. For Derrida, on the con-trary, the other person is simply wholly other, *tout autre*, not a mediator of the Infinite or of God, though Derrida, in *The Gift of Death*, concerns himself with the demand made without intermediary on Abraham by Jeho-vah. The other person, for Derrida, generates in me nothing more nor less than an experience of complete alterity. I cannot even be sure that my neighbor is a "person" like me. In a more indirect way, as I shall try to show, Derrida's notion of community is also consonant with his assertions that every other is wholly other.

How is the peculiar late Derridean concept of community as self-de-structively autoimmunitary related to his view of the always constructed and therefore deconstructible nature of every *Mitsein*? As Tom Mitchell has gently instructed me in his response to an earlier version of this essay, I need to explain that relation, not just take it for granted. First, what does Derrida mean by calling every community "autoimmunitary"?

Derrida sees every community as inhabited by something like the human or animal body's immune system. The immune system repels for-eign invaders, but sometimes disastrously turns against itself in what is called "autoimmunity." Derrida makes a brilliant exploitation of this fig-ure in "Faith and Knowledge" ("Foi et Savoir") and elsewhere. I owe to

Tom Mitchell, however, the recognition that there is something strange about this figure, namely, that it is a figure of a figure, whichever way you look at it.[53] The stem *mun* in *immune system* is the same as the *mun* in *community*. It comes from Latin *munus*, meaning the obligation owed within the group, as the price of my citizenship, also a gift I may give to the community. *Immune* was originally a social term applying to those, for instance, the clergy, who were in one way or another exempt from the ordinary citizen's obligations. They were immune, indemnified, just as those who took sanctuary in a church were immune from arrest or just as legislators in some democracies today are immune from prosecution for some crimes. Biologists appropriated an entire social and political vocabulary, including the notion of aliens to the community or foreign invaders who must be repelled, to name the operation of the body's immune system and the catastrophe of autoimmunity. When foreign cells or antigens invade the body, the immune system cleverly assesses those cells and then creates and multiplies antibodies designed to destroy the antigens, thereby securing the body's immunity. "Flu shots" create antibodies that are supposed to make a person immune to flu viruses, safe, protected, indemnified, invulnerable. In autoimmunity something goes wrong with the immune system. It starts creating antibodies that attack the body's own cells, as in diabetes, in Crohn's disease (experts assume), and in rheumatoid arthritis, or as in some even more deadly forms of autoimmunity in which a whole organ is attacked and destroyed. Derrida takes this already metaphorical system of terms back from biology and applies it again to the social body, the body of the community and its members, from which the terminological system originally came. As Mitchell observes, whichever side you look at is the metaphor of the other.

Derrida's strikingly original insight, made with the exuberance and even wildness characteristic of "the late Derrida," is the claim that both immunity and autoimmunity are in one way or another characteristics of every community. Therefore community cannot be understood except by way of this structure. "[W]e feel ourselves," says Derrida, "authorized to make this expansion and to speak of a sort of general logic of autoimmunization. It seems indispensable to us today for thinking the relations between faith and knowledge, religion and science, as well as the duplicity of sources in general" (FK, 80, trans. modified; FS, 59). "Duplicity of sources in general" is a reference to Henri Bergson's *The Two Sources of Morality and Religion (Les deux sources de la morale et de la religion)*, referred to more than once in Derrida's "Faith and Knowledge." Derrida emphasizes that immunity and autoimmunity operate in any community mechanically, spontaneously, inevitably, willy-nilly, not as a result of choices members of the community make or that the community collectively makes. Every community strives to keep itself pure, safe, "sacrosanct," uncontaminated by aliens. At the same time, every community is inhabited by a suicidal tendency to shoot itself in the foot, as we say, in the act of trying to shoot the invader.

Here is Derrida's careful formulation of the way every community generates its own autoimmune reaction against itself, as well as using its immune system to repel foreign invaders:

> But the auto-immunitary haunts the community and its system of immunitary survival like the hyperbole of its own possibility. Nothing in *common*, nothing immune, safe and sound, *heilig* and holy, nothing unscathed in the most autonomous living present without a risk of auto-immunity. . . . This excess above and beyond the living, whose life only has absolute value by being worth more than life, more than itself—this, in short, is what opens the space of death that is linked to the automaton (exemplarily "phallic"), to technics, the machine, the prosthesis, virtuality: in a word, to the dimensions of the auto-immune and self-sacrificial supplementarity, to this death drive that is silently at work in every community, every *auto-co-immunity*, constituting it in truth as such in its iterability, its heritage, its spectral tradition. Community as *com-mon auto-immunity*: no community [is possible] that would not cultivate its own auto-immunity, a principle of sacrificial self-destruction ruining the principle of self-protection (that of maintaining its self-integrity intact), and this in view of some sort of invisible and spectral sur-vival. This self-contesting attestation keeps the auto-immune community alive, which is to say, open to something other and more than itself: the other, the future, death, freedom, the coming or the love of the other, the space and time of a spectralizing messianicity beyond all messianism. It is there that the possibility of religion persists: the *religious* bond (scrupulous, respectful, modest, reticent, inhibited) between the value of life, its absolute "dignity," and the theological machine, the "machine for making gods." (FK, 82, 87, trans. modified; FS, 62, 68–69)

This dense passage says a mouthful, as they say. It could be the object of virtually endless meditation, commentary, and interrogation. Several different figurative, semantic, or lexical systems are superimposed, in a characteristically late Derridean punning or etymologically echoing way. Multiple references to other work, Derrida's own or that of others, are obliquely made: to the concept of messianicity without messianism and that of spectrality from his own *Specters of Marx*; to Kant's work entitled *Religion Within the Limits of Reason Alone* (*Die Religion innerhalb der Grenzen der blossen Vernunft*), and to Kant's notion of the priceless price of human life; to Bergson's definition of human society as a machine for making gods in *The Two Sources of Morality and Religion*; to Freud and anthropologists for the role of the phallic in all religions; to the whole vocabulary, crisscrossing biology and human society, of words in *mun* or *mon, common, community, immunity, autoimmunity*; to the concepts of the machinal, the phallic, and the prosthetic as fundamental features of tele-techno-mediatic-capitalism. Derrida's concept of auto-co-immunity is discussed further in Chapter 11.

The notion of the machinal is here applied to the religious concept of self-sacrificing autoimmunity. It is a feature of the body's immune system, as of the endocrine system, that it works automatically, on its own, machinelike, without any control by consciousness. Derrida affirms that the self-destructive autoimmunity of any community works in the same way. The words *heilig*, "holy" (in English in the original), and "sacrificial" connect Derrida's concept of the autoimmunitary to his earlier thinking about religion and about sacrifice as an essential feature of the three "religions of the Book." Reflections about sacrifice are central in *Glas* and in *The Gift of Death*. The essay about autoimmunitary communities is, after all, called "Faith and Knowledge." It is included in books called *Religion* (*La religion*) and *Acts of Religion*. The word *sacrifice* comes from *sacer*, "holy, sacred," and *facere*, "to do, to make." To sacrifice is to do something holy, that is, something in some way related to what Derrida, echoing Jan Patočka, calls, in *The Gift of Death*, the *mysterium tremendum*. The self-sacrificial impulse in any community derives from its exposure to a secret, supernatural "wholly other" and from its desire to be saved by being transported to that place, to survive after its self-sacrifice. That is an extremely important aspect of Derrida's concept of auto-co-immunity. The tendency of any community, such as a nation-state, sooner or later to over-reach itself and destroy itself, as the United States may be doing today, cannot be detached from its religious aspect, from the openness of any community to the "wholly other" and from its desire for survival after death.

Central in the passage is a definition of a viable community as committed to preserving itself uncontaminated, safe and sound, pure, sequestered, hail and holy, while being inhabited by an irresistible tendency to turn its self-protective mechanisms against itself, to sacrifice itself in an attempt to protect itself against itself and in order to preserve its relation to the holy and to achieve "spectral sur-vival." Derrida takes for granted here and throughout the whole essay, or collection of fifty-two segments that makes up "Faith and Knowledge," that every community, in spite of its desire for safe self-enclosure, is open to some limitless other. Derrida here gives various contradictory names to this otherness, including "death" and "the future," though he scrupulously avoids calling it "God" or "heaven." Every community, whether it wants to be or not, however much it tries to enclose itself in itself, is open to "the other, the future, death, freedom, the coming or the love of the other, the space and time of a spectralizing messianicity beyond all messianism." A messiancity without messianism, as *Specters of Marx* makes clear, is an inherent structural collective belief in some happy millennial future, such as "the democracy to come." This belief, however, is detached from any belief that an actual Messiah will come.

A more recent work by Derrida, the interview included in *Philosophy in a Time of Terror* (*Le "concept" du 11 septembre*), would add the word *terror* to this list of names for the spectral outside/inside other. The title of the interview Giovanna Borradori conducted with Derrida for this book, shortly after the destruction of the World Trade Center but before the invasion of Iraq, is: "Autoimmunities: Real and Symbolic Suicides" ("Auto-immunités, suicides réels et symboliques"). As this name suggests, the interview is an analysis of the post–9/11 so-called War on Terror. It appropriates, from "Faith and Knowledge," the notion that autoimmunity is a characteristic of every community, for example, the community of so-called terrorists and the community of those who call the United States their homeland, in an inextricable interpenetration of the two, terrorists and terrorized. Both, for example, shared an interest in having the images of the Twin Towers falling broadcast throughout the world as often as possible and for as long as possible. Osama bin Laden must have rejoiced every time he saw those videos, but our government authorities also rejoiced. They rejoiced because they needed the effect of those images to justify the repressive measures they wanted to put in place. Terror is not stark fear of what has happened, but, as Derrida recognizes, of what is certain to happen again at some indefinite time in the future. What is certain to happen, sooner or later, is another "terrorist attack," as our government authorities, for example, the Secretary of Homeland Security or the Director of the CIA, keep periodically telling us, just in case we might start forgetting to live in a state of abject terror and so begin wondering where our civil liberties have gone. What is most terrifying is the conviction that the terrorists are not outside but within, secretly present as antigens, "terrorist cells," against which it is extremely difficult, in the end impossible, to develop effective antibodies. The "other" is not outside

but inside, as an uncanny, ghostly presence within the house. These terrorists might be anybody, the family next door, someone we see at the
grocery store, at the gas station, perhaps even, unbeknownst to us, our
own selves. As Pogo says, "We have met the enemy, and he is us." Derrida
uses the concept of autoimmunity to describe, for example, the way every
attempt to repress or forget post-traumatic terror just brings it back more
violently:

> Yet all these efforts to attenuate or neutralize the effect of the traumatism
> (to deny, repress, or forget it, to get over it [*pour en faire son deuil*], etc.) are,
> they also, but so many desperate attempts. And so many autoimmunitary
> movements. Which produce, invent, and feed the very monstrosity they
> claim to overcome.
>
> What will never let itself be forgotten is thus the perverse effect of the
> autoimmunitary itself. For we now know that repression in both its psycho-
> analytical sense and its political sense—whether it be through the police,
> the military, or the economy [*au sens politico-policier, politico-militaire, polit-
> ico-économique*]—ends up producing, reproducing, and regenerating the
> very thing it seeks to disarm. (PTT, 99, trans. modified; C11S, 152)

This double, self-defeating effort can be seen at work in the U.S. "War
on Terror." We spend billions on "homeland security," while sacrificing
the lives of thousands of our citizens in the Iraq war, not to speak of the
tens of thousands of Iraqi citizens we have killed. We often direct our
immunity army, the FBI, the CIA, and the more hidden security forces,
against our own citizens or against refugees, immigrants, or victims of
repressive regimes to whom we ought to owe hospitality. We do this under
the authority of the "Patriot Act," an Orwellian name if there ever was
one, since it is designed to take away the civil liberties of all patriotic U.S.
citizens, as well as of the alien "terrorists" we *must* be harboring in our
midst, like ghosts who have invaded the homeland. The Patriot Act does
the "homeland" serious harm and makes it less secure, as in the exclusion
of foreign students, scientists, and scholars on whom the successful working of American capitalism depends, or as in the failure to prepare adequately for the possibility of Hurricane Katrina because the Department
of Homeland Security was so focused on a potential terrorist attack.

Another striking example of self-destructive auto-co-immunity is the
gigantic subprime mortgage pyramid scheme that has led banks and other
financial institutions to the verge of bankruptcy. This is requiring an esti-
mated seven trillion dollars of government bailout funds to be poured into
banks and other financial institutions in the United States alone. The bailout has been necessary in order to keep the whole global financial system

from collapsing. In an attempt to get rich safely, and in view of a capitalist millennium, the community of investment officers at financial institutions like Citigroup divided the risky subprime mortgages they had bought into what are called by the quaint French name of *tranches*, slices. These slices were mixed with solider investments to spread the risk so widely and thinly, it was assumed, that it would in effect disappear. These "toxic" investments were in turn made protected, safe, by way of what were fool-ishly assumed to be immunity antibodies, financial instruments called "de-rivatives" and "credit default swaps." These were supposed to eliminate the risk just as immune system antibodies neutralize foreign antigens that have invaded the human body. When the housing bubble burst, as any sane person could have foreseen would happen, the hollow derivatives and default swaps, "toxic" themselves because they were worthless, turned against the financial institutions they were meant to protect. The deriva-tives and default swaps would have destroyed the banks, in a spectacular example of autoimmunity, if government bailouts, funded primarily by printing more money, had not rescued them. This is a yet further example of auto-co-immunity, since the huge increase in government deficits will in the end weaken the United States further by inflating the currency and by having even more of the United States owned by China in the form of U.S. Treasury Bonds. The applicability of Derrida's autoimmumity model to the current world financial crisis is a good example of how powerful a means of understanding it is. Investment bankers seem to have been led willy-nilly to destroy themselves and their institutions in a way that con-firms Derrida's notion of the inevitability of autoimmunitary self-destruc-tion as inherent in any community.[54] The whole enormous Ponzi scheme, it is worth noting, depended at every step on new telecommunication technologies like email and complex computer programs, which produced derivatives and swaps that even experts cannot understand. That matches Derrida's insistence on the role of the prosthetic machinal in auto-co-immunity.

A fissure, fault-line, or cleft seems to exist, however, when what Derrida says about auto-co-immunity in "Faith and Knowledge" is juxtaposed to what he says about the isolation of each "I" in the passage already cited from his last set of seminars. Derrida's theory of each community's self-destructive autoimmunity presupposes an organic or collective concept of community that determines, whether they wish it or not, the lives of the individuals within it, while my citation from "The Beast and the Sovereign (Two)" defines each individual as entirely separate from any community, marooned on a bridgeless, isthmusless island.

How can these two features of the late Derrida's thought be reconciled? What bridge will allow a crossing from one to the other? A somewhat paradoxical connection between these two ideas is implied in a remarkable passage in *A Taste for the Secret*. Derrida, in one interview in that book, echoing Gide's denunciation of the family, resolutely defines himself as unwilling to belong to any family or community: "I am not one of the family [*Je ne suis pas de la famille*]." Why not? It is because every family, nation, or community is an artificial, deconstructible structure built precariously on some agreed-upon code. For Derrida, as opposed to Heidgger, it seems that only one kind of community exists, something quite close to Heidegger's *das Man*, "the they." Derrida gives it, in the English translation, at least, the dyslogistic name "the herd." There is, in Derrida, no glorification of the nation's "folk," such as Heidegger, notoriously, pronounced.

Every community, moreover, for Derrida, is inhabited by the self-destructive autoimmunity he describes so eloquently in "Faith and Knowledge," written more or less at the same time as he gave the interviews in *A Taste for the Secret*. Who would want to participate in something doomed to self-destruct? It would seem reasonable to want to hold oneself aloof from such a *Mitsein*, even though some people might argue that we should make do the best we can with what we have. We are all in the same boat and should love our neighbor within the context of whatever community we have. Derrida, however, above all refuses to belong to any family or community because it is only in isolation from such belonging that a responsible, responsive ethical relation to another person can take place. For Derrida, the strange "with" of I/other relations between two persons, two persons who are wholly other to one another, can only happen in isolation from any family or community. In *The Gift of Death*, Derrida sees Abraham's willingness to obey Jehovah and sacrifice his beloved son, Isaac, as paradigmatic of this isolation from family and community of true ethical decision. Abraham says nothing about Jehovah's command to his wife Sarah or to any other member of his family, or to Isaac himself, when he takes Isaac off to sacrifice him (GD, 53–81; DM, 79–114; GD2 121–29; DM 163–73.)

I would add to what Derrida says that Jesus affirmed one must leave father and mother in order to follow him: "And every one that hath forsaken houses, or brethren, or sisters, or father, or mother, or wife, for my name's sake, shall receive an hundredfold, and shall inherit everlasting life" (Matt. 19:29).[55] Here is Derrida's eloquent expression of his refusal to belong:

Let me get back to my saying "I am not one of the family." Clearly, I was playing on a formula that has multiple registers of resonance. I'm not one of the family means, in general, "I do not define myself on the basis of my belonging to the family," or to civil society, or to the state; I do not define myself on the basis of elementary forms of kinship. But it also means, more figuratively, that I am not part of any group, that I do not identify myself with a linguistic community, a national community, a political party, or with any group or clique whatsoever, with any philosophical or literary school. "I am not one of the family" means: do not consider me "one of you," "don't count me in," I want to keep my freedom, always: this, for me, is the condition not only for being singular and other, but also for entering into relation with the singularity and alterity of others. When someone is one of the family, not only does he lose himself in the herd [*gregge*, in the Italian version[56]], but he loses the others as well; the others become simply places, family functions, or places or functions in the organic totality that constitutes a group, school, nation, or community of subjects speaking the same language. (TS, 27)

On the next page Derrida claims we would not say we want to belong to the family or community if we really did belong to one or the other: "The desire to belong to any community whatsoever, the desire for belonging *tout court*, implies that one *does not belong*" (TS, 28). This is our happy chance, since my only road to responsible ethical relations to my neighbor, the "wholly other," is by detaching myself from family or community, or by recognizing that I am always already and for good detached, enisled. I must detach myself from the herd, or appropriate my detachment, in order to escape the doom of autoimmune self-destruction that always awaits such deconstructible agglomerations. I must come to know that I am detached, and that it's a good thing too.

The different concepts of being with represented by Derrida and by all those modern thinkers of being with I began by identifying are incompatible. They cannot be synthesized or reconciled. *Il faut choisir*. Which do I choose? I wish with all my heart I could believe in Williams's ideal of a happy, classless community or in Heidegger's assumption that *Mitsein* is a fundamental aspect of being human, but I fear that each man or woman may be an island unto himself or herself, and that real communities are more like the communities of self-destructive autoimmunity Derrida describes. Certainly the United States these days, if you can dare to think of it as one immense community, is a better example of Derrida's self-destructive autoimmune community than of Williams's community of kindness and mutuality.

I claim, moreover, to have confirmed through several examples the triple hypothesis with which I started: (1) that the concept of community, in a given thinker, is consonant with his or her concept of relations between self and other; (2) that you cannot get from *Dasein* to *Mitsein* unless you assume from the start that *Dasein* is *Mitsein*; (3) that Derrida in his last seminars, almost uniquely among modern philosophers and theorists, affirms the fundamental and irremediable isolation of each *Dasein*. For Derrida, no isthmus, no bridge, no road, no communication or transfer connects or can ever connect my enisled self to other selves. There is no common world. There are only islands. Any community is an artificial, deconstructible, construct fabricated out of words or other signs. Any community, moreover, is self-destructively autoimmunitary to boot. One should not underestimate the consequences of holding that each human being is, throughout his or her lifetime, enisled.

CHAPTER 7

Derrida's Special Theory of Performativity

The hypotheses that ground (or unground) this chapter are as follows.

1. Performativity in the sense of the way a dance, a musical composition, or a part in a play is performed has practically nothing to do with performativity in the sense of the ability a given enunciation has to function as a performative speech act. "He gave a spectacular performance of Hamlet" does not exemplify, nor does it refer to, the same use of language as does saying "He gave his solemn promise that he would be here at ten," even though both are forms of enunciation, of speaking out, of uttering words, even of doing something with words. I call these performativity sub one (the speech act), and performativity sub two (the performance of a role, or of a dance or musical composition).

2. Derrida's late work proposes a special theory of performativity. This theory is without antecedent in previous theorists of speech acts.

A hypothesis, such as the ones I have just proposed, *is* a genuine performative. A hypothesis fits the standard definition of a performative in traditional speech act theory. Proffering a hypothesis is like a bet. "I bet you I can show that performativity as performance style and performativity as the felicitous operation of a speech act have almost nothing to do with one another. Considerable confusion, I hazard to say, has resulted, in some quarters, from thinking the two kinds of performativity are the same, or almost the same."

These pages are an extended version of what the admirable online encyclopedia, *Wikipedia*,[1] calls a "Disambiguation Page," that is, a page that discriminates among the various more or less incompatible meanings of a given term. *Wikipedia*, for example, distinguishes nine different referents for *catastrophe*. I hold that it would be a catastrophe to blur different meanings of *performativity*.

A hypothesis is something set down underneath as a foundation on the basis of which further inquiry may be carried out, from Greek *hupo* ("under") and *tithenai* ("to place"). A valid scientific hypothesis must be capable of being falsified if it is mistaken. That is why religious fundamentalists' claims that God created the world in 4004 B.C. or that the "creation" manifests "intelligent design" are not valid hypotheses. They can neither be proved true nor proved false. You have to take them on faith. If I hypothesize that the moon is all made of green cheese, my hypothesis can be proved false by a trip to the moon and bringing back moonrock, no cheese, or indeed proved true if green cheese turns up there. My hypothesis about the more or less complete disjunction between the two kinds of performativity will, I hope, be confirmed by the investigation of some examples, even though it ungrounds some widely established disciplinary assumptions.

First, however, a word about the words *performative* and *performativity*. Neither word exists in *The American Heritage Dictionary of the English Language*, nor does my computer dictionary recognize these as valid words. My computer draws red lines under both words when I type them on the screen, even though many people, mostly academic people, now use both words all the time, in the most natural way possible. Usage becomes the norm.

Performance is a word, all right. Here are the three relevant meanings of the five given in *The American Heritage Dictionary*: "the act of performing, or the state of being performed"; "the act or style of performing a work or role before an audience"; and "a presentation, especially a theatrical one, before an audience." That seems clear enough. "Performativity," though it is not a word but a neologism, must mean the quality of a performance, the condition of someone who is capable of performing, or, perhaps, the object of investigation in "performance studies." Here is part of what *Wikipedia* says under "Performativity." I am using *Wikipedia* here, and in what I say about Judith Butler later, as the best source I know for often highly informed and current received opinion about a given topic or writer. *Wikipedia*, like any encyclopedia, printed or online, should be used with vigilant suspicion. Any encyclopedia entry will be an oversimplification. The presumed "authority" may not be an authority at all, or may not be disinterested. Other sources should be consulted. *Wikipedia* makes that somewhat easier by often providing links to other texts. My primary concern here is with what people think about "performativity," or about Judith Butler's *Gender Trouble*. In particular, I am interested in figuring out how a certain confusion in the "academic mind" came about:

> *Performativity* is a concept that is related to speech acts theory, to the pragmatics of language, and to the work of John L. Austin. It accounts for situations where a proposition may constitute or instaurate the object to which it is meant to refer, as in so-called "performative utterances." [That, by the way, is a skewed definition. A performative utterance, according to Austin, does not constitute the object to which it refers. It changes objects and people that already exist, as when the minister's "I pronounce you man and wife," uttered in the right circumstances, brings it about that the couple is married.]
>
> The concept of performativity has also been used in science and technology studies and in economic sociology. Andrew Pickering has proposed to shift from a "representational idiom" to a "performative idiom" in the study of science. Michel Callon has proposed to study the performative aspects of economics, i.e. the extent to which economic science plays an important role not only in describing markets and economies, but also in framing them. ["Framing them"? Just what does that mean? If economics are performative, as the author has just said, they would not just "frame" markets and economies, in the sense of setting them into a framework allowing understanding, but actively change them, as a way of doing things with words.]
>
> Other uses of the notion of performativity in the social sciences include the daily behavior (or performance) of individuals based on social norms or habits. Philosopher and feminist theorist Judith Butler has used the concept of performativity in her analysis of gender development, as well as in her analysis of political speech. Eve Kosofsky Sedgwick describes *Queer Performativity* as an ongoing project for transforming the way we may define—and break—boundaries to identity.[2]

Wikipedia's entry "Performance Studies" says this topic, according to one "origin narrative," was created as an academic discipline in the 1960s by Richard Schechner, Victor Turner, and others—all men, I note. It was first institutionalized at New York University and at Northwestern University. According to *Wikipedia*:

Performance studies is a growing field of "academic" study focusing on the critical analysis of performance and performativity. The field or post-discipline engages performance as both an object of study and as a method of analysis. Examining events as performance provides insight into how we perform ourselves and our lives. And understanding the performative nature of speech-acts introduces an element of reflexivity and critique to otherwise descriptive accounts of social phenomena.

Though performance studies has an anthropological component, as Victor Turner's role as a founder indicates, it centers on performances in dance, music, and drama, as well as on the performance of roles in daily life. If "performance studies" was created in the 1960s, it precedes the work or the wide influence of Foucault, Derrida, and Butler. It even precedes, I believe, any substantial academic influence of Austin's speech act theory. The first edition of *How to Do Things with Words* was in 1962, but it was not, I suspect, widely noticed at the time. The original French version of Foucault's *The Order of Things* (*Les mots et les choses*) dates from 1966. "Performativity theory" and current "performance studies," I suggest, are somewhat later hybrids combining speech act theory, Foucault, and the original performance studies. The lines of filiation here, to use a sexist word, are complex and inextricably entangled, as is the case with modern theory generally.

The newest entries in *Wikipedia*, quite different from the ones I cited just two years ago in the first version of this chapter, confirm this duplicity. The changes in the entries are a good example of the way *Wikipedia* is constantly being revised and updated. You have to move fast to keep up with *Wikipedia*. Who knows what these entries will be by the time this book appears in print? The change is also a sign that "performance studies" and "performativity studies" are dynamic disciplines. Someone or several someones care enough about them to have made a radical revision of the earlier entries. *Wikipedia* now says about "performance studies":

> An alternative origin narrative stresses the development of speech-act theory by philosophers J. L. Austin and Judith Butler and literary critic Eve Kosofsky Sedgwick. Performance studies has also had a strong relationship to the fields of feminism, psychoanalysis, and queer theory. Theorists like Peggy Phelan, Butler, Sedgwick, José Esteban Muñoz, Rebecca Schneider, and André Lepecki have been equally influential in both performance studies and these related fields. Performance studies incorporates theories of drama, dance, art, anthropology, folkloristics, philosophy, cultural studies, sociology, and more and more, music performance.[3]

So how does one get from "performance studies" to "performativity"? As I suspected when I began thinking about the genesis of "performativity," Judith Butler's work, or the way it has been read or misread, is the missing link. When I click on the link to "Judith Butler" in *Wikipedia*'s entry for "performativity," I get a little closer to the heart of the matter, or to the root of the confusion. The reader will remember that I am more interested here in what people think Butler said than in what she may actually have said. Her work has perhaps not always been read accurately. This may be a case in which misreadings have wide influence and consequences. People often see what they want to see or expect to see. This happens sometimes in reading. Butler may not have meant what *Wikipedia* says she meant, but she was read as meaning to say that. Once more, the current entry (February 2008) is quite different from the one I cited two years ago:

> The crux of Butler's argument in *Gender Trouble* is that the coherence of the categories of sex, gender, and sexuality—the natural-seeming coherence, for example, of masculine gender and heterosexual desire in male bodies—is culturally constructed through the repetition of stylized acts in time. These stylized bodily acts, in their repetition, establish the appearance of an essential, ontological "core" gender. This is the sense in which Butler famously theorizes gender, along with sex and sexuality, as performative.[4]

"The concept of performativity is," *Wikipedia* holds, "at the core of Butler's work. It extends beyond the doing of gender and can be understood as a full-fledged theory of subjectivity. Indeed, if her more recent books have shifted focus away from gender, they still treat performativity as theoretically central" (ibid.). Several of Butler's more recent books— *Bodies That Matter* (1993), *Excitable Speech: A Politics of the Performative* (1997), and *Undoing Gender* (2004), as well as the new preface of 1999 for *Gender Trouble*—do some disambiguating of their own. They make amends, to some degree, for the confusion between performativity as performance and performativity as speech act that *Gender Trouble* can be read as fostering, if *Wikipedia* is to be believed. *Gender Trouble*, with its account of a certain performativity, has remained, however, immensely influential. Over a hundred thousand copies are out there in various languages.

If I turn from *Wikipedia*'s account of *Gender Trouble* to the book itself, I find a much more complex and nuanced argument. This is especially the case if I read the new edition that includes the preface of 1999. A full account of *Gender Trouble* would require many pages and would take me away from my focus in this chapter on Derrida's new theory of performatives. A paragraph by paragraph and sentence by sentence interrogative reading of, for example, the preface of 1999, not to speak of all Butler's subsequent work, would be demanded. My much more limited aim is to understand and account for Butler's use of the word *performativity*.

Gender Trouble has done much good in the world. It has done good by persuasively putting in question "normative" binary heterosexuality and thereby making a space for gay and lesbian sexuality and gender. Butler's primary target in *Gender Trouble* is not just habitual notions that sex and gender are innate, natural, and unalterable but, more specifically, the dependence of the feminism current in 1990 on just the ideas of normative heterosexuality that it ought to have contested. Feminism's acceptance of heterosexuality led it to exclude gays and lesbians from the "real" and the "intelligible," almost as violently as did (and still does) the hegemony of primarily straight male social and legal power. Butler contests the reigning ideology of sex and gender by tirelessly, patiently, with passion and with much nuance, arguing that sex and gender are not natural, biological, innate, and pre-existent but the violent product of iterated discursive formations that sequester as unnatural and "unreal" sexual and gender minorities in their considerable variation: "Juridical power inevitably 'produces' what it claims merely to represent; hence, politics must be concerned with this dual function of power: the juridical and the productive. In effect, the law produces and then conceals the notion of 'a subject before the law' in order to invoke that discursive formation as a naturalized foundational premise that subsequently legitimates that law's own regulatory hegemony."[5]

Gender Trouble culminates in a "Conclusion: From Parody to Politics," which makes a powerful argument for political agency, for the possibility of changing the almost universal acceptance of binary heterosexuality as the norm. Since binary heterosexuality is not innate but an illusion, a fiction, a "phantasmatic construction"(199), it could be otherwise. As Butler says in the preface of 1999:

> One might wonder what use "opening up possibilities" finally is, but no one who has understood what it is to live in the social world as what is "impossible," illegible, unrealizable, unreal, and illegitimate is likely to pose that question. . . . There is no political position purified of power, and perhaps that impurity is what produces agency as the potential interruption and reversal of regulatory regimes. Those who are deemed "unreal" nevertheless lay hold of the real, a laying hold that happens in concert, and a vital instability is produced by that performative surprise. (viii, xxviii)

"A vital instability is produced by that performative surprise": this is an amazing formulation. It defines a performative as a "laying hold," and it defines that laying hold as creating an "instability" that comes as a "surprise." You cannot foresee this instability. It comes as a surprise, and by then it is too late. The instability gives a space for an "agency" that can dismantle normative heterosexuality.

My primary interest here, however, is in the role of the terms and concepts of *performance, performative*, and, especially, *performativity* in Butler's discourse. The word *performative*, as a name for a speech act, a use of words to do something rather than constatively name something, was J. L. Austin's invention in *How To Do Things with Words*. Strangely enough, Austin is never mentioned in *Gender Trouble*, though the term *speech act* occasionally appears.[6] Speech act theory is taken for granted in *Gender Trouble*, and the word *performative* is, as Derrida would put it, "exappropriated." No shame in that. Derrida himself more than once praises creative (mis)reading, that is, strictly speaking, unfaithful appropriation as the right way to go. An example is what he says about our responsibility to make a rupture with authority: "there is no responsibility without a dissident and inventive rupture with respect to tradition, authority, orthodoxy, rule, or doctrine" (GD, 27; DM, 47). Derrida says more or less the same thing in *Specters of Marx* about his reading of Marx, in a passage cited at greater length in Chapter 5 of this book: "This dimension of a performative interpretation, that is, of an interpretation that transforms the very thing it interprets, will play an indispensable role in what I would like to say this evening" (SMe, 51; SMf, 89). (Both these passages are cited again in a different context in Chapter 9 of this book.) Even so, it would have been helpful if Butler had specified just how her use of *performative* differs from Austin's. For more on Butler's theory of speech acts, in this case the performative effects of hate speech, it would be necessary to go to a later book, *Excitable Speech: A Politics of the Performative* (1997).

If Austin is never mentioned in *Gender Trouble*, Derrida is mentioned a few times, though crucially, as I shall show. The overt theoretical references in *Gender Trouble* are to Foucault (the most explicit theoretical foundation), to Lévi-Strauss, to Lacan and Freud in the psychoanalytical second chapter, and to certain feminists, French and otherwise—Simone de Beauvoir, Luce Irigaray, Monique Wittig, and many others. Moreover, the word *performativity* is hardly salient until the last sections of *Gender Trouble*, and even then it appears only sparingly, alongside *performance* and *performative*, and even *performativeness*, often in proximity to *act, theatricality, masquerade, drag*, and *acting out*. The preface of 1999, however, is to a considerable degree an attempt to explain just what Butler means by *performativity*. The word appears over and over in that preface. The conflation of performativity sub one and performativity sub two is present in many of Butler's formulations, as when she says, "As the effects of a subtle and politically enforced performativity, gender is an 'act,' as it were, that is open to splittings, self-parody, self-criticism, and those hyperbolic exhibitions of 'the natural' that, in their very exaggeration, reveal its fundamentally phantasmatic status"(200). The phrase "as it were" indicates a wavering that is explicitly and somewhat uneasily acknowledged in the preface of 1999, under the name *waffle*: "*Gender Trouble* sometimes reads as if gender is simply a self-invention or that the psychic meaning of a gendered presentation might be read directly off its surface. Both of these postulates have had to be refined over time. Moreover, my theory sometimes waffles between understanding performativity as linguistic and casting it as theatrical" (xxvi).

Having posed a distinction between what I have been calling performativity sub one and performativity sub two, and confessed to having waffled about that distinction, Butler goes on immediately to take back with one hand what she has offered with the other. She does this by way of a claim that a linguistic speech act and a theatrical performance are always related, "chiasmically," though what she says hardly supports the claim that one is the crisscross reversal of the other, which is what a chiasmus is: "I have come to think that the two are invariably related, chiasmically so, and that a reconsideration of the speech act as an instance of power invariably draws attention to both its theatrical and linguistic dimensions. In *Excitable Speech*, I sought to show that the speech act is at once performed (and thus theatrical, presented to an audience, subject to interpretation), and linguistic, inducing a set of effects through its implied relation to linguistic conventions" (xxvi–xxvii). The two kinds of performativity are then superimposed once more in the next sentences, and not in the crisscross of a chiasm: "If one wonders how a linguistic theory of the speech act relates to bodily gestures, one need only consider that speech itself is a bodily act with specific linguistic consequences. Thus speech belongs exclusively neither to corporeal presentation nor to language, and its status as word and deed is necessarily ambiguous. This ambiguity has consequences for the practice of coming out, for the insurrectionary power of the speech act, for language as a condition of both bodily seduction and the threat of injury" (xxvii).

It is true that language always has some form of embodiment, whether as inky marks on the page of my copy of *Gender Trouble* or as the sounds I breathe forth when I speak, accompanying my speech, perhaps, with significant gestures. It is also true that Austin allows that a bodily gesture, such as a judge donning a black hood to condemn a criminal to be hanged, can substitute for a literal speech act, such as "I sentence you to be hanged by the neck until dead." The materiality of language, however, is an exceedingly peculiar kind of nonmaterial materiality, as Derrida, Paul de Man, and others have in different ways argued.[7] The relation of language to bodily gestures hardly supports the assertion that the theatrical and the linguistic are "always related," even chiasmically. A given piece of language can go on functioning performatively in an infinite variety of material embodiments and circumstances, including many that are not in any direct way incarnated in a human body.

I conclude this brief attempt to read something of what Butler actually says in *Gender Trouble*, as opposed to what *Wikipedia* says she says, with a look at a crucial paragraph in the preface of 1999. In this paragraph, Derrida's "Before the Law" is unexpectedly, at least for me, in a "performative surprise," identified as the initial instigator of the thinking that went into *Gender Trouble*, especially Butler's thinking about performativity. The surprise is generated by the fact that neither Kafka's parable "Before the Law" nor Derrida's essay "Before the Law" has anything to say about the way gender and sex are the result of a performative power that seems to come from an implacable social law that is actually not there but is phantasmatic, an illusion, the projection of something that we fruitlessly expect will reveal itself in the future.

Kafka's "law" is a transcendent entity something like the Mosaic law of the Old Testament, and though Derrida's project may be the "deconstruction" of that law by way of showing that it is always contaminated with "literature," that is, with the fictional, nevertheless Derrida's essay is haunted by the undeconstructible possibility that this transcendent law exists but just is forever inaccessible. "The inaccessible incites from its place of hiding [*l'inaccessible provoque depuis son retranchement*]" (BL, 191; DL, 109), says Derrida in one of the more provocative formulations in his "Before the Law." Derrida's essay, moreover, was originally written as part of a series of seminars at the École normale on Kant's *Critique of Practical Reason*, that is, as a commentary on Kant's idea of a categorical moral law. A section of Derrida's essay sets Kafka's parable in the context of what Freud has to say about the origin of the moral law in a shame about genital and anal smells that led *homo sapiens* to walk upright. Freud's myth in *Totem and Taboo* about the primal murder of the father by the sons is also invoked, as is, in a footnote, Freud's friend Fliess's interest in bisexuality. Derrida, moreover, has provocative things inspired by Freud to say about the way Kafka's man from the country is intimidated by the nose, beard, and fur coat of the guardian of the law, but nothing overtly is said about the way either Freud's or Kafka's law imposes heterosexual gender distinctions (see BL, 192–99; DL, 110–17).

Nevertheless, Derrida's invocation of Freud, in relation to Kant's idea of respect, may have started Butler's thinking. In the initial footnote to the long central chapter of *Gender Trouble*, "Prohibition, Psychoanalysis, and the Production of the Heterosexual Matrix," Butler says that she was teaching Kafka's "In the Penal Colony" while she was writing this chapter. The footnote refers directly to Derrida's "Before the Law." This is almost the only overt reference to that essay in the 1990 *Gender Trouble*, though the phrase "before the law" is at one point put within quotation marks, with a footnote to Derrida's essay (3, 206). Referring in the first-mentioned footnote to Foucault's idea that power has become so diffuse that it no longer exists as "a systematic totality," Butler goes on to say: "Derrida interrogates the problematic authority of such a law in the context of Kafka's 'Before the Law.' . . . He underscores the radical unjustifiability of this repression through a narrative recapitulation of a time before the law. Significantly, it also remains impossible to articulate a critique of that law through recourse to a time before the law" (215). One of Derrida's primary concerns in "Before the Law" is the question of what makes a text literature, who decides a given text is literature and on what authority. This issue does not interest Butler in *Gender Trouble*. I conclude that if *Gender Trouble* was instigated by Butler's reading of Derrida's "Before the Law," this is a spectacular case of the "dissident and inventive rupture" that Derrida praises as the most responsible response "to tradition, authority, orthodoxy, rule, or doctrine." Butler's reading of Derrida's essay invoked the performative surprise of a new theory of sex and gender that could not have been predicted by its source, any more than Derrida's *Specters of Marx* can be predicted by Marx's writings. Both formed a radically innovative break or rupture with tradition and received doctrine, in Butler's case with the then dominant feminism as it excluded lesbians.

Butler begins, in the paragraph in question in the preface of 1999, by making overt the way *performativity*, a relatively infrequent word in *Gender Trouble*, has in subsequent years become the central focus of its influence. It is, moreover, Butler says, a topic she has turned to again and again in subsequent work, in a constant process of modification:

> Much of my work in recent years has been devoted to clarifying and revising the theory of performativity that is outlined in *Gender Trouble*. It is

difficult to say precisely what performativity is not only because my own views on what "performativity" might mean have changed over time, most often in response to excellent criticisms, but because so many others have taken it up and given it their own formulations. (xv)

Performativity was a word whose time had come, like the word *deconstruction*, and, like *deconstruction*, it has come to mean whatever people "formulate" it to mean or use it to mean to say, including the different meanings over time that a given theorist, such as Butler, ascribes to it. Another example is the use of the word in the discipline of Performance Studies. Though Butler, as I have shown, uses the words *performance* and *theatricality* in *Gender Trouble*, she nowhere mentions Performance Studies, just as she does not mention Lyotard's prior use of the word *performativity*. It may be that she independently invented the word and a version of its concept, even though others had already used it.

What immediately follows the citation from *Gender Trouble* I have just made is the crucial reference to Derrida's "Before the Law" as the text that started Butler thinking about what she came to call *performativity*. That reference leads to what looks to me like a quite coherent and comprehensive expression of the theory of performativity that is essential to *Gender Trouble*. At the same time it is a remarkably dissident, performatively surprising, productively transposing, reading of Kafka's "Before the Law" and of Derrida's "Before the Law." The passage is eloquent and cogent. I cite it in extenso to give Butler the last word on what she means by *performativity*. What I have found by turning from *Wikipedia* to *Gender Trouble* itself complicates quite a bit the genealogical story *Wikipedia* tells:

> I originally took my clue on how to read the performativity of gender from Jacques Derrida's reading of Kafka's "Before the Law." There the one who waits for the law, sits before the door of the law, attributes a certain force to the law for which one waits. The anticipation of an authoritative disclosure of meaning is the means by which that authority is attributed and installed: the anticipation conjures its object. I wondered whether we do not labor under a similar expectation concerning gender, that it operates as an interior essence that might be disclosed, an expectation that ends up producing the very phenomenon that it anticipates. In the first instance, then, the performativity of gender revolves around this metalepsis, the way in which the anticipation of a gendered essence produces that which it posits as outside itself. Secondly, performativity is not a singular act, but a repetition and a ritual, which achieves its effects through its naturalization in the context of a body, understood, in part, as a culturally sustained temporal duration. (xv)

A footnote to this paragraph connects the notion of performativity's dependence on repetition to Pierre Bourdieu's work (206), but surely the context is also Derrida's idea of the "iterability" of performative speech acts. That might imply, however, that Butler's had by 1990 read Derrida's *Limited Inc.* The new edition of *Gender Trouble* offers no evidence that this is the case.

The genealogy I began trying to trace by way of Butler's work as an intersection or place of crossing is further complicated by the way Jean-François Lyotard was already in 1979, eleven years before *Gender Trouble*, in *The Postmodern Condition: A Report on Knowledge* (1984; *La condition postmoderne: Rapport sur le savoir*; 1979), using *performativity* as a key word and a key concept. I shall now look briefly at that. Examples of Lyotard's use of the word are two chapter titles: "Research and Its Legitimation Through Performativity," and "Education and Its Legitimation Through Performativity." Lyotard meant by "the performativity criterion" more or less that science, technology, education, and other social enterprises, in the postmodern period, do not depend upon preexisting principles of legitimation. They produce their own grounds through the performance of research, education, or other such "language games," as Lyotard calls them, following Wittgenstein's use of this term in his *Philosophical Investigations*.[8] The rules or principles depend upon a social contract or bond. We agree to abide by certain rules in playing a game or in deciding what counts as new "truth" in science, and so on. Speaking of the way technology "masters" "reality," Lyotard affirms:

> This is how legitimation by power takes shape. Power is not only good performativity, but also effective verification and good verdicts. It legitimates science and the law on the basis of their efficiency, and legitimates this efficiency on the basis of science and law. It is self-legitimating, in the way a system organized around performance maximization seems to be. Now it is precisely this kind of context control that a generalized computerization of society may bring. The performativity of an utterance, be it denotative or prescriptive, increases proportionally to the amount of information about its referent one has at one's disposal. Thus the growth of power, and its self-legitimation, are now taking the route of data storage and accessibility, and the operativity of information. (47)

This is an amazingly prophetic statement, when one reflects that it was written in 1979. Think, if you can remember that far back, what was the state of computing in 1979! *Wikipedia*, as a self-generating and self-regulating online encyclopedia, collectively created, is a splendid example of the problematic self-legitimating databases that Lyotard so presciently foresaw.

Though space here does not permit detailed demonstration, I think it can be shown that Lyotard's use of the term *performativity* is an example of the confusion I am attempting to disambiguate. Lyotard begins with a more or less orthodox account of performative speech acts à la Austin (9). He then shifts, by way of Wittgenstein's theory of language games (10), to the "pragmatic" (his word, 23) notion of performativity as know-how (21), and, as the citation above indicates, to performativity as legitimation by an exercise of power, whether by denotative or prescriptive utterances. By this final shift, Lyotard has come a long way from Austin. It is not unreasonable to assume that Lyotard's celebrated work may have had some influence on Butler (though she nowhere, as I have said, refers to Lyotard in *Gender Trouble*) and certainly on widespread received ideas about performativity in the eighties and nineties. To put this another way, it almost seems as if the widespread (mis)understanding of Butler's theory of performatively produced gender in *Gender Trouble* is a special case of the "legitimation by power" Lyotard describes as a central feature of the postmodern condition.

The entries in *Wikipedia*, plus what I have found in Lyotard, succinctly tell a story, the story of how university disciplines wandered away from Austin's quite definite concept of performative utterances in *How to Do Things with Words* to the institutionalizing of something called, on Butler's example, "performativity" or even "performativity theory." Here is the little genealogical story: Judith Butler, so this story assumes, appropriated Derrida's modification of Austin's speech act theory and married it, under the impetus of feminism and nascent queer theory, to something more or less alien to Derrida's work, namely, Foucault's *Discipline and Punish* and his *History of Sexuality: Volume I*, with Lyotard perhaps hovering in the background. On that basis, Butler invented a new and immensely influential theory called performativity, that is, the notion that gender is not inherent but is engendered by disciplinary pressures that coerce us into performing, that is, behaving, in a way society assumes is appropriate for a certain gender. "That very repetitive performance," once upon a time said *Wikipedia*, with eloquent succinctness, in the old entry that has now disappeared, "produces the imaginary fiction of a 'core gender,' as well as the distinction between the surface/exterior of 'the body' and the 'interior core.' Paradoxically, it is a kind of forced, repetitive 'doing' of gender that itself produces the *fiction* that an individual 'has' a stable 'gender' that 'she/ he' is just 'expressing' in 'her/his actions.'" This notion of what has come to be called "social construction" was so powerful and so attractive, it explained so much, that it has been appropriated, as *Wikipedia* tells us, under the name "performativity," in a variety of disciplines: in science and technology, sociology, economics, anthropology, drama studies, and the study of the "performances" of everyday life, as in "my son put on quite a performance when I tried to get him to do his homework." Performativity theory has now become a discipline or an interdisciplinary project, for example, at the conference where the first part of this chapter was origi-nally presented in an earlier form. (See the Acknowledgments.) "Perform-ativity theory" has become an alternative name for what used to be called "performance studies."

"Performativity," it now appears, means, among other things, the as-sumption that human beings have no innate selfhood or subjectivity but become what they are through more or less forced repetition of a certain role. It is as though someone who plays the role of Hamlet or Ophelia on the stage is in danger of becoming Hamlet or Ophelia, or perhaps no one at all, as the antitheatrical tradition from the Renaissance to Henry James's *The Tragic Muse* and beyond feared.[9] That is what "social construction" means. Everyday life is something like acting on the stage. You play the role of being straight, or gay, or an English professor long enough and you become straight, or gay, or an English professor.

This is both a depressing and at the same time a tremendously attractive notion. It is something in the social world akin to what Freud called the "family romance," that is, the child's belief that he or she is not really the offspring of his or her parents but a princess or prince in disguise. Though I am not Prince Hamlet nor was meant to be, I am not really an English professor either. I have been forced to become one by surrounding social circumstances and by playing at being an English professor for so long that it finally has come to seem like what I really am, at my heart's core. This is a depressing theory because it assumes I am not innately anything. It is an exhilarating theory because, apparently, it blows the gaff on the familial, social, ideological, and political forces that have made me what I now think I am by forcing me to enact repetitive performances of that role. Once I understand that, the way is open to change society so I can be different or even, so it appears, however difficult that might be to do, to take my identity into my own hands and "perform" myself into becom-ing some other person, some other gender, or some mixture of genders, or one person or gender today and another person or gender tomorrow.

I find this genealogy of performativity theory fascinating. The wide influence of "performativity" shows the performative force of a theoretical formulation whose time has come. Of course, Butlerian performativity, as understood by her readers, has drifted pretty far away from what either Austin or Derrida meant by a performative utterance. That in itself, one might argue, is no great matter. We can make words mean whatever we like. "The question is . . . , which is to be master—that's all," as Humpty Dumpty said.[10] Intellectual life moves forward widdershins, through creative misinterpretation or exappropriation. It does matter somewhat, however, if performativity theory, the theory that we are nothing, initially, but potentiality and are forced to perform ourselves, under external discipline, into what we become, is identified too closely, and, I believe, illicitly, with Austin's or Derrida's theories of performative utterances. It *is* important not to confuse kinds. It is important not to be misled by the multiple incompatible uses of the same word, its heterogeneity or plurisignificance, into seeing identities where there are essential differences. We must disambiguate. Austin, Derrida, and Butler have radically different concepts of "performativity," though one can see how the first, Austin's, evolved into the other two along somewhat different paths.

Just what are those differences?

Austin's *How to Do Things with Words* is one of the most important philosophical works of the Anglo-American analytical or "ordinary language" school. It is a wonderfully witty, intelligent, and disarmingly complex book. Its essential claim, however, seems simple enough. Certain intelligible sentences, Austin claims, are not constative statements that can be proved to be either true or false but what Austin calls, in a made-up word, "performatives." He considered at first calling them "performatories," or "operatives," or "contractuals," or "declaratories" but decided, in a performative decision of naming, to call them "performatives." A performative is an utterance "in which to *say* something is to *do* something; or in which *by* saying something we are doing something."[11] A performative speech act is a sentence in "the first person singular present indicative active form" (150) that, uttered by the right person in the right circumstances, brings about what it says. Examples would be: "I pronounce you man and wife"; "I promise to finish this chapter in less than fifty manuscript pages" (a promise I have failed to keep); "I bequeath my watch to my brother"; "I christen thee the Queen Mary"; "I bet you sixpence it will rain tomorrow"; or "we may christen those infelicities where the act *is* achieved ABUSES" (16). Such sentences do not make statements of fact that can be proved true or false. They bring something about, for example, that the couple is married, that the ship is now named the Queen Mary, or that a certain kind of speech act is to be called an "abuse."

All this seems simple and straightforward enough, though it was a revolutionary idea in philosophical thinking. The Austinian performative has, so far as I can see, almost nothing to do with the idea that I am disciplined into becoming such and such a person or gender by performing that role repeatedly. Austin's theory, as critics of it have noted, presupposes a preexisting, stable, and perdurable selfhood as a condition of what he calls a "felicitous performative." That enduring selfhood allows me to say "I," as in "I promise," and to be held responsible for fulfilling that promise tomorrow or whenever, without any possibility of saying, "Well, that was yesterday. I am now a different person. You can't be so naïve as to hold me to a promise I made when I was a different 'I'?"

Austin, moreover, far from thinking that "performance," in the sense of a performance of Hamlet in *Hamlet* or a performance of the prima ballerina's role in *Swan Lake*, can be an efficacious performative, has an ingrained distaste for playacting or for pretending of any kind. *How to Do Things with Words* repeatedly stresses this distaste. "I must not be joking, for example, nor writing a poem," avers Austin (9), linking the hollowness of joking with a similar triviality and lack of seriousness in poetry. A "performative utterance," he roundly asserts,

> will, for example, be *in a peculiar way* hollow or void if said by an actor on the stage, or if introduced in a poem, or spoken in soliloquy. This applies in a similar manner to any and every utterance—a sea-change in special circumstances. Language in such circumstances is in special ways—intelligibly—used not seriously, but in ways *parasitic* upon its normal use—ways which fall under the doctrine of the *etiolations* of language. (22)

"Etiolation" means whitening, enfeebling, as in etiolated asparagus, which is bred in straw away from sunlight and so remains white, tender, and never turns green. It is, in a manner of speaking, ghostly asparagus. So much for the idea that "performativity theory" in "performance studies" or in Butler's theory of gender has any consonance with, any resonance or *Stimmung* with, Austin's theory of performative speech acts! One might even claim that Butlerian performativity theory, as understood by *Wikipedia*, is the opposite of the Austinian theory of performatives.

Matters are not by any means so simple with Austin, however, though a full explanation of that complexity would take me many more pages. The essential complications can, however, be stated succinctly. Austin himself describes the series of lectures that makes up *How to Do Things with Words* as a process whereby he "bog[s], by logical stages, down" (13). This bogging down happens by way of the investigation of examples. These show the idea that we sometimes do something by saying something getting ever more complex and even contradictory. The bogging down also happens through a proliferation of terms. Constative versus performative becomes the tripartite distinction among locutionary, illocutionary, and perlocutionary utterances, and those three further divide into five names for classes of speech acts: verdictives, exercitives, commissives, behabitives, expositives. The mind boggles or bogs down! Moreover, the apparently firm and clear "dichotomy" between constative and performative utterances breaks down almost completely. It "has to be abandoned in favor of more general *families* of related and overlapping speech-acts" (150). All constatives, Austin is forced to recognize, by examination of examples from ordinary language, are a little bit performative, and all performatives are a little bit constative.

This bogging down is an extraordinary example of a great philosopher forced by his own thinking to qualify radically what he thought he was going to demonstrate. Moreover, in spite of Austin's stern, even Puritanical assertion that we must not be joking or writing a poem, *How to Do Things with Words* is full of jokes and of that form of poetry we call narration or storytelling. All of his examples, when you come to think of it, reveal themselves to be miniature stories or synecdoches for implicit stories, for example, "I give and bequeath my watch to my brother" (5). Many memorable Austinian examples are more extended stories, often ironic or joking stories, such as the example of the way you can accuse a woman of adultery "by asking her whether it was not her handkerchief which was in X's bedroom, or by stating that it was hers" (111). This is an allusion to *Othello*, by the way. *How to Do Things with Words* is full of allusions, many of them Shakespearean, as in "sea-change," quoted above, an allusion to *The Tempest*. Another story is an example of an infelicitous performative: when someone without authority and in the wrong circumstances breaks a bottle over a great new British warship and says, "I name this ship the *Mr. Stalin*" (23). Austin disproves the necessity of a first person singular pronoun with a present active indicative verb for a felicitous performative by way of another story. If you want to warn someone a ferocious bull is in the field and about to charge, you do not say, "I warn you that a ferocious bull is in the field about to charge." You just say, "Bull!" (59).

Austin cannot proceed with his argument without using, over and over, in a serious way, the mode of language he calls etiolated, nonserious, parasitical on normal uses. No doubt he would say he is just mentioning these examples, not using them, but, as anyone knows who has thought a bit about this distinction, it no more holds up than the constative/performative distinction. You cannot mention a performative utterance without to some degree using it.

I draw two conclusions from this spectacular bogging down.

1. Austin's philosophical argumentation is not systematic and consistent but heterogeneous, just as is Butler's supposed performativity doctrine, which is simultaneously distressing ("I am not innately anybody or anything"), and liberating ("I can therefore, perhaps, become anything or anyone I like").

2. It follows that Austin is, perhaps unwillingly and unwittingly, granting some performative felicity to performances, such as the performance of a wedding on the stage and in a play. After all, a "real" wedding is the repetition of a script that has been performed countless times before. This iteration does not disqualify a wedding, in Austin's eyes, from being felicitous, from being a happy way to do things with words. Far from it, since its iterability (to use Derrida's term) is what makes a wedding ceremony "a conventional procedure having a certain conventional effect" (14). Butler's exappropriation (to borrow another word Derrida uses) of Austinian speech act theory in her performativity theory is, I conclude, after all not entirely unfaithful to its progenitor. This is so even though, so far as I remember, Austin never uses, nor would have been likely to use, the word "performativity."

What then about Derrida, whom *Wikipedia* sees, correctly, I believe, as the intermediary between Austin and Butler? Derrida is an essential stage in the progress toward present-day performativity theory. His concept of performatives is, however, fundamentally different not only from Austin's but also from Butler's. The bare facts of Derrida's own exappropriation of Austin are easy enough to specify. Derrida published in 1972 a strong critique of Austin's speech act theory entitled "Signature Event Context." A hapless American philosopher named John Searle then published an incautious attack on Derrida's essay entitled "Reiterating the Differences: A Reply to Derrida." I say "hapless" and "incautious" because Searle's essay called forth a long, often funny, and certainly violently polemical response from Derrida entitled "Limited Inc a b c . . ." All these (except Searle's essay, which he, for some unstated reason, but one can guess why, refused to have included) were collected, in English translation, with a new "Afterword: Toward an Ethic of Discussion" by Derrida, in *Limited Inc.*

The gravamen of Derrida's accusation of Austin is the following, delivered with Derridean panache but not without respect for Austin, though hardly for Searle: any form of words used in a performative utterance (e.g.,

"I pronounce you man and wife") can be used in more than one, indeed in innumerable different situations and contexts. Therefore, what Derrida calls "iterability" is a fundamental feature of performatives. This iterability has more than one consequence. I shall name the three most important.

For one thing, iterability means that, as Derrida puts it, the context of a performative can never be "saturated," that is, exhaustively identified, whereas it is a feature of felicitous performatives, in Austin's theory, that they must occur in the correct "circumstances," so those circumstances must, in a given case, be capable of exhaustive inventory. That, says Derrida, is impossible. Therefore the distinction between felicitous and infelicitous performatives, so important for Austin, breaks down.

Second, iterability means that the parasitical or etiolated performatives—writing a poem, acting on the stage, uttering a soliloquy, or making a joke, and so on—that Austin wants to "exclude," in a resolute anathema, cannot be excluded. No such thing as a fully "serious" performative utterance exists as a unique, one-time-only event in the present. The possibility of the abnormal is an intrinsic part of the normal.

Iterability, finally, disqualifies the requirement that a felicitous performative must depend on the self-consciousness of the ego and its "intentions," the "I" who says "I promise" and means to keep that promise. Here are Derrida's own words, in "Signature Event Context":

> For, ultimately, isn't it true that what Austin excludes as anomaly, exception, "non-serious," *citation* (on stage, in a poem, or a soliloquy) is the determined modification of a general citationality—or rather, a general iterability—without which there would not even be a "successful" performative? So that—a paradoxical but unavoidable conclusion—a successful performative is necessarily an "impure" performative, to adopt the word advanced later on by Austin when he acknowledges that there is no "pure" performative.
>
> . . . given that structure of iteration, the intention animating the utterance will never be through and through present to itself and to its content. The iteration structuring it a priori introduces into it a dehiscence [this word names the bursting open of a seed-pod] and a cleft [*brisure*] which are essential. The "non-serious," the *oratio obliqua* will no longer be able to be excluded, as Austin wished, from, "ordinary" language. . . . Above all, this essential absence of intending in the actuality of utterance, this structural unconsciousness, if you like, prohibits any saturation of the context. In order for a context to be exhaustively determinable, in the sense required by Austin, conscious intention would at the very least have to be totally present and immediately transparent to itself and to others, since it is a

determining center [*foyer*] of context. The concept of—or the search for—the context thus seems to suffer at this point from the same theoretical and "interested" uncertainty as the concept of the "ordinary," from the same metaphysical origins: the ethical and teleological discourse of consciousness. (LIe, 17–18; LIf, 44, 46)

This seems a clear enough and more or less complete dismantling of the theoretical scaffolding that Austin so elaborately constructs (only to dismantle it himself) in *How to Do Things with Words*. Why, then, does Derrida go on using, in the long years after publishing "Signature Event Context" and "Limited Inc a b c . . . ," the notion of performatives as an essential feature of his own philosophical argumentation? The idea of the performative speech act appears in many, perhaps most, of Derrida's many essays, seminars, and interviews after 1977. The performative is an essential aspect of Derrida's ideas about the secret, literature, friendship, hospitality, perjury, decision, sovereignty, politics, responsibility, justice, death, temporality, religion, and so on. Performativity sub one permeates every corner of Derrida's late work. Why? The answer lies in the quite special and even scandalous concept of the performative that Derrida developed in his late work by exappropriation, that is, through a taking over by way of creative distortion, of Austin's ideas. "Exappropriation" names the heterogeneity of Derrida's relation to speech act theory. On the one hand, he ferociously ridicules it, "deconstructs" it. On the other hand, his own later work would be impossible without it.

In all the regions of Derrida's thought I have named, a more or less similar and quite un-Austinian paradigm of the performative utterance is an essential ingredient. The performative is seen as a response to a demand made on me by "the wholly other" (*le tout autre*), a response that, far from depending on preexisting rules or laws, on a preexisting ego, I, or self, or on preexisting circumstances or "context," creates the self, the context, and new rules or laws in the act of its enunciation. This happens in a way that is anticipated by Austin's extraordinary statement: "As official acts, a judge's ruling makes law; a jury's finding makes a convicted felon" (154). Judith Butler's recent *Giving an Account of Oneself* presents a different account of my response to the other, a more coercive one. What she says might usefully be set against Derrida's paradigm.[12]

Derridean performatives are essentially linked to his special concept of time as "out of joint," as *différance*. A Derridean performative creates an absolute rupture between the present and the past. It inaugurates a future that Derrida calls a future anterior, or an unpredictable *à-venir*, as in Derrida's iterated phrase in his late work *la démocratie à venir*, "the democracy to come." My response to the call made on me is essentially a reciprocal performative. I must say "yes" to a performative demand issued initially by the wholly other. My "yes" is a countersigning or the co-performative validating of a performative command that comes from outside me. One model would be Derrida's analysis, in "Ulysses Gramophone: Hear Say Yes in Joyce" ("Ulysse gramophone: Ouï-dire de Joyce") of Molly Bloom's "yes I said yes I will Yes." Another would be Derrida's extraordinary two-hour, as yet unpublished, seminar on the French locution *je t'aime* ("I love you"; the "you" is second person singular in the French). To say *je t'aime*, said Derrida, is not a constative statement of fact. It is a performative that creates my condition of being in love. This makes me into a new person, the one who is in love with someone. That other person, in turn, has no access to my interiority and therefore no way of knowing whether I am lying or telling the truth. My performative utterance, *je t'aime*, must be endorsed by your return performative, though you have no certain evidence that I mean what I say. You must say, in effect, "I swear that I believe that you love me. I love you in return." Another example of this saying yes, analyzed at length by Derrida in *The Gift of Death*, is Abraham's response to Jehovah's demand that he sacrifice Isaac. Jehovah says, "Abraham," and Abraham answers, "Behold, here I am" (Genesis 22:1).

The admirably eloquent final pages of "Psyche: Invention of the Other" express succinctly Derrida's anti-Austinian concept of performative speech acts:

> The very movement of this fabulous repetition can, through a crossing of chance and necessity, produce the new of an event. Not only with the singular invention of a performative, since every performative presupposes conventions and institutional rules—but by bending these rules with respect for the rules themselves in order to allow the other to come [*laisser l'autre venir*] or to announce its coming in the opening of this dehiscence. That is perhaps what is called deconstruction. (Pe, 44; Pf, 58–59)

This passage offers an opportunity to distinguish further Derrida's thought from that of Levinas. This distinction was a topic in the previous chapter. The "other" is equally importunate for Derrida and for Levinas, and equally dissymmetrical to the I, but that other is more explicitly personified in Levinas, more a matter of my face to face encounter with my neighbor. The dissymmetry for Derrida, furthermore, is primarily a result of the complete otherness of the other, whereas it is for Levinas a matter of the disjunction between the infinite demands each neighbor or *autrui* makes on me and my own finitude as a respondent. Moreover, my response, for Levinas, is more programmed by the other in the form of any "neighbor" and by traditional religious and ethical formulations of my responsibilities toward my neighbor. For Derrida, the other is "wholly other," and not much more than that can be said about that other. In addition, my response to the demand made on me by the wholly other is seen as radically innovative. It is seen as a performative instituting the *à-venir* in an event that allows the other to come, all right, but that takes off from coming in a way that installs, in a "rupture," something altogether new, something gesturing toward the future, the *avenir*. For that novelty and that rupture I must take full responsibility. In a passage in "Force of Law," Derrida specifies this difference from Levinas, at least in part, while saying that there would be much more to say about his differences from Levinas:

> Levinas speaks of an infinite right: in what he calls "Jewish humanism," whose basis is not "the concept of man," but rather the other; "the extent of the right of the other" is that of "a practically infinite right" ["*l'étendue du droit d'autrui [est] un droit pratiquement infini*"] ("Un droit infini," in *Du Sacré au Saint, Cinq Nouvelles Lectures Talmudiques*, pp. 17–18). (FLe, 22; FLf, 49)

This passage challenges Levinas's use of the word *droit* by developing a characteristically Derridean discussion of the three "aporias," as he puts it, of the relation between law and justice, *droit* and justice. These are discussed in Chapter 2 of this book.

I conclude this discussion of performativity in Derrida with a passage from *Specters of Marx* in which the word *performativity* actually appears, the only time I have noticed it used by Derrida. The passage admirably encapsulates the Derridean paradigm I have been identifying:

> it is a matter there [in our relation to Marx's works and for Marx himself in relation to what enjoined him to write] of an ethical and political impera-tive, an appeal as unconditional as the appeal of thinking from which it is not separated. It is a matter of the injunction itself [*l'injonction même*]—if there is one.
>
> What also resonates in "Marx's Three Voices" [the Blanchot essay Der-rida is discussing] is the *appeal* [l'appel] or the political injunction, the pledge or the promise (the oath, if one prefers: "swear!" [a reference to the ghost scene at the beginning of *Hamlet*, a constant presence in *Specters of Marx*]), the originary performativity [*cette performativité originaire*] that does not conform to preexisting conventions, unlike all the performatives ana-lyzed by the theoreticians of *speech acts* [in English in the original], but whose force of *rupture* produces the institution or the constitution, the law

itself [*la loi même*], which is to say also the meaning that appears to, that ought to, or that appears to have to guarantee it in return. *Violence* of the law before the law and before meaning, violence that interrupts time, disarticulates it, dislodges it, displaces it out of its natural lodging: "out of joint" [in English in the original; another citation from *Hamlet*]. It is there that différ*a*nce, if it remains irreducible, irreducibly required by the spacing of any promise and by the future-to-come that comes to open it [*l'à-venir qui vient à l'ouvrir*], does not mean only (as some people have too often believed and so naively) deferral, lateness, delay, postponement. . . . The pledge [*Le gage*] is given here and now, even before, perhaps, a decision confirms it. It thus responds without delay to the demand of justice. The latter by definition is impatient, uncompromising, and unconditional. (SMe, 30–31; SMf, 59–60)

The reader will see how far both from Austin's performative and from Butler's performativity, as understood by *Wikipedia*, is this concept of the political performative as a response to an injunction that comes from the other, as the ghost's injunction to Hamlet does in Shakespeare's play. What is a bad thing for Butler, at least as presented by *Wikipedia*, being solicited and coerced by society to perform a certain gender role, is a good thing for Derrida when it takes the form of an injunction that comes from the wholly other. I conclude that one must discriminate quite sharply among different notions of performativity. We must disambiguate them in order to avoid confusion of thought. We must resist thinking that gender socially constructed by performativity is like an Austinian promise, that either is like a Derridean performative response, a saying yes to the wholly other, or that the performance of a Mozart piano sonata is like any of these.

And yet . . . And yet . . . And yet—after all my efforts of disambiguation, I must nevertheless assert that these various forms of performativity, different as they are from one another, have a family resemblance, in the Wittgensteinian sense of that phrase. The social construction of gender is somehow a little bit like my first falling in love by saying "I love you." Both of these are a little bit like the way I am changed by playing Mozart and change Mozart's music too in the same performance of performativity. All of these examples show the power of words or other signs to do something, to act.

I now turn to two moments in George Eliot's *Daniel Deronda* that demonstrate the fundamental usefulness of performativity theory both for understanding what happens in literary works and for seeing the essential function of literary study as a way of understanding what is at stake in performativity studies.[13]

In one of those passages the heroine, Gwendolen Harleth, betrays the shallowness and inauthenticity of her selfhood, the person her society has coached her into becoming, by the way she sings an aria by Bellini. Both her performance and the aria itself are sharply criticized by the true musician in the novel, Klesmer, modeled on Franz Liszt:

> Yes, it is true; you have not been well taught. . . . Still, you are not quite without gifts. You sing in tune, and you have a pretty fair organ. But you produce your notes badly; and that music which you sing is beneath you. It is a form of melody which expresses a puerile state of culture—a dangling, canting, see-saw kind of stuff—the passion and thought of people without any breadth of horizon.[14]

In the other passage, which comes much later in the novel, Daniel Deronda, the hero in this double-plotted novel, utters a solemn promise to the dying Jewish scholar Mordecai. Daniel promises to carry on Mordecai's work after the latter's death: "Everything I can in conscience do to make your life effective I will do" (600). This echoes Deronda's earlier promise to Mordecai: "I will be faithful" (564). Both these statements are, in all strictness, forms of the speech act Austin calls a "performative." They are examples of how to do things with words. What do they do? They put Daniel in a new position, the position of someone who in the future will either keep his promise or fail to keep it. All promises do that. Promises are paradigmatic examples of performatives in *How to Do Things with Words*. Daniel, it happens, keeps his promises.

Deronda's promises look at first like Austinian performatives. A case can be made, however, that they fit better the Derridean paradigm of political, ethical, and religious commitment. Deronda's promise is a response made to a demand made indirectly on him by the "wholly other," by the Judaic Jehovah, operating by way of Mordecai as intermediary or medium. Daniel at this point has no knowledge that he is actually a Jew, so the promise is made without the context such certainty would provide. It is a Derridean leap in the dark, a fortuitous commitment. It is a proof that, as Kierkegaard said, in a passage Derrida more than once cited, "The instant of decision is a madness" (FLe, 26; FLf, 58). Deronda's promise makes a sharp rupture or break in his life. It makes him henceforth, in a sense, a different person, a proto-Jew. Daniel's promise is proleptic of his eventual retrospective discovery that he *is* a Jew and of his commitment to the cause of Zionism, as well as of his marriage to the Jewess Mirah. These events form the dénouement of the novel. What grounds and justifies his decision comes after the decision, not before. The decision works metaleptically, the cart before the horse. Alternatively, one might say that the decision seems magically to produce its own ground and justification.

I am not sure this tempting reading is right. One must "disambiguate." Looked at a bit more closely, Deronda's two promises to Mordecai reveal themselves to be perhaps something sui generis, neither quite Austinian nor quite Derridean. They fit Austin's description of a felicitous performative, all right, in that both take the form of a first person pronoun plus a present tense active verb, or at least an implicit one: "[I promise] I will be faithful" and "[I promise] that everything I can in conscience do to make your life effective I will do." Daniel's promises, moreover, are based on a preexisting "I" or "ego." He is presented throughout the novel as an earnest, self-conscious man of thoughtful rectitude. He is determined to do his duty when he can see it clearly. The whole fabric of English morality is firmly in place as a context for his promise making. He is free to commit himself to a vocation. His problem is that no overwhelming, life-determining duty has as yet presented itself nor does he yet know just who he is. He is, in the whole early part of the novel, without a vocation and without knowledge of his selfhood. Now an irresistible duty does present itself.

Mordecai's appeal to Deronda is based on a notion, borrowed from the Kabbalah, of metempsychosis. They are one soul in two persons. After Mordecai's death, Mordecai believes, his soul will pass into Daniel, and Daniel will continue his work of furthering the Jewish cause. He will work toward the establishment of a new Jewish nation. Mordecai is convinced, correctly as it turns out, that Daniel must really be Jewish. Daniel's promises are made, though he does not yet know it, on the solid basis of his actual Jewish identity. It is not the case, as with Derridean performatives, that he becomes a new self when he utters a performative speech act in response to an appeal made to him by someone or something "wholly other" or that he is a blank slate that becomes a social self through the enforced, repressive, iteration of some form of role playing.

Both Derrida's performativity theory and the one ascribed to Butler would have seemed appalling to George Eliot. She believed, with some nuances in that belief, in fixed, innate selfhood, or she saw those who lacked such a thing as in a parlous state. The drama of the Daniel Deronda part of the novel is that Daniel discovers who he already is, that is, that he is a Jew. Once he discovers that, he has no choice but to be faithful to his discovery. He joyfully does that. He keeps his promises to Mordecai.

To many modern readers, me included, this seems almost too easy. It is a strange wish-fulfillment version of the Freudian "family romance." The child's fantasies that his parents are not really his parents, that he is a prince in disguise, do actually come true. How nice it would be, a modern reader thinks (that is, someone who feels himself or herself, in Montaigne's phrase, as "wavering and diverse [*ondoyant et divers*]"), if some unquestionable power would tell me who I already inalterably am. In George Eliot's defense, it must be said that the somewhat absurd fable of the Daniel Deronda part of *Daniel Deronda* was a response to a full sense of what might be so disastrous, from one angle of her double perspective, about the alternative Derridean or social constructionist theories of the self. These possibilities, it can be argued, she foresaw. Eliot's novels were written at the historical transition point between the sense that the self is innate, inalterably fixed, and the more modern idea that the self is alterable, possibly a matter of free choice or of shaping by experience. The latter notion, however, has historical antecedents, not only in Montaigne but also, for example, in eighteenth-century French fiction.

The aporia between reading Deronda's vocation in his promise to Mordecai as a Derridean performative and reading it as an Austinian one is inscribed in the novel itself. Cynthia Chase, long ago, in a brilliant and still decisive essay,[15] put this aporia under the aegis of a contradiction between the metalepsis that makes Deronda's promise to Mordecai the cause of its cause and the more traditional narrative logic that marches toward the inevitable and even, after a certain point, predictable discovery that Deronda has always been a Jew. Being a Jew is what he "really is." Basing her reading on a phrase in a letter to Deronda from Hans Meyrick, a minor character in the novel: "the present causes of past effects" (704), Chase identifies the narrative structure of *Daniel Deronda* as "a chiasmus or a metalepsis, a reversal of the temporal status of effect and cause: cause is relocated in the present and effect in the past" (162–63). "It is not the event of Deronda's birth as a Jew that is decisive for his story," Chase says, "but the knowledge or affirmation of it" (162). In "naming the cause as an effect of its effects, and the effects as the cause of their cause," Eliot is, Chase says, "identifying the contradictory relationship between the claims of realistic fiction and the narrative strategy actually employed" (163). Chase identifies the latter as like "the kind of magical metamorphosis found in fairy tales" (168). The frog turns into a prince; Deronda turns into a Jew. As Chase recognizes, the result is that the novel expresses two different notions of identity. In the more traditional one, identity is inalterably determined by origin, and Deronda has only to say "yes" to his discovery of his Jewish birth. He really is a Jew. In the other notion of identity, Deronda's promise to Mordecai "presents character and attributes as preceding and causing the inference of origin" (163). Because Deronda makes his promise to Mordecai, he finds out that he is a Jew. Though Chase makes astute reference to speech act theory later in her essay, she does not explicitly observe that one of her own phrases suggests a problematic conflation between constative and performative utterances. She says Deronda's "knowledge or affirmation" of his Jewish identity, not "the event of his birth as Jew," is decisive for his story. This makes it sound as though knowledge and affirmation are perhaps equivalents. The metaleptic aporia she identifies, however, is expressed in that juxtaposition. Deronda "affirms" his Jewishness before he has "knowledge" of it. This is both like and unlike a Derridean performative assertion of a vocation, since, for Derrida, you can never know for certain that the call you think you have heard from the "wholly other" within yourself is a genuine command or that it is intended for you. I shall discuss Derrida's quite un-Derondalike relation to his own Jewish descent, as expressed in "Abraham, the Other," later in this chapter.

Chase also mentions a faintly amusing or embarrassing feature of *Daniel Deronda*. This feature is the visible scar of its aporia. That aporia can be defined as Eliot's desire to have it, impossibly, both ways with the question of identity as it is related to performative affirmations. The novel depends on Deronda's ignorance of his Jewish birth up until the moment, late in the novel, when his mother reveals to him the truth. In those days, however, only male Jews were circumcised, not Gentiles. How could Deronda not have known he was a Jew? Steven Marcus recognizes this problem in an essay of 1976 that Chase cites in a footnote. He writes:

> It is only when he is a grown man having been to Eton and Cambridge, that he discovers that he is a Jew. What this has to mean—given the conventions of medical practice at the time [that Gentiles were not circumcised]—is that he never looked down. In order for the plot of *Daniel Deronda* to work, Deronda's circumcised penis must be invisible, or nonexistent—which is one more demonstration in detail of why the plot does not in fact work.[16]

"Does not in fact work" is Marcus's epithet for the aporia Chase, and I following her, have identified.

The context in the present book for the lapse on Eliot's part is all the elaborate attention Derrida pays, in many texts, to his own circumcision, to Freud's, to Celan's, and to that of Jews in general, as the mark or scar of their election. Circumcision is an essential motif in *Glas*, in "Circumfession," in *The Post Card*, in *Schibboleth*, in *Archive Fever*, and in "Abraham, the Other." What Eliot forgot, Derrida obsessively remembered. That might serve as an allegorical sign of the differences between them on the issue of performative promises. What does it mean to be faithful to the covenant that circumcision seals? Does circumcision bind you to that covenant? Derrida was not so sure about that.

The other half of *Daniel Deronda*, the catastrophic story of Gwendolen Harleth, can be read as a proleptic presentation and critique of the theory of performativity ascribed to Butler. The portrait of Gwendolen is one of the greatest and most complex character representations in Victorian fiction. It is comparable to Tolstoy's representation of Anna Karenina in subtlety. It is not easy to say something worthy of Gwendolen's complexity in a few paragraphs. A shorthand approach can be made by way of saying that she is only one of many characters in *Daniel Deronda* who are presented by way of their performances. An essential theme of *Daniel Deronda* is singing and acting in public, literal performance, and what doing that means for selfhood.

The novel offers itself to modern-day performance studies as a wonderful reservoir of Victorian theories of performativity sub two. Klesmer, modeled, as I have said, on Franz Liszt, whose work George Eliot much admired, is a great composer and pianist. Deronda's Jewish mother, he finally discovers, was a famous singer and actress, whose stage name was "Alcharisi." Mirah, foil to Gwendolen, is a good Jewish girl whom Deronda saves from drowning herself in despair and ultimately marries, in anticipation of his ultimate role as a rescuer of the Jewish people. Mirah has been forced by her father to become a singer and actress, though she continues to resist these artificialities as alienations of her true self. This alienation drives her to suicidal despair. Gwendolen, on the contrary, is always deliberately playing a role. She is repeatedly measured by her futile attempts to become a distinguished singer and actress.

Eliot's theory of performativity sub two is complex and perhaps even contradictory. On the one hand, Klesmer's compositions and performances are praised because they come directly from his powerful and commanding personality. In his performativity he expresses a preexisting self:

> Herr Klesmer played a composition of his own, a fantasia called *Freudvoll, Leidvoll, Gedankenvoll* ["Joyful, Sorrowful, Thankful"]—an extensive commentary on some melodic ideas not too grossly evident; and he certainly fetched as much variety and depth of passion out of the piano as that moderately responsive instrument lends itself to, having an imperious magic in

his fingers that seemed to send a nerve-thrill through ivory key and wooden hammer, and compel the strings to make a quivering lingering speech for him. (79–80)

On the other hand, Klesmer's performances are the result of the long and arduous acquisition of a skill that is like a craft. That craft you must study and be taught by masters, as a patient apprentice. You do not just sit down at the piano and express yourself. You must also submit yourself to the limitations of your instrument, in this case the "moderately responsive" piano. Nevertheless, Klesmer can compel the strings to make a quivering, lingering speech for him, as though he himself were speaking through the sounds he makes. Gwendolen's singing, unlike Klesmer's playing, is self-conscious and artificial, whereas Mirah sings from the heart. Moreover, Mirah has been well trained. Klesmer praises Mirah's singing and severely criticizes Gwendolen's singing, in the passage cited in part above, to the latter's dismay, since she thinks she can rise in the world through her singing and acting. She has no idea how much work that will be or how uncertain success will be. Klesmer disillusions her.

Mirah is another cup of tea. Her bad father has forcibly separated her from her mother and from her mother's Jewish piety. He has compelled her to become an actor and singer. She tells the assembled Meyrick family, which has given her sanctuary, that she has always hated acting. Her father's mistress and her teacher, "an Italian lady, a singer" (252), predicts her failure: "She will never be an artist; she has no notion of being anybody but herself" (253). This conforms to the antitheatrical tradition that says being a good actor or actress is a priori incompatible with the integrity of a fixed selfhood that can commit itself in loving attachment to another person. Henry James's *The Tragic Muse* is an admirably subtle exploration of this theme. Mirah confirms her happy limitation (from George Eliot's perspective) when she says, "I knew that my acting was not good except when it was not really acting, but the part was one that I could be myself in, and some feeling within me carried me along" (258). This propensity, somewhat paradoxically, makes her a gifted singer of songs that she can use as a means of self-expression. When she sings for Herr Klesmer, to get his judgment on her chances of making a living in London as a singer, he shakes her hand afterward and says, "You are a musician" (541), though he says she should perform only in private drawing rooms, since her voice is not strong enough for the concert stage. Singing, for Eliot, seems to differ from acting in that good singing is not incompatible with having a solid, fixed self.

That leaves Gwendolen, the most complex case in the novel of the relation between performativity and selfhood. Her performances should be judged in the context of the presentations of Klesmer, Alcharisi, and Mirah. Gwendolen is a good demonstration of Butler's claim that society coerces people, particularly women, to be something artificial and limited. Society imposes on women the ideological presuppositions of gender difference, as if they were natural and innate. Gwendolen has been coerced to be what she is, interpellated. Her ideas and her feeble ability to play and sing are those of the ordinary genteel, middle-class, marriageable young woman of the Victorian period. She thinks she is a gifted singer, but Klesmer passes remorseless judgment. She has a "pretty fair organ," as he tells her, but she has "not been well taught," and her choice of Bellini is a disaster, since his music "expresses a puerile state of culture," "no cries of deep, mysterious passion—no conflict—no sense of the universal" (79), such as Mirah's singing exemplifies.

Gwendolen's singing, as opposed to Mirah's, expresses her lack of authentic selfhood rather than her possession of it. When faced with the horrible, to her, prospect of becoming a governess, she arranges an interview with Klesmer to get him to assure her that she can have a great career as an actress-singer. She says to him, "I know that my method of singing is very defective; but I have been ill taught. I could be better taught; I could study. And you will understand my wish;—to sing and act too, like Grisi, is a much higher position. Naturally, I should wish to take as high a rank as I can" (296). Klesmer tells her, as gently but as firmly as he can, and at length, that she has no hope of becoming a second Grisi. She is starting far too late, and even with years of arduous training she "will hardly achieve more than mediocrity" (303).

Does this mean that Gwendolen has no fixed self? Not quite. Her presentation is a wonderfully perceptive portrait of what Freud was to call a hysteric, though without Freud's etiology of hysterical symptoms. She is subject to what today we would call "panic attacks." Gwendolen's self is a strange combination of "an inborn energy of egoistic desire" (71), a foolish desire for mastery over others, such as she quite mistakenly thinks she will exercise over her cruel husband Grandcourt, and a deep underlying hysterical fear of open spaces, of reality, and of death. After the panic attack I describe below, Eliot comments that "She was ashamed and frightened, as at what might happen again, in remembering her tremor on suddenly feeling herself alone, when, for example, she was walking without companionship and there came some rapid change in the light. Solitude in any wide scene impressed her with an undefined feeling of immeasurable existence aloof from her, in the midst of which she was helplessly incapable of asserting herself" (94–95).

In the remarkable event involving performativity sub two that Eliot is here commenting on, Gwendolen thinks to dazzle her family and the other guests at Offendene by performing the scene in Shakespeare's *The Winter's Tale* in which Hermione is wakened by music from her statuelike fixity: "Music, awake her, strike!" It is a fine irony that Shakespeare's scene ascribes to music the power to awake someone from a sleep that is like death, for example, the trancelike sleep of Gwendolen's everyday alienation from herself. It is a further irony that Klesmer should play the music that awakens this pseudo-Hermione. When Klesmer strikes a thunderous chord on the piano, a wall panel flies open and Gwendolen is faced with a hitherto hidden picture. The picture shows a dead face and a fleeing figure. Gwendolen's sudden sight of the dead face and the fleeing figure brings on a hysterical fit of extreme terror. She stops her lifelong playacting for a few instants, becoming for a few moments what she really is. She is a person dominated by a hidden fear, fear not of anything in particular but of life itself, of its open, ungovernable spaces, which are forever beyond her control. For a moment she is not performing at all: "Everyone was startled, but all eyes in the act of turning towards the opened panel were recalled by a piercing cry from Gwendolen, who stood without change of attitude, but with a change of expression that was terrifying in its terror. She looked like a statue in which a soul of Fear had entered: her pallid lips were parted; her eyes, usually narrowed under their long lashes, were dilated and fixed. . . . Gwendolen fell on her knees and put her hands before her face. She was still trembling, but mute" (91–92).

This powerful episode is proleptic of a scene much later in the novel dramatizing Gwendolen's guilty inability to help the drowning Grandcourt when he falls overboard from their yacht in the Mediterranean. "I saw my wish outside me," she tells Daniel when she confesses to him her complicity in Grandcourt's death (761). Gwendolen's confession to Daniel comes late in the novel. It involves two more somewhat anomalous speech acts, authentic cases of performativity sub one. A confession is a performative use of language in the sense that the one who confesses not only speaks the truth, constatively, but also does so in a way that may have consequences. A confession may be a way of doing something with words. It may, for example, bring about a trial and conviction if what is confessed is a criminal act. Since Daniel does not make Gwendolen's confession public, just as a priest keeps the secrets of the confessional, her confession leads only to Daniel's response. That response is an odd kind of promise,

quite unlike the ones Daniel makes to Mordecai. The scene of Gwendolen's confession is quite painful, even embarrassing, to read, not only because it marks the breakdown of Gwendolen's self-possession, but also
because it makes clear that Gwendolen sees in Daniel not only a moral
savior but also a possible husband. For the first time she is capable of a
genuine love for someone other than herself. Daniel's destiny, however, is
to marry Mirah, even though some readers may expect or hope that the
two halves of the novel will come together in a triumphant union of
Gwendolen and Daniel. Eliot raises that hope only to dash it in a way that
seems a somewhat cruel punishment of Gwendolen, however much she
may deserve it.

Daniel listens with immense sympathy and sorrow to Gwendolen's confession. He consoles her as best he can by saying that Grandcourt would
almost certainly have drowned even if she had made extravagant efforts to
save him. At one point Daniel's response to her detailed confession and
pitiable hope that he will not forsake her is just to hold her hand. This is
an unspoken promise that is defined, in a striking formulation, as like putting your name to a blank sheet of paper, signing a blank check, as we
might say today: "He took one of her hands and clasped it as if they were
going to walk together like two children: it was the only way in which he
could answer, 'I will not forsake you.' And all the while he felt as if he
were putting his name to a blank paper which might be filled up terribly"
(755). Here a gesture, the handholding, substitutes for a literal speech act,
in a way that Austin's theories allow. Daniel fears, however, that the blank
sheet of paper with his signature on it, another performative, will be filled
up by Gwendolen's expectation that he will marry her. Later in the scene,
after Gwendolen has described her "wickedness" in allowing Grandcourt
to drown, she beseeches him once more, "You will not forsake me?" and
he answers, "It could never be my impulse to forsake you," but "with the
painful consciousness that to her ear his words might carry a promise
which one day would seem unfulfilled: he was making an indefinite promise to an indefinite hope" (765).

Is this what Austin calls a "felicitous" promise or not? Yes and no. Daniel certainly means it when he says it will never be his impulse to forsake
Gwendolen, but she takes his words in a way different from his intention,
which is simply to be kind to Gwendolen in her extreme distress. Daniel
has a foreboding that he may be misunderstood. He has spoken his promise "with that voice which, like his eyes, had the unintentional effect of
making his ready sympathy seem more personal and special than it really
was. And in that moment he was not himself quite free from a foreboding

of some such self-committing effect" (765). Daniel has not meant to commit himself, but his words, his voice, and his eyes commit themselves for him. This is a splendid example of the way a speech act may have unintended consequences. It may make something happen all right. It may be a way of doing something with words. It may, however, act on its own to do something quite different from what the speaker means to do.

This doctrine of the unintended results of a speech act anticipates Paul de Man's notion of speech acts in "Promises (*Social Contract*)" in *Allegories of Reading*,[17] as well as elsewhere in his late work.[18] I remember hearing him encapsulate this in a seminar by saying, "You aim at a bear, and an innocent bird falls out of the sky." The words you utter enter the interpersonal, social, and political world, where they have the consequences they do when they are taken in a certain way. Sometimes your well-meant words may have violent or cruel effects, as when Daniel unintentionally misleads Gwendolen into thinking he might love her. His words operate on their own, independent of his intention or will, as he half suspects. Any performative I utter is like signing my name to a blank check or on a blank sheet of paper, leaving someone else to insert the amount I owe or the obligation I have incurred.

Can Daniel be held responsible for a breach of promise? That is a difficult question. He has, after all, uttered those words and must take responsibility for having uttered them. He has held Gwendolen's hand and promised never to forsake her. Dickens, in *Pickwick Papers*, dramatizes this question in a comic but nevertheless profound way. Pickwick's innocent note to his landlady, Mrs. Bardell, ordering supper, "Dear Mrs B.—Chops and tomata sauce. Yours, PICKWICK,"[19] seems to her and her lawyers, absurdly enough, a proposal of marriage. This leads to a suit for breach of promise, the trial of Bardell against Pickwick, which lands Pickwick in prison. Any form of words may have an unforeseen and unintended performative effect, such as getting you imprisoned. It might be better to keep silence.

Derrida's theory of performatives is even more radical and disturbing. He affirms that even silence does not protect you from radical breaches of promises you have never explicitly made. Derrida holds in *The Gift of Death*, as I shall show in detail in Chapter 9, that I have made an implicit promise to care for every person and animal in the world, every "other" whatsoever, even if I have never uttered a word that can be taken as an overt promise. That limitless obligation leads to the aporia of responsibility. I have no hope of fulfilling all my responsibilities to all those others, each and every one of them. I take care of my one cat, but I ought to be feeding and housing all the cats in the world, all those cats that are dying of starvation and exposure every day. A thoughtful reading of the episode of Gwendolen's confession in *Daniel Deronda* is a good example of the way literature is an exemplary place to investigate the complexities of performativity sub one in its difference from performativity sub two. All the other characters in the novel offer other examples, in a spectrum of possibilities.

Deronda's mother, "Alcharisi," is another case in point. She is no doubt modeled on such famous actresses or singers as the Jewess Rachel (mentioned in the novel) and the Italian Grisi (also mentioned). Alcharisi is "a born singer and actress" (696). This suggests that her talents are innate, part of her selfhood as a gifted person. She was, however, also arduously trained. She became a celebrated actress and singer until she began to lose her voice and sing out of tune. She then married a Russian nobleman and became the Princess Halm-Eberstein. Even that persona, however, is make-believe, pretense: "I made believe that I preferred being the wife of a Russian noble to being the greatest lyric actress of Europe; I made believe—I acted that part" (703).

The novel leaves no doubt about Alcharisi's great gifts and great success. These did not, however, make her a good or happy person. She deliberately betrayed her Jewish heritage and her father's piety to become a singer and actress. She gave her son, Daniel, away to be brought up as an Englishman by one of the many men who loved her, Sir Hugo Mallinger. She thereby has cruelly prevented Daniel for many years from learning that he is a Jew, that is, from learning who he really is. Eliot is discreet about whether Alcharisi became Sir Hugo's mistress or the mistress of any of her many other suitors. Perhaps yes; perhaps no.

Alcharisi's repudiation of her Jewish heritage can be read in a way ironically like *Wikipedia*'s version of Butler's early position, since Eliot disapproves of what Butler is said to enjoin. Moreover, in a further irony, Butler is in her current work embracing her own Jewish heritage, for example, by interpreting Levinas, in a way more like Daniel Deronda than like his mother. Alcharisi deliberately repudiates the self her father and her Jewish community wanted her to be, that is, a good, subordinate, obedient Jewish daughter and wife. She chooses, rather, the freedom of becoming a great singer and actress. Alcharisi embodies the possible disconnect between acting and singing, on the one hand, and personal integrity such as might lead one to make promises and keep them, on the other. Her marriage to Prince Halm-Eberstein was a piece of insubstantial playacting not based on a solid selfhood.

In a wonderful passage in the scene in which the Princess tells her son Daniel of his Jewish origins and the story of her life in an attempt to justify her abandonment of him to Sir Hugo, Eliot describes her highly theatrical performance before Daniel, a mixture of defiant self-defense and confession, by way of an oxymoron, "sincere acting":

> The varied transitions of tone with which this speech was delivered were as perfect as the most accomplished actress could have made them. The speech was in fact a piece of what may be called sincere acting: this woman's nature was one in which all feeling—and all the more when it was tragic as well as real—immediately became matter of conscious representation: experience immediately passed into drama, and she acted her own emotions. In a minor degree that is nothing uncommon, but in the Princess the acting had a rare perfection of physiognomy, voice, and gesture. It would not be true to say that she felt less because of this double consciousness: she felt—that is, her mind went through—all the more, but with a difference: each nucleus of pain or pleasure had a deep atmosphere of the excitement of spiritual intoxication which at once exalts and deadens. (691–92)

"Spiritual intoxication" names a spurious exaltation brought on by acting a part. It has no solid base in self. Alcharisi's performance for Daniel is presented as a battle between her real self and the false self she has trained herself to become. "It was as if," says Eliot, "her mind were breaking into several, one jarring the other into impulsive action" (700). She has decided to tell Daniel of his Jewishness in a victory of her real, Jewish self, what Eliot calls "the poor, solitary, forsaken remains of self, that can resist nothing" (699), and of her father's desires for her over her false, artificial, acting self. Eliot is here again faithful to her presupposition that each of us has an innate, ultimately inalienable self, whatever games the metaleptic structure of Daniel's story may play with that assumption.

It happens that we have in Derrida's "Abraham, the Other" a story parallel to Daniel Deronda's story as Eliot tells it. Derrida's relation to his own Jewishness, however, was quite different from the one George Eliot ascribes to Daniel Deronda. This supports my claim that Deronda's promises cannot be seen as straightforwardly Derridean performatives. Deronda enthusiastically accepts his Jewishness when he discovers it. He accepts it as what he really is, as a calling from Jehovah. He makes that preexisting selfhood the basis of family and political commitments: his marriage to Mirah and his work for the Zionist cause. Derrida, on the contrary, was reticent, intricately involuted, and even self-contradictory in his public statements about his relations to his Jewishness and to Judaism.

I discuss "Abraham, the Other" ("Abraham, l'autre") briefly again in Chapter 11 but need to identify here Derrida's essential hesitations, in contrast to Deronda's eager acceptance of his Jewish identity. This will help confirm my claim that Deronda's promises are only quasi-Derridean. Doing full justice to this complex topic in Derrida's work, following justly just this one thread in its intricate texture, would be a virtually interminable task. It would involve reading not only the essays and books, mentioned above, in which circumcision figures but also other essays, such as "How to Avoid Speaking: Denials," *Monolingualism of the Other*, or the essays by Derrida collected in *Acts of Religion*, plus all the important, though scarcely distinterested, "secondary" literature on Derrida's relation to his Jewish heritage, such as the other essays in *Judeities: Questions for Jacques Derrida*, the volume in which "Abraham, the Other," appears, Gil Anidjar's introduction to *Acts of Religion* (AR, 1–39), and, especially, Hélène Cixous's admirable *Portrait of Jacques Derrida as a Young Jewish Saint*.[20] Moreover, "Abraham, the Other," like many of Derrida's late essays, touches on most of the important topics in his work: responsibility, the gift, hospitality, forgiveness, sovereignty, testimony, the question of the third as witness, *khōra*, messianicity without messianism, the new International, the democracy to come, and so on, not to speak of his concept of speech acts. I limit myself here to a brief sketch, a hypotyposis, of what Derrida says in "Abraham, the Other," with a focus on what this essay has to say about Derrida's special theory of performativity. That is my topic, after all, in this chapter.

On the one hand, in "Abraham, the Other" Derrida wholeheartedly accepts his "jewish descent": "I have never, absolutely never [*au grand jamais*], hidden my jewish descent [*ma filiation juive*], and I have always been honored to claim it" (AO, 6; AA, 16). On the other hand, Derrida immediately goes on to explain why it is that he cannot just say, Derondalike, "I am a Jew. I pledge my allegiance to my Jewish identity. I promise that everything I can in conscience do to further the Jewish cause I will do." Matters, moreover, rapidly get intricately complicated, overdetermined, and even contradictory or, as Derrida says, "vertiginous" (AO, 28; AA, 36) when he begins giving the reasons why he cannot just say "Yes, I am a Jew" but must, rather, define it as "the question of my belonging without belonging to jewishness or to Judaism [*la question de mon appartenance sans appartenance à la judéité ou au judaïsme*]" (AO, 8; AA, 17). Derrida, you can see, poses another question, not an answer, to the questions posed to him at the conference Judéités: Questions pour Jacques Derrida.[21] Derrida's responding question, moreover, can only be posed in a Blanchotian self-contradictory formula: "belonging without belonging."

Derrida begins by saying he is subject to a strange injunction to keep silent on this topic, though of course he breaks that silence by talking at length in this lecture. Perhaps his talking is a way to "avoid speaking." He goes on to say he does not know what it means to say "I am a Jew" or "I am a jew," or how important the capitalization, or lack of it, is. Sometimes he capitalizes "Jew," sometimes not. He says he does not know just how these locutions differ from someone saying to him: "You are a Jew," "They say you are a Jew," or just "Dirty Jew! [*sale Juif!*]" (AO, 10; AA, 19). He says that he does not know what it means to be an "exemplary" Jew, that he is extremely suspicious of the logic of exemplarity. At the same time, he recalls that he had, in "Circumfession," cited a notebook of 1976 in which he "played without playing" at calling himself "the last and least of the Jews [*le dernier des Juifs*]" (Ce, 154; Cf, 145). He goes on, in "Circumfession," to try to define "my religion about which nobody understands anything" and to speak of the way "the constancy of God in my life is called by other names [*s'appelle d'autres noms*]" (Ce, 154, 155; Cf, 146), names such as, I suppose, *le tout autre*, the wholly other. To call himself the last of the Jews, in the double sense of being the last real Jew left and of being hardly Jewish at all, echoes, perhaps, Mary Shelley's novel *The Last Man* and Maurice Blanchot's *récit The Last Man* (*Le dernier homme*). The latter is cited in the "Border Lines" part of "Living On / Border Lines" ("Survivre / Journal de bord"): "But with me [the narrator] present, he would be the most alone of men, without even himself, without that last one that he was—thus the last of all [*Mais moi présent, il serait le plus seul des hommes, sans même soi, sans ce dernier qu'il était,—ainsi le tout dernier*]" (LO/BL, 132–34, trans. altered; P, 176–79).

Derrida's phrase "the last of the Jews" also echoes, perhaps, a motif in the prophetic writings of the Hebrew Bible and of the Christian Old Testament. This is the theme of the righteous or saving remnant, that is, the few Jews who remained faithful to Jehovah rather than whoring after strange gods: "Except the Lord of hosts had left unto us a small remnant, we should have been as Sodom, and we should have been like unto Gomorrah" (Isaiah 1:9); "The remnant shall return, even the remnant of Jacob, unto the mighty God" (Isaiah 10:21; see also Isaiah 4:2); "Yet will I leave a remnant, that ye may have some that shall escape the sword among the nations, when ye shall be scattered through the countries" (Ezekiel 6:8). To be a remnant, the last of the Jews, is to be what remains, a remainder, a *reste* or *restance* (*sherit* in Hebrew).[22] (For *reste*, see Chapter 5.)

Derrida's explanation of what it means to call himself *le dernier des Juifs* is an extraordinary, long, and characteristically aporetic or self-contradictory sentence that goes on for twenty lines in the English translation. The sentence turns this way and that in a twisting that gives a good idea of the complex rhetoric of "Abraham, the Other." Derrida's formulations invoke, in the sentence just following the one I am about to cite, "the figure of the marrano," that is, the covert or hidden Jew in Renaissance Spain or Portugal who practiced his or her faith in secret, while apparently a convert to Catholicism, in order to avoid the Inquisition:

> I introduce myself [in "Circumfession"] both as the least Jewish, the most unworthy Jew, the last to deserve the title of authentic Jew, and at the same time, because of all this, by reason of a force of rupture that uproots and universalizes the place [*lieu*], the local, the familial, the communal, the national, and so on, he who plays at playing the role of the most Jewish of all [this "playing at playing a role" would make Derrida more like Gwendolen or like Deronda's mother than like Deronda himself], the last and therefore the only survivor fated to assume the legacy of generations, to save the response or responsibility before the assignation, or before the election, always at risk of taking himself for another, something that belongs to the essence of an experience of election; as if the least could do the most, but also as if (you will have noted, no doubt, that I often have recourse to the "as if" [*comme si*], and I do so intentionally [*à dessein*], without playing, without being facile, because I believe that a certain *perhaps of the as if*, the poetical or the literary, in sum, beats at the heart of what I want to entrust to you)—*as if* the one who disavowed the most, and who appeared to betray the dogmas of belonging, be it the belonging to the community, the religion, even to the people, the nation and the state, and so on—*as if* this individual alone represented the last demand, the hyperbolic request of the very thing he appears to betray by perjuring himself. (AO, 13; AA, 21–22, trans. modified)

I have cited this long sentence partly because it introduces two other features of Derrida's denegations in "Abraham, the Other." First is his belief that ethical decision is genuine only if it is free from every preexisting law or prescription. (See Chapter 2.) He calls this "a deconstruction as well as an ethics of decision, an ethics of responsibility, exposed to the endurance of the undecidable, to the law of *my* decision as *decision of the other* in me, dedicated and devoted [*vouée, dévouée*] to aporia, to a not-being-able-to or not-being-obligated-to [*au ne-pas-pouvoir ou au ne-pas-devoir*] trust an oppositional border between two, for example, concepts that are apparently dissociable" (AO, 17; AA, 25–26). Second, Derrida firmly declares once more his refusal to identify himself with any family, community, group, nation, or congregation. (See Chapters 6 and 8.) Elsewhere in "Abraham, the Other," Derrida traces his resolute refraining, his saying "Don't count me in" to every appeal to belonging (including belonging to any Jewish community), to the experience of official French anti-Semitism he had as a schoolboy in El Biar in Algeria:

> Ultimately, the paradoxical effect I wanted to describe schematically is that my suffering as a persecuted young Jew (common enough, after all, and not comparable to those endured in Europe—something that adds to all the reserve and decency that prevent me from speaking of it), this suffering has no doubt killed in me an elementary confidence in any community, in any fusional gregariousness, whatever its nature, and beginning of course with any anti-Semitic herding [*attroupement*] that alleges ethnic, religious, or national roots. . . . an obscure feeling took shape in me, at first uncultivated, then more and more reasoned, of interrupted belonging, a relation vexed *from both sides*: from the side of the declared enemy, of course, the anti-Semite, but also from the side of "my own" [*du côté des "miens"*], if I may say so. (AO, 15; AA, 23–24)

To accept the judgment of those others who say "You are a Jew" and, as a consequence, to join the Jewish community, as Daniel Deronda so enthusiastically does in Eliot's novel, is, Derrida asserts, paradoxically an anti-Semitic gesture. It plays into the enemy's hands by accepting the distinction between Jew and Gentile anti-Semitism prescribes. The young Derrida hated the Jewish school in Algiers he was sent to after he was expelled because of his Jewish descent from the French one. He soon played truant.

This originary refusal to belong to any group is, Derrida explains, the necessary basis of any valid ethical act. This includes the performative response, the "yes" of vocational reaffirmation of a call made on me, or apparently made, by the "wholly other." As opposed to Deronda, who saw his discovery that he was of Jewish birth as an unambiguous sign of election, to which had only to assent obediently, Derrida sees election as extremely problematic and uncertain. It is something that must be put under the rubric of the fictional "as if." You can never be sure that you have really been called or that the call was meant for you and not for someone else. This means that the life-determining vocational performative "yes" or the Abrahamic "Behold, here I am" is, for Derrida, in accord with his special theory of performativity, always an uncertain leap in the dark. "The instant of decision is a madness." You cannot justify it by way of any preexisting grounds. It creates its own grounds, as well as the self of the decider, in the act of its enunciation. Derrida explicitly relates this to his theory of performativity. To say "I am a Jew" is a performative utterance, not a constative one. In this it is like saying *je t'aime*. Like "I love you," however, "I am a Jew" is a performative utterance of a peculiar, anti-Austinian kind. It creates the self of the one who utters it, rather than grounding itself on a preexisting self.

A perpetual disjunction, moreover, exists between faith and knowledge in this, as in any other, speech act, or, rather, you know without knowing. The utterance precedes knowledge, and you can never be sure, even afterward, just what you did in that utterance, even though that nonknowledge is the ground without ground of the "felicity," the responsible responsiveness, of your speech act. "To say 'I am a jew' [*je suis juif*], as I do," says Derrida, "while knowing and meaning [*en voulant dire*] what one says, is very difficult and vertiginous. One can only attempt to think it after having said it, and therefore, in a certain manner [*d'une certaine manière*], without yet knowing what one does there, the *doing* [*le* faire] preceding the *knowing* [*le* savoir] and remaining, more than ever [*plus que jamais*], heterogeneous to it" (AO, 28; AA, 36). "In a certain manner"? What manner is that? What does saying that include or exclude? "More than ever"? More than what preceding speech act events? Why "more than ever"? Derrida's careful reservations and nuances do not really add clarity, except to indicate, perhaps, that there is something exceptional ("exemplary"?) about saying, "I am a Jew."

I have said that this nonknowledge is the groundless ground of the efficacy of this speech act. Derrida several pages later says just that:

> It is possible that I have not been called, me, and it is not even excluded that no one, no One, nobody, ever called any One, any unique one, anybody. The possibility of an originary misunderstanding in destination [cf. Chapter 3 on "destinerrance"] is not an evil, it is the structure, perhaps the very vocation, of any call worthy of that name, of all nomination, of all response and responsibility. (AO, 34; AA, 41–42)

This dubiety is quite different from Levinas's assumption that the *visage* of the other peremptorily invokes my response. As I shall mention again in a different context in Chapter 11, Derrida puts this strange form of unverifiable election under the aegis of Franz Kafka's disturbingly comic imagination, in his parable "Abraham," of more than one possible Abraham, including one who comes "unsummoned [*ungerufen*]." This "other Abraham" is like the bad student in the back of a schoolroom who mistakenly thinks his name is being called when it is the good student instead who is being summoned, in order to be rewarded for his good work. Derrida's special theory of performativity puts him, in relation to his Jewishness, and puts all of us at any moment of decision, perpetually in the situation of that bad student. "And perhaps," Kafka's parable concludes, "he had made no mistake at all, his name really was called [*wirklich genannt*], it having been the teacher's intention to make the rewarding of the best student at the same time a punishment [*Bestrafung*] for the worst one."[23] "Is it really to me," asks Derrida, "at the back of the class, in the last row, that such questions must be addressed or destined?" (AO, 4; AA, 14). He means the questions that were asked him at the Judeities conference. The reader will see how far this is from Eliot's notion of Deronda's joyful and unquestioning acquiescence in his election.

I conclude this chapter by asking which kind of performativity does *Daniel Deronda* itself, I mean the whole novel, exemplify, if either? It is an example of both kinds of performativity, performativity sub one and performativity sub two. *Daniel Deronda* is a performance, or reading it is a performance, like performing a Mozart sonata by following the score or, in this case, since the novel is long, complex, and *echt* Victorian, like performing a Liszt piano composition. *Daniel Deronda* is also an extended performative utterance of a peculiar kind. It generates a virtual literary reality that can be "accessed" only by way of the performative efficacy of the words on the page as I read them. Those words call or conjure into existence, like ghosts in broad daylight, Gwendolen, Daniel, all the other characters, their "worlds," and all that they do and say. The words do this in response to a spectral preexistence of the novel in potential form before Eliot wrote it. This happens according to the quasi-Husserlian theory of literature that Derrida proposes in "The Time of a Thesis: Punctuations" (TT, 37–38; DDP, 443–44). The novel's words on the page, in exercising this sovereign power, in their break in temporal sequence (since nothing in Eliot's life, social circumstances, or previous writings could have predicted that she would write just this novel), and in their source as inventions or discoveries coming from something wholly other, are more like Derridean performatives than like Austinian ones or like Butlerian performativity as understood by *Wikipedia*.

I have shown in this chapter that one must distinguish carefully among several different kinds of performativity in order to identify what is distinctive about Derrida's "special theory." I have also shown that these discriminations are powerful tools for reading literary works. They are "edge tools," however, so they must be used carefully, to avoid cutting oneself.

CHAPTER 8

"Don't Count Me In":
Derrida's Refraining

Simon Morgan Wortham's admirably penetrating and comprehensive *Counter-institutions: Jacques Derrida and the Question of the University* has traced in detail Jacques Derrida's complex relations over the years both to the institutions in place with which he has been associated and to the counter-institutions of various kinds that he was involved in founding.[1] As Morgan Wortham shows, a contradictory "with-against" movement has always characterized Derrida's relation to academic institutions, to institutions generally, and to the traditions of philosophy as an academic discipline.

The "third," neither/nor, or both/and is a fundamental feature of Derrida's thought or, better put, of his characteristic style, if one can speak of such a thing in a multitudinous writing that is so heterogeneous in styles. The opening pages of *A Taste for the Secret*, for example, give several examples of this in rapid-fire sequence. Derrida begins by saying that "there is an injunction to the system that I have never renounced" (TS, 3). He then immediately goes on to say that "deconstruction, without being anti-systematic, is on the contrary, and nevertheless, not only a search for, but itself a consequence of the fact that the system is impossible" (TS, 4). Odd syntax! What is the object of "search for"? Search for what? Search for systematic coherence or search for proof that system is impossible? The sentence seems to want to say both things at once. (I have been unable to consult the original French, or the Italian, to see if they have the same ambiguity.) In the next paragraph, Derrida simultaneously asserts his allegiance to doing philosophy, even "systematic philosophy," and his non-allegiance, his commitment to doing something that "exceeds" the philosophical: "Mine, then, is an *excessively* philosophical gesture: a gesture that is philosophical and, at the same time, in excess of the philosophical" (TS, 4). Two paragraphs later, he defines his interest in the question of imagination in Aristotle, Kant, or Hegel as resulting from the way imagination is two things at once: "there is something about it that has made it a threat to truth, intellect, and reality—yet a resource as well" (TS, 5). Derrida goes on immediately to generalize this as an interest in "the 'third'" as something that both participates and does not participate, both at once, in any system built on oppositions: "And in the end everything we have said about the system comes down to a question of the 'third.' This third term can be taken as the mediator that permits synthesis, reconciliation, participation; in which case that which is neither this nor that permits the synthesis of this and that . . . the third of neither-this-nor-that and this-and-that can indeed also be interpreted as that whose absolute heterogeneity resists all integration, participation and system, thus designating the place where the system does not close" (TS, 5). The third is a dialectical *Aufhebung* that does not sublate but rather prohibits sublation.

Some readers are driven up the wall by such formulations. If you have a taste for Derrida you must, on the contrary, find such formulations tantalizing and challenging. You must be inspired to further thought by them. This first segment of the first interview in *A Taste for the Secret* ends with one more example, in remarks about the way time is out of joint, *aus den Fugen*, and about the way this undoes any periodization in the history of philosophy and makes our so-called contemporaries, that is, philosophers since Hegel, "non-contemporary" either to us or to one another, since "this dislocation of the present . . . renders the present non-contemporary to itself" (TS, 7).

All these *X*-not-*X* formulations occur in the first five pages of the first interview in *A Taste for the Secret*! Another large-scale example, touched on only briefly in *A Taste for the Secret*, is what Derrida has to say about friendship in *The Politics of Friendship*. On the one hand, Derrida was a touchingly loyal friend, for example, in my unclouded friendship with him over almost forty years. On the other hand, a leitmotif of *The Politics of Friendship* is a sentence from Montaigne, often attributed to Aristotle, that says "O my friends, there is no friend [*O mes amis, il n'y a nul amy*]" (PF,

1; PA, 11). The book can be defined as a deconstruction, or at least a making extremely problematic, of the usual idea of friendship. On the first hand, again, Derrida, in the inscription in the copy of this book he gave to me, has crossed out "Politiques de" and made it read: "pour Dorothy, / pour Hillis / l'amitié, l'affection / et l'admiration de / Jacques."

My citation about the "third" also exemplifies another somewhat exasperating feature of Derrida's style (if "style" is the right word for it). This might be called the continually displaced middle. Lost in the scintillating abundance of Derrida's writings, the reader, this reader at least, seeks a solid rock or anchor in the flux, something around which the "whole," if it is a whole, even a nonsystematic whole, can be organized. Derrida appears to give us such anchors, as when he says, "And in the end everything we have said about the system comes down to a question of the third ["in the end"? Why say that? When do we get to the end? Where is the end? And "we"? Who is this we? Is Derrida a plurality, other to himself, heterogeneous to himself, a divided or fissioned signature? He often says so: "Every time there is a name—by which we mean proper name—the word can remain the same while naming something new each time. The very possibility of the name is iterability: the possibility of repeating the same, but each time to name an other or to name the same otherwise" (TS, 68)]. Let me repeat the citation, after this interpolation: "And in the end everything we have said about the system comes down to a question of the third" (TS, 5). That seems to give the reader solid ground to stand on, a fundament. The problem is that before long Derrida is offering yet another quite different center around which his writing can be organized, as when, in a later interview in *A Taste for the Secret*, he says, " I think about nothing but death, I think about it all the time. . . . And at bottom it is what commands everything—what I do, what I am, what I write, what I say" (TS, 88). Well, which is the bottom, the third or death? I would like to know.

The series of interviews of Derrida by Maurizio Ferraris and Gianni Vattimo of 1993–95 collected in *A Taste for the Secret* contains here and there statements by Derrida that succinctly summarize his with-against relations to institutions and counter-institutions over the years. These relations are a salient example of Derrida's "third." Morgan Wortham's book fills out the historical details about these relations.

On the one hand, Derrida repeatedly, in many places in his writing, pledges his fidelity to the academic institutions already in place and especially to the European philosophical tradition and to the protocols for studying and teaching it in France, even though no French university ever appointed him a professor. He taught always at prestigious but to some degree marginal institutions, since neither was a university proper: the École Normale Supérieure and the École des Hautes Études en Sciences Sociales. At the former he was, at least initially, an *agrégé-répétiteur.* "A repeater, the agrégé-répétiteur," Derrida tells us in "Where a Teaching Body Begins and How It Ends," "should produce nothing, at least if to produce means to innovate, to transform, to bring about the new [*faire advenir le nouveau*]. He is destined to repeat and make others repeat, to reproduce and make others reproduce: forms, norms, and a content" (WAP, 75; DDP, 122). The mind boggles at the thought of Derrida as a "repeater." Much later, after promotions at the École Normale, he became "Director of Studies" at the École des Hautes Études. He chose "Philosophical Institutions" as his topic of research and teaching. "My principal interests," he said, "have tended towards the great canon of philosophy—Plato, Kant, Hegel, Husserl" (TS, 4), to which Nietzsche and Heidegger must surely be added. An immense proportion of Derrida's seminars over the years focused on careful, slow, patient readings of passages or texts by Heidegger, as for example, the reading, in his last seminars, of 2002–3, "The Beast and the Sovereign (Two)," of a few passages from Heidegger's seminars of 1929–30, *The Fundamental Concepts of Metaphysics*.[2] More than once Derrida asserted his continued commitment to Husserlian phenomenological procedures, the *epochē* or transcendental reduction, and so on. In "The Time of a Thesis: Punctuations," he says he still sees Husserlian phenomenology as "a discipline of incomparable rigor" (TT, 38; DDP, 444). In *A Taste for the Secret*, Derrida speaks of his fidelity to the French tradition of microscopic reading as a way of identifying the systematic hanging together of philosophical writings, "the way the text works" (TS, 45). He learned this, he says, at the École Normale, especially from a certain Martial Guéroult: "Even if I protested against that discipline, against the unspoken norms of the discipline of reading, it's true that they continue to inspire in me an ineradicable respect. Those models of philological, micrological, I'd even say grammatico-logical demands, for me have never lost their irrecusable authority" (TS, 42–43).

Derrida's interest in counter-institutions would appear to go counter to this commitment to the institutions already firmly in place. "The idea of a counter-institution, neither spontaneous, wild nor immediate," says Derrida, "is the most permanent motif that, in a way, has guided me in my work" (TS, 50). Here is yet another assertion of what forms the center of Derrida's work, to be added to death and the third. Altogether too many centers! Nor was the counter-institution just an "idea" for Derrida. As Morgan Wortham has shown in detail, and as Ferraris in one of his questions to Derrida in *A Taste for the Secret* succinctly summarizes, Derrida was directly involved in the setting up at least four counter-institutions: Greph, that is, the Groupe de recherché sur l'enseignement philosophique in 1974; the Estates General of Philosophy, held at the Sorbonne in 1979; the Jan Hus Association in 1981, which got him arrested in Prague when he went there to run a clandestine seminar; and the foundation in 1983 of the Collège internationale de philosophie, of which he was the first director.

Four features of these counter-institutions can be identified. (1) They are not "counter" in the sense of being wholly different, subversive, revolutionary, unfaithful. They are, rather, attempts to put the institution of philosophy study back on track, so to speak, to make it more faithful to a tradition to which the institutions then in place were, in Derrida's view, being unfaithful, were betraying. (2) Derrida never remained associated with these counter-institutions for long. Though he was the first director of the Collège internationale, he soon gave that up. His relation to this, as to the other counter-institutions he helped found, tended to become more and more marginal as time passed. (3) None of these counter-institutions has had much influence or has changed institutional organizations all that much in France or elsewhere. All of them, says Derrida, were "counter-institutions with original and paradoxical ideas (albeit unrealized) on the subject of counter-institutionality" (TS, 51). The operative word here is "unrealized." (4) In a strange way, Derrida moved counter to the institutions to which he belonged by fulfilling to the letter the protocols of interpretation he had been taught by those institutions themselves, by Guéroult, Hyppolite, and others of his teachers, for example. Something of the same sort, to compare the lesser with the greater, can be said of my own movement from American New Criticism to the rhetorical criticism I now practice. I just did what the New Critics told me to do: "Read closely. Ask questions of the text. Ask just why is this or that feature there. What is its function? What does it do? Do not say anything about a text that cannot be supported by the words on the page." Strange things happen, as I discovered, when you do that conscientiously and with as open a mind as possible. In Derrida's case, the age-old assumption that a great philosopher's works form a system, plus the exhortation to micrological reading, led him to try to fit everything in. Behold! He found that you cannot do that.

The distance between trying honestly and patiently to fit everything in and a taste for aspects of a given philosopher's work that turn out not to be capable of being fitted in is so narrow as to be almost nothing. After having said that his interests have tended toward the great canon of philosophy, from Plato to Husserl, Derrida goes on to say, "but, at the same time, towards the so-called 'minor' loci of their texts, neglected problematics, or footnotes—things that can irritate the system and at the same time account for the subterranean region in which the system constitutes itself by repressing what makes it possible, which is not systematic" (TS, 4–5). Well, is that being faithful to Guéroult's micrological reading or not? As any schoolchild knows, nothing can be more insolent or subversive than a slightly ironic exact repetition of what someone in authority has said. Derrida, as an *agrégé-répétiteur* at the École Normale was supposed to perform such iteration in his teaching. He was supposed to avoid thinking for himself. He was supposed just to repeat what Plato, Hegel, Kant, or Husserl had said. As Derrida tirelessly demonstrated, under the aegis of what he called "iterability," every repetition both iterates and alters. This happens at a minimum in the sense that the same words are uttered in a different socio-institutional context and at a different historical time.

Though Derrida never defended himself by saying what I am about to say, I think he would nevertheless have been justified in asserting: "I have been an obedient student. I have done exactly what you told me to do. I have remained faithfully inside the institution or discipline of philosophy. I have repeated exactly and micrologically, and look what happened! The 'system' disarticulated itself, deconstructed itself before my very eyes. My obedient reading revealed what the system depends on but that cannot be incorporated into the system, for example, the *pharmakon* in Plato."

I conclude that, for Derrida, the opposition between institution and counter-institution is not really an opposition. It is, rather, a question of supplementarity. The counter-institution supplements the institution by more adequately fulfilling its goals, that is, the goal of a collective working together on the basis of some kind of consensus. At the same time, the counter-institution brings into the open what keeps the institution from ever fulfilling its goals. No doubt the counter-institutions Derrida founded or helped found were, not so secretly, attempts to institutionalize deconstruction and its abyssal basis in respect for the otherness of every other. Nevertheless, a counter-institution is still an institution, with its own destined incompletion. That may explain why Derrida tended to remain for so short a time in each of his counter-institutions.

Everything I have said so far still follows from my earlier "on the one hand," that is, a tracing out of Derrida's allegiance to professional institutions. I have not yet got to the other hand. I hope my readers have noticed that and have been waiting with bated breath for the other shoe to drop or for me to turn from one hand to the other.

On the other hand, then, Derrida remains, in spite of his allegiance to institutions and counter-institutions, deeply suspicious of any form of collectivity or togetherness, any institution, however "counter." His most deep-seated and spontaneous reaction to invitations to join something is what William Faulkner, using a Southernism or at least a "Faulknerism," calls "refraining." This is, for example, the violent gesture made by a horse when it rears back, rolls its eyes, arches its neck, and resists being put in a truck or corral. The resistance to saying "X" without also immediately saying "not X" or "at the same time Y" is the stylistic marker of this refraining. Why is this? Why all this rearing back? What is the logical, illogical, or logical-illogical basis of this refraining?

A full answer would take a more or less interminable reading of all Derrida's work, including all the unpublished seminars. Nevertheless, a sketch or hypotyposis of an answer may be given in the rest of this chapter. I begin this sketch by looking at a paragraph about community in *A Taste for the Secret*, already cited in part in Chapter 6. It is characteristically double, with and against, taking away with one hand what it has given with the other. In response to a question from Ferraris about whether he would still be willing to subscribe to "a community of interpretation and allegoresis," Derrida begins by saying that he has no problem with using the word or the concept of community to name those associations of people described in such recent works as Agamben's *The Community to Come*, Nancy's *The Inoperable Community*, and Blanchot's *The Inavowable Community*, to which I would add Alfonso Lingis's *The Community of Those Who Have Nothing in Common*. As the two paragraphs on community develop, however, Derrida radically puts in question the use of this word to name such associations: "Why call it community?" he asks. He goes on, in sentences not cited in Chapter 6, to say, "If I have always hesitated to use this word, it is because too often the word 'community' resounds with the 'common' [*commun*], the as-one [*comme-un*]. . . . [Blanchot's communism] is a communism where the common is anything but common: it is the placing in common [*mise en commun*] of that which is no longer of the order of subjectivities, or of intersubjectivity as a relation—however paradoxical—between presences. Everything we have been saying here is a certain way of questioning community in the classical sense, and intersubjectivity as well" (TS, 24–25). Derrida's allegiance to Blanchot, beyond almost all his other French contemporaries, is, by the way, evident here.

Well, just what is wrong, for Derrida, with community in the classical sense, or with intersubjectivity in the usual sense of the word, that is, as a name for the interaction between two subjectivities, present to themselves in the present, which have some sort of access to one another? Why does he recoil or refrain from using these words or concepts? The answer is that everything in Derrida's thought follows from the fundamental assumption that every self or *Dasein* is absolutely isolated from all the others. I have discussed in Chapter 6 a remarkable passage on this topic in Derrida's last, so far unpublished, seminars. I cite it in part again here for its stubborn, iterated, intransigent refusal to allow for any sort of communication between one so-called subjectivity and another. The passage, in its bleak refraining, has great importance for my understanding of Derrida:

> Between my world, the "my world," what I call "my world," and there is no other for me, every other world making up part of it, between my world and every other world, there is initially the space and the time of an infinite difference, of an interruption incommensurable with all the attempts at passage, of bridge, isthmus, communication, translation, trope, and transfer that the desire for a world and the sickness of the world [*mal du monde*], the being in sickness of the world [*l'être en mal de monde*] will attempt to pose, to impose, to propose, to stabilize. There is no world, there are only islands. (BS, 1st seminar, my trans.)[3]

This passage, if I may say so, says a mouthful, as they say. Its iterative phrasing of words in apposition, such as the late Derrida was wont to use, saying the same thing over and over in slightly different terms, seems calculated to make sure the reader or listener does not think the slightest chink out of my windowless monad exists as anything other than an ideological phantasm. As Derrida says just a moment before the passage cited above, "the community of the world [is] always constructed, simulated by a group of stabilizing positings [*dispositifs*], more or less stable, therefore also never natural, language in the broad sense, codes of traces being destined, with all the living, to construct a unity of the world always deconstructible and nowhere and never given in nature" (ibid., my trans.). What this implies for the question of Derrida's belonging, in any serious way, to any institution, counter or otherwise, is a devastating refusal, since it asserts clearly enough that both any institution and any counter-institution are fragile, spectral constructs, always deconstructible, never based on any other than a phantasmal community or on any true intersubjective communication between the members of the institution. Who would want to belong to an institution like that?

Nor is this an isolated formulation.

Another example is a passage in a somewhat cheeky, defiant, and even to a degree insolent answer to a survey by the journal *Lignes*, published in October 1997. This survey asked Derrida, among many others, one supposes, to answer in two or three pages a whole series of global questions about "intellectuals" today. Derrida's answer runs to eight pages and is entitled, "But . . . No, but . . . Never . . . , and Yet . . . , as to the Media" ("Mais . . . , non mais . . . , jamais . . . , et pourtant . . . , quant aux médias"). Early on, Derrida says he has difficulty answering because he is more than one person: "—well, there is (perhaps, perhaps) someone within me who decides (perhaps) to keep quiet. I say 'someone within me' because there are several of us [*nous sommes plusieurs*], as you know, and 'I' will begin by positively claiming this plurality, close to dizzying heights [*au bord des vertiges*], especially juridical and political ones, which are already turning my head 'within me'" (PMe, 34, trans. modified; PMf, 230). How can he be expected to commit himself to answer all those hard questions if he is more than one person? He is in a state of dizziness to boot, as a result of that interior plurality. On the next page, Derrida speaks for this dizzy-making "someone within me" in a forceful Derridean gesture of total refraining that ridicules the terms used so blithely in the survey questions:

> When he thinks, teaches, speaks, reads, or writes, and works too in his own way, this "someone in me apart from me" *endeavors* (there is also an endeavor—a duty and a responsibility) no longer to *function*: either as an "intellectual" or even (if the word *intellectual* mainly defines a belonging—social, political, or cultural) as the citizen of a community (culture, nation, language, religion, and so on), as the citizen of a nation-state (were this a "citizen of the world"), or even as a "man" (whence my unquenchable interest in "the animal"—a crucial question, to be developed elsewhere, with much more space and time).
>
> For this "someone in me" (undersigned "so-and-so"), these concepts and the prescriptions attached to them will always remain themes, problems, and even presuppositions that, in their general form or in particular determinations they can be given, are submitted to a questioning, a critique—a "deconstruction," if you like; the necessity of it corresponds to an *unconditional affirmation*.
>
> Thus in a place of *absolute* resistance and remaining [*de résistance et de restance* absolues]. (PMe, 35, trans. modified and a missing phrase inserted; PMf, 231)

"*Absolute* resistance and remaining": this hyperbolically total rejection expresses in a single phrase the gesture of rearing back, clenching teeth and lips, turning the head aside, that I am calling, in this chapter, "Derrida's refraining." "Absolute" means, etymologically, totally "untied," detached. The use of the word *restance* here gives another twist to the words *reste* and *restance*, to which I have devoted Chapter 5. Derrida does not just remain on the sidelines, outside the intellectual game. He insists in another interview in *Paper Machine*, you will remember from that earlier chapter, that what "remains" is not just a leftover part of something whole but "inscribes in itself something of the infinitely other" (PMe, 151; PMf, 385). Using the word *restance* to help define his absolute resistance to being incorporated into any community and his unconditional affirmation of his right to put everything in question, for example, the clichés in the survey questions, indicates that this refraining is in the name, so Derrida is affirming, of a demand made on him by the wholly other that has a higher claim on him than any survey questions might have, any request that he speak as part of the "intellectual community."

A passage in *A Taste for the Secret* also echoes the one cited above from the last seminars. Each person's isolation is expressed somewhat less hyperbolically in this text, with a significantly different twist, but just as firmly. Here is one of the relatively few places where Derrida uses the word *God* more or less affirmatively, proffering and withdrawing it at the same time. Someone might be tempted to say, "Ah ha! Derrida has come out of the closet. He really *does* believe in God. We can recuperate him within one form or another of traditional theology, perhaps so-called 'negative theology,' perhaps even within some institutionalized religion or other." That "someone" would do well to be wary, however. It is true that Derrida was fascinated by the question of religious faith and wrote often about it, for example, in "Faith and Knowledge," in the admirable prolonged discussion of Kierkegaard's interpretation of the Abraham and Isaac story in *The Gift of Death*, in the investigation of negative theology in "How to Avoid Speaking: Denials" ("Comment ne pas parler: Dénégations"), or in what he has to say about the religious basis of ideology in *Specters of Marx* (SMe, 148; SMf, 236). "In the end," nevertheless, Derrida always refrains. He always says, once more, "I refuse to answer that question." In "How To Avoid Speaking," Derrida argues forcefully that deconstruction is *not* a form of negative theology. The title suggests that the whole essay is an evasive refusal to answer, though, as the reader of Derrida may have come to expect, the title has a double meaning:

Between the two interpretations of "Comment ne pas dire?" [*dire* rather
than *parler* was apparently Derrida's first formulation] the meaning of the
uneasiness thus seems to get reversed: from "How to be silent?" (How to
avoid speaking at all?) one passes—moreover, in a completely necessary
way and as if from within—to the question, which can always become the
prescriptive heading of a recommendation: How not to speak, what words
to avoid, in order to speak *well?* (PIIe, 154; PIIf, 157)

About refusing to speak as a form of refraining I shall say more below.
Derrida can hardly be said to affirm straightforwardly any sort of religious
faith. Far from it. "Faith and Knowledge," for example, sees religious faith
as a basic feature of the strange structure of "auto-co-immunity" that leads
every community to turn its self-protective mechanisms, its immune system, against itself in the terrifying reversal called "autoimmunity" (FK,
87; FS, 68–69). In *Specters of Marx*, Derrida follows Marx, as I have said,
in asserting that all ideological aberrations are built on the basic spectral
and baseless mystification of religious belief.

And yet . . . and yet . . . Derrida *does* believe in the solicitations of a
nameless something he calls *le tout autre*. If *tout autre est tout autre*, if every
other is wholly other, according to the formula Derrida proposes and
comments on at length in *The Gift of Death* (GD, 82ff.; DM, 114ff.), then
nothing more can be said about it, in spite of the urgent and irresistible
demands that wholly other makes on me. The word *Dieu* ("God") in the
passage I am about to cite must ultimately appear as just one more catachresis for what has no proper name, along with "Jehovah," "Jaweh,"
"Elohim," *le secret*, *le don*, *la justice*, and *l'autre* itself. Derrida's reading of
the Abraham and Isaac story in Genesis, originary moment, according to
him, of the three great religions of the book, Judaism, Islam, and Christianity, is deflected in Derrida's reading to become a story of the secret
demand made on the singular individual by the wholly other. I shall read
this reading in some detail in Chapter 9.

I turn now to the passage in *A Taste for the Secret*. Just as Derrida says,
in "The Time of a Thesis: Punctuations," that in 1957 "it was then for
me a matter of bending [*de ployer*], more or less violently, the techniques
of transcendental phenomenology to the needs of elaborating a new theory of literature, of that very peculiar type of ideal object that is the literary
object" (TT, 37; DDP, 443), so in *A Taste for the Secret* he bends Leibnizian monadology more or less violently to the need to elaborate a new
theory of the absolute singularity and isolation of every "I," every ego.
The passage begins with an assertion that most people can accept: each of

us sees the world differently from the way anyone else sees it, especially when I am looking at you looking at me. What is unusual, perhaps, is the claim that this difference is "absolute": "the eyes meet, and what one sees is absolutely other than what the other sees" (TS, 70). Also a little peculiar and a little surprising, at least to me, is the corollary Derrida derives from this absolute otherness. It is because I am so absolutely different from my neighbor, enisled in my own ego, that I can understand you and that you can understand me. Just why this is the case Derrida does not explain, but he insists on its necessity:

> What I see at this moment has no relation [he does not say it is somewhat different, but that it has *no relation* whatsoever] to what you see, and we understand each other: you understand what I'm saying to you, and for that to happen it is necessary, really necessary, that what you have facing you should have no relation, no commensurability, with what I myself see facing you. And it is this infinite difference that makes us always ingenuous, always absolutely new. (TS, 70)

Why is this so? It seems counter-intuitive. It would seem that each person understands what his or her neighbor means because the two have something, quite a lot in fact, in common—a common language, for example. It would seem that this, in turn, turns on the way you and I both go on being the same person from moment to moment, day to day, year to year. Derrida, however, insists that I am always, each moment, ingenuous, like a newborn, always new. He insists, paradoxically, moreover, that it is just because we are infinitely different that we understand one another. Why is that?

A hint at an answer is given in Derrida's assertion that I am not only wholly other to my neighbor but also wholly other to myself. I hide a secret from myself. I am radically heterogeneous to myself. On the grounds of these rather strange assertions, Derrida brings in Leibniz and relates what he says so forcefully in the later-written passage from the last seminar, cited above, to what he calls "a Leibnizianism without God, so to speak." "So to speak"? What reservation lurks in this refraining? Here is Derrida's description of what he defines as our Godless monadism, though God, says Derrida, is "*there* where he is not there":

> Call it monadology—the fact that between my monad—the world as it appears to me—and yours, no relation is possible: hence the hypothesis of God, who thinks of compossibility, pre-established harmony, etc. But from monad to monad, and even when monads speak to one another, there is no relation, no passage. The translation totally changes the text.[4] From this

point of view, it is a question for me of a Leibnizianism without God, so to
speak: which means that, *nevertheless*, in these monads, in this hypersolipsism, the appeal of God finds place; God sees from your side and from
mine at once, as absolute third; and so *there* where he is not there, he is
there; *there* where he is not there, is his place. (TS, 70–71)

This quite extraordinary passage is a hyperbolic example of taking away
with one hand what it gives with the other, and then giving it back again.
On the one hand, Derrida asserts that each person's isolation within his
or her windowless monad is absolute. "No relation is possible," no trope,
transfer, bridge, isthmus, or translation. No translation carries anything
over from the original text. God is a baseless Leibnizian hypothesis to
provide an escape from this truly desperate situation, the situation of a
hypersolipsism, a Leibnizianism without God. On the other hand, in a
formulation that says "both/and" or "this and that," Derrida recognizes
the "place" of "the hypothesis of God," "the appeal of God." The reader
may remember my discussion in Chapter 6 of a passage by Walter Benjamin that shows overtly the sometimes hidden theological basis of any belief, even the most apparently secular, in a happy "intersubjectivity."
"Only a God can save us," Heidegger, notoriously, said in a late interview
in *Der Spiegel*. The word *place* (presumably *lieu* in Derrida's original
French) is crucial here, along with the twice-italicized word *there*, as is the
reappearance of the nondialectical third that, as I have shown, Derrida
says, earlier in *A Taste for the Secret*, is essential to his way of thinking, his
way of making way without making way. God is, after all, *there* where he
is not there. That is his place. I suppose Derrida means by this that, even
if a God exists as the absolute third who sees from your side and my side
at once, he is not there as a presence available to either of us as a bridge
to the other. Therefore we are left in our solitude, as islands or windowless
monads.

Though Derrida appeals here to Leibniz, he makes clear in many other
passages in his work that the section on our "analogical apperception" of
the other transcendental ego in Husserl's Fifth Cartesian Meditation is
the crucial reference for Derrida's assumption that each singularity has no
direct access whatsoever to the interiority of any other singularity. (See,
for example, R, 161; B, 75–76.) Each singularity is an island. We can only
guess, by analogy and by a perception without perception, an apperception, that the other has an interiority like my own.

It is on the basis of this double postulation, the postulation of the radical isolation and singularity of each "I" and the postulation of a wholly

other, a "God" who is "*there* where he is not there," that Derrida asserts, in an earlier passage in *A Taste for the Secret*, that he is not one of the family, that he refrains from belonging to any institution, regular or counter. He also tells us why he refrains. He tells us what precious value, a price beyond price, is protected by this nonbelonging, this refraining. My entire chapter so far has been working toward the citation of this remarkable passage and toward saying a few words about it in conclusion. Ferraris has asked Derrida why he is fond of echoing Gide's indictment of the family and why he gives, as his "own private translation" of what Gide says, "I am not one of the family [*je ne suis pas de la famille*]":

> let me get back to my saying "I am not one of the family." Clearly, I was playing on a formula that has multiple registers of resonance. I'm not one of the family means, in general, "I do not define myself on the basis of my belonging to the family," or to civil society, or to the state; I do not define myself on the basis of elementary forms of kinship [an ironic reference here to Lévi-Strauss and structural anthropology]. But it also means, more figuratively, that I am not part of any group, that I do not identify myself with a linguistic community, a national community, a political party, or with any group or clique whatsoever, with any philosophical or literary school. "I am not one of the family" means: do not consider me "one of you," "don't count me in." (TS, 27)

"Don't count me in"! This is the most violent and total expression of Derrida's fundamental gesture or speech act of refraining that I know anywhere in his writings. Not only *is* Derrida an island, a windowless monad without access to God as third (if God does indeed exist as more than a placeless place or an unprovable hypothesis). Derrida also *wants*, and must want, to be an island. He defines himself as an island by refusing to belong to any community, group, or institution whatsoever (counter or otherwise), including, for example, the community of deconstructionists or that famous "Gang of Four," the so-called Yale Mafia. Like Melville's Bartleby, Derrida just says no, or rather, he says no without saying no, or yes either. "He doesn't say no and he doesn't say yes," says Derrida of Bartleby. Derrida says, like Bartleby, politely but firmly, "I would prefer not to" (TS, 27).

In "Passions," Derrida puts forward the concept of an absolute right not to answer. This right is associated by him especially with democracy and with its concomitant, literature, in its modern sense as the right to say or write anything and not be held responsible for it (POOe, 19–20,

28–29; POOf, 47, 65–67). "Passions" was written to fulfill an obligation to respond to a book of essays by various scholars about Derrida's work. Derrida conspicuously refrains from doing that, though he says it is impolite to do so. "How to Avoid Speaking: Denials " shows, perhaps, how to talk without talking, without saying anything. In "The University Without Condition," Derrida projects a utopian university that allows putting everything in question, even the right to put everything in question.

Derrida *is* this multiple and many-layered gesture of refraining, through and through. To express this total refraining in terms of not belonging to his family, as a synecdoche for all the other forms of not belonging—disciplinary, political, and institutional—makes it all the more violent and even improbable. How can I not be a member of my own family? Derrida's presupposition is that even this most intimate and apparently irrefutable form of belonging is an illusion, an ideological assumption. Each man or woman is an island, cut off entirely, without any bridge or isthmus to any other island, even to members of his or her family. Moreover, he or she ought to *want* this separation.

Derrida therefore chooses his enisled separation. He desires it. He prizes it above all else. Why? The rest of the passage from *A Taste for the Secret* cited above explains why:

> I want to keep my freedom, always: this, for me, is the condition not only for being singular and other, but also for entering into relation with the singularity and alterity of others. When someone is one of the family, not only does he lose himself in the herd, but he loses the others as well; the others become simply places, family functions, or places or functions in the organic totality that constitutes a group, school, nation or community of subjects speaking the same language. (TS, 27)

Derrida's logic here is clear enough. He presumes that what I really am is that always renewed, always different, always diverse and multiple, always ingenuous, newborn, always unique, windowless monad. All other people are like me in being absolute singularities. True ethical relations must be between these monads. Such relations are to be defined as my response to the demand made on me by the version of the wholly other each other person is. It is my infinite responsibility to respond without reservation to that demand.

The model for this responding is religious, not, strictly speaking, ethical. The elaborate analysis of Kierkegaard's analysis of the Abraham and Isaac story in *The Gift of Death*, discussed in detail in Chapter 9, is the fullest exploration of the quasi-religious, "pro/con," basis of Derrida's ethics. As soon as I am one of the family, a member of any group or institution, or see others as such members, I become "one of the herd." The others also become herdlike. I lose myself, but I lose the others as well. Only by retaining my separate singularity, outside of any family or institution, can I respond to other singularities as unique versions of the wholly other.

In what follows this passage, Derrida relates his resolute refraining from any belonging to his "unusual family history," his situation, as he puts it in "Circumfession," as "a little black and very Arab Jew [*un petit Juif noir et très arabe*]" (Ce, 58; Cf, 57), who did not feel that he belonged to any of his local communities, not to the Arab one, not to the French one (which all his life treated him as an outsider), and not to the Jewish one, either:

> The fact is that I have a predisposition to not being one of the family, it
> wasn't just my choice. I am a Jew from Algeria, from a certain type of
> community, in which belonging to Judaism was problematic, belonging to
> Algeria was problematic, belonging to France was problematic, etc. So all
> this predisposed me to not-belonging; but, beyond the particular idiosyn-
> crasies of my own story, I wanted to indicate the sense in which an "I" does
> not have to be "one of the family." (TS, 27–28)

It would be a mistake, in my judgment, and a cop-out, to seize on this autobiographical explanation and conclude: "Well, that explains it. It is special to Derrida's subject position. I can heave a sigh of relief and belong with a clear conscience to my family, my nation, my university, my group of like-minded scholars." No, we are, in Derrida's view, all in some form or another of his situation. His situation was no more than a singular form, *his* form, of the general human situation of not having to be one of the family, of having an urgent obligation not to be one of the family. My obligation to respond without mediation to the wholly other means I must refrain from responding to any institution's demands. I must respond, rather, to an infinite demand for justice, as opposed to right or law. This call comes from no existing institution or counter-institution. While taking account of the context in which I find myself, my response enters the context to change it in response to a call from the future, the to-come, *l'à-venir*. Derrida calls this "a messianism without religion, even a messianic without messianism," and a fidelity to the "democracy to come" (SMe, 59, 64–65; SMf, 102, 110–11). One important feature of her or his context, for an academic, is the circumambient institutions already in place, including counter-institutions that have been installed. The latter then also become part of my context. I *must*, with the utmost urgency, refrain from belonging to any of these. This gesture of refraining is Derrida's fundamental and defining act, his ground without ground.

CHAPTER 9

Derrida's Ethics of Irresponsibilization; or, How to Get Irresponsible, in Two Easy Lessons

My signature is the moment of highest responsibility
in a deep irresponsibility.

—TS, 85

The ethical can therefore end up making us irresponsible.

—GD, 61

Literature as Irresponsible Son of Scripture

What in the world does Derrida mean by saying "the ethical can therefore end up making us irresponsible [*L'ethique peut donc être destinée à irresponsabiliser*]" (GD, 61; DM, 89)? That is my central question in this chapter. It was first prepared for a conference on "irresponsibility" held at Nanyang Technological University from September 28 to September 30, 2006, though only the few first sentences plus the second half were presented there. My goal is to show how one gets irresponsible, how one irresponsibilizes oneself. I shall get help from Derrida, especially his *The Gift of Death*. I need all the help I can get.

I seriously considered going all the way to Singapore from Deer Isle, Maine, standing up before my audience, and saying "I'm sorry if it seems irresponsible of me, but I regret to say that I have not succeeded in preparing a paper for this conference." I would have then left the podium. Doing that was a big temptation. It would have saved me the bother of writing a paper. Moreover, it would have performatively manifested irresponsibility. It would have been performative in two senses: as a speech act and as a staged performance. Instead of that, I ended up, irresponsibly, with a manuscript twice too long to be read in fifty minutes. I read only part of it.

Like speaking for two hours, such an act as saying "I have no paper" and then sitting down would have been grossly irresponsible of me, most people would agree. It would have been a little like John Cage's famous musical composition 4'33", which consisted of four minutes and thirty-three seconds of silence, to which the audience was supposed to listen attentively. Was that silence, punctuated by whatever circumambient noise happened to be around, really music? A lot of any music consists of the silences between movements, sections, phrases, and notes. Silence is an important part of music, indicated by "rests" on the score. "Rest" in this case means the musician takes a rest, not "rest" in the Derridean sense of "remains" I have explored in Chapter 5. Nevertheless, "rest" in the musical sense of silence might be defined as what remains when the music pauses. Cage's performance just gave the silence, the "rest" in all senses, without the interrupting notes. Was that irresponsible of him? At least it performatively (in both senses I have mentioned) made an important point about music. A good bit of most music in any tradition is silence. Music is not all organized noise. To hear a lot of silence is a way of learning that. In a similar way, I might have argued that the best way I could get you to understand irresponsibility would be to perform before your eyes an act of gross irresponsibility, so you could see me in the very moment of getting irresponsible, of "irresponsibilizing" myself.

How do I get irresponsible? How may I, might I, can I, should I, get irresponsible? Please, sir, how do I get irresponsible? I have deliberately chosen a phrase and its musical variations, which sound more or less idiomatic, though nevertheless they also sound a little odd. Any one of them might conceivably be used in ordinary speech, but perhaps not all that often. I have also chosen a phrase using the remarkable English word *get*. Idiomatic sentences using that word hover halfway between active and passive. I claim, by way of this word, that it is hard to decide whether one just passively becomes irresponsible, by some strange, perhaps impersonal, process of irresponsibilization, or whether one has to do something for which one can be held responsible. Which is it? Is it perhaps both?

In English, or at least in American, one says "How do I get to Peoria?" but also "I want to get some chocolate bars" or "I got mugged on the way to the subway," "How did I get to be so old?" or "Get ready!" Recently I saw a T-shirt with the half-ironic exhortation "Git It Done," vernacular for "Get It Done," whatever "it" may be. One might say, when confronted with any difficult task, "Let's get it done." Matthew Arnold, in *Friendship's Garland*, has his imaginary German philosopher, Arminius, no doubt a post-Hegelian, urgently adjure the English to *"Get 'Geist'"* (whatever, exactly, *that* means).[1] Arminius speaks as though the English do not have enough *Geist* now and as though getting more were something they could deliberately decide to do. Many English, and Americans too, remain even today relatively *Geistlos*, without spirit in the sense of a gift for the dangerous irony or wit Arnold so prized and so admirably exemplified in his writing. An example of Arnold's irony is the idea that the English should be told to *"Get 'Geist'"* and that they might conceivably do so.

Somewhat surprisingly, to me at least, Derrida inserted a long and exuberantly perceptive footnote concerning Arnold's *"Get 'Geist'"* in *Of Spirit* (OS, 125–7; DE, 114–16). Derrida comments on the untranslatability not only of German *Geist* but also of English *get*, so the phrase is "Babelian." "By the way [in English in the original]," says Derrida:

> *Get Geist* is barely translatable into French, and not only because of *Geist*, but because of *Get*. *Profoundly* untranslatable [Profondément *intraduisible*] is the hidden profundity of the word *Get* which means *have, become,* and *be,* all three. *Get Geist*: (1) have, obtain, gain, or apprehend (some) *Geist*. (2) Be or become, learn how to become, *yourself, Geist*. And *Geist* then functions as an attribute (become "spirit" as one would say "get mad," "get drunk," "get married," "get lost," "get sick," "get well," or "get better" and as a noun ("get religion," convert yourself)—in short, *become or have, yourself, spirit itself* [devenez ou ayez, vous-même, l'esprit lui-même]. (OS, 126, trans. modified; DE, 115–16)

Derrida's "get mad," "get drunk," "get lost," down to "get religion" are in English in his original French, to indicate their untranslatability. My citation and commentary, in their confusion of languages, are abyssally, profoundly, Babelian. Derrida's examples may be added to my list of locutions in "get," along with his observation that "get" says at one and the same time "have it," "become it," and "be it."

One abbreviation used in emails and in instant messaging by computer adepts is "GAL": "Get a life." The person to whom this ironic command or performative adjuration is addressed is presumably too uptight now to have a life. He or she could, the phrase implies, get a life by deliberately choosing to act differently, in a more relaxed and "cool" fashion. Jesus promised those who forsook father and mother to follow him that they would get a new life, one more abundant, and everlasting to boot (Matt. 19:29; the Bible says "inherit everlasting life"). I have written an essay on what it means to "Get a life" by way of the computer.[2] One final, in this case obscene, use of "get" is "Where can I get laid?" asked by a male in search of a prostitute, as though getting laid is something that passively happens to a man rather than something he does and for which he can be held responsible. Putting it that way has always struck me as an extremely odd and irresponsible locution.

So how do I get irresponsible? Normally, in these secular days, in everyday life and speaking in everyday language, most people, I believe, think of getting irresponsible as some act or other whereby I fail to fulfill a manifest familial, social, ethical, or political responsibility, a clear public obligation that everyone sees and accepts as mine. I ought to do, and I know I ought to do, and everyone else knows I ought to do, something or other, or refrain from doing something or other, and I do otherwise. As Ovid put this, "I see and approve the better course, but I follow the worse [*Video meliora proboque, deteriora sequor*]" (*Metamorphoses*, 8.20.) I fail to show up on time for dinner with my family because I have been out drinking beer with friends, and my wife says, with every justification, "How unpardonably irresponsible of you!" Or I invest in the lottery the weekly wages on which my family depends for food, clothing, and shelter. Everybody I know, the whole circle of my community, my wife, my children, my friends, my employer, those with whom I attend church, condemn me for acting irresponsibly. At the other end of the social scale and the scale of power, many people would condemn as irresponsible, and worse, George W. Bush and more or less the whole U.S. elected and appointed government for deceiving the American people about Saddam Hussein's presumed weapons of mass destruction, launching the Iraq war, which will cost at least two trillion dollars and already over six hundred thousand dead Iraqis, by some counts, and for passing tax breaks for the rich that, taking the two acts together, are running up huge budget deficits that in the long or short run will ruin the U.S. economy. We are, at the moment I am revising this essay (March 3, 2008), either in a recession or on the verge of one. Or the U.S. government can be held unpardonably irresponsible for failing to do anything about our part in causing global warming. Some legislators, as well as other people, still call it "a great hoax." The evidence that global warming is happening and that it is caused by human beings is more or less irrefutable. It is accepted by 99 percent of responsible scientists. It is irresponsible to pretend otherwise, or to keep saying "The evidence is not yet in."

In all these cases (and one can think of innumerable other examples), irresponsibility is defined as some act or other, perhaps a physical act or perhaps a speech act, like a lie, that goes against some manifest and publicly agreed-upon responsible course of action or expected speech. One of

Austin's examples of a speech act situation gone awry is the marriage ceremony in which the bride says "I will not" rather than "I will."[3] That is
irresponsible of her or, perhaps, who knows, the highest act of responsible
refraining from giving herself away. Perhaps she has already given herself,
as we say, to another man. In either case, irresponsibility is an act or
speech that is defined in relation to a clear, responsible way I should act
or speak. "Video meliora proboque, deteriora sequor." I see the better
way, approve of it, and everyone else does too. But I do otherwise. That
makes me get irresponsible.

This simple paradigm is, in my responsible judgment, a drastic oversimplification or, rather, a misreading of the actual human ethical situation. I shall argue, following Derrida and against what most people think
about how to get irresponsible, that the act of acting or speaking responsibly, the act of fulfilling one's obligations to one's neighbor, family, community, nation, or God, leads directly and inevitably to irresponsibility.
Acting responsibly is itself irresponsibilization. The Bible says we should
pray unceasingly. Christopher Smart, the great mad eighteenth-century
English poet, caused much trouble to those around him by taking that
injunction seriously. Smart was in the habit of falling on his knees in the
streets of London and publicly praying. Samuel Johnson, in a memorable
response, said he would as lief pray with Kit Smart as with any other man.
What, exactly, is prayer? How would I know I am praying? Can I ever
know whether or not my prayers are answered? Is prayer by definition
solitary, a direct and private address to the deity? Is it responsible to ask
God for help, or will I act more responsibly if I depend on myself alone?
Does such a thing as public or collective prayer exist? How is it different
from private prayer?[4] Derrida, as I mentioned in Chapter 4, devotes a long
section of the eighth seminar of "The Beast and the Sovereign (Two)" to
the question of prayer. Families that pray together stay together. Was
Smart acting responsibly when he blocked traffic and made a spectacle of
himself by praying publicly? Would Johnson have been acting responsibly
if, as he suggests he might have done, he had fallen on his own creaky
knees beside Smart and joined him in praying?

To shift to another example and to speak (irresponsibly) of a fictive
character as though she were a real person, did Sethe, in Toni Morrison's
Beloved, act responsibly when she cut her beloved baby daughter's throat
with a handsaw to prevent her from being taken back into slavery? In all
these cases, I shall argue, the person made himself or herself irresponsible
by acting responsibly, in a strange act of irresponsibilization.

Is it unforgivably irresponsible of me to talk about a fictional character as if she were a real person? Christopher Smart and Samuel Johnson were flesh and blood people. Though now long dead, they once walked (and prayed) in the streets of London. Belief in their once bodily existence is based on more or less irrefutable historical evidence. Morrison's Sethe is based on a historical personage, true enough, though Morrison changed the historical facts in crucial ways, as a novelist is privileged to do. Just what does it mean, in any case, to say "based on a historical personage"? Sethe is, despite that relation to history, a fictional construction, a virtual person created through language. She can be met only on the pages of *Beloved*. The words about Sethe are references without referent, like literary language in general.

It is irresponsible to confuse kinds. Derrida's chief example in *The Gift of Death* of what he calls "irresponsibilization" is Abraham's willingness to sacrifice his beloved son Isaac in response to Jehovah's secret command. I shall discuss this later on. What is the difference between these three kinds: a historical example, a literary example, and an example from a sacred text like Genesis? Derrida, in the second essay in *The Gift of* Death, "Literature in Secret: An Impossible Filiation," distinguishes more or less sharply between a sacred text and a literary text, though asserting their "impossible filiation" and seeing each as always contaminated by the other. What is the difference among these three kinds of writing? I need to know, since it would be irresponsible to confuse them.

On the one hand, a literary text, such as *Beloved*, is referentiality without reference. As Derrida puts this in "Literature in Secret":

> Every text that is consigned to public space, that is relatively legible or intelligible, but whose content, sense, referent, signatory, and addressee are not fully determinable *realities*—realities that are at the same time *non-fictive* or *immune from all fiction* [*des* réalités *pleinement déterminables, des réalités à la fois* non-fictives *ou* pures de toute fiction], realities that are delivered as such, by some intuition, to a determinate judgment—can become a *literary* object. (GD2, 131; DM, 173, 175)

A literary text hangs in the air, like something unearthly, revealing itself in a flash, in an instant of illumination, and then disappearing, like a meteorite, to borrow Derrida's metaphor (GD2, 132–33, 139–40; DM, 177–78; 185–86). It is impossible to be sure, for a text taken as literature, who is the signatory, who is speaking, to whom, and just what is being said. I say "taken as" because, as Derrida often asserts, nothing identifiable in grammar, diction, syntax, or rhetoric distinguishes a literary text from a referential one, such as a newspaper story. Any text can be taken as literature, though it might in some cases seem perverse to do so. A literary text keeps its secrets, whereas you can, at least hypothetically, find out whether the newspaper account is lying or not by checking it against extra-textual facts. It is impossible to do that with literature. For Derrida, this connection of literature with the secret, "if there is one" (as he often says), is fundamental, as many assertions by him attest. Here is one categorical assertion. Speaking of the enigmatic phrase he uses as a leitmotif in "Literature in Secret," "Pardon for not meaning [*Pardon de ne pas vouloir dire*]," Derrida says: "And being up in the air is what it keeps its secret of, the secret of a secret which is perhaps not one, and which, because of that fact, announces literature" (GD2, 132; DM, 176). If you cannot figure it out, decipher its secret, or even tell for sure whether or not it hides a secret, it must be literature.

On the other hand, a sacred text, such as the story of Abraham and Isaac in Genesis or the infinitely moving story of Mary Magdalene's recognition of the risen Christ in the Book of John, is, fundamentalist believers assume, historical fact. These events really happened. We know they really happened because the accounts of them are the word of God. Moses may have written the Pentateuch, which includes Genesis, but he wrote it at God's dictation. God guarantees the historical truth of the Abraham and Isaac story and the rest of the Bible. "Jesus loves me. This I know. / 'Cause the Bible tells me so," as the hymn I was taught in Sunday School as a child puts it. Jesus' disciple John wrote the Book of John, so believers assume, as an act of bearing responsible witness to what really happened and what he knows really happened.

Derrida nevertheless asserts an "impossible filiation" between literature and the Bible. What is the connection, the filiation, the sonship, the affiliation? The answer is that both depend absolutely on the secret. No one among the human characters in the story, including Abraham, has any way of knowing just what was in Jehovah's mind when he spoke to Abraham, just what was his motive or intent in demanding that Abraham sacrifice Isaac. Abraham in his turn, as the sacred text affirms, keeps both Jehovah's command and his (Abraham's) intention to obey it secret from his wife Sarah, from the rest of his family and retinue, and from the destined lamb for the sacrifice, his beloved only son, Isaac. Kierkegaard, in *Fear and Trembling*, makes much of Abraham's silence. Jehovah is "wholly other." He cannot be fathomed. He keeps his secrets. Abraham keeps his secrets too. The Abraham and Isaac story is a story of secrets, in the strict sense of the secret as something hidden that may not by any means be told.

Literature, however, if Derrida is right, even a strange linguistic mete-orite like "Pardon de ne pas vouloir dire," taken as literature, also depends on the secret and keeps its secrets. The difference is that literature illicitly borrows from Scripture in order to compose secular texts, as religious peo-ple call them. Secular texts, what we call literature—novels, poems, and plays—exploit the possibility of writing in such a way that the words hang in the air and keep an impenetrable secret or secrets. After having said that a mark of literature is that it hides its secret, Derrida goes on to ask:

> Literature? At least that which, for several centuries, we have been calling literature, what is called literature, in Europe, but within a tradition that cannot not be inherited from the Bible, drawing its sense of forgiveness from it while at the same time asking forgiveness for betraying it [*y puissant son sens du pardon mais lui demandant à la fois pardon de la trahit*]. That is why I am here inscribing the question of secrecy as the secret of literature under the seemingly improbable sign of an Abrahamic origin. As though the es-sence of literature, in its strict sense, in the sense that this Western word retains in the West, were essentially descended from Abrahamic rather than Greek culture. (GD2, 132; DM, 176–77)

Derrida says "Abrahamic" rather than "biblical" to be faithful to his claim that all three "religions of the Book," Judaism, Islam, and Christianity, depend equally and absolutely on the Abraham and Isaac story as their enigmatic foundation. All three, it follows, would have the same concep-tion of literature. This is a quite specific historical and cultural assertion. It supports Derrida's claim about the "impossible filiation" of literature and the Bible.

It is perhaps worth noting, in passing, that this would disqualify any conception of "world literature" that assumes the word *literature* is univo-cal and means the same thing when applied to Chinese or Indian poetry as it does when applied to *Hamlet*, "Tintern Abbey," or *Bleak House*. It would be irresponsible to assume such univocity. Considerable conse-quences for pedagogy, in these days of globalization and the proliferation of textbooks and courses in world literature, would follow from this heterogeneity.

Derrida's cryptic phrase "Pardon de ne pas vouloir dire" is more or less untranslatably idiomatic, resonant, and full of shimmering contradictory implications. It may mean "I beg your pardon for not meaning anything" but also "I beg pardon for not wishing to speak." *Vouloir dire* literally means "to wish to say," but it really, strangely enough, means "means" in French. *Je veux dire* so and so means "I mean so and so." Derrida proffers his odd phrase as a miniature example of literature. The word *pardon* in the phrase suggests, according to Derrida, that literature, as the betrayal of Scripture, sacred texts, the Bible, must continually, in one way or another, beg pardon (from whom? from God? from constituted authorities? from the reader?) for falsely imitating Scripture, for pretending to be what it is not. Or, on the contrary, literature must beg pardon just because it does, blasphemously, succeed in being Scripture, in hiding secrets just as Scripture does.

The first great text in the vernacular in Western early modernity, Dante's *The Divine Comedy*, great-grandfather of its filial descendents, all those works of modern Western literature, both does and does not pretend to be Scripture, or like Scripture. In the "Letter to Can Grande,"⁵ Dante discusses allegory but does not make it clear whether he means *The Divine Comedy* to be taken as what used to be called "allegory of the theologians" or as "allegory of the poets." Dante scholars have been arguing ever since about which *The Divine Comedy* is. On the one hand, in the letter Dante defines allegory in the traditional four-level way that definition was used to read the Bible. He affirms that the *Comedy* should be read the same way. On the other hand, he also refers to Horace and to medieval poetic genre theory in describing it as a "comedy," that is, as a form of poetry. He says that in the *Comedy* "The form or the mode of treatment is poetic, fictive, descriptive, digressive, transumptive; and along with this definitive, divisive, probative, improbative, and setting examples [*Forma sive modus tractandi est poeticus, fictivus, descriptivus, digressivus, transumptivus; et cum hoc definitivus, divisivus, probativus, improbativus, et exemplorum positivus*]." If the form is poetic and fictive, however "transumptive," it can hardly be like Scripture, which is assumed to be, at the first level, literal, representational truth. On the first hand, again, Dante cites Paul in Corinthians 2 12:2–4, as if it applies to the pilgrim-protagonist in the *Comedy*: "I know a man . . . (whether in the body, or out of the body, I know not; God knoweth), caught up to the third heaven . . . , and [he saw secret things of God], which it is not granted to man to utter." (I cite the translation of Dante's Vulgate Latin, not the King James Bible.) The "man" here is no doubt Paul himself, however much he demurs in 12:5: "Of such an one will I glory: yet of myself I will not glory, but in mine infirmities" (King James version). But who is the protagonist, "actor," or "agent" of the *Comedy*? Is it Dante himself or a poetic, fictive invention? Everything hangs on the answer to this question. Here the "Letter to Can Grande" is ambiguous. Dante refers to the protagonist or agent as "he," for example, in saying of the speaker in the poem "he says [*dicit*]." Who is this "he"? Dante says, "The agent (protagonist), then, of the whole as well as the part is he who has been mentioned, and throughout he will be seen to be [*Agens igitur totius et partis est ille qui dictus est, et totaliter videtur esse*]." Translating *agens* as "protagonist" strikes me as a little hazardous. The reader looks in vain, however, for any previous identification or definition of the "agent," though he has been mentioned in passing as the same person in the *Paradiso* as in the *Inferno* and the *Purgatorio*. It might be argued that the title Dante gives his poem in the "Letter to Can Grande" indicates that the protagonist is Dante himself and that the poet is describing his own actual visionary experiences: "Begins the Comedy of Dante Alighieri, Florentine in birth, not in custom [*Incipit Comoedia Dantis Alagherii, Florentini natione, non moribus*]." The fatal ambiguity of the little word "of," or of the possessive in Latin, means that the title may mean "by Dante," "concerning Dante," or both. I conclude that the question is undecidable. The "Letter" does not give a firm textual basis for a decision.

The great Dante scholar Charles S. Singleton, who can be presumed to have known better than I do about these matters, claims the *Comedy* must be allegory of the theologians and therefore, so to speak, a form of Scripture, not poetry, like, say, Wordsworth's *The Prelude*, also a long autobiographical poem. No one, to my knowledge, has claimed *The Prelude* is Scripture, though why not? A good case could be made. In the case of *The Divine Comedy*, in my judgment it is impossible to choose, for a reason that is intrinsic to the question of the text's validity. On the one hand, unless the experiences Dante's pilgrim claims to have had really happened, in visionary reality, the poem loses all validity. Who cares what Dante Alighieri imagined, on his own hook, so to speak, hell, purgatory, and heaven to be like? That would make *The Divine Comedy* an early example of science fiction, which perhaps it is. On the other hand, if *The Divine Comedy* is granted, uniquely among texts in modern Western vernaculars, status as allegory of the theologians, then it is a blasphemous imitation of the unique, the one and only sacred text, the Bible. Secular literature, as the faithful-unfaithful son of Scripture, is permeated by this aporia.

The Abraham and Isaac story in Genesis and Morrison's *Beloved* are two quite different uses of language, though strangely affiliated. That seems clear enough. Matters are made somewhat more complicated, however, by a feature of the Abraham and Isaac story that Derrida (so far as I had remembered when I began to write this essay) nowhere mentions in all his lengthy analysis in *The Gift of Death* of the story and of Kierkegaard's analysis of it in *Fear and Trembling*. Derrida emphasizes that Jehovah's eternal secret from Abraham and Abraham's silence, his eternal secret from his family and from Isaac, are essential to the event. The biblical text, however, does give away both secrets by writing them down. Readers over the centuries of all three of the religions of the Book have been in on the secret. The reader is told that "God did tempt Abraham" (Gen. 22:1), something he does not say to Abraham himself, though after the event God tells Abraham that "because thou hast done this thing, and hast not withheld thy son, thine only son"(Gen. 22:16) he will hyperbolically bless him and all his descendents and give them great power and sovereignty:

> And the Angel of the LORD called unto Abraham out of heaven the second time, And said, By myself have I sworn, saith the LORD, for because thou hast done this thing, and hast not withheld thy son, thine only son: That in blessing I will bless thee, and in multiplying I will multiply thy seed as the stars of the heaven, and as the sand which is upon the sea shore; and thy seed shall possess the gate of his enemies; And in thy seed shall all the nations of the earth be blessed; because thou hast obeyed my voice. (Gen. 22:15–18)

Wow! That is quite a promise! The careful reader will note at least two peculiarities of this text, at least in the King James translation. First, in Genesis 22:1 God speaks directly to Abraham. In the verses just quoted, it is the Angel of the Lord as intermediary who speaks to Abraham, even though he speaks in the first person, as Jehovah. *Angel*, etymologically, means "messenger," from Greek *angelos*. Why the change? Can it be that we mortals, even Abraham, can, at least some of the time, only hear the voice of God indirectly, by way of some intermediary, some messenger of the word of God, an angel, or Moses, or whoever wrote Genesis? Second, Jehovah explicitly gives away an oath that he says he has secretly sworn for himself alone. He says, "By myself I have sworn." This is another way this text gives secrets away. God's oath is a speech act. For mortals, a felicitous speech act must be in some way publicly attested, and it must be based on something outside itself, a sovereign authority, as when someone swears an oath with her or his hand on the Bible. A secret engagement to marry is no valid alliance. Perhaps only God, or a god, can felicitously swear an oath in secret or swear an oath "by himself," on his own, not basing the oath on anything outside he who swears it.

It is true that the biblical text says nothing whatsoever about what went on in Abraham's mind. The Bible reader, however, is told that God called out Abraham's name and that Abraham answered, "Behold, here I am" (Gen. 22:1). Abraham keeps absolutely silent about this exchange both to his wife Sarah and to Isaac, the destined sacrificial lamb, just as only the reader of the Bible knows what Abraham said to Isaac when Isaac asked, "where is the lamb for a burnt offering?" (Gen. 22:7): "And Abraham said, My son, God will provide himself a lamb for a burnt offering" (Gen. 22:8). This is a wonderful double irony, since Abraham tells Isaac the truth without divulging the truth, whereas, though it is a secret from Abraham at that moment, God does provide a lamb for the burnt offering in the form of a ram caught by its horns in a nearby thicket.

Some of my sympathy goes out to the ram, by the way, which might well have said "Why does it have to be me?" Derrida looks at the story from the ram's perspective in "Rams": "One imagines the anger of Abraham's and Aaron's ram, the infinite revolt of the ram of all holocausts. But also, figuratively, the violent rebellion of all scapegoats, all substitutes. Why me? [*Pourquoi moi?*]" (R, 157; B, 65). Some biblical scholars claim that this story marks the immemorial moment of the shift from human sacrifice to animal sacrifice.

The Bible does not say that Abraham, or Isaac, or the two young men Abraham brought with him, ever said anything to anyone about this strange double event. Abraham, at Jehovah's command, raised his knife over Isaac's throat. No reader can doubt that he would have fulfilled God's command. Abraham then stayed his hand and substituted the ram at the command of the Angel of the Lord. Abraham and Isaac kept all this secret. We only know about it because someone—God, or Moses as amanuensis of God, or whoever wrote Genesis, betrayed the secret, gave the secret away, as we say, and told the story on which the three great religions of the Book are based. Anyone who can read the Bible in any language or who can hear the story read aloud in church can know the secret that even Abraham did not completely know.

Though I thought I had seen something in the biblical text that Derrida missed, I was wrong, as I might have expected. In a forceful passage in "Literature in Secret," Derrida compares Kafka's "Letter to His Father" to the Abraham and Isaac story. Kafka never meant his letter to be seen by his father, or by anyone else. It was imaginary, a fiction, a literary work meant to remain secret. One remembers that Kafka commanded his friend Max Brod to destroy all his manuscripts after his (Kafka's) death, something happily (or unhappily) Brod did not do. Kafka thought they were "failures," which in a sense they are, both in the sense of being ultimately inscrutable and in the sense of often being incomplete. Kafka's "Letter to His Father" contains a fiction within a fiction, an imaginary letter from the father to the son holding the son responsible for all his own troubles and for the father's troubles too. Derrida takes evident pleasure in formulating the vertiginous exchanges of imaginary accusations and pardons. The son imagines the father pardoning him for his transgressions in a fiction within a fiction, but this is really Kafka pardoning himself for, or accusing himself of, forever unpardonable filial ingratitude. All this, however, is done in secret, in a letter that Kafka had no intention of sending to his father and no intention of having published so all the world could read this amazing fiction or literary work. In a similar way, it is only by a kind of accident that Jehovah's secrets, Abraham's secrets, and Isaac's secrets are given away, turned, one might even argue, into literature and published in innumerable languages where all who can may read. Here is what Derrida says. The brief segment (GD2, 143–45; DM, 191–92) should be responsibly read and commented on at length, but I, more or less irresponsibly, cite only the essential sentences of the comparison, and I cite them in English translation, with only a little of Derrida's French:

> this secret letter becomes literature, in the literality of its letter(s), only once it exposes itself and risks becoming something public and publishable, an archive to be inherited, still a phenomenon, one of inheritance, or a will that Kafka doesn't destroy. For, as in the sacrifice of Isaac, which took place without witnesses, or whose only surviving witness was the son, namely a chosen beneficiary who saw his father's tortured visage at the moment he lifted the knife over him, it all comes down to us only in the trace left by an inheritance, a trace that remains legible but equally illegible. This trace left behind, this legacy, also represents, whether by design or by unconscious imprudence, the chance or risk of becoming a testamentary utterance within a literary corpus, becoming literary just by being left behind [*la chance ou le risque de devenir une parole testamentaire dans un corpus littéraire, devenant littéraire par cet abandon même*]. (GD2, 144; DM, 191)

Does writing down God's, Abraham's, and Isaac's secrets, "abandoning" them to public language, necessarily and inevitably turn the story into literature? It is not entirely easy to answer that question, as Derrida's formulations indicate. It is only "a chance" or "a risk." Derrida stresses the way literature depends upon making public a text that has meaning but that is detached from any ascertainable referent. The Bible makes the Abraham and Isaac story public, therefore, perhaps, turning it into literature.

Matters are not quite so simple, however. One distinction between the Bible and secular literature is that the later is freely open to translation into any language, whatever the losses may be in doing that, whereas the former was for centuries kept in the original languages and was considered by the Roman Catholic Church to be bound to those languages, as though we know for sure that Jehovah spoke Hebrew. Theologians puzzled for centuries over that question. This notion of sacred languages holds, however, even though the Book of Acts asserts that the worldwide spread of Christianity depends on the gift of tongues bestowed on the apostles at Pentecost. This gave them the ability to spread the Word everywhere in every language. God's Word, the Gospel, the Good News that the Messiah has come, was, the New Testament implies, translatable without loss into any language. In an analogous way, American book publishers, even "academic" ones, tend to assume that anything, including all literary works, can be translated into English without loss. For Roman Catholicism, nevertheless, Hebrew (or Aramaic), and Koinē Greek were viewed as the only faithful carriers of the word of God, with Latin translations having a secondary authority. That meant the Bible was unreadable by all but the learned, in effect, the priests and clergy. Mass was said in Latin, a language many members of the congregation did not understand.

Only within my lifetime have Masses been allowed to be said in the vernacular. For many ordinary parishioners, for almost two thousand years, it could be said that the Bible and the Mass were, as the adage has it, "Greek to them." The faithful had to take it on trust that the priests were truthful reporters in their (sometimes) vernacular sermons of what the Bible says. The great revolution performed by the Protestant Reformation was not only a new stress on the direct relation between the believer and God, bypassing the intermediaries of all those priests, saints, and icons, but also the systematic translation of the Bible into all the world's vernaculars, so any literate person could read the Bible for herself or himself. Those vernacular versions included, signally, Luther's great German translation, but also the early English translations, including the Wycliffe Bible, Tyndale's Bible, the "Breeches" Bible, and ultimately the King James Bible, from which I have been making my citations, for I am not a learned man.

If we think of the Abraham and Isaac story for a moment as "literature" in our ordinary Western sense of the word, then it has that peculiarity essential to literary narrative that the storyteller knows more than the characters do, even implausibly more. An example from literature proper is the episode in *Remembrance of Things Past* in which Proust's narrator, Marcel, is endowed with miraculous knowledge of what was going on in Bergotte's mind at the moment of his death.[6] Bergotte is the distinguished writer in Proust's novel. Bergotte dies in a Paris museum, sitting on a bench looking at the little patch of yellow wall in Jan Vermeer's great painting *View of Delft* and thinking that he must make his own writing style more like that, more chaste and pure.

Marcel claims to know what Bergotte was thinking and feeling even though he was not there. He would not have been able to penetrate Bergotte's mind even if he had been present. It is certainly irresponsible of Marcel to pretend to secret knowledge he could not possibly have had. It is, moreover, one might argue, irresponsible of Proust, by a "literary fiction," to ascribe to his narrator such knowledge. Only Bergotte knew what he was thinking at the moment of his death, as he looked at the great Vermeer, and he took that secret to the grave.

The convention of free indirect discourse in third person narration presupposes the quite implausible transparency of the characters' minds to the narrator's clairvoyance. This is so even though the characters are not shown as being aware that the narrator is spying on them. Literature and the Bible may keep their secrets, but they also abundantly, and perhaps irresponsibly, give those secrets away. The reader of Genesis knows more than Sarah or Isaac knew, even more than Abraham knew. If we think of the Genesis story as being written by Moses under Jehovah's dictation, then a reasonable explanation for how the text knows all those secrets is given. It still remains, nevertheless, an impenetrable secret as to why Jehovah would have chosen to make public, where anybody can read them, the secrets that, if Derrida is right, remain eternally occult, hidden by the silence of God and by the echoing silence of Abraham. Jesus promised his disciples, in his explanation of the parable of the sower, that they would learn God's secrets. The disciples ask, "Why speakest thou unto them in parables?" And Jesus answers: "Because it is given unto you to know the mysteries of the kingdom of heaven, but to them it is not given" (Matt. 13:10–11). A little later Matthew says, echoing Psalms 49:4 and 78:2: "All these things spake Jesus unto the multitude in parables; and without a parable spake he not to them: That it might be fulfilled which was spoken by the prophet, saying, I will open my mouth in parables; I will utter things which have been kept secret from the foundation of the world" (Matt. 13:34–35). The New Testament, and especially the parables of Jesus, can be defined as giving away the secrets that the Old Testament had already kept secret by giving them away, for example, in the readable/unreadable story of Abraham and Isaac in Genesis.

Thinking of all this boggles the mind just a little, my mind at least. Does giving away God's secrets, along with Abraham's and Isaac's, make the Abraham and Isaac story literature? It would be grossly irresponsible of me to say so. Courses in "The Bible as Literature" are taught with the best will in the world and do much good. Nevertheless, they are subject to a double danger: either to smuggle in too much religion along with the "literature" or to falsify the Bible by treating it as if it were merely a literary text, not sacred Scripture, which makes special demands on the reader. But how can you, or should you, avoid doing both if you read the Bible stories seriously?

And yet . . . and yet . . . I believe Derrida is right to say that all Occidental literature is the unfaithful or perjuring son of the Bible. This means literature uses the Bible's ways of storytelling. All allegory of the poets is perhaps a guilty, unpardonable form of allegory of the theologians. Dante irresponsibilized himself when he walked into this double bind by writing *The Divine Comedy*, even though the *Comedy*, like all Western literature, has an "impossible filiation" to Scripture.

Well, How Then Can I Get Irresponsible?

With these examples of responsible irresponsibility in mind, I ask again my guiding question: How can it be that one gets irresponsible by acting responsibly? I had thought, once more, of, irresponsibly, stopping just here, after this long prolegomenon, still on the threshold of coming clean about irresponsibility. However, since I am, of course, nothing if not scrupulously responsible, I shall continue. I shall continue by trying to show how one gets irresponsible, how one irresponsibilizes oneself. I shall get help from Derrida, especially his *The Gift of Death*, already more than once cited, just as I have used Ovid to help me express the ordinary conception of irresponsibility. I need all the help I can get.

Is it irresponsible of me to use Derrida in this way, to speak for myself by way of using Derrida's words and argument, as though they were my own? How can I responsibly, in conscience, as we say, sign with my own name a chapter that owes so much to his thought and writing? I answer that my excuse is that I am only following Derrida's own practice. All that he says so eloquently and persuasively about irresponsibilization in *The Gift of Death* is said in commentary on, often more or less in paraphrase of, what had already been said by the contemporary Czech philosopher Jan Patočka, in his *Heretical Essays on the Philosophy of History*,[7] and by Kierkegaard in *Fear and Trembling*. It is as though Derrida were possessed by their ghosts and speaks for them, like a spirit medium. Derrida is so dependent on Patočka and Kierkegaard that at one point he feels obliged to draw himself up and assert his heretical difference from Patočka's heresy: "What I have said might seem faithful to the spirit of Patočka's heresy at the same time that it is heretical with respect to that very heresy" (GD, 27; DM, 47). This is an odd moment. Does Derrida protest too much? Does he reveal in *The Gift of Death*, perhaps inadvertently or unconsciously, his own irresponsibility? At the end of the paragraph from which I have just cited, Derrida relates this "heresy" regarding Patočka to the necessity of an odd sort of irresponsibility in the heart of responsibility: "there is no responsibility without a dissident and inventive rupture with respect to tradition, authority, orthodoxy, rule, or doctrine" (GD, 27; DM, 47). He says more or less the same thing in *Specters of Marx* about his reading of Marx, in a passage cited at greater length in Chapter 5 of this book: "This dimension of a performative interpretation, that is, of an interpretation that transforms the very thing it interprets, will play an indispensable role in what I would like to say this evening" (SMe, 51; SMf, 89). Though I do not lay claim to anything at all like Derrida's inventive rigor, I am prepared to say the same thing as Derrida says about his heresy in relation to Patočka, concerning my saying again in my own words what Derrida already has said about what Patočka and Kierkegaard have already said about what the Bible (in the case of Kierkegaard) has already said. I am, I claim, inevitably speaking for myself, however hard I try to be no more than faithful to what Derrida said. What I say is, no doubt, another case of performative interpretation. Even an exact repetition alters what it repeats, at the very least with a soupçon of irony or by way of the violence involved in wresting a citation out of its context.

Is it unforgivably irresponsible of me to speak about Derrida, Patočka, Kierkegaard, and the Bible in claiming to speak for myself, or can I, or anyone else, for that matter, perhaps never do otherwise? Are we perhaps condemned to speak for ourselves by respeaking the words of the other or the words of an interminable string of others, going back to vanish somewhere near the "things which have been kept secret from the foundation of the world" that Jesus claimed to expose (Matt. 13:35)? I shall therefore cheerfully and somewhat defiantly, responsibly and irresponsibly at once, sign this essay with my own name.

Derrida may allude to this double bind in the first of my epigraphs: "My signature is the moment of highest responsibility in a deep irresponsibility." As the surrounding context in *A Taste for the Secret* makes clear, signing my name to a contract or to something I have written is the moment of highest responsibility because it is a way of saying: "I wrote this. I take responsibility for doing so, along with all its consequences, whatever they may be, and however unpredictable and unintended they may be." At the same time, because my signature implicitly claims, falsely, that I am one unified person, ego, or consciousness and that I go on perdurably remaining the same person from moment to moment, day to day, month to month, year to year, throughout my whole life, my signature is an act of "deep irresponsibility" because it makes an illicit claim that I am one I. "The other is in me before me: the ego (even the collective ego) implies alterity as its own condition," says Derrida in the sentences in *A Taste for the Secret* leading up to the citation I have made in the epigraph. "There is no 'I' that ethically makes room for the other, but rather an 'I' that is structured by the alterity within it, an 'I' that is itself in a state of self-deconstruction, of dislocation. . . . I am not the proprietor of my 'I,' I am not proprietor of the place open to hospitality. Whoever gives hospitality ought to know that he is not even proprietor of what he would appear to give. The case of the signature is analogous: usually interpreted as one's very own mark, it is instead what I cannot appropriate, cannot make my own" (TS, 84, 85). Then follows my epigraph. If Derrida is right, then who do I think I am, at this moment, to claim to be signing responsibly for all that congeries of heterogeneous other people I am from time to time, as I speak through, or am spoken through, ventriloquized, by a swarm of others: the Bible, Kierkegaard, Kafka, Patočka, and, especially, Derrida? This is a Babelian babble of confused voices in different languages—Hebrew, Danish, German, Czech, and French—all speaking at once, through me, though in English translation. This happens by a form of speaking in tongues that can be called mechanical, prosthetic, mediatic, or mediumistic—all those printed translations on my bookshelves. Speaking or writing at all is a way to get irresponsible by becoming multiple, legion.

Well, just what in the world does Derrida mean by "irresponsibilization"? Or by saying, as my second epigraph from Derrida puts it: "The ethical can therefore end up making us irresponsible [*L'éthique peut donc être destinée à irrresponsibiliser*]" (GD, 61; DM, 89)? I return once more to that initial question. *Irresponsibiliser* and *irresponsibilisation* are not French words, at least not in my *Petit Robert: Dictionnaire de la Langue Française*, though Derrida uses both. Their English cognates also do not exist in any dictionary I know, not even in the *Oxford English Dictionary*, though "irresponsibleness" is given in the latter and defined as "the quality of being irresponsible, irresponsibility." Is using those words irresponsible of Derrida? Does he commit an act of irresponsibility toward the French language, which he so often claims so much to respect? He says it is the only language that is his, though, as he also says, it is not his, but that of the French colonizers of Algeria. The reason Derrida needs these words must be that he wants to move from calling irresponsibility the quality of being irresponsible, or calling irresponsible the quality of an act, to making irresponsibility the *result* of an act, sometimes perhaps a speech act, an act that is in any case explicitly defined as ethical. I make myself irresponsible by acting responsibly, in an act of auto-irresponsibilization. What in the world does this mean? How does it happen that I irresponsibilize myself in the act of making an ethical choice or behaving ethically?

The word or the concept of irresponsibilization appears in four related registers, strata, or sediments in *The Gift of Death*. All derive from, or are at least apparently special to, Occidental culture, with its twin roots in Greece and Palestine. These four forms of irresponsibilization appear to come in historical sequence from pre-Platonic mystery religions or Dionysiac religions, religions that seek or endure spirit possession, to the daylight of Platonic dialectic and the birth of individual human ethical responsibility in the West, to the biblical disqualification of Greek and Roman philosophy, to present-day, everyday, ordinary, post-Enlightenment acts of taking responsibility or performing apparently ethically responsible acts that may not, at least in appearance, have or need any religious sanction at all for their validity, for the way I have "done the right thing." An example, a scandalous example to some, that Derrida proffers is feeding and caring for my pet cat, surely an innocently responsible way of doing the right thing.

Nevertheless, in spite of this four-stage historicity in Western ethical history, Derrida indicates that the first stage does not disappear in the next stage, the Dionysiac in the Platonic, nor any of the previous stages in any of the later ones, but that all the previous ones are mysteriously, secretly, perhaps disastrously or ruinously, perhaps happily, present in each successive stage after the first. Derrida, following Patočka, puts this afterlife, this survival, under the psychoanalytical aegis of the terms *incorporation* and *repression*, and under the aegis of the Platonic, Christian, political, and Heideggerian term *conversion*. "The word 'conversion,'" says Derrida, "is regularly rendered [by Patočka] by such words as 'turning back' (*obrácení*, 114) or 'about turn' (*obrat*, 115–17).⁸ The history of secrecy [*du secret*], the combined history of responsibility and of the gift, has the spiral form of these turns [*tours*], intricacies [*tournures*], versions, turnings back, bends [*virages*], and conversions. One could compare it to a history of revolutions, even to history as revolution" (GD, 8; DM, 23).

Nevertheless, as the historical line spirals back on itself in continual revolutionary conversions, each new turn does not lose entirely the previous ones. Each new circling carries within itself all the previous ones, in either incorporation or conversion, as Derrida eloquently asserts:

> Historical conversions to responsibility, such as Patočka analyzes in both cases, well describe this movement by which the event of a second mystery does not destroy the first. On the contrary, it keeps it inside unconsciously, after having effected a topical displacement and a hierarchical subordination: one secret is at the same time enclosed and dominated by the other. Platonic mystery thus *incorporates* orgiastic mystery and Christian mystery *represses* Platonic mystery. (GD, 9; DM, 25–26)

What does it mean for my question about irresponsibilization to say that the orgiastic is nevertheless retained as incorporation in the Platonic turning from the dark cave of the mystery religions to the sunlight of the soul's gathering itself into itself responsibility and ascending to the sun of the Good? What does it mean for irresponsibilization to say that the Platonic, including its incorporated orgiastic remnant, is retained as repression in the *mysterium tremendum* of the Christian mystery? It means that an element of irresponsibility is present in all these historical turns. What irresponsibility? It is the irresponsibility of orgiastic ecstasy. In the orgiastic I am taken out of myself, am put "beside myself," as we say, and am no longer responsible for what I say or do. I get irresponsible. Who can blame me for what I do when I am in a trance, am possessed, or am in a Dionysiac frenzy? Socrates had his *daemon*, who (or "which"—which is it?) gave him orders in dreams: " 'Socrates,' it [the dream] said, 'make music and work at it.' "[9] Abraham was ordered by Jehovah to do the most irresponsible and hideous act imaginable, to kill his beloved only son, in a return of the repressed orgiastic in Old Testament religious mystery, just as Jesus, speaking as the Son of God, as a member of the Trinity, said to his followers: "And everyone that hath forsaken houses, or brethren, or sisters, or father, or mother, or wife, or children, or lands, for my name's sake, shall receive an hundredfold, and shall inherit everlasting life" (Matt. 19:29). All Christian believers must pass the test God set for Abraham. All Christians must repeat Abraham's willingness to sacrifice Isaac and abnegate all family alliances and responsibilities. One must choose. Either family and social responsibilities or Jesus. Jesus was pretty clear about this. Similar admonitions are repeated in all the first three Gospel accounts. Few nominal, church-going Christians, at least to my knowledge, follow Christ's clear command. Christianity, moreover, is explicitly defined as the rejection of both Judaism and of Greek philosophy. As Paul says in 1 Corinthians 1:23: "But we preach Christ crucified, unto the Jews a stumbling block, and unto the Greeks foolishness."

Patočka sees authentic religion, by which he means Christianity, as fundamentally requiring a sense of the responsible self. "In the proper sense of the word," says Derrida, speaking for Patočka and for himself at the same time:

> religion exists [*il y a religion*] once the secret of the sacred, orgiastic, or demonic mystery has been, if not destroyed, at least dominated, integrated, and finally subjected to the sphere of responsibility. . . . "The demonic is to be related to responsibility; in the beginning such a relation did not exist" (Patočka, 110). In other words, the demonic is originally defined as irresponsibility, or, if one wishes, as nonresponsibility. (GD, 2, 3, trans. modified; DM, 16–17, 17)

If the second turn is the replacement of orgiastic prereligion with Platonism, though the orgiastic is still incorporated in Platonism, and the third turn is the repression of the Platonic in Christianity, though it is still retained in repressed form, what is the fourth conversion or *Kehre*?

The fourth turn of the screw is the turning of the previous three stages into secular Enlightenment ethics of intersubjective, familial, civic, and political responsibility, with its accompanying notion of irresponsibility. About this fourth stage I shall speak in a moment. Here is Derrida's most succinct account of the first three as Patočka (and Derrida as ventriloquist for Patočka) see them:

> The history of the responsible self [*moi responsible*] is built upon the heritage and *patrimony* of secrecy, through a chain reaction of ruptures and repressions that assure the very tradition they punctuate with their interruptions. Plato breaks with orgiastic mystery and installs a first experience based on the notion of responsibility, but there remains something of demonic mystery and thaumaturgy, as well as some of responsibility's corresponding political dimension, in Platonism as in Neoplatonism. Then comes the *mysterium tremendum* of the responsible Christian [*du chrétien responsible*], second tremor in the genesis of responsibility as a history of secrecy. (GD, 7, trans. modified; DM, 22–23)

The third and fourth turns, however, are investigated most extensively, in *The Gift of Death*, not by way of Patočka's *Heretical Essays* but, in the last two chapters of the book, by way of the Abraham and Isaac story in

Genesis and by way of Kierkegaard's reading of that story in *Fear and Trembling*. Derrida reads Kierkegaard reading Genesis. I read Derrida reading Kierkegaard reading Genesis. It is in these chapters that Derrida discovers or invents the word *irresponsibilization*. I focus on chapter 3, "À qui donner (savoir ne pas savoir)," translated by David Wills as "Whom to Give to (Knowing Not to Know)" (GD, 53–81; DM, 79–114). The word *irresponsibilization* appears in that chapter. To whom should I give this essay? To Jacques Derrida? To the memory of Jacques Derrida? It isn't much of a gift. At least it would be a true gift, since I could expect no compensating return. It was difficult to give Derrida gifts. He always, or almost always, for example, insisted on paying for lunches we shared. Now that he is dead, I can at last give him a gift, such as it is, that he cannot pay back in return.

The word *irresponsibilization* appears in the section of "Whom to Give to (Knowing Not to Know)" that comes after Derrida has been reading Kierkegaard's focus on Abraham's silence. That silence is not simply an unwillingness to hear his wife Sarah's reproaches or to respond to his son Isaac's horror at being the victim of filicide, nor is it simply a desire to keep the secret (a secret that he absolutely does not understand) of Jehovah's command to him to sacrifice his son. No, Abraham's silence is based on his recognition of a total incommensurability between absolute ethics and the language of universal ethics. Universal ethics can be publicly expressed and publicly shared. I can, do, and often must justify what I do by showing that it is based on a responsible response to my universally acknowledged obligations to my fellow human beings. Absolute ethics, on the contrary, Abraham's saying "yes" or "Here I am" to God's command, his one-sided compact with God, could not be expressed in any language, even if Abraham were willing to try to do so. He could not explain himself if he would. He can only express himself in ironic riddles that speak without saying anything, as in what he says to Isaac: "God will provide himself a lamb for the burnt offering" (Gen. 22:8). As long as he is faithful to Jehovah's terrible command, Abraham is condemned to silence, however much he speaks. "Tyrannically, jealously [*Farouchement, jalousement*], it [this absolute responsibility] refuses to present itself before the violence that consists of asking for accounts and justifications, to require summonses to appear [*à exiger la comparution*] before the law of men" (GD, 62, trans. modified; DM, 89–90).

It follows that acting according to absolute responsibility is a process that leads straight to irresponsibility by a temporal sequence that can be named in the neologism *irresponsibilization*. First you are responsible, and then you do something, saying "yes" to God's incomprehensible and secret demand, for example, and by doing that you get irresponsible. Here is the sequence in which the word *irresponsibilisation* appears, in an act of inauguration. I mean by this that Derrida uses a word unheard of before and not in any dictionary. This happens as if in response to a demand made by Derrida's process of thinking or writing on Derrida himself or on his fingers as they type. He needs the word, though up to that moment it did not yet exist. A fairly long extract is necessary in order to show the tendons and sinews, so to speak, of Derrida's robust thought process as he thinks again in his own words what Kierkegaard has thought or, to tell the truth, thinks beyond or around, in extraordinary arabesques or flourishes, what Kierkegaard says in *Fear and Trembling*:

> The ethical involves me in substitution, as does speaking. Whence the insolence of the paradox: for Abraham, Kierkegaard declares, *the ethical is a temptation* [l'éthique est la tentation]. He must therefore resist it. He keeps quiet in order to avoid the moral temptation which, under the pretext of calling him to responsibility, to self-justification, would make him lose his ultimate responsibility along with his singularity, make him lose his unjustifiable, secret, and absolute responsibility before God. This is ethics as "irresponsibilization" [*irresponsibilisation*], as an insoluble and paradoxical contradiction between responsibility *in general* and *absolute* responsibility. Absolute responsibility is not a responsibility, at least it is not general responsibility or responsibility in general. It needs to be exceptional or extraordinary, and it needs to be that absolutely and par excellence: it is as if absolute responsibility could not be derived from a *concept* of responsibility and therefore, in order for it to be what it must be it must remain inconceivable, indeed unthinkable: it must therefore be irresponsible in order to be absolutely responsible. "Abraham *cannot* speak, because he cannot say that which would explain everything . . . that it is an ordeal such that, please note, the ethical is the temptation" (115).[10]
>
> The ethical can therefore end up making us irresponsible. [*L'ethique peut donc être destinée à irresponsibiliser.*] (GD, 61; DM, 89)

A more literal translation of that last sentence would be: "The ethical can therefore be destined to irrresponsibilize." Derrida needs here an active verb, even if it is an invented one, not an adjective. The reader will note that Derrida's thinking here, like Kierkegaard's, depends on a kind of super-Protestantism. Derrida insists on the absolute singularity of each person, his or her incommensurability with any other person, and therefore his or her eternal inscrutability or secrecy. Each person is "exceptional or extraordinary," hence inconceivable, unthinkable, and, strictly speaking, unspeakable. That is because language deals in concepts and generalities, whereas "absolute responsibility" has to do with "uniqueness, absolute singularity, hence nonsubstitution, nonrepetition, silence, and the secret" (GD, 61, trans. modified; DM, 88–89).

Ordinary language involves the possibility of substitution and repetition. Any apple can in speech be substituted for any other apple, and each apple repeats all the others, at least in the sense that it is yet another apple, whereas absolute responsibility is like a singular apple that is unlike any other apple that is now or ever was, like the apple Eve offered to Adam. I am, according to Derrida, an eternal secret to my fellows, and they are eternal secrets to me, even those closest to me—my wife or my children, for example. I have discussed in Chapter 6 a passage in *A Taste for the Secret* that defines this presumption or basic Derridean presupposition as a Leibnizian monadism without God as guarantee of harmony between one monad and another (TS, 71).

Chapter 6 also cites a remarkably intransigent passage in Derrida's last seminars. This passage asserts that there is no passage. It categorically asserts that each of us is marooned, like Robinson Crusoe, on an island that is my singular world, separated by "the space and time of an infinite difference, of an interruption incommensurable with all the attempts at passage, of bridge, of isthmus, of communication, of translation, of trope, and of transfer," from any other island world (BS, lst seminar, my trans.). For Derrida, it is "Every man is an island," not Donne's cheerful and hopeful, conventionally Christian, appeal to the human community: "No man is an island unto himself."

The reader will also note that the long passage I cited above must use the same words to describe two kinds of responsibility and irresponsibility. What is irresponsible in general ethics is responsible in absolute ethics, and vice versa, but we do not have special words for these two uses. Absolute responsibility is "indeed unthinkable." This means also that ordinary language, French or English, stumbles and stutters in trying to express it. Derrida stammers, and contradicts his word usage, in trying to say how the highest responsibility, Abraham's before God, is also the most unforgivable irresponsibility. Responsibility is irresponsibility, and irresponsibility is responsibility, in a whirling that boggles the mind, like being caught in a revolving door.

The reader will also note, finally, that, in a way characteristic of Derrida, what he says here depends not only on a rhetoric of paradox, even "insolent" paradox, but also on what might be called an "all or nothing" rhetoric. That contributes to making it a rhetoric of aporia and impasse, in which you have "had it" whichever way you turn. This impasse results to a considerable degree from the way what Derrida says is carried instantly to a kind of hyperbolic extreme, where no room is left for compromise or for some middle term, half this and half that, for somehow having it both ways: "Absolute responsibility . . . needs to be exceptional or extraordinary, and it needs to be that absolutely and par excellence."

This third turn in Derrida's four-turn vortex or corkscrew is relatively easy for someone brought up in a Protestant Christian tradition, as I was, to understand and perhaps even accept. Of course my responsibility to God is secret, absolutely demanding, and absolutely incommensurate with my responsibility to my fellows. The Bible tells me so. The most important prayer is private prayer, a secret between me and God. Jesus said the "first and great commandment" is: "Thou shalt love the Lord thy God with all thy heart, and with all thy soul, and with all thy mind." Jesus then added, as a kind of afterthought, the second commandment, which is "like unto" the first, but not said to be "great": "Thou shalt love thy neighbor as thyself" (Matt. 22:37–39). What is the likeness? An analogy in difference? A mere similarity in grammatical expression? Is love of God the same love as I have for my neighbor? Probably not. Though the passage in Matthew may sound as if you can love God with your whole heart and at the same time love your neighbor as yourself, it is pretty clear elsewhere in the Bible, from the story of Abraham and Isaac on down to the sayings of Jesus, that this is not the case. You cannot do both things at once, have your cake and eat it too. That is one reason it is so hard to get to heaven, as hard as getting a camel through a needle's eye. Which takes precedence, love of God or love of my neighbor, is made clear in what Jesus said, in what Kierkegaard, in *Fear and Trembling*, calls a "hard saying [*parole . . . rude*]" (as cited by Derrida, GD, 64; DM, 92). The text in question is Luke 14:26, cited by both Kierkegaard and Derrida (GD, 64; DM, 92). The text in Luke echoes a text I have already cited from Matthew. Here is the way Luke puts it: "If any man come to me, and hate not his father, and mother, and wife, and children, and brethren, and sisters, yea, and his own life also, he cannot be my disciple" (Luke 14:26). Hard, or "rude," saying though this is, all this part of Derrida's discourse makes good sense within a certain Protestant or even specifically Kierkegaardian tradition. This is so, however intransigent, paradoxical, unthinkable, scandalous, and even incommensurate with language is what the Bible, Kierkegaard, and Derrida say, and however unlikely it may be that good, church-going Protestants will not figure out a way to wiggle out of becoming Jesus' disciples on the terms Jesus proposes.

The fourth revolution, however, is the specifically Derridean twist in his doctrine of inevitable irresponsibilization. It is also, perhaps, the most scandalous and troubling. What Derrida says in the fourth turn builds on the third but is actually quite different from what Kierkegaard, or indeed the Bible, says. It is closer to Levinasian ethics, as Derrida indirectly indicates in a footnote spelling out "the logic of an objection made by Levinas to Kierkegaard" (GD, 78–79; DM, 110–11). Nevertheless, Derrida goes well beyond Levinas's discourse about the "visage" of the other to develop a theory that I irresponsibilize myself just through responding, as Levinas might put it, to the face of the other. Kierkegaard sees Abraham's willingness to sacrifice Isaac as beyond the ethical and its general rules, as properly religious, whereas Levinas sees the crucial moment of the story to be the return to the ethical when the Angel stays Abraham's hand and reinstitutes the prohibition against murder that Levinas sees as the crucial effect of the face-to-face encounter with the other, with *autrui*.

Derrida's version of the fourth turn goes by way of a shift or sleight of hand in transition from the third that the reader may not even notice, so much is it an effect of prestidigitation. One odd feature of Derrida's account of Kierkegaard's *Fear and Trembling* is that he conspicuously refrains from using the distinction between the ethical and the religious that is so important for Kierkegaard. That distinction has vanished from Derrida's account. He speaks, rather, of absolute ethics as against general ethics or of Abraham's "hyper-ethical sacrifice" (GD, 71; DM, 101). Similarly, Derrida repeatedly makes clear that he thinks "God," "Jehovah," "Jaweh," "JWH," "Elohim," and so on are just names for the unnamable, the absolute other, as when he says "the absolute other: God, if you wish" (GD, 69; DM, 98) or:

> And this name which must always be singular is here none other than the name of God as completely other, the nameless name [*le nom sans nom*] of God, the unpronounceable name of God as other to which [*auquel*; not "whom" but "which"; I am bound to the unpronounceable name, not to God as a person] I am bound by an absolute, unconditional obligation, by an incomparable, non-negotiable duty. (GD, 67; DM, 96)

This is the first, almost imperceptible shift. It is imperceptible because it agrees so closely with the tradition of negative theology to which Derrida had such a complex relation of denegation, as in "How to Avoid Speaking: Denials." Nevertheless, these slight linguistic touches get Derrida off the hook of being a Kierkegaardian Christian.

The second shift, or twist within a twist, is even more important. Derrida asserts, or takes for granted, that my neighbor, or indeed each living thing, is just as singular, just as wholly other, as is the absolute other we may name God, if we wish. Derrida says, "I can respond only to the one (or to the One) [*Je ne peux répondre à l'un (ou à l'Un)*], that is, to the other, only by sacrificing the other other to this other [*qu'en lui sacrifiant l'autre*]" (GD, 70, trans. modified; DM, 101). A lot hangs on assimilating lowercase "one" to uppercase "One," my neighbor to God. What hangs on this assimilation, this little "or," as if you could say it either way, is the fourth turn. This is a new form of irresponsibilization in which by fulfilling my responsibility to one neighbor I inevitably and automatically get irresponsible in relation to all the others.

> I am responsible to any one (that is to say to any other) only by failing in my responsibilities to all the others, to the ethical or political generality. And I can never justify this sacrifice, I must always hold my peace about it. Whether I want to or not, I can never justify the fact that I prefer or sacrifice the one (an other) to the other. I will always be secretive, held to secrecy in respect of this, for there is nothing to say about it. (GD, 70–71, trans. modified; DM, 101)

One example Derrida gives of this wholly unjustifiable preference has given scandal to some, since it seems, to some, to trivialize ethics. However, they miss Derrida's point. Every hour of every day, he forcefully asserts, we are like Abraham on Mount Moriah with his knife raised over his son's throat. The experience of this form of irresponsibilization, this way of learning how to get irresponsible, is, Derrida insists, the most everyday and ordinary thing imaginable. It is not some high falutin', philosophical, or theoretical construct, a mere thing of language. It happens to anyone all the time, and is proved on his or her pulses, whether they acknowledge it or not. Anyone who loves cats, as I do, will understand the force of Derrida's example of this fourth form of irresponsibilization:

> How would you ever justify the fact that you sacrifice all the cats in the world to the cat that you feed at home every day for years, whereas other cats die of hunger at every instant? And other people? How would you justify your presence here speaking French, rather than there speaking to others in another language? And yet we also do our duty by behaving thus. There is no language, no reason, no generality or mediation to justify this ultimate responsibility which leads us to absolute sacrifice. Absolute sacrifice that is not the sacrifice of irresponsibility on the altar of responsibility, but the sacrifice of the most imperative duty (that which binds me to the other as a singularity in general) in favor of another absolutely imperative duty binding us to every other. (GD, 71, trans. modified; DM, 101)

You will see how Derrida's argument here depends on his all or nothing rhetoric. Just taking care of a lot of cats is not enough. That would still leave me behaving irresponsibly toward all the other cats in the world that are dying of hunger every day, as well as other people. One feature of teletechnologicomediatic globalization is that we get instant information, complete with graphic pictures and videos, about all the famines, plagues, and natural disasters all over the world, about AIDS in Africa, starvation and genocide in Darfur, murders by the dozen every day in Iraq, earth-quakes and tsunamis in South Asia, hurricanes in New Orleans, floods in India. How can we fulfill our responsibilities toward all these suffering ones and at the same time fulfill our responsibilities to our immediate neighbors?

Here is Derrida's most eloquent and most exigent expression of this everyday but universal double bind. This double bind, according to him, exceeds any particular religion or culture. It is a universal feature of the human condition anywhere at any time. The passage turns on the formula-tion that becomes, later on, the topic of extended discussion in chapter 4, entitled "Every Other Is Wholly Other" ("Tout autre est tout autre"):

> I am responsible to the other as other, I answer to him and I answer for
> what I do before him. But of course, what binds me thus in my singularity
> to the absolute singularity of the other, immediately propels me into the
> space or risk of absolute sacrifice. There are also others, an infinite number
> of them, the innumerable generality of others to whom I should be bound
> by the same responsibility, a general and universal responsibility (what
> Kierkegaard calls the ethical order). I cannot respond to the call, the re-
> quest [*la demande*], the obligation, or even the love of another without sacri-
> ficing the other other, the other others. *Every other (one) is every (bit) other*
> [Tout autre est tout autre], every one else is completely or wholly other.
> (GD, 68; DM, 97–98)

The reader will see the remorseless, watertight logic of what Derrida is saying. You could escape this logic only by denying one or another of his premises. He assumes, first of all, that each person, each living creature, such as my cat, is absolutely singular. That means that the other, every other, is completely other to me, foreign, incomprehensible, secret, as well as other to every other other. *Tout autre est tout autre*. Even though I have no access to the other, however, every other (second assumption) makes an absolute demand on me, imposes on me an irresistible obligation, a call to respond responsibly, to take responsibility, as I take responsibility for my wife, my children, my cats. Since there are so many others, an infinite number, each of whom makes the same ethical demand on me, I cannot possibly fulfill my obligation to all of them (third assumption). It follows, therefore, that I must sacrifice all the others in order to act responsibly toward the one I choose, my one cat, for example, over all the other cats (and people) who will starve because I do not respond to their cries of hunger. I cannot in any rational way justify that choice or that decision, any more than I can justify falling in love with one woman over all the other women in the world I might have married.

Derrida's expression of the way this entirely logical and irrefutable conclusion (if you accept the premises) leads to "paradox, scandal, and aporia," at the limit of conceptual linking, is eloquent and intransigent. It does not leave any way out. The concepts involved are bound together in a tight net that is an inescapable trap. The reader becomes like the mouse in Kafka's parable who comes to a dead end in its attempt to flee the cat. "'You only need to change your direction,' said the cat, and ate it up."[11]

> The simple concepts of alterity and of singularity constitute the concept of duty as much as that of responsibility. As a result, the concepts of responsibility, of decision, or of duty, are condemned to paradox, scandal, and aporia. Paradox, scandal, and aporia are themselves nothing other than sacrifice, the exposition of conceptual thinking at its limit, at its death and finitude. As soon as I enter into a relation with the other, with the gaze, look, request [*la demande*], love, command, or call of the other, I know that I can respond only by sacrificing ethics, that is, by sacrificing whatever obliges me also to respond, in the same way, in the same instant, to all the others. I offer a gift of death, I betray, I don't need to raise my knife over my son on Mount Moriah for that. Day and night, at every instant, on all the Mount Moriahs of this world, I am doing that, raising my knife over what I love and must love, over the other, this or that other to whom I owe absolute fidelity, incommensurably. (GD, 68, trans. modified; DM, 98)

One might think, or hope, that Abraham's case was exceptional. He was, after all, a great patriarch. His act was the basis of the three great religions of the Book. His progeny, by way of Isaac, ultimately included Jesus Christ, the Messiah. Abraham is not so much to be emulated as admired. Surely God (if you want to call the "nameless" that) will not require of you or me anything like Abraham's sacrifice of his love for his only son to his love for God. The radical strength of Derrida's argument here is to say "no" to this cop-out. No, he says, each one of us, every instant of every day, is in exactly the same situation as Abraham on Mount Moriah with his knife raised over Isaac. Abraham's situation is exemplary, paradigmatic, not exceptional.

The other, more than a little scandalous, and certainly radical feature of Derrida's argument is to transfer Abraham's relation to Jehovah and Isaac to my relation to any two of my fellow men and women, or to any two cats. The concept and practice of sacrifice are religious through and through, fundamental aspects of more or less any religion in the world. Derrida has paradoxically, scandalously, and aporetically transferred by analogy the concept and practice of sacrifice to everyday ethical situations. He has done this by what might be called an allegorical transfer or an allegorical reading of the Abraham and Isaac story. I must sacrifice all the other cats to my loving care of my one cat, just as Abraham sacrificed Sarah, Isaac, and all his social obligations to his willingness to obey God's terrifying command and just as Jesus demanded that we should hate father, mother, and all the rest if we want to follow him. Derrida has put that one cat I care for in the place of God in the biblical story.

This is, to say the least, an extravagant and hyperbolic, not to say paradoxical and even scandalous way to describe the concrete facts of my everyday situation, whether I am religious or not. Nevertheless, I confess in conclusion, my own life experience confirms the truth of what Derrida says. On the next page after the citation I just made, Derrida explicitly applies what he has said to his own life situation:

> By preferring what I do right now, simply by giving it my time and attention, in choosing my work, my activity as a citizen or as a professorial and professional philosopher, writing and speaking here in a public language, French in my case, I am perhaps fulfilling my duty. But I am sacrificing and betraying at every moment all my other obligations: my obligations to the other others whom I know or don't know, the billions of my fellows (without mentioning the animals that are even more other others than my fellows), my fellows who are dying of starvation or sickness. (GD, 69, trans. modified; DM, 98–99)

Derrida goes on to say that fulfilling his professional duties also means betraying his family, his son (he had two), "each of whom is the only son I sacrifice to the other, every one being sacrificed to every one else in this land of Moriah that is our habitat every second of every day" (GD, 69; DM, 99).

This comes home to me, in the most intimate, personal, and singular way. I began this chapter by asking "How do I get irresponsible?" Going to Singapore to give part of the chapter as a lecture was a way to get irresponsible, since I had to betray all my exigent family obligations for the time I was away from home, including washing the dishes, feeding the cats, buying groceries, all the thousand little things one must do in a household. During the time I was department chair at Yale, I used to think all the time, more or less every instant of every day, about how impossible it was to satisfy three equally exigent obligations: the obligation to my colleagues and to my university in my capacity as chair, my obligation to my true vocation of teaching and writing about literature, and my obligations to my wife, children (and cats). It was paradox, scandal, and aporia, felt in the blood and felt along the bone. I have in my own life proved on my pulses the process of irresponsibilization. Over many years, day and night, at every instant, I have become better and better at this serious game of "how to." I have learned more and more every day about how to get irresponsible.

Derrida's Politics of Autoimmunity

This chapter was first drafted for a conference at the University of Florida in Gainesville, held from October 9 to October 11, 2006. Some of the first part of the chapter is "time sensitive," as one says. It describes the political situation in the United States as it was in the fall of 2006. A lot of water has flowed over the dam since then. Some interpolations added since then bring the chapter up to date at least to the time of the interpolations.

Now, in February 2008, as I revise and augment the essay once more to make it a chapter for this book, I realize that the situation in the United States has not changed all that much in the intervening sixteen months. Our troops are still occupying Iraq. Though the "surge" has to some marginal degree brought stability, suicide bombs still go off almost daily, U.S. troops are still being killed by roadside bombs every few days. No effective political resolution among Sunnis, Shiites, and Kurds has been achieved, though some legislation has been passed, at last. The talk now from our leaders is of postponing the promised troop drawdown, probably indefinitely, for years or for decades. Over six hundred thousand Iraqis, by some calculations, have died since our invasion. Many millions more are displaced from their homes or in exile outside of Iraq. In the United States, forty-seven million persons are without health insurance. Little or nothing has been done in the United States to stave off catastrophic climate change that is already happening, with rapid ice-melt in Greenland, the North Pole, and Antarctica. A modest fuel-efficiency standard for gas-powered vehicles has been passed and signed into law. The United States is still resisting global mandatory carbon-emission standards. No solution has been legislated for the problem of the eleven million "illegal immigrants" living in the United States. Hardly anything has been done to make health care universal. The sub-prime mortgage debacle has precipitated what many economists say is already a recession. This recession, if it is that, has been brought on by tax cuts for the rich, gigantic deficits, huge military spending, and the limitless greed of what is called, with unintentional irony, the "banking and financial industry." That sounds as if they manu-factured something, whereas they just make money out of money. Many overseas investors are shifting from the dollar to the euro as a more stable currency.

By the time this book is published, in the summer of 2009, the United States will have had presidential and congressional elections. These elec-tions will determine the future, if there is any, of U.S. constitutional de-mocracy—government of the people, by the people, and for the people. This is our hope for what Derrida calls "the democracy to come." This chapter focuses on the question of what aid Derrida's political thought can give us, you and me, in deciding what to do in the way of political action, now, at this moment. Of one thing I am sure, however, and that is that it is our duty to vote in November 2008. This chapter ends with an identifi-cation of Derrida's concept of political duty. That concept may help to understand what it might mean to say it is our duty to vote.

Final update, December 14, 2008: Since I added the previous para-graphs, much has happened in the United States. The bad news is that the greed and stupidity of a few hundred people in the banking and financial "industry" have plunged not just the United States but also the whole world into the worst recession since the 1930s, with no end in sight. They have done this with a gigantic Ponzi scheme based on subprime mortgages and their derivatives. This airy pyramid was aided and abetted by the de-regulators in Congress and by the executive branch of our government. The financial collapse has also happened with the connivance of rating companies like Moody's, which are supposed to identify risky or worthless paper. The stock market has lost much of its value. Unemployment is way up. Thousands of people are losing their homes through foreclosure. U.S. auto companies are on the verge of bankruptcy. The bailout of the banks and financial institutions has put American taxpayers on the line for as much as seven trillion dollars. This enormous sum, some experts say, will be required to put the banks back in a position to lend to one another and to citizen borrowers. See the Op-Ed piece by Frank Rich in the *New York Times* for December 14, 2008, for a good account of this catastrophe: http://www.nytimes.com/2008/12/14/opinion/14rich.html?_r=1&th& emc=th. Talk about self-destructive autoimmunity!

Meanwhile, practically nothing has been done in the United States to stop global warming, to save the environment, to improve health care, or to fix the education system. The infamous prison at Guantánamo Bay still flourishes. Our reconstruction of Iraq has been a costly catastrophe, costing billions and billions, much of it wasted or purloined. An Iraqi journalist just today threw two shoes at George W. Bush during a press conference in Baghdad called to celebrate an agreement with the Iraqi government that will keep U.S. troops there three more years. Throwing shoes at someone is a Muslim insult. "This is a goodbye kiss, you dog," the journalist shouted.

The good news is that Barack Obama has been elected President of the United States, along with an increased majority of Democrats in the House and Senate. This gives some reason for hope. I was much touched by the way people from all over the world e-mailed me to congratulate me on this event, as though it were a personal triumph for me, which it was. Obama is appointing an impressive centrist group of distinguished experts to Cabinet and Agency posts. They differ considerably from one another. That means Obama will have much power and responsibility to choose among contradictory pieces of advice. That situation will require from him immense courage, intelligence, and bold action. The problems he faces are gigantic. A recent essay in *Harper's*, for example, is entitled "The $10 Trillion Hangover: Paying the Price for Eight Years of Bush."[1] Nevertheless, I and millions of other Americans now have a glimpse of light at the end of the dark tunnel of the last eight nightmare years.

I return now to what I wrote in the fall of 2006:

Things are not going at all well in the United States today, not to speak of the rest of the world. Our sad situation is clear enough, though many of our citizens are still in denial of it. We are engaged in a disastrous war in Iraq that was based on two great lies and a lot of smaller ones. We were told that Saddam Hussein had weapons of mass destruction and that he was in cahoots with Al Quaeda, both lies. We were told that we would be greeted with open arms and with bouquets of flowers, whereas just the opposite has happened. We were told that the war in Iraq would cost perhaps forty billion dollars and that Iraq oil would pay for the rest, whereas no oil revenue from Iraq is footing the bill and the present estimate of the war's cost is two trillion dollars, probably still an underestimate. Everything that could go wrong in Iraq has gone wrong. Iraq at the moment I write this is in the midst of full-scale sectarian civil war. Bush and Co. are still in denial about the gravity of this situation, though they are beginning to admit there are some problems. They think a "troop surge," that is, escalation of our occupation, will bring stability to Iraq.

We were promised that invading and occupying Iraq would make us safer at home. Exactly the opposite has happened. Iraq has now become what it was not before our occupation, a breeding ground for terrorists. Iran is winning control of Iraq as a result of our invasion. Our standing or credit in the world has diminished immeasurably. We are now the object of widespread hatred, distrust, and disdain, in part because we are a rogue state that ignores international law and the Geneva convention, not to speak of our own Constitution. Nobody can be sure what mad act we will next commit. We torture and hold indefinitely without charge detainees in a prison falsely claimed to be extra-territorial. We operate secret prisons around the world, where prisoners are held and tortured through what is called, in an extraordinary example of doublespeak, "Extraordinary Rendition." We have suspended our own precious civil liberties through something with the chilling Orwellian name, doublespeak once more, of "The Patriot Act." The Department of Homeland Security has conspicuously failed to secure our ports, our borders, or our chemical plants and nuclear power plants. We are immensely more insecure than we were before, trembling in a terror that we have ourselves created, like Robinson Crusoe when he sees the print of a naked foot in the sand and thinks it may be his own footprint. The War on Terror has conspicuously failed to do anything more than multiply the terrorists, in spite of Bush's boast that we would capture Osama bin Laden, "dead or alive," and eliminate the terrorist threat. That does not mean that we have not captured or killed some terrorists or "foiled" some terrorist plots, but the international terrorists are an invisible, anonymous, hydra-headed monster that is everywhere at once, especially, we fear, in our own homeland. That monster multiplies exponentially the more we make war on it.

The misnamed War on Terror has made us live in terror. As Derrida has argued in *Philosophy in a Time of Terror*, this terror is directed not toward what *has* happened, the destruction of the World Trade Center twin towers and part of the Pentagon, but toward what we are all taught to believe *will* happen in the future, something worse than the Cold War, something without precedent, "the worst." It will be nothing less than the end of the "world" as we have come to think of in these days of teletechno-economicomediatic globalization. That end may come by way of global warming or by way of a "nuclear winter," but our absolute terror tells us it is bound to happen sooner or later. Derrida focuses on the "nuclear menace," with a prophetic anticipation (his long interview-essay about 9/11 was given in October 2001, five weeks after 9/11) of our present anxiety about Iran's development of nuclear weapons or about some anonymous terrorist armed with a nuclear bomb or a "dirty bomb" in a suitcase:

> From now on, the nuclear threat, the "total" threat, no longer comes from a state but from anonymous forces that are absolutely unforeseeable and incalculable. And since this absolute threat will have been secreted by the end of the Cold War and the "victory" of the U.S. camp, since it threatens what is supposed to sustain world order, the very possibility of a world and of any worldwide effort [*mondialisation*] (international law, a world market, a universal language, and so on), what is thus put at risk by this *terrifying* autoimmunitary logic [more about that terrifying logic later on; I have already discussed it in Chapter 6] is nothing less than the existence of the world, of the worldwide itself. . . . Absolute evil, absolute threat, because what is at stake is nothing less than the *mondialisation* or the worldwide movement of the world, life on earth and elsewhere, without remainder [*sans reste et rien de moins*]. (PTT, 98–99; C11S, 150–51)

Meanwhile, while we tremble in terror, we are almost completely failing to take care of ourselves at home, much less guarantee a happy globalization in fulfillment of what Bush defines as his and our "mission." "Mission" is a Christian word. Bush and the rest of us Americans have been sent by God to bring democracy (and capitalism) to the whole world, the "religion of capital," as Derrida calls it in *The Other Heading* (OH, 77; AC, 76).

Think what we could have done at home with two trillion dollars to fight global warming, to improve education, to make good health care a universal right, to guarantee social security for our old people, to reduce poverty and homelessness, not to speak of fighting AIDS here and around the world, preparing seriously for natural disasters here or elsewhere, many caused or exacerbated by man-made global warming, and so on! Instead of that, many of our lawmakers have been bribed by lobbyists and contributions made by pharmaceutical companies, oil companies, automobile companies, and the like to pass laws, like Medicare Part D, that benefit primarily not ordinary people but, in this case, the pharmaceutical companies. Medicare Part D was written by the pharmaceutical industry for the pharmaceutical industry, for example, by prohibiting the Federal Government from negotiating drug prices. Real income for ordinary wage earners has remained about the same or even somewhat lower over the last forty years. Health care and pension situations are worse for such people, whereas the average income of the top one and a half percent of our citizens have gone up by several hundred percent, about 328 percent, according to one figure I saw. The United States is at this point not a democracy but a postdemocracy, a plutocracy, government by and for the rich. Our national elections are stolen by way of systematic "irregularities" and discriminatory registration laws that would give the most crooked third-world country some lessons in how to rig elections. Our tax system has been skewed in favor of the very rich and in such a way (cutting taxes while vastly increasing government spending) that what was only six years ago a budget surplus under President Clinton has become a gigantic and ballooning budget deficit under President Bush. This means, among other things, that the Peoples' Republic of China owns and controls a large part of our economy in the form of U.S. Treasury Bonds. They have only to pull the plug in a massive sell-off to bring us economic and social chaos. Our present tax system, plus run-away military spending, also means that our government and our economy are headed straight toward bankruptcy, fiscal collapse, and depression. It may be ten years or it may be twenty, but that is the direction we are going, unless things are turned around. Meanwhile, many of our citizens, legislators, and elected leaders continue to deny and even to define as a hoax the irrefutable evidence of the man-made global warming caused by air pollution that will soon irreversibly change our climate, inundate our coasts, turn farmland into desert, and, incidentally, turn my family's two acres of beautiful coastal property in Deer Isle, Maine, into two more acres of clam flats. By the end of this century, scientists like Edward O. Wilson believe, half the species of plants and animals on earth will be extinct or scheduled for extinction. No solid Arctic icecap any longer exists during the summer, as anyone who flies to China over the North Pole can see, on a clear day. Our warming oceans are already causing more frequent and more violent hurricanes, like Katrina, the one that destroyed New Orleans. Our government's response to this is to give tax and mileage credits to the car manufacturers that, under the guise of encouraging the use of ethanol, a boon to the corn industry, actually subsidize the production of more gas-guzzling SUVs. This is because artificially high gas-mileage ratings of thirty-five mpg are given to SUVs that run on both gasoline and ethanol but will most likely never be run on ethanol because it is not available in most of the country. One SUV

Consumer Reports tested got fourteen mpg on gasoline and ten mpg on ethanol. Not one single ethanol station, I am told, exists as yet anywhere in the whole Northeast. Our health-care system is a shambles, as are our pension systems and our educational system at the primary and secondary levels. We have enormous, urgent domestic problems that are not being addressed by our laws and regulations, but exacerbated.

Our situation is truly terrorizing, but most frightening of all is that hardly anyone is doing anything about it. (I add now, on January 14, 2007, that the winning of the House and Senate by the Democrats in the November 2006 elections has meant the passage of a whole series of laws by the House in the first hundred hours of the new session. These laws would begin to address some of the problems I have listed, if they make it through the Senate and are not vetoed by President Bush, a big if.) (A further addition, February 12, 2008: Bush has vetoed some progressive laws. Some he has signed with the explicit proviso that he has no intention of carrying them out. He has signed them with his fingers crossed, so to speak, thereby nullifying any good effect they might possibly have had.) The sadness is that we have the scientific and technological knowledge, plus the economic resources, to address all these terrifyingly urgent problems, as well as give everyone in the world the equivalent of what is at least a lower-middle-class existence in the United States today, plus health care and retirement security. We could still turn things around if we act fast enough and decisively enough. So far, the new Democratic Congress has made only a beginning.

How has this suicidal situation come about? What possible explanation can be found for such auto-destructive behavior on so many fronts at once? What can or should we (I mean you and me, here and now) do about it? These are the most immediate questions that face any thinking person today in the United States (and in other countries around our globalized world): How are we to understand our situation and how are we to act to ameliorate it? How are we to hold off the end that terrorizes us, like a specter in broad daylight? My question in this chapter is more limited. I ask whether Derrida's political thought can help us citizens of globalization to understand this emergency and to decide how to act. We need all the help we can get.

It used to be said (first canard) that Derrida's writing and deconstruction generally are apolitical. They have nothing to do with politics. Derrida is interested more or less exclusively, it was thought, in such arcane theoretical issues as whether writing preceded speech (who cares?), or whether human temporality and human language can be defined as "differantial" (with an "a") or whether speech acts are a product of "iterability." The presumption that Derrida was apolitical was always false. Look at *Positions* (1972) or at the political features of the discussion of Rousseau in *Of Grammatology* (1967)!

With the publication of *Specters of Marx, The Politics of Friendship, Aporias,* and other such late works as *Philosophy in a Time of Terror* and *Rogues,* not to speak of ten seminars on "Kant, the Jew, the German," on hospitality, on witnessing, on perjury, on capital punishment, and on sovereignty (two sets of ten for the latter), it became more or less impossible any longer to say that Derrida was not concerned with politics.

People who were bad readers or just in bad faith then shifted to the claim (second canard) that Derrida and deconstruction are conservative or reactionary politically. That claim is no more viable than the first, but it does require reading Derrida, no easy matter, to decide just what his politics were. Derrida wrote so much about politics in his last decades that it might even be possible to assert (not quite truthfully) that he became almost exclusively a political philosopher, a political theorist, or even a political scientist in the strict, disciplinary sense. He wrote so much about politics that it would take a long book to give a full account of his political thought. In a short chapter like this one, I can only make a sketch.

Nor did Derrida's politics remain purely theoretical. He did not remain in his armchair in his study or safely before his computer screen. He took stands. He acted politically, often in ways that were risky. He suffered anti-Semitic persecution by the French in Algeria during World War II. He resigned from *Tel Quel* because he was opposed to Maoism. He chose never to join the Communist Party, at a time when it was difficult not to join it if you were, as he was, an intellectual on the left. He took a public and somewhat unpopular stand of qualified solidarity during the student rebellions in France in '68. Years later, Derrida got himself arrested in Czechoslovakia for giving a clandestine seminar there. He attacked apartheid vigorously and visited Nelson Mandela in South Africa. *Specters of Marx* is dedicated to Chris Hani, an avowed Communist and a hero of the resistance against apartheid. Hani was assassinated in South Africa on April 10, 1993, just as Derrida was finishing his book on Marx. That book, with its measured praise of Marx and criticism of capitalism, was given as lectures at the University of California at Riverside on April 22 and 23, 1993. Doing that was a courageous political act in itself. Derrida often spoke out in the United States against U.S. legalization of capital punishment. He accused us, correctly, vigorously, and publicly, of being the only so-called first-world country still to have capital punishment. He harbored a homeless African immigrant in his home outside Paris, allowing that man to use Derrida's address as his address in order to avoid deportation. At that time in France, an immigrant could stay if he or she had a valid address. Derrida did not just sit around and think or write about politics, however complex, contradictory, "aporetic," and ambiguous he may have seen political action to be. That should never be forgotten.

Derrida is in many places quite explicit and specific about our obligation to act as well as to think politically. Here is one example in "Force of Law," part of which I have already cited in Chapter 2. In this passage, Derrida declares our obligation to pass new emancipatory laws to deal with a whole series of specific contemporary social problems, and he explains the precarious ground of unpredictability on the basis of which we should enact such legislation:

> Left to itself, the incalculable and giving [*donatrice*] idea of justice is always very close to the bad, even to the worst for it can always be reappropriated by the most perverse calculation [*le calcul le plus pervers*]. It's always possible.[2] . . . This requirement [*L'ordre de ce il faut*] does not properly belong either to justice or law. It only belongs to either of these two domains by exceeding each one in the direction of the other. Politicization, for example, is interminable even if it cannot and should not ever be total. To keep this from being a truism or a triviality, we must recognize in it the following consequence: each advance in politicization obliges one to reconsider, and so to reinterpret the very foundations of law [*les fondements mêmes du droit*] such as they had previously been calculated or delimited. This was true for example in the Declaration of the Rights of Man, in the abolition of slavery, in all the emancipatory battles that remain and will have to remain in progress, everywhere in the world, for men and for women. Nothing seems to me less outdated than the classical emancipatory ideal. . . . But beyond these identified territories of juridico-politicization on the grand geopolitical scale, beyond all self-serving interpretations [*au-delà de tous les détournements et arraisonnements intéressés*], beyond all determined and particular reappropriations of international law, other areas must constantly open up that at first seem like secondary or marginal areas. This marginality also signifies that a violence, indeed a terrorism and other forms of hostage-taking are at work (the examples closest to us would be found in the area of laws on the teaching and practice of languages, the legitimization of canons, the military use of scientific research, abortion, euthanasia, problems of organ transplant, extra-uterine conception, bio-engineering [Derrida might now have added "stem-cell research"], medical experimentation, the

social treatment of AIDS, the macro- or micro-politics of drugs, the home-less, and so on, without forgetting, of course, the treatment of what we call animal life, animality [*l'énorme question dite de l'animalité*]. (FLe, 28–29; FLf, 61, 62, 63)

Well, what are the main contours, the chief presuppositions, of what my title calls "Derrida's Politics of Autoimmunity"? These presuppositions might be called the conceptual foundations of Derrida's political thought and political action. The reader should be not too certain ahead of time that all these concepts will seem transparently reasonable and open to clear cognition. Derrida deliberately and self-consciously works at the margins of conceptual clarity, in a borderland realm of paradox and aporia, as any careful reader of his work knows. One feature of the "event" of 9/11, the destruction of the World Trade Center, according to Derrida, is that it exceeds the concepts and language that we had in place, before that event, in the discourse of politicians and the media, even though, as Der-rida insisted in the weeks after 9/11, it was not an event in his sense of the word because it could have been predicted. If 9/11 was nevertheless a gen-uine "event," as Derrida came later to hold, that was because, predictable though it was, when it happened it was incommensurate with previous forms of understanding. That does not mean we should not try our best to understand it, along with the other features of our present situation that I began by sketching out. It does mean, however, that new conceptual formulations are necessary in order to try to do that.

The passage I have just cited gives some important indications about Derrida's political thought and action.

1. It tells us that Derrida remains faithful to what he calls "the classical emancipatory ideal." I think he means by this phrase the Enlightenment ideals that led, for example, to the U.S. Declaration of Independence and Bill of Rights, that is, the dream of an egalitarian democracy that would be government of the people, by the people, and for the people. This ideal is a "democracy to come," in Derrida's phrase, something never, of course, anywhere fully accomplished. Derrida recognizes this when he speaks of "emancipatory battles that remain and will have to remain in progress, everywhere in the world, for men and for women." The United States is at this point hardly a good model of such a democracy.

2. The passage cited above also tells the reader that Derrida sees useful political action as often taking place in what "at first can seem like second-ary and marginal areas," such as the need for new and better laws on the teaching and practice of languages, the legitimization of canons, and all

the other quite specific, local, and what might be called nitty-gritty problems in Derrida's list. Useful political action is not abstract and high-falutin', "juridico-politicization on the grand geo-political scale," such as Bush's declared mission to bring Western-style democracy (meaning capitalism and Christianity) to the whole world. Good political action is local and specific, such as passing good laws and then enforcing them, about abortion, bio-engineering and stem-cell research, the treatment of animals, legal gas mileage for our automobiles, permitted air pollution by our factories, or universalizing health insurance.

3. The context of the passage I have cited is the distinction Derrida draws between law and justice. To act lawfully is not to act justly. Preexisting laws preprogram decision and act, for example, a judge's decision in a court of law, whereas justice is always new, inaugural, and unheard of. I have discussed, in Chapter 2, Derrida's distinction between law and justice. A just judge, according to Derrida, remakes the laws in every just judgment, because he or she acts in response to the uniqueness and singularity of each case. Justice is a response to what Derrida calls "the wholly other." That means justice is "incalculable." It resists rational calculation either beforehand or after the fact. This concept of justice is an example of the resistance to cognition I spoke of above as fundamental to Derrida's thinking and action. No one and nothing, no general command, no Kantian imperative, tells him he must allow that African immigrant to Paris to use his address or that he should feed and take care of one single cat out of all the others who are dying of hunger every day, to cite a somewhat scandalous example Derrida gives in *The Gift of Death* (GD, 71; DM, 101). I have discussed that example in Chapter 9. Since justice is "incalculable," this means that it can easily be appropriated by the bad or by the worst. A bad person can always say "I acted unlawfully because the 'wholly other' commanded me to do so and so. I claim I acted according to a higher justice."

This means that "incalculable justice *requires* us to calculate" in order to try to avoid the bad or the worst, totalitarianism, fascism, or some unjust authoritarian regime claiming sovereignty. Calculating in this case means measuring what we do against that "classical emancipatory ideal." It also means calculating as best we can what will be the actual practical effect, for example, of new laws about stem-cell research, something that in its novelty and promise does not fit earlier paradigms of medical research. Derrida stresses that we get no help in doing this from pre-existing laws. We are forced to remake the very foundations of law: "each advance in politicization obliges one to reconsider, and so to reinterpret the very foundations of law such as they had previously been calculated or delimited." Moreover, since what Derrida calls *destinerrance*, discussed in detail here in Chapter 3, means that we can never anticipate just what will be the results of our political choices and decisions, our calculations about the incalculable are always risky and dangerous. Nevertheless, a decision is demanded of us. Derrida stresses the urgency and immediacy of the obligation to decide. I must decide, *now*, even though I never have enough information to make my decision and act anything other than a more or less complete leap in the dark, as when I propose marriage to this one woman out of all the other possible ones or vote for one given candidate rather than another.

4. One phrase, uttered almost in passing, in the passage I have cited is of great importance in understanding Derrida's politics. "Politicization, for example," says Derrida, "is interminable even if it cannot and should not ever be total." The development of the humanities in recent years toward becoming a branch of the social sciences, toward cultural studies, women's studies, postcolonialism, identity politics, and so on, admirable as these developments are, might be defined as an example of interminable politicization gradually taking over the whole field. The slogan now might be, not Jameson's "always historicize" but, for many scholars in the humanities, a new gesture that could be expressed as "always politicize." Derrida conspicuously, in the final phrase of the sentence just quoted, resists that totalization: "even if it cannot and should not ever be total." Derrida in a number of other places explicitly refrains from being totally engulfed by the politicization of everything. Signs here and there, for example, in papers given at social science or anthropology conferences, suggest a turn in those fields to questions of language and literature. If humanists in recent years have been influenced by political scientists and anthropologists, the latter have, in turn, been deflected by work in the humanities toward a new interest in literature.

Why resist the politicization of everything? A striking passage in *A Taste for the Secret*, analyzed in detail in Chapter 6, gives the answer. In that passage Derrida says, firmly and defiantly, "I am not one of the family" and "Don't count me in." The passage makes clear that "family" here is a synecdoche for all forms of belonging, intellectual, social, and political (TS, 27). Why does Derrida resist being one of the family? His answer is specific and cogent. He must refrain from identifying himself with any of these forms of belonging, including any political belonging, because what he really *is* is something entirely singular, sui generis. Therefore his most important transactions are extra-political responses to the demands made on him by the complete otherness of other singularities.

If matters are going as badly in the United States and in the world as I began by specifying, it is easy to understand why someone might want to refrain from defining himself or herself entirely, or even at all, as, say, a citizen of the United States with the right to vote. What I have said so far, however, does not explain how Derrida's political thinking and action helps me, or you, to understand how we ever got into this truly cata-strophic national and global situation or what we should do about it. It is a situation in which the news of the day, every day, tells of more car bombs and suicide bombers in Iraq, more gigantic quarterly losses and more "downsizings" (meaning firing or "buyouts" of workers) in U.S. industries like automobile manufacturing, more bad or unconstitutional laws passed by our legislatures, such as the renewal of the electronic surveillance law that adds a provision to exempt the complicit telecommunications compa-nies for being sued for unconstitutional invasion of citizens' privacy. This has just been passed, or repassed, by the Senate (February 12, 2008), with the exemption feature added, but the House of Representatives has (Feb-ruary 14, 2008) refused to include the exemption in its bill. Another exam-ple of un-American legislation is the laws in several states requiring photo IDs for voter registration, thereby disenfranchising with a stroke of the pen untold numbers of old people and people of color, all—surprise!— most likely to vote Democratic.

I am coming to Derrida's explanation. I promise to get there. Derrida's political thought and political action can be put under the aegis of a series of key words or phrases. These might be called "aporias," or oppositions without opposition, several of which have been identified already. These include justice as against law, performative as against constative enuncia-tions, faith as against knowledge, messianicity without messianism, the democracy to come, the new international, teletechnoeconomicocultural-mediatic globalization or, as Derrida prefers to call it, *mondialisation*, which might be translated as "worldwideification," the instant of decision, duty, the event, sovereignty without sovereignty, promise, the wholly other, *des-tinerrance*, the "dangerous perhaps," responsibility, *irresponsibilisation*, and, above all, the "terrifying" general logic of autoimmunization. Each of these terms demands or asks for an elaborate, more or less interminable, development and analysis, as the twists and turns of Derrida's uses of the terms could be followed from work to work. Other chapters of this book investigate many of these terms from one perspective or another.

These terms, however, are not just a random series, each segregated from all the others, each having its own separate logic. Nor do they, taken together, form an easily definable, coherent system. They are, rather, a reticulated or wrinkled intellectual surface in which each concept is defined by all the others and each is necessary, in its turn, to define each of the others. Or, rather, each is a way of working that depends on the others to function and is necessary, in turn, to the working of the others. In innumerable aleatory combinations, they work. They do work. Used rightly, they are a way of doing something, or they name the doing of something that can be called a political action.

Let me move out onto this surface by way of Derrida's concept of the event, in French, *événement*, something that comes from French for "to come," *venir*. A true event, for Derrida, is a happening that is unpredictable, that comes from who knows where, from the wholly other, that comes suddenly, unexpectedly, without precedent, and that constitutes an inaugural break with what came before. A true event is something incommensurate with our pre-existing conceptual grids. Examples are, perhaps, the destruction of the World Trade Center, though Derrida denied that, at least at first, or a just act or decision, as opposed to a merely lawful one. Perhaps the real event of 9/11 was the stupid, self-defeating, autoimmune reaction to it by the Bush administration. The extent of the damage they have done to the United States was to some degree unpredictable because it was so hyperbolic and happened in so many areas at once: the seemingly interminable wars in Iraq and Afghanistan, worsening health care, the unconstitutional Patriot Act, torture of prisoners, ignoring the human causes of global warming, further suicidal deregulation of financial institutions, and so on. The Bush years have formed a decisive break in American and world history.

One of the most conspicuous events, or set of events, these days, is what we English-speakers call "globalization," or what the French call *mondialisation*. Derrida prefers the latter term because it calls attention to the source of the concept in the Christian idea of "the world" as a unity waiting to hear the Gospel and be Christianized. Our present-day globalization is a more or less secular version of biblical or Augustinian thinking in terms of the whole world, considered to be a totality under God's providence. I say "more or less secular" because the Christian roots remain in even the most secular versions of "the religion of capital." The traditional notion of separate and sovereign nation-states does not prepare us to deal with teletechnicoeconomicomediatic globalization. Globalization has been facilitated or, rather, made possible and even inevitable by new tele-communication devices: telephone, radio, cinema, television, fiber-optic cables, communication satellites, cellphones, i-Pods, and, finally, most powerful of all, computers connected to the Internet or the World Wide Web. The Web makes possible emails to and from anywhere in the world, text messaging, the instantaneous transfer anywhere in the world of large or small sums of money, the division by way of sophisticated computer programs of financial instruments like subprime mortgages into "deriva-tives." Computers distribute these mortgages into multiple small pieces called *tranches*, so no human mind can any longer track what has become of them or how much they are worth, if anything. As Tom Cohen puts this in a fine phrase in an e-mail to me, it is "the revolt of the autoimmune robots."

Both "Internet" and "World Wide Web" suggest the more than a little misleading figure of spatial reticulation I began by naming and using. The terms are misleading because the "Net" is neither a net nor a web, nor is it spatial. It is rather an immense, temporalized, constantly moving, changing, and developing system of nodes, each more or less the same distance from all the others, that is, the distance of an instant, the "click of a mouse," as we say. I can, for example, with a few clicks of the mouse on "Google Earth," zoom in from a satellite in outer space to see, from 1,475 feet up, my own house on Deer Isle, where I now (that was in 2006) sit typing this into my Portable Mac, connected to the Web by "Wild Blue Satellite." It makes me more than a little dizzy to look at the image and to think of it, since I seem to be in two places at the same time, in my study and 1,475 feet in the air above it, looking down on its roof from above, spying on myself. Economic, cultural, military, capitalist, and mediatic globalization depend absolutely on such technological "advances," includ-ing not just telecommunication gadgets but jet planes, high-powered ex-plosives, "smart" missiles, and, alas, nuclear bombs.

The destruction of the World Trade Center would not have been possi-ble without these "high tech" devices, passenger jets turned into missiles, cell-phones and e-mail used for communication during the planning of the attack, and so on, just as the roadside bombs in Iraq require powerful and compact explosives, along with cell-phones. The latter are often used as detonation devices, as well as for communication among the "terrorists" or "insurgents." Globalization, facilitated by new technologies, is also in-evitably weakening the separate sovereignty of nation-states and making possible new forms of worldwide political organization. What Derrida in *Specters of Marx* and elsewhere calls "the new International" is the promise without promise, or untenable promise, of this new form of globalization. Speaking of Heidegger's saying, without elaboration, "yes," when asked, in a famous interview in *Spiegel* in 1976, whether he foresaw the coming of an absolutely technologized state, Derrida comments, "It goes without saying that nothing resembles an 'absolute technological state' [*État absolument technique*] less than that which I have spoken about under the terms *faith, messianicity, democracy to come* [démocratie à venir], the untenable promise of a *just international institution*, an institution that is strong in its justice, *sovereign without sovereignty*, and so on" (PTT, 191; C11S, 171).

The proper response to an event, whether that event is good or bad, for Derrida, is an active saying "yes" that sees the event as making a demand on me for a responsible response. The proper responsible response is to use the occasion to work toward fulfilling the promise of the democracy to come in the light of the nondenominational messianicity without messianism that is an inextinguishable faith seemingly built into human nature. Derrida calls it a "universal structure" (PTT, 190; C11S, 171). I suppose he means an indestructible belief that, perhaps, just perhaps, according to the strange Nietzschean and Heideggerian logic of "perhaps," which he discusses so eloquently in *Politics of Friendship* (PF, 26–48 ; PA, 43–66), perhaps the good time will come. Nevertheless, like the utopian democracy to come, with which the messianicity without messianism is closely associated, the messiah, as Derrida insists repeatedly, will never come. The democracy to come will always remain an unfulfilled "perhaps," always still yet "to come." It is this faith or hope, this untenable promise, that leads Derrida to make those small political acts I have named, even though he recognizes that the law of *destinerrance* means that our acts, like whatever we write—letters for example, or this essay—are destined to wander and err. They reach their destination only by fortuitous and aleatory accident.

> I have often tried, elsewhere [says Derrida in "No Apocalypse, Not Now," commenting on Heidegger's confidence in a *Geschick des Seins*, a sending of Being], to stress the divisibility and the irreducible dissemination of the plurality of *envois* ["dispatches"]. What I have called "destinerring" [*destinerrance*] no longer gives us even the assurance of *a sending* of Being [*d'*un envoi *de l'être*], of a gathered-up [*rassemblement*] sending of Being. . . . The destinerring of the *envois* is linked to a structure in which randomness and incalculability are irreducible. I am not speaking here of an undecidability or incalculability that can be factored into a calculable decision. I am not speaking of the margin of indeterminacy that is still homogeneous to the

order of the decidable and the calculable. As in the lecture "Psyche: Invention of the Other," it would be a question here of an aleatory dimension that is still heterogeneous to every possible calculation and every possible decision. (Pe, 405–6; Pf, 381)[3]

This formulation leads me back to the Derridean concept that is most useful for understanding and perhaps responding constructively to the disastrous situation we are now in, in the United States and in the world: the terrifying logic of autoimmunization. What is this logic? As I have demonstrated in Chapter 6, the logic in question arises from Derrida's appropriation for politics of the terminology of autoimmunity in the living body. Here is the essence of what Derrida says: any community, such as a nation-state, has a built-in, "unconscious," and incurable tendency to destroy itself, in a suicidal act that Derrida calls "auto-co-immunity." Just as the body may turn its immune system against its own organs, so any community or state, in its attempt to protect its borders, to achieve homeland security, and to make itself safe and sound inevitably turns its self-protective mechanisms against itself. This makes things worse rather than better. It can lead to the auto-destruction of the community or state. The most alarming aspect of what Derrida says about political autoimmunity is his insistence on its inevitability and universality. Just knowing about it does not prevent it from happening. It applies everywhere at all times whenever human beings gather themselves into a community or state.

In a brilliant analysis, in *Philosophy in a Time of Terror* (PTT, 94–99; C11S, 144–52), of the way the destruction of the World Trade Center on 9/11 was, perhaps, a true event, Derrida uses this frightening general logic of autoimmunity to illuminate, better than I have seen any other commentator do, the way 9/11 was a case of autoimmune suicide, real suicide for the "terrorists," symbolic suicide for the United States and for the globalized world that depended on the United States as its economic, military, cultural, and technological sovereign power. Derrida does not much emphasize, in this case, as he does in "Faith and Knowledge," the religious base of auto-co-immunity in notions of sacrifice, holiness, survival, and messianicity. He emphasizes more, in *Philosophy in a Time of Terror*, Freudian notions of mourning, repression, the unconscious, and traumatism. Derrida stresses the way 9/11 was a consequence and extension of the Cold War, since the United States had, during the Cold War, in one way or another trained and supported many of the terrorist groups. This training was part of its clandestine, CIA-operated opposition to the Soviet and then Russian occupation of Afghanistan. (The collapse of the Russian occupation, by the way, ought to have forewarned us about the eventual outcome of our invasion and occupation of Afghanistan. It was and is doomed to failure, as it was for the British in the nineteenth century and for the Russians much more recently.) The 9/11 terrorists were trained to fly in the United States, used our own planes as bombs, and employed devices, like cell-phones and computers, developed in the United States. Their hatred of the United States was generated by U.S. acts of terror and imperialist aggression abroad, though those were intended to protect our security and sovereignty. It was a spectacular example of autoimmunitary logic, the suicidal turning against ourselves of weapons, machinery, and ideology that we had developed as a kind of immune system to protect us, to keep the United States safe, indemnified, even holy, the sacred "home-land." Derrida also stresses, as I have said, the way the "terror" generated by 9/11 and kept alive by the media (endless shots of the twin towers falling) and by the Department of Homeland Security (heightened alerts to "yellow" or "red" whenever it is decided we might be forgetting and might begin to notice that our basic civil rights are being taken away) was not a terror of what had already happened. It was fear of something worse, "the worst," something that has not yet happened, something certain to happen in the future, for example, a rain of nuclear bombs from North Korea or from Iran, or a "dirty bomb" exploded in the streets of New York or Los Angeles by some unknown and anonymous terrorist group. The Republicans, in the lead-up to the 2008 presidential election, attempted to exacerbate that terror of some immanent act of terrorism, "worse than 9/11," as Bush said in mid February 2008. Only the Republicans, they argued, can protect us from the terror that they have generated. Derrida also, finally, in a passage I have already cited in Chapter 6, asserts that all efforts to repress or forget the terror that is firmly lodged in the unconscious of every U.S. citizen just makes the terror worse, in a fearful and terrifying return of the repressed (PTT, 99; C11S, 152).

Everything that has happened in Iraq, in the United States, and in the world since Derrida gave that interview in October 2001 has confirmed how prophetically right he was. All the suicidal autoimmunitary actions I detailed at the beginning of this essay attest to that. Everything we have done to attenuate our terror has only made it worse. Our right-wing politicians capitalize on this terror, endlessly and deliberately regenerate it, in order to keep U.S. citizens in subjection.

What should we do in this terrifying situation? What does Derrida suggest that we should do? The logic of autoimmunization, the reader will have noted, has one positive aspect. It keeps a community, a political entity, open to the wholly other—for example, to the democracy to come.

That means we can, must, and should still work, according to the classic emancipatory ideal, as best we can in the concrete situation in which we find ourselves, to move, even if only an inch or a centimeter, closer to the democracy (perhaps) to come. It is our responsibility, our duty, to do so. The present Democratic Congress is making some moves in that direction. We may even dare to hope that our political situation may change after the 2008 election. (Added December 26, 2008: as has now happened.)

Nevertheless, it will not do to be too cheerful or sanguine about our ability to fulfill this measureless responsibility. One reason for this, as Derrida powerfully argues in *The Gift of Death*, is that the fulfillment of one specific, exigent political responsibility means "irresponsibilizing" oneself in relation to all the other equally exigent political obligations. Each responsibility is wholly other to all the others. One cannot fulfill them all, though each is equally demanding. Beyond that, however, as Derrida says in a remarkably concentrated passage in *Rogues* (*Voyous*), the last book for which he was able to read proofs during his mortal illness, the punctual or stigmatic instant act of exercising sovereign decision, by way of the *cracy* in "democracy" ("rule of the people"; etymologically, *cracy* means 'rule,' *demos* means "people"), inevitably infects the self of the one who acts with suicidal autoimmunity. The passage is a good example of the way a swarm of Derrida's key terms are often at work in a given short passage:

> Finally, and especially, however one understands *cratic* sovereignty [*la sou-veraineté cratique*], it has appeared as a stigmatic indivisibility that always contracts duration into the timeless instant of the exceptional decision. Sovereignty neither gives nor gives itself the time; it does not take time. Here begins the cruel autoimmunity with which sovereignty sovereignly affects itself but with which it also cruelly infects itself. Autoimmunity is always, in the same time without duration, cruelty itself, the autoinfection of all autoaffection. It is not some particular thing [*quelque chose, ceci ou cela*] that is affected in autoimmunity, but the self, the *ipse*, the *autos* that finds itself infected. As soon as it needs heteronomy, the event, time and the other. (Rog, 109, trans. modified; Vf, 154)

This concentrated passage says a mouthful, as they say. Its aporetic logic is extremely concentrated and even enigmatic. "*Cratic* sovereignty" would appear to name the sort of authoritative, unreserved power a sovereign or a chief executive, such as the president of the United States, has or sometimes claims to have. The immediate contexts in *Rogues* and Derrida's many discussions of sovereignty in relation to ethical or political decision indicate, however, that each of us, in a "demo-cracy," in which sovereign power is vested in the people, is sovereign in the moment of ethical or political decision and act. An example is the act of voting. The moment of decision, such as deciding to put an *X* beside such and such a candidate's name when I am in the voting booth, is without time, outside of time. This means that it is not based on anything prior, such as a conclusive calculation that this will be the best choice, nor can it be certain of its future consequences. In that moment, moreover, the decider cruelly affects and infects himself in an event of autoimmunity.

Just what does that mean? It sounds pretty frightening, since it makes any political decision or act, such as voting, in some sense suicidal. Derrida insists that it is not some thing or other, this or that, that is infected and affected by autoimmunity in the moment of decision, but the self itself, *ipse*, *autos*, just as my body is mortally endangered by autoimmune reactions. This is certainly a cruel and intransigent claim. It is the basis of a "radical" and apparently "pessimistic" politics, and then some. One would do well not to take what Derrida says too lightly, and just move on. Derrida must mean that the most acute place and time where the logic of autoimmunity operates is in the time outside of time of ethical or political decision, what I have called the "moment of decision." I mean to do my duty by voting or by doing something green. I end up making things worse in the act of doing my best to do the best. Instead of making myself safer, I expose myself to limitless danger.

The final sentence, however, suggests the glimmer of a way out of what appears to be a dead end supporting the conclusion that it might be better not to commit any political act at all. The paragraph ends with the assertion that the self infects itself with autoimmunity "as soon as it needs [*dès lors qu'il lui faut*] heteronomy, the event, time and the other." It needs these whenever it makes a genuine political decision. I suppose, on the basis of what Derrida says elsewhere about decision and responsibility (see Chapters 3 and 9 of this book), that he means a true decision is a responsible/irresponsible response to the call of the wholly other, *le tout autre*. This call and response is an event that is outside the law or that establishes its own, heteronomous law. An example is Jehovah's command to Abraham to sacrifice Isaac and Abraham's saying "Here I am," always paradigmatic for Derrida of the moment of decision. The consequences of such an act are devastating for the decider, but at the same time they are altogether necessary as a move toward the "democracy to come." Abraham becomes willing to murder his only beloved son, guilty of an intent to commit filicide. As Abraham could not yet have known, since Moses on Mt. Sinai came later, but as those who redacted the Bible did retroactively know, this would have been a failure to obey one of the Ten Commandments: "Thou shalt not kill" (Exod. 20: 13). That willingness, however, is necessary to the founding of the Jewish people, since, as Jehovah says, "because thou hast done this thing, and hast not withheld thy son, thine only son: That in blessing I will bless thee, and in multiplying I will multiply thy seed as the stars of the heaven, and as the sand which is upon the sea shore" (Gen. 22:16–17). Such autoimmunitary acts, according to Derrida, are the only way forward, the only way to break the catastrophic, endless repetition of the same institutionalized injustice.

Several intricate pages in *Aporias* that comment on passages in *The Other Heading* about political duty (*devoir*) will, as a conclusion for this chapter, perhaps clarify Derrida's hard, even cruel wisdom about political action. It is hard not only in the sense that it is hard to take but also because it is perhaps more than a little obscure, hard to understand. Derrida is quite specific about what our political duty is. He speaks in terms of the duty of those who have inherited European traditions. He speaks as a European. *The Other Heading*, as Derrida observes, was written during the first Gulf War. His question then was: "What should we good Europeans, dwelling on this isthmus, this 'cape,' do now, in this situation?" *The Other Heading* gives ten minus one or plus one commandments or duties, for that moment, seven of which he cites in *Aporias*, though they are all the "same duty," as he says. All are exemplifications of what Derrida means by "aporia." Europeans' "duty," first, is "to respond to the call of European memory," the memory of Europe, Europe, that is, as a unified and self-enclosed tradition within which the concept of duty was developed. It is equally Europeans' duty, however, to open up Europe's shoreland to what "is not, never was, and never will be Europe." What Derrida calls, repeatedly, the "*same duty* [même devoir]" dictates "welcoming foreigners." It dictates criticizing, "'in-both-theory-and-practice,' and relentlessly," both Communist "totalitarian dogmatism that, under the pretense of putting an end to capital, destroyed democracy and the European heritage" and, at the same time, "a religion of capital that institutes its dogmatism under new guises." The *same duty* enjoins being faithful to the tradition of "critique" while subjecting that tradition to "a deconstructive genealogy that thinks and exceeds it without compromising it," a neat trick if you can do it. The *same duty* enjoins faithfulness to the "democracy to come," "a democracy that must have the structure of a promise." The *same duty*, finally, dictates "respecting differences, idioms, minorities, singularities," while, contradictorily, respecting "the universality of formal law" (cited from OH, 76–78; AC, 75–77, in Ae, 18–19; Af, 40–41). This seems clear enough. It gives answers to the question Derrida goes on to pose in *The Other Heading*, "What are you going to do TODAY?" (OH, 79; AC, 77). Each one of us should act today, for example, as Europeans, in the midst of the first Gulf War, by casting a vote, sending a letter to the Editor, or marching in a protest, so as to do our best to advance specified causes. It is also easy enough to see how these injunctions can be adapted to fit my situation now, as a citizen of the United States, in the midst of the endless War on Terror. Some small, in the end insurmountable problems remain, however. The duties that Derrida identifies are contradictory, "aporetic." How can we respect the enclosed unity of Europe while welcoming foreigners to our shores? How can we respect differences while respecting the universality of law? To act responsibly in response to one of these duties is to act irresponsibly toward its contradictory counterpart. Moreover, the reader might well wonder just what is the basis, the foundation, the ground of this so-called duty? Who or what enjoins me to do these possible/impossible things? How can I be sure this is really my duty, the "same duty" in different, contradictory forms?

Derrida's answer is given in the intricate argumentation of the pages just preceding and following the citations from *The Other Heading* I have made. You must read these pages for yourself, meticulously, but I give here a succinct and sketchy précis. Derrida asserts, explicitly contra Kant, that the duty he has in mind is an "*over-duty [sur-devoir]*," "whose *hubris* and essential excess dictate transgressing not only the action that *conforms to duty* [conforme au devoir] (*Pflichtmässig*) but also the action undertaken *out of the sense of duty* [par devoir] (*aus Pflicht*), that is, what Kant defines as the very condition of morality" (Ae, 16; Af, 38). Well, if Derridean duty is not Kantian, then what is it? It is, says Derrida, an "aporetic" duty, a "single 'double, contradictory imperative'" (Ae, 16; Af, 37).

What in the world can that mean? Derrida has here defined "aporia" both as a dead end, an impasse, a "no thoroughfare" and, at the same time, as an "experience" in the root sense of a transgression, a passing through. To say "the experience of aporia" is to utter an oxymoron, since "experience" means living through, passing across, while "aporia" means being stuck in a dead end. In an initial, more usual sense, an aporia is the encounter with a border, an edge, a frontier, a barrier or closed door. In the second sense, an aporia is an experience of the limitless, the interminable. An aporia in the second sense differs from an antinomy, which might suffice for the first sense, that is, as a name for a hovering between two contradictory but equally imperative concepts or demands. The second sense of aporia names the contradictory demand made on each of us by the

"wholly other." The other asks me both to act in an entirely new, unspon-
sored, unprecedented, even lawless way, while acting in conformity with
law. I have discussed at greater length this strange Derridean concept of
decision in Chapter 2 of this book, though with a focus on ethical rather
than political decision. "In order to be responsible and truly decisive,"
says Derrida, "a decision should not limit itself to putting into operation
a determinable and determining knowledge, the consequence of some pre-
established order. But, conversely, who would call a decision that is without rule, without norm, without determinable and determined law, a
decision?" (Ae, 17; Af, 38). Nevertheless, the contradictory political decisions and acts Derrida enjoins in *The Other Heading* under the heading of
"the *same duty*" are, precisely, without rule, without norm. Only such political acts will, perhaps, move forward toward the endlessly receding horizon of the "democracy to come." This is expressed in challenging and
even scandalous terms in the sentences that just precede the ones I have
cited about the anti-Kantian "over-duty": "The most general and therefore most indeterminate form of this double and single duty is that a responsible decision must obey an 'it is necessary' that owes nothing, it must
obey *a duty that owes nothing, that must owe nothing in order to be a duty*, a
duty that has no debt to pay back, a duty without debt and therefore without duty" (Ae, 16; Af, 37).

"A duty without duty," "a duty that owes nothing"—these are the
aporetic formulations that best define our permanent political situation.
They also may explain why this duty without debt, which is enjoined by
the wholly other, exposes us, always, to the terrifying logic of autoimmunity I identified earlier in its political dimension. Nevertheless, each of us
must take political action now, whatever the risks. It is our duty to do
so. This duty, however, owes nothing. It does not obey any identifiable
injunction to act in such and such a way. Since such a duty without duty
always invokes "heteronomy, the event, time and the other" in all their
aporetic uncertainty, it also puts into play our collective irresistible, ineradicable penchant toward autoimmune reactions. Each of us, and all of
us collectively as we are segregated into communities or states, are "at
war with ourselves," to echo the original title of Derrida's last interview.[4]
Political action, for Derrida, is therefore always a leap in the dark. This
leap is always shadowed by auto-co-immunity, but it is nevertheless our
duty to take it.

CHAPTER II

Touching Derrida Touching Nancy

But O for the touch of a vanished hand,
And the sound of a voice that is still.

—TENNYSON, "Break, Break, Break"

They hand in hand with wandring steps and slow,
Through *Eden* took thier solitarie way.

—MILTON, *Paradise Lost*

Of touch they are, that, without touch, doth touch.

—SYDNEY, *Astrophil and Stella*, 9

Here, "to touch" means to say [*veut dire*], to tamper with, to change,
to displace, to call into question; thus it is invariably a setting in
motion, a kinetic experience.

DERRIDA, *Le toucher, Jean-Luc Nancy*

How to Get a Handle on Le toucher

How can I touch Derrida, now that he is dead? How can I touch, in a
shapely chapter, on the immense and immensely complex text he wrote
touching touching, the tactile, tactility, the contingent, the tangential as a
theme in Nancy's immense work,[1] and as a theme in Western philosophy
from Aristotle to Husserl, Heidegger, Levinas, Didier Franck, Jean-Louis
Chrétien, and, by way of Immanuel Kant, Félix Ravaisson, Maine de Biran,
and others? One little touch, that's all I want, such as the touch at one
point the tangent line makes on a curved line before flying off at a tangent.[2] This chapter will show that, if Derrida is right, what I want is im-
possible/possible.

It would seem, at first touchdown, that the way to touch Derrida or to
be touched by him is to read what he wrote, such as his immense text on
Nancy, *Le toucher, Jean-Luc Nancy*. Problems of translation arise from the
word go, as always. They inhibit getting in touch with this book in a chapter in English, given that its title has been rendered as *On Touching—Jean-
Luc Nancy*. What is the difference between a dash in the English and a

comma in the French between the two segments of the title? The appositive comma connects the second half of the title more intimately to the first half than the vaguer dash, which may indicate separation as much as connection. The French article and noun *Le toucher* can certainly be translated as "touch" or "touching," taking *toucher* as a substantive. But *toucher* is also a verb in French, so Derrida's title also means "to touch it." The referent of *le*, taken as a pronoun, seems to be, or may be taken as, the proper name Jean-Luc Nancy, as the comma of apposition perhaps indicates. The French title can mean "touching Jean-Luc Nancy" or "touching that, I mean Jean-Luc Nancy."[3] Or the proper name might be an apostrophe: "Touch that if you can, Jean-Luc Nancy." Derrida in the book more than once speaks directly to Nancy, as I shall show. Like the text itself, the French title shimmers with multiple idiomatic meanings, which cannot easily or fully be carried over into English. I shall keep in touch with these problems as best I can as I go along.

Alfred Lord Tennyson's dead friend Arthur Hallam touched him when Tennyson read Hallam's letters. At least that is what Tennyson says in a famous passage in his *In Memoriam*:

> So word by word, and line by line,
> The dead man touched me from the past,
> And all at once it seem'd at last
> The living soul was flash'd on mine,
>
> And mine in this was wound, and whirl'd
> About empyreal heights of thought,
> And came on that which is, and caught
> The deep pulsations of the world.[4]

To this I can only say "Wow!" "That which is"! "The deep pulsations of the world"! Who would not wish to "come on" or "catch" *them*? And to reach, through words, the dead other! At the small expense of a little reading. Does anything of this sort happen when I read Derrida? It would seem possible, since Derrida's writings have a distinctive, inimitable voice that makes it possible to say of a given fragment "Derrida must have written this." Or rather, since it is a question of writing, not talking, I should more appropriately say that Derrida has an inimitable "hand." That is an old-fashioned, metonymic way to speak of the distinctive features of a given person's handwriting. Lady Dedlock, in Dickens's *Bleak House*, recognizes the law document she glimpses, among those Tulkinghorn has in hand, as being in her dead lover's hand. That recognition is the beginning of the end for her.

English, like French, is full of idioms using "hand." We say "Let's shake hands on it" when patching up a quarrel or "I give you my hand on it" when making a promise or sealing a contract. The French say, or used to say, according to Nancy, "*Touchez là!* in order to conclude an accord or to terminate a disagreement [*"Touchez là!"* . . . *pour conclure un accord ou pour terminer un différend*]."[5] That is the way grain sales are concluded by Henchard in Hardy's *The Mayor of Casterbridge*, before Farfrae comes along and changes that to the indirection, the prosthetic technicity, of a paper contract. I say I am "touched to the heart" by something or other, but heart and hand are connected by the idea that the third finger of the left hand (counting as first the one next to the thumb) is "heart in hand." I suppose that is because it has a vein or artery coming directly from the heart. Hence we wear wedding rings on that finger. At least that is what my mother taught me. I "put my hand on my heart" when swearing allegiance or when making a solemn promise. I may also sanctify an oath by swearing with my hand on the Bible, for example, when in the witness box I promise to tell the truth, the whole truth, and nothing but the truth, so help me God. A recently elected member of the U.S. House of Representatives, Keith Ellison, the first Muslim in that august body, gave offense by suggesting that he might take the oath of office with his hand on the Qur'an rather than the Bible. "Give the little lady a hand" is an invitation to a round of applause by clapping hands. It is extremely odd, when you think of it, to say I can *give* my hand. Surely that is a gift that is taken back in the moment of giving, except, perhaps, when you say "I'd give my right hand for it," though I never heard of anyone who actually did that. A famous Zen koan says: "This is the sound of two hands clapping." Clap! "What is the sound of one hand clapping?" Dickens's Pip, in *Great Expectations*, was "brought up by hand." When I need help, I say, "Please give me a hand." In English, we engage in "hand-to-hand combat," though the French say *corps-à-corps*. We play a hand of cards or deal someone a hand. We say "Fate has dealt me a losing (or winning, usually losing) hand." The heroine in melodramas says to the hissing villain "Unhand me, sir!" I ask: "How can I get a handle on Derrida's book on Nancy?" We say: "Don't you lay a hand on me" or "He didn't lay a hand on me." "I'll see if I can lay my hands on it" is a promise to look for something you have misplaced. Spiritual power passes from person to person by a "laying on of hands," as in the biblical story of Isaac's blind blessing of Jacob rather than Esau, the younger son in place of the eldest. The thief or policeman says "Hands up!" A "handmade" object of manufacture, a piece of handwork, or handiwork, is assumed to be better than a machine-made one, for example, a piece of lace. One says "Please hand me the salt." The "Get-Ready Man," in James Thurber's sketch, shouts out through a megaphone, "GET READY! GET READ-Y! THE WORLLLD IS COM-ING TO AN END!"[6] He might just as idiomatically (and religiously) have said "The end of the world is at hand!" Heidegger, notoriously, makes use of German idioms using *Hand* in *Being and Time*. He speaks of the way some-thing is *zur Hand*, "to hand," and he makes a crucial distinction between material objects that just happen to be there, *vorhanden*, "present-at-hand," and other things, such as tools, that are for man's use, prepared for manipulation by human hands, *zuhanden*, "ready-to-hand." My hammer, my pen, or even my computer is *zuhanden*, though Heidegger hated the typewriter and would have hated the computer even more. He thought handwriting was the only valid writing. Derrida has written an admirable essay about the motif of the hand in Heidegger, "Heidegger's Hand (*Geschlecht* II)" ("La main de Heidegger [*Geschlecht II*]"). I shall return later to this essay. A wonderfully specific passage near the beginning of Hardy's *The Mayor of Casterbridge* gives a list of ready-to-hand farm implements as they were offered for sale in Casterbridge shop windows:

> Scythes, reap-hooks, sheep-shears, bill-hooks, spades, mattocks, and hoes at the iron-monger's; bee-hives, butter-firkins, churns, milking stools and pails, hay-rakes, field-flagons, and seed-lips at the cooper's; cart-ropes and plough-harness at the saddler's; carts, wheel-barrows, and mill-gear at the wheelwright's and machinist's; horse-embrocations at the chemist's; at the glover's and leather-cutter's, hedging-gloves, thatchers' knee-caps, plough-mens' leggings, villagers' pattens and clogs.[7]

The hyphens here indicate the inherence of these manmade objects in the uses for which they were intended, while the apostrophes indicate the way these shopkeepers make by hand what they sell, in that doubling of making and made that distinguishes even the most primitive manufacture. One must make a tool to use to make a tool, use one hand-crafted stone to chip away another stone to make it a spearhead or a flint-scraping tool. As Helen Tartar reminds me, the Confucian *Analects* say, "When making an axehead, the model is not far away." A "hay-rake" is for raking hay, while "the saddler's" is a shop where cart-ropes and plough-harness are made by means of other hand tools and then sold. All these items depend on the hand for their use. They are prosthetic extensions of the hand. The hand is already, in a manner of speaking, a prosthetic extension of the body, a signal example of what Nancy calls "ecotechnicity."

To continue my list of hand idioms: a woman "gives her hand in mar-riage," as in Hardy's *The Hand of Ethelberta*. We say that someone who is good at fixing things is "handy." A jack of all trades is a "handyman." We "manhandle" something into place. Of an errant child who was corrected, we say, "His parents took him in hand." A used article, usually clothing, that you receive from an older sibling, from your parents or grandparents, or from some older relative is called a "hand-me-down." Often a hand-me-down is a relic of the dead. "The back of my hand to you" is an insult, like thumbing one's nose, which, as Joyce puts it in the Aeolus section of *Ulysses*, means "K. M. R. I. A.," or "Kiss my royal Irish Arse."[8] I have elsewhere discussed kisses, though not of the "arse," as they appear in *Le toucher*.[9] Kisses will reappear here later on.

"Hand" in the sense of idiosyncratic style is one item in this tangled, interlaced multitude, which includes manipulation of things with the hands, hand gestures, or hand signs—pointing, waving, clapping, "thumbs up" (or down), and so on—as well as hands shaking one another, clasping one hand with the other in prayer, or just holding hands with another person, as in the touching last lines of *Paradise Lost* describing Adam and Eve after the fall. They have been exiled from Paradise into the thorny wilderness. Nevertheless, they walk hand in hand, as earthly fallen lovers still do, hand touching hand in a way that is almost a self-touching: "They hand in hand with wandring steps and slow / Through *Eden* took thier solitarie way" (12:648–49). I shall return to this by way of Derrida's commentary on Nancy's linguistic "invention" *se toucher toi*, "touching myself touching you." That is what Milton's Adam and Eve do. The tangle of idioms is not quite the same in French. We do not say, as the French do, *maintenant*, literally "holding in the hand," for "now," but we do say "manoeuvre," "manage," "manufacture," "maintain," and "maintenance," all of which have the French word for "hand" buried within them.

Derrida, in *Le toucher*, is most interested in the hand as being, for so many philosophers, the premier "organ" of touch and in the idea that the hand as tool, sign, or means of self-touch is, for so many philosophers, the exclusive attribute of "man," what Derrida calls the "humanual." I shall return to this.

Derrida certainly had an inimitable "hand." His handwriting was more or less indecipherable, except by adepts, if then. Paul de Man and I used to spend a whole lunch hour trying to decipher some letter or other Derrida had sent me from Paris to New Haven. The most important parts came at the end and were the least legible. The difference between Heidegger and Derrida might be identified by observing that, while Heidegger stuck to *Handschrift*, handwriting, Derrida began by writing out his seminars with a pen, then changed to the typewriter, and finally moved to the computer, though he resisted e-mail until the end. Scholars are at this moment struggling to decipher his handwriting in his early seminars in preparation for publishing them all.

By a further metonymic extension one might mean, by Derrida's "hand," the distinctive features of his "style" in a given piece of writing. Derrida, as we know from other essays, for example, *Spurs: Nietzsche's Styles / Éperons: Les Styles de Nietzsche* (Sp, 36, 37), was aware that *style* comes from *stylus*. This happens by way of a metonymy, a sideways displacement, that is, from the writing implement to what we ordinarily think of as the special features of a given author's way of writing. I read something or other by Derrida. Its distinctive stylistic features lead me to say, with confidence, "Derrida must have had a hand in this," "I recognize Derrida's hand here," or "This must come from Derrida's hand." "Hand," in this sense, survives as distinctive, *pace* Heidegger, through changes in the various technological mediations used, from pen to manual typewriter to electric typewriter to computer to printed book.

I shall follow, in this chapter, the guiding thread or pointing finger of the hand as a recurrent theme or motif in *Le toucher*. The chapters in the present book each focus on a single term or theme in Derrida's work: the word *reste*, the term *irresponsibilisation*, the theme of being late, and so on. Only in this way can the requisite micrological attention, word by word, line by line, and page by page, to what Derrida wrote be reflected, perhaps, in what I write in my turn. I follow Derrida's own methodology in doing this, as I shall specify later in this chapter.

My choice of the hand theme in *Le toucher* is made somewhat arbitrarily, since the hand is only one among many salient and recurrent motifs in this book. Derrida touches again and again on each of these motifs, in different contexts each time. I might have chosen heart. Or body. Or spacing: *partes extra partes*. Or the strange phrase in Freud's penultimate note, written a year before his death, that says "Psyche is extended, knows nothing about it [*Psyche ist ausgedehnt, weiss nichts davon*]." Both Nancy and Derrida have made extended commentaries on this note. I discuss it in Chapter 12.

Or I might have focused on the motif of the limit that is touchable-untouchable. Here are examples of this recurrent theme:

> We can touch only on a surface, which is to say, the skin or thin peel [*pellicule*] of a limit (and the expressions "to touch at the limit," "to touch the limit" irresistibly come back as leitmotifs in many of Nancy's texts that we shall have to interpret). But by definition limit, *limit itself*, seems deprived of a body. Limit is not touched and does not touch itself, it does not

let itself be touched, and it evades touch [*Elle ne se touche pas, elle ne se laisse pas toucher, elle se dérobe au toucher*], which either never reaches it or transgresses it always. (OT, 6; LT, 16, trans. modified)

The superficies of these surfaces, as noted earlier, are limits—exposed as such [*comme telles*] to a touch that can only ever leave them intact, untouched and untouchable. (OT, 14; LT, 26)

The infinite leap that separates thinking from pondering [*Le saut infini qui sépare la pensée de la pesée; pesée* also means "weighing"], just where they remain inseparable (at least insofar as thought is not limited to representation or the body to the objectivity of neurons) is but the leap, in the very experience of touching, between the touchable and the touchable, at the limit, thus between the touchable and itself as untouchable limit. It is touching that touches on the limit, the limit that is its own and not its own, that is to say, on the untouchable whose border it touches. To touch on the limit is not, for contact, just one experience among others or a particular figure: one never touches except by touching a limit *at the limit* (OT, 297; LT, 333, trans. modified)

Or I might have chosen the theme of the exactitude for which Derrida so often praises Nancy. The watchers around Psyche's extended body, sleeping or dead, know exactly what she does not know, that she is extended and that she knows nothing about it: "They know it with a knowledge that is *exact* (one of Nancy's master words, to which we will frequently return: *exactitude* is the very thing, the big deal for this thinker [exactitude *est la chose, la grande affaire de ce penseur*], who thinks *exactly* something other than what one thinks [*pense*] in general or ponders [*pèse*] too easily under the word *exactitude*, and yet . . .)" (OT, 15, trans. modified; LT, 27).

Or much could be said about the theme in *Le toucher* of syncope or interruption (diastole without systole, thesis without antithesis, a suspension breaking dialectic). The word *syncope*, according to the *American Heritage Dictionary*, means: (1) the omission of part of a word, as in "bos'n" for "boatswain"; (2) "A brief loss of consciousness caused by transient anemia; a swoon." Syncopated music puts the stress on a normally weak beat. It skips a beat. One of Nancy's books is called *The Discourse of the Syncope: Logodaedalus* (*Le discours de la syncope: I. Logodaedalus*).[10] Derrida refers often to this book. He also uses the word *syncope* to allude to Nancy's heart-transplant operation.

Or I might have focused on what Derrida says about vision in relation to touching, as in the odd recurrent phrase in *Le toucher*, "when our eyes touch, is it day or is it night? [*quand nos yeux se touchent, fait-il jour ou fait-il nuit?*]" (OT, 1–4; LT, 11–14), which Derrida looks at so carefully, trying to reach out, somewhat blindly, and touch it. He says he first saw it as graffiti on a wall in Paris.

Or I could have taken as the way into *Le toucher* what Derrida says about the kiss, whose salience in this book I have elsewhere discussed and will discuss again in this chapter, from another perspective.[11] Or, finally, I might have approached *Le toucher* by way of prosthetics, transplants, techniques, technicity, technics, and ecotechnics as they make immediate touch impossible while keeping the self from being touched by death.

Prosthetics is a particularly rich vein. It takes a long time before Derrida, after mentioning the issue here and there, makes clear just what is at stake, for Nancy and for Derrida too, in the appeal to a universal distancing or nonimmediacy by way of "prosthesis, transplant [*greffe*], metonymic substitute, and so forth" (OT, 286, trans. modified; LT, 322). What is at stake is no less than the dispersion of essence into multitude. Fundamental to Nancy's thought, for example, in *The Inoperative Community*, in his other, as yet untranslated, book on community,[12] or in *Being Singular Plural*, his book about intersubjectivity,[13] is the conviction that division, *partage*, goes all the way down to the bottom, so to speak. It is, nevertheless, a shared division, as in the other side of the pun in *partage*. The word means both "shearing" and "sharing." Though Nancy tends to emphasize the idea of sharing in *partage*, as in "share a meal," the primary meaning of "divide in parts for distribution" is still there as an overtone in his uses, for example, in the title of one of his books: *Le partage des voix* (*The Division/Sharing of Voices*). Food must be divided in order to be shared, *partagé*. What might be called "a shared plurality" is, for Nancy, aboriginal. I have written elsewhere concerning Nancy's ideas about *partage* in relation to community and intersubjectivity.[14]

As Derrida observes, saying "there is no 'the' something or other" is a key locution in Nancy, as in "There is no 'the' body; there is no 'the' touch; there is no 'the' *res extensa*."[15] Derrida adds the hand to this list: "This multiplicity . . . challenges every presupposed unity of whatever sort: of the self, the body proper, and the flesh [*du soi, du corps propre et de la chair*]. And of the hand, I would add" (OT, 289; LT, 324; trans. modified). This universal multiplicity means there is no "the" hand. Saying "there is no 'the' technical," as Nancy also says, is, however, as Derrida recognizes, not just one example in a series. Why? Because saying there is no "the" technical "compromises the unity or oneness [*l'unité ou l'unicité*] proper of essences" (OT, 287; LT, 323). Derrida's expression of this adds an important touch to his reading of Nancy, as well as to the reader's understanding of Derrida's own sense of what is at stake in *technē*, in these days of robots, prosthetic limbs (including hands), organ transplants (including hearts), cloning, stem-cell research, gene alteration (which someday might save people from dying of the pancreatic cancer that killed Derrida).

I must look a little closely at the sequence in which Derrida discusses technicity. Derrida begins (well, *continues*) by citing three passages from Nancy, all from "A Finite Thinking":[16] "And this is why . . . there is no 'the' technical [*"la technique"*], merely a multiplicity of technologies"; " 'The' technical is nothing other than the 'technique' of compensating for [*de suppléer*] the nonimmanence of existence in the given"; " 'The' technical—understood this time as the 'essential' technicity that is *also* [aussi bien] the irreducible multiplicity *of* technologies—compensates for the absence of *nothing* [rien]; it fills in for and supplements *nothing*" (OT, 287; LT, 322–23). These passages are more than a little odd, if you look at them closely and think about them a little, even out of their contexts—always a dangerous thing to do. It seems intuitively correct to say that there is no "the" technical, merely a multiplicity of technologies. Of course that's true, the reader thinks. Right on. Then that reader may realize that the target here is a celebrated essay by Heidegger, "The Question Concerning Technology" ("Die Frage nach der Teknik").[17] That essay certainly does assume there is an essence of technology, a "the" technology. One quarrels with Heidegger at one's peril. A lot is at stake in "The Question Concerning Technology," as numerous commentators, including Derrida himself, have demonstrated. Nancy dismisses Heidegger a little too casually and obliquely, without really arguing, at least here, with what Heidegger says. Derrida, on the contrary, has engaged Heidegger on technology in hand-to-hand combat, or in a wrestling match, in numerous seminars.

The second and third citations from Nancy are even more odd. Generally speaking, we are likely to assume that technologies, even if they are always a plurality with no common essence, are a replacement or an extension of something or other positive, as the telephone allows us to talk and hear one another at a distance, as a supplement to talking to someone close by, that is, as a supplement to the limitations of voice and hearing, which exist and are not nothing. No, says Nancy firmly, "the 'essential' technicity [so technicity *does* have an essence after all, even though one suspended by the clothespins of quotation marks, like a word hung out to dry!] that is *also* the irreducible multiplicity *of* technologies" does not extend some human power or other or supplement it. It "compensates for the absence of *nothing* [a phrase that can be read two ways, as saying, on the one hand, that nothing is absent, that technicity compensates for a hole, an absence, nothing, and, on the other hand, that technicity compensates for a substantive nothing, like Heidegger's *das Nichts* or Stevens's "nothing that is not there and the nothing that is," in "The Snow Man"[18]]; it ["the" technical] fills in for and supplements *nothing*." One sees what Nancy is saying. If my heart were gone and there were nothing there in my chest, I would be, "technically," dead. I must, so to speak, die and be resurrected from the dead in a heart-transplant operation. When I have lost my hand in an accident, the prosthetic hand fills in a place in my body where there is nothing. A little more is at stake here, however. Nancy, I think, wants to assert that technicity compensates for a nothing at the base or origin. For Nancy, however, there is no "the" base or origin, such as Heidegger's Being with a capital *B*.

Derrida's commentary on the three citations he makes from Nancy on technicity seizes a different handhold from mine in the passages. Derrida stresses in his own way that Nancy deconstructs essence at the same time as he reaffirms essence. This duplicity is, Derrida affirms, the center of what Nancy says. It is an exemplary moment in Derrida's commentary. It is also a good example of the way Derrida takes with one hand what he gives with the other. I shall return to this formulation. Derrida praises Nancy for his "exactitude," his radical rigor, and at the same time shows the limits of Nancy's thought, tactfully putting what Nancy says in question:

> As regards this example (which would be precisely more than an example, an exemplary example) I would be tempted to up the ante a little more [*de pousser la suenchère un peu plus loin*]. The "there is no 'the' technical" isn't just another "there is no 'the' . . ." among others [*un "il n'y a pas 'le' ou 'la' " parmi les autres*], a sample in a homogeneous series. No, it would give us a privileged access, under this name or another, to all the instances of "there is no 'the' . . ." 's, and thus to something like the "essence of technicity" that precisely "there is not." Hence a quasi-transcendental dizziness [*le vertige quasi transcendantal*]. For there is the process opening onto the possibility of a supplementary substitution, onto a metonymy that compromises the unity or proper oneness of essence. It is because there is *some* [de la] technology (which there is not) that there isn't this or that, and so forth, and that one can repeat or multiply examples to infinity, gestures that deconstruct the unity *itself* or the properness *itself* of all essence or even all "being" [*le propre même de toute essence voire de tout "étant"*]. (OT, 287, trans. modified; LT, 323)

So far so good. Nancy is here praised for having, with his own hands, so to speak, or with his own words as tools, "deconstructed" unity and properness, propriety, ownness, oneness, all down the line. That phrase about "quasi-transcendental dizziness" is a little ominous, however. It doesn't quite sound like a good thing to bring about in readers, this quasi-transcendental dizziness. The word "quasi-transcendental" has appeared more than once earlier in the book and will reappear later as the name for Nancy's implicit appeal to something like a Kantian transcendental that is not really a Kantian transcendental but only a "quasi-transcendental," whatever that means. In this case, Nancy appeals to an essence of technicity that really is not a transcendental essence but a kind of counterfeit or "quasi" essence.

The notion that Nancy turns concepts into funny money that could not be invested, draw interest, or be used to buy something appears elsewhere in *Le toucher*, as in the following exuberant passage describing Nancy as a spendthrift wasting the great lexicon of the Western philosophical tradition. Nancy uses all those august words, such as "essence," but in such a way as to use them up, usuriously. "Transcendentalizing or ontologizing everything that comes down to 'touching,' he spends like a madman, to the point of ruin [*il dépense comme un fou, jusqu'à la ruine*], the resources, the credit, the capital, and the interest of the transcendental-ontological. He reduces them, it seems to me, to monetary simulacra" (OT, 271, trans. modified; LT, 306). This is devastatingly funny, but to call Nancy a spendthrift madman hardly seems like high praise.

What is at stake here is made clear in what follows the long paragraph I cited above. Saying there is no "the" technical, the reader will remember, is, according to Derrida, a way to "deconstruct the unity *itself* or the properness *itself* of all essence or even all 'being' [*étant*]." (The French word *étant*, used by Derrida here, corresponds to Heidegger's *Seiendes*, something in being, as opposed to his hypostatized *Sein*, which would be *être* in French. The distinction does not exist in English words.) Deconstructing essence and properness seems to be an unequivocally good thing, if one believes that believing in essence, as the great tradition of Western philosophy has tended to do, is a mystification.

Alas, however, matters are not quite so simple, as the next paragraph asserts. It is impossible, Derrida argues, to do without the "the" or "the the," as Wallace Stevens calls it. ("Where was it one first heard of the truth? The the," asks Stevens in "The Man on the Dump."[19]) You cannot use conceptual words without an implicit appeal to the "the." You cannot

"do philosophy" without recourse to words that reify or generalize themselves into concepts. Saying there is no "the," says Derrida, "would risk
depriving him [Nancy] of all conceptual determination and, at the limit,
of all discourse [*à la limite de tout discours*]—handing over discourse to the
most irresponsible empiricism" (OT, 287, trans. modified; LT, 323). The
latter, I suppose, would be, in this context, an endless enumeration and
description of different kinds of what are all, falsely, called "techniques,"
though Nancy is not far from an "irresponsible empiricism" when, at the
very end of *Corpus*, in a passage Derrida cites a couple of pages on, Nancy
disintegrates "the" body, since there is no "the" body, into a potentially
endless grotesque list of body parts. He does this in such a way as to turn
"the living body" of myself or the other into a fragmented, dismembered,
corpse, or into the "images" thereof, though Derrida, in his generosity
toward Nancy, denies that this is the case. The list, he says, is "exactly
calculated [*très exactement calculé*]" (OT, 289; LT, 325): "A body is an
image [*une image*] offered to other bodies, a whole corpus of images
stretched from body to body, local colors and shadows, fragments, moles,
areolas, half-moons [*lunules*], nails, hairs, tendons, skulls, ribs, pelvises, bel-
lies, meatuses, foams, tears, teeth, droolings, slits, blocks, tongues, sweat,
liquids [*liqueurs*], veins, pains, and joys, and me, and you [*et moi, et toi*]."[20]

What is the force of the repeated word *image* in this extraordinary list
of apparently heterogeneous items, in which body parts both visible and
invisible are set side by side with "blocks [*blocs*]" and "pains, and joys, and
me, and you"? The list may be "very exactly calculated" to accumulate
toward a climax in "and me, and you," but its main effect is the disintegra-
tion of "the" body into disparate "images," whatever that word means,
along with the pluralization of a body into multiple examples of any one
of "its" body parts, that is, perhaps, into "images" that are always multiple.
Nancy, just before the passage just cited, in sentences not quoted by Derrida, tells the reader what these images are not—not, exactly, what they
are. The explanation is a little obscure, since it works by negations: "The
between-bodies is their images' taking-place. The images are not like-
nesses, still less phantoms or phantasms. It's how bodies are offered to one
another, it's being born into the world [*mise au monde*], the setting on
edge, the setting into glory of limit and radiance."[21] Well, if images aren't
semblances, phantoms, or phantasms—all, one might say, technical prostheses for the things themselves—then what are they? I suppose, on the
basis of what Nancy says in general about touch no touch, and the improper proper, that images are the way I offer my body to the other person, to "you," and the way "you" offer your body to me, in an immediacy

that is intermediate or always mediated, a "birth to presence,"[22] or bringing into the world (*mise au monde*) that is a glorious visible manifestation or éclat that is at the same time indirect, intangible, metonymic, and ungraspable, no more than "images."

As soon as you open your mouth and speak, or put pen to paper or hand to computer keys, Derrida wants to say, you are in complicity with the assumption of essence. The only escape would be silence. Philosophers, we know, do not go in much for silence. Derrida imagines a diabolically or daemonically ironic Socrates saying to Nancy, "I'm not asking you, he says, for an enumeration of techniques, but what you mean to say when you term them techniques in the plural. In what way are they techniques? [*En quoi sont-elles des techniques?*] and so forth" (OT, 287; LT, 323). Neither Nancy nor anyone else, I included, can escape the "the." It fatally enters into any locutions one uses to deconstruct the "the": "The definite or defining [*défini ou définissant*] article is already engaged or required by the discourse that disputes it. It is with this limit and within this transaction that Nancy is to be understood, in this wrestling match of thinking [*en ce corps à corps de la pensée*]" (OT, 287, trans. modified; LT, 323). It is a hand-to-hand combat one always, it appears, loses.

Derrida then goes on to draw the conclusion that not only is there no "the" deconstruction but also no "the" deconstruction*s* either, since Nancy's goal might be defined as an attempt to deconstruct the "the." It follows from the nonexistence of "the" deconstruction(s), as Derrida says on the next page, that Nancy's project of deconstructing Christianity, often mentioned in *Le toucher*, is doomed to failure. This is so not only because there is no "the" Christianity to be deconstructed but also because there is/are no "the" deconstruction(s) either. That has not stopped Nancy from publishing, after Derrida's death, a book called *Dis-Enclosure: The Deconstruction of Christianity* (*La Déclosion [Déconstruction du christianisme, 1]*).[23]

I shall return to this question of who gets the last word, or the last fall, in this little wrestling match between Derrida and Nancy. The ineradicable presence of Christian presuppositions in apparently secular or "Enlightenment" concepts like *mondialisation* (the French word for "globalization"), "the materiality of the body,"[24] or political "sovereignty" is something Derrida never tired of demonstrating. It is one of the leitmotifs of his late seminars and books.

On the way to his assertion that "Christianity" cannot be "deconstructed," Derrida makes an instructive contrast between Nancy's "typical syntagma, "there is no the . . . ," and his own "if there is any," such as "the gift, if there is any [*s'il y en a*]," or "forgiving, if there is any." It is an instructive contrast because it goes to the heart of Derrida's difference from Nancy. Though Derrida doesn't exactly say so but affirms, rather, that Nancy's locution and his are just "two irreducibly different deconstructive gestures," nevertheless one may read between the lines and see that Nancy's locution, "a *negative modality* ('there is no . . .')," sets for Nancy the trap Derrida has identified of using the "the" to confute the "the," whereas in Derrida's "if there is any [*s'il y en a*]," "the 'there is' turns *to a conditional* [au conditionnel]" and thereby escapes that trap: "And 'if there is any' doesn't say 'there is none' [*il n'y en a pas*], but rather, there isn't anything that could make room for any proof, knowledge, constative or theoretical determination, for any judgment—especially not any determinant judgment" (OT, 288, trans. modified; LT, 324, 323). The last phrase is another passing tangential swipe at Kant. Derrida would never have the temerity to propose to try to deconstruct Christianity, not only for the reasons I have given, that is, because there is no "the" Christianity and no "the" deconstruction(s), but also because the most that can be said about Christianity is "Christianity, *s'il y en a*."

After this exorbitant digression or deflection at a tangent from the curve I was following, I return to that curve and assert again that I choose the hand as my guiding thread, as just one handy way among many ways to get a handle on *Le toucher*. I do this with a somewhat despairing sense that *Le toucher* calls for a virtually endless line by line and page by page reading, sticking to what Derrida calls "the letter of the text." You see what happened, dear reader, when I allowed myself to be inveigled into a brief discussion of Derrida on Nancy on technicity, as one of the lines I *might* have followed, but chose not to follow. Things rapidly got out of hand. Even in the case of hands, or other topics I discuss, I must choose synecdochic examples read somewhat carefully (it is never careful enough), rather than an exhaustive repertoire, to avoid that interminable reading. Nevertheless, I fear my chapter will be exorbitant, the longest in this book, even though it fails ever really to touch Derrida. I shall return later to this micrological methodology of reading as practiced by Derrida *passim*, but especially in this book.

I also want, at the same time as I single out the hand from the tangle of motifs in *Le toucher*, to identify distinctive features of Derrida's "hand" in this book. I want to figure out, hypothetically, just why Derrida writes about Nancy in just the way he does. I want to understand what is at stake in Derrida's using just this style or hand, since he had more than one nib in his penholder, more than one hand to choose from. I want to engage in a wrestling match with Derrida, *mano a mano*, one in which I am certain to lose, or, rather, I want to do combat with *Le toucher*, to see if I can actually touch him or it. I would then be able to cry "Touché," as in a fencing match. Derrida at least once calls attention to this locution, as I shall show. "Touché" is pronounced the same as *toucher*.

Whenever I hear the word *touché*, I think of the Thurber cartoon in which one fencer has just severed the head of his adversary, with a single swipe of his sword, so that the head is flying off from the body. The victor calls out "Touché!" Is touching the other, if it ever happens, always lethal, a beheading? If so, it would be a piece of good luck if I can never touch the other, get in touch with him or her. I also remember another cartoon in *The New Yorker* that was made up of a sequence of pictures showing a sculptor working with a hammer and chisel on a monumental sculpture of a human figure. In the end, in the last frame, the sculptor gives one final small tap with his hammer on the chisel, a finishing touch, a last touch. The whole thing instantly disintegrates into a thousand fragments.

Why are these cartoons funny? Is the disintegrating sculpture cartoon an allegory of so-called deconstruction? Deconstruction, as practiced by Derrida, most often respectfully, "gratefully," and at length, reads a given text with the most sympathetic intimacy. The reading then makes one final "timid" interrogation or statement of demur, upon which the whole text falls into fragments. I shall return to this catastrophic happening later. It might be called a catastrophe theory or a chaos theory of what so-called deconstruction does. Some small butterfly wingbeat of a question leads to a hurricane in which a system of thought collapses wholesale. If Heidegger, for example, is wrong in distinguishing so sharply between man and the other animals,[25] as every Western philosopher from Plato and Aristotle to Lacan has done, then his whole theory of *Dasein*, of *Menschheit*, cornerstone of his thinking, is invalidated, along with his philosophy as a whole. Derrida tactfully suggests just this in his last seminars, "The Beast and the Sovereign (Two)," which I have discussed in other chapters in this book.

Le toucher, I begin my hand to hand, or face to face, eyes touching eyes, encounter by saying, is one of Derrida's most extravagant, strange, and hyperbolic, even outrageous books. It is unusual, for one thing, in the conditions of its composition. Unlike much of Derrida's work, the whole was not prepared for oral delivery as seminars or lectures. Only the first part was written in response to a commission. Peggy Kamuf had asked Derrida to contribute an essay for an issue on Nancy of *Paragraph*, an issue that she was editing. He did that, in 1992. The essay came out in 1993. Derrida was, for some reason, not satisfied with that. My present essay could be defined as an attempt to guess why he was dissatisfied and why his book got so long. In subsequent years Derrida added and added to the first essay until finally he published in 2000 a big book, *Le toucher, Jean-Luc Nancy.* As Derrida says in the Foreword, dated September 1998–September 1999:

> Unable [*Incapable*] today [Why was he incapable? Not enough time, or was it intrinsically impossible?] to transform the central topic of this essay and make it less unworthy of Nancy's thought, and particularly of the powerful books he has published during the past five years [*cinq dernières années*; he means, I guess, between the time of the first essay in 1992 and the publication of *Le toucher, Jean-Luc Nancy* in 2000, though that would be more than five years], I have contented myself here with changes in the form of the text, interpolated passages [*d'incises*]—some of them admittedly long ones—and notes added retrospectively.
>
> The age of this text is thus manifold. [*Ce texte a donc plusieurs âges.*] It sometimes skips several years from one sentence to the next. And so, together with the reader, I could have played at coloring in the strata of an archive. (OT, x; LT, 10)

It would be interesting to have such a version. The reader could then see what were first thoughts and what were afterthoughts. The finished book is not really finished, as Derrida more than once observes in the book itself. It is only arbitrarily closed off. *Le toucher* is made of different archival strata laid down at different times, visible, if the interpolations were colored differently, like a cross-section cut in igneous rock formed in layers at different times by successive volcanic eruptions. It certainly would be interesting, and possible with today's computer programs, to have a version of *Le toucher* with the different strata dated and marked in different colors. Probably the dates of the interpolations are lost forever by the technical conditions of composition on the computer. Perhaps, however, Derrida's hard drives, *s'il y en a*, retain dated traces, like those the "Deconstruction Machine," described in footnote 28 of this chapter, is designed to pulverize. Those strata may include, if we could recover them, for all I know, though Derrida does not say so, material imported and then revised from seminars given years and years prior to *Le toucher*, seminars on Husserl or Aristotle or Maine de Biran or Ravaisson. This is the case, as Jason Smith has shown in a brilliant dissertation,[26] with the part of *Specters of Marx* on *The German Ideology* and the "Theses on Feuerbach" that takes up the argument Marx makes that all ideology is basically religious. For Marx, as Derrida notes, mystified religious belief is the basis of all ideological mystification.

The composition of *Le toucher* coincides with Derrida's transition from writing on the typewriter to writing on the computer, just as he had much earlier moved from handwriting his seminars to typing them. Derrida was a demon typist, like Northrop Frye. I remember on two occasions accidentally overhearing the staccato, machine-gun-like sound of Derrida typing. This happened once in Zürich when I was outside his hotel window on the ground below and heard him typing in his room up on the second floor what was, it happens, "La différance." This essay was presented orally later that week in Paris before France's important philosophers assembled. I heard this daunting sound once much later when Harold Bloom and I heard Derrida's ferocious typing when we came up the stairs to his apartment in Ezra Styles College at Yale to pick him up for lunch. "Shall we interrupt him?" we asked one another, eyes touching eyes. "Yes!" we said. Who knows what important insight or invention, what intellectual event, was lost forever through our mischievous malice.

Composition on the word processor, as anyone knows who does it, though it is more silent than the typewriter, much less open to touch by way of the ear, lends itself much more easily than writing on the typewriter to virtually endless revision and interpolation. The traces of just when those changes were made disappear forever, unless you make extraordinary and awkward efforts to preserve each successive version, for example, by keeping innumerable backups of each stage of the writing. Talk about prostheses and technicity! Heidegger, as I have said, hated the typewriter, just as Plato devalued writing as opposed to speaking, and Heidegger would have really detested the "word processor." It would have seemed to him a salient example of the way technicity is cutting Western civilization off from "Being." The computer is reinforcing the oblivion of Being by suspending handwriting, *Handschrift*, as an essential concomitant of "thinking." This seems, I must say, nonsense to me. Writing on the computer is as much done "by hand" as were Heidegger's scribblings with pen on paper, which he wanted to think were so much more immediate, were kept so much closer to "what is called thinking" and therefore to Being. The pen is as much a technical prosthesis as is the computer. Try writing with your naked finger! "The" hand itself, not to speak of the pen, though there is no "the" hand, is already a technical, prosthetic, extension of the brain or of the heart that thinks. Those who are computer adept have the feeling that the fingers on the keyboard are doing the thinking, that the keyboard, the computer, and the screen are extensions of the hand and fingers, and that the whole assemblage is doing the thinking for you. The computer, when I take it in hand and "touch" the keyboard, thinks for me and writes down those thoughts as they occur to me as a small voice speaking more or less on its own inside of me / outside of me and then turned into words that ultimately appear on the screen at the endpoint of this highly mediated transaction.

The existence of a doubling in Derrida's process of thinking is indicated by all those places where he holds a dialogue with himself. An example is a passage I cite below in which he imagines himself talking to himself and at the same time addressing an imaginary reproach to Nancy. This was not Derrida's "unconscious" engaged in conversation with the "conscious" Derrida, the id talking to the ego, but two perfectly conscious Derridas talking to one another, each of which had a perfect right to claim itself to be "the real Derrida." The immensely complicated and invisible series of relays from the keyboard to the word processing "application," such as Microsoft Word or the more primitive MacWrite that Derrida persisted, somewhat perversely, in using, to the "chip" with its "Random Access Memory" (Intel Core 2 Duo running at 2.33 Gigahertz in my laptop, a MacBookPro), to the "hard drive," whose extraordinary powers (two gigabytes in my present machine, that is 2,000,000,000 bytes by decimal measurement, or 2 times 1,073,741,824 bytes, that is, 2 times 1024^3 by another common definition; a byte is eight bits; a bit is either a zero or a one in the binary counting system computers use) the word processing "program" appropriates and organizes, and then in an instant to the screen, where zeroes and ones are turned back into letters and words, is a spectacular example of what Derrida (and Nancy in his own somewhat different way) mean by the absence of any direct immediacy or presence in a ubiquitous detouring technicity that is already present in the unaided hand touching its own other hand or the hand of another, touching oneself touching the other, *se toucher toi*, or picking up the pen to write. This impossibly long sentence is meant to mime the series of relays that take place in an instant as soon as I press one of the keyboard's keys.

As I might have foreknown, Derrida himself talks about the technicity of the computer in the opening paragraph of the last section of *Le toucher*, "Salve (Untimely Postscript, for Want of a Final Retouch)." "Salve" was apparently begun and then abandoned, "stalled" on Derrida's computer for seven years, as one says a computer "stalls" or "freezes." This leads him to reflect on the intervening dramatic changes in computer technology and on the way the computer is a spectacular example of "technicity" as a short circuit or obstacle to immediacy that comes up against the hard, stubborn resistance of the "hard drive," associated by Derrida, in an earlier footnote, with Kant's hardness (*die Härte*), as held against him by

Hegel, and with Nancy's obdurate rigor, exactitude, and a certain emotional hardness, all examples of the resistance at the limit of "exscription," where touch touches the untouchable:

> (A supplementary touch or past retouch left stalled long ago [*laisée naguère en panne*], almost seven years ago, on my computer, that is, in a place where the relation between thought, pondering [*la pensée, la pesée*], language, and digital [a play on "digit, finger" and the computer's "digital" code of ones and zeroes] touch will have undergone an essential mutation of ex-scribing [*de l'ex-crire*] over the past ten years. A description is needed of [*Il faudrait décrire*] the surfaces, the volumes, and the limits of this new magic writing pad [an allusion to a famous essay by Freud, about which Derrida had, many years before, written a brilliant essay, "Freud and the Scene of Writing" ("Freud et la scène de l'écriture"; WD, 196–231; ED, 293–340)], which exscription touches in another way, with another kind of "exactitude," precisely, or "punctuality," from the keyboard to the memory of a disk said to be "hard." All I have written, then, is—see Chapter 13 n. 26—on *die Härte*, about the hard, hardness, hardship—obduracy of duration or enduring [*sur la dureté de ce qui dure ou s'endure*]. On resistance, as it were [*en somme*] . . . .) (OT, 300, trans. modified; LT 337)

"As it were"! Writing on the computer is a form of exscription in which what one writes vanishes, at the limit, when it comes up against the obdurate hardness of the hard disk, though of course it comes back again, most of the time but not always, when I "retrieve" it.

Derrida's (and Nancy's somewhat different) universalizing of technicity means that Derrida saw even lovemaking, counter-intuitively, as an example of touch as touch at a distance, not immediate touching. In a passage early in *Le toucher* he imagines something that in the jargon of youthful computer nerds is called "tiny sex," though I don't suppose he had ever heard that computerized youths' term. David Crystal in *Language and the Internet* quotes a student as claiming that he can do his mathematics homework and have tiny sex at the same time.[27] It's a neat trick if you can do it, but young people these days are adept at multitasking.

Sex on the Internet does come up in *Le toucher*, as part of a claim that touch, not just the visual, can be virtualized. Apropos of a description of the Integrated Media Systems Center at the University of Southern California, a center that is devoted, among other things, to virtualizing and digitizing touch, Derrida observes that "Tomorrow's Sigmund Freud will have to refine his magic writing pad. But also the topography of bodies during psychoanalytical sessions. Not to mention erogenous 'touching at a distance' and the amorous body-to-body wrestling match in the sheets of the Web [*corps à corps amoureux dans les draps du Web*]" (OT, 301, trans. modified; LT, 338). That's "tiny sex," as I understand it. Derrida's somewhat scandalous claim is that sex on the telephone or by postcard, as in *The Post Card*, or, I suppose, between the sheets of the Web, is not narcissistic or masturbatory but, on the contrary, that even the most "immediate," "intimate" "contact" of two bodies entwined, one penetrating the other, is no more immediate than making love by telephone, postcard, or computer, since there is no "the" touch, no immediate touch, only metonymically displaced and mediated touch, touch at a distance. Derrida says, "at the heart of the syncope, between touching and the untouchable—an absolute untouchable that is untouchable not because it is of the order of sight or hearing, or any other sense, but untouchable in the order of touching, untouchable touchable, untouchable right at [*à même*] the touchable—there is the originary intrusion, the ageless intrusion of technics, which is to say of transplantation [*greffe*] or of the prosthesis" (OT, 113, trans. modified; LT, 131). Derrida had just illustrated this in an extraordinary parenthetical interpolation that follows his assertion that "It is time to speak of the voice that touches—always at a distance, like the eye—and the telephonic caress, if not the (striking) phone call [du coup de téléphone]" (OT, 112, trans. modified; LT, 130):

> (Imagine lovers separated for life. Wherever they may find themselves and each other. On the phone, through their vocal inflections, timbres, and accents, through elevations and interruptions in breath, through moments of silence, they cultivate all the differences necessary to arouse sight, and touch, and even smell [*le parfum même*], so many caresses, up to the ecstasy from which they are forever weaned—but never deprived. They know that they will never find it again, never save across the cordless cord of these entwined voices. A tragedy. But they also know themselves to be intertwined, at times only through the memory they keep of it, through the spectral phantasm [*spectre phantasmatique*] of ecstatic pleasure [*jouissance*; is that spectral phantasm, that phantasmatic specter, the same as Nancy's "images"? Probably not quite. Nancy explicitly denies that his images are "phantasms." That is probably a sign of the strangely intangible, but nevertheless fathomless, gulf that separates them, Derrida from Nancy], without whose possibility, they know this too, a pleasure would never be promised. They have faith in the telephonic memory of a touch. A phantasm gratifies them. Almost, each in their monadic insularity. Even if the shore of a "phantasm," precisely, seems to have more affinity with *phainesthai*, that is, with the appearance or the brilliance of the visible.) (OT, 112–13, trans, modified; LT, 130)

In all the careful complexity of this "imaginative" invention ("Imagine lovers separated for life," says Derrida), one phrase, for me, stands out. It is salient as a way to touch the heart of Derrida's thought and also to touch the difference between Derrida's thought and Nancy's thought: "each in their monadic insularity [*chacun dans leur insularité monadique*]." Nancy would never use such a phrase. For him, as he argues at length in *Being Singular Plural*, each of us, though caught in our singularities, is in touch without touch, from the beginning and primordially, with the other. We are singular and plural at once. For Derrida, however, as I have demonstrated in Chapter 6, "Derrida Enisled," each of us, as Derrida says in a striking passage in *A Taste for the Secret*, is like a Leibnizian windowless monad in a world without God to guarantee the monads' harmony, their resonance or *Stimmung*, or anything like what Husserl called their "analogical apperception" of one another. Each of us, for Derrida, as not for Nancy, is enclosed in a private world with no bridge, isthmus, passageway, or translation across to the equally private worlds of others, including those with whom I make love.

The phantasm or invention of touching another by telephone appears once more in *Le toucher*, as if it were a recurrent waking dream. This time the intimate second person singular is used: "When I speak to you, I touch you [*Quand je te parle, je te touche*], and you touch me when I hear you, from however far off it comes to me, and even if it is by telephone, the recollection of a voice's inflection on the phone, or by letter or e-mail, too" (OT, 291; LT, 326–27). Here the inflection is more positive, perhaps because it is part of a paraphrastic commentary on Nancy's phrase *se toucher toi*, Derrida goes on to negate this happy touching by telephone or e-mail by saying that you could not be touched by the other's voice unless you were able to touch yourself, which he holds you cannot do.

The Main Traits of Derrida's Hand

Just what is so strange and outrageous about Derrida's "hand," in the sense of manner of writing, in *Le toucher*? I herewith identify eight distinctive, extravagant features of its "style" or "manner." It might seem that I am interested only in Derrida's "rhetorical strategies" but, as Derrida himself asserts more than once in *Le toucher*, both as a general fact about philosophy and as strikingly exemplified by Nancy, style is meaning. If we look at the superficial "surroundings and clothing of thought [*entours et . . . vêtement de la pensée*]" in Nancy's work, he sometimes appears to be saying the same thing as Merleau-Ponty or Chrétien. Nevertheless, Nancy's way of writing brings into the open "the *gaps* [*les* écarts] that we [he means "I, Derrida"] are continually measuring." He does this measuring by paying close attention to "the tone, the connotations, the mise-en-scène, indeed in ob-scene [*la mise en scène, voire en ob-scène*]: for these gaps [*écarts*] are also powerful and inventive gaps of language [*écarts de langage*]" (OT, 286, trans. modified; LT, 322). In the coinage *ob-scène*, Derrida plays on the prefix *ob* as, in one of its antithetical meanings, "against, in opposition to," meaning by *ob-scène* "outside the scene and the seen," offstage, so to speak. The *mise en scène* or staging is perhaps even the *ob-scène*, with an elided repetition of the *mise* in *mise en scène*, literally "put." The obscene is what should not or cannot be seen. It is a hiatus or *écart* in the visible. *Obscene* in both French and English derives from a Latin word originally meaning "inauspicious." Later it took on the meaning of "offensive or repulsive to the senses," especially sexually repulsive, indecent, most often its modern meaning. Derrida plays with that origin and with the nuances of *obscène* in French, which are not quite the same as its nuances in English. Nevertheless, the sexual meaning is not absent in Derrida's formulation. Characteristically, however, he plays on the word inventively by adding a hyphen and thereby producing a new word whose meaning I have tried to tease out. It is a good example of the difficulties of *Le toucher* and of Derrida's writing in general.

Reading Derrida requires careful attention to details of semantics, syntax, and punctuation (e.g., the hyphen in *ob-scène* and the doubling of the *en* in *mise en scène* and *voire en ob-scène*). This attention often requires a return to the French original. *Voire*, for example, is an antithetical word. It comes from Latin *vera*, "true," and is either, according to my *Petit Robert*, "an exclamation which marks doubt," as when one says "truly? really?" or an expression "used to reinforce an assertion," *de même*, in French, "even," in this case to say, "not only a *mise en scène*, but perhaps even a *mise en ob-scène*." The reader needs to remember that Derrida is using these expressions to characterize the way Nancy's style not only stages its meanings out in the open but also uses powerful and inventive gaps in language to say what it means to say, or at least to allude to what is unsayable.

This use of gaps, the ob-scene, in the mise-en-scène of language means that Nancy's writing and his concomitant way of thinking are singular, unique. The way style is meaning entails a certain untranslatability that I am defying here by citing Derrida in English, with some of the original French interpolated here and there where the French contains something

idiomatic and hard to translate. The entire effort of *Le toucher* is, following
Nancy, to find ways to speak of the unspeakable, to touch in language the
untouchable, using the resources of French. It is an effort doomed to failure, of course, but that is not a reason not to keep trying, even though
whatever you say gets "exscribed," that is, in one sense of Nancy's neologism, written away or effaced. This happens on the skin, so to speak, that
is, at the untouchable limit of what you are trying to touch. Almost at the
end of *Le toucher* Derrida says, "one still has the impression that we are
always going to be at a loss for a meta-language with which to say anything
whatever about touch, touching, or the touchable that is not in advance
accommodated by the skin, exscribed right on the skin [*excrit à même la
peau*]" (OT, 303; LT, 339). If whatever he says is exscribed right on the
skin, then, according to Derrida's doctrine of the limit, discussed earlier,
it does not cross that limit and touch touch.

   This doom is what, it may be, led Derrida, a page earlier, to say he
wanted his whole book erased from all the hard disks, deleted from all the
memory banks: "I'm now sincerely asking that this book be forgotten or
effaced, and I'm asking this as I wouldn't have done—with as much sincer-
ity—for any of my other books. Wipe it all away [*Qu'on efface tout*], and
start or start again to read him, Nancy in his *corpus*" (OT, 301, trans.
modified; LT, 338). This imperative command is addressed both to the
reader and to himself, though of course Derrida never erased the hard
drive that contained *Le toucher*.[28] On the contrary, he anxiously kept backups of everything he wrote. In spite of this foredoomed failure to read
justly, anyone (you, I, he, she) should always start over and keep trying, as
Derrida does for over three hundred pages. You never know. You might
get it right by accident. Here are the features of Derrida's hand I find
most salient, most standing out to be almost touched. Most of these are
exemplified in citations already made.

   One: Derrida takes away with one hand what he gives with the other.
This is so important that I shall return to it after sketching out the other
seven stylistic features. The whole of *Le toucher* is one immense act of
taking back with one hand what is given with the other. The book also
constantly performs that double act in local, characteristically Blanchotian
locutions. In just two pages well along in *Le toucher*, for example, in an
attempt to do justice to Nancy's thought, Derrida says "inevitable-impos-
sible," "returning to me without returning to me," and "gathers, without
gathering [*rassemble, sans rassembler*]" (OT, 283–84; LT, 319–20). A few
pages later, another locution in the strictly Blanchotian form of *X* without
X appears: "suspending without suspending" (OT, 288; LT, 324). A large

number of other examples could be adduced of this small-scale simultaneous giving and taking. They punctuate *Le toucher*. The aim of all the book,
however, is to put in question, with Nancy's slightly ambiguous help, the
age-old intuitive tradition holding that touch is immediate, a "(continuous
and continuistic) haptocentric [*haptocentrique*: a neologism built on the
Greek stem for touch, *haphē*] intuitionism" (OT, 300; LT, 337). Those
places, here and there, where the aim of Derrida's book is encapsulated in
a total back of the hand to the whole Western tradition holding that touch
is immediate use extravagant forms of the X without X expression to give
and take away in a single double gesture requiring perhaps two hands.
Here is the best example, near the end of the book. The passage is addressed in praise of Nancy for breaking with this tradition:

> This *quasi*-hyper-transcendental-ontologization of tact (and not of touch)
> must remain paradoxical: it *exscribes* itself instead of inscribing or writing
> itself. [*Elle* s'excrit *au lieu de s'inscrire ou de s'écrire*; "exscribes," as earlier
> examples have shown, is Nancy's neologism for an act of writing that puts
> something beyond writing or acknowledges that it cannot be touched by
> writing.] For that which touches on it or that about which one speaks under
> the name of touch is also the *intangible*. To touch, with tact, is to touch
> without touching that which does not let itself be touched: to embrace eyes
> [*t'embrasser des yeux*], in a word or several words, and the word always brings
> to your [*ton*: second person singular in the French throughout this passage;
> he is addressing, perhaps, Nancy] ear the modest reserve of a kiss on the
> mouth. To touch with tact is, thanks to you, because of you, what can break
> with immediacy, with the immediate given, which one wrongly associates
> with touch and on which always rests, as on self-presence, intuitionism in
> general, transcendental idealism (Kantian or Husserlian intuitionism) or
> ontology, the thinking of the presence of being [*de l'étant*] or of being-*there*
> *as such* in its Being [The reference is to Heidegger's *Dasein*], the thinking
> of the body proper or of flesh [*chair*: as in all those present-day feminist
> appeals to the "materiality of the body," as well as in discussion in the male
> philosophical tradition, recapitulated by Derrida, of the "body proper" or
> of flesh—*Leib* in the German philosophical idiom, as opposed to *Körper*,
> body]. (OT, 292–93, trans. modified; LT, 328)

In a characteristic gesture, Derrida follows this admirable giving of a
summary by taking it all back. He says, in effect, I have gone too precipi-
tously to the end: "I have gone too quickly" (OT, 293, trans. modified;
LT, 328). I must go back and read Nancy carefully again, read what he
says about the weight of thought: "In order to demonstrate that the great

thinker of touch is interested, as is finally only right, in nothing but the intangible—and this is not something else—one would need, once again, to think, to weigh, to weigh *exactly* [*penser, peser, peser* exactement] what he says about the relation between *thinking* [pensée] and *weighing* [pesée]. One would have to read and meditate here step by step *Le poids d'une pensée* [*The Weight of a Thought*, the title of a book by Nancy]"[29] (OT, 293, trans. modified; LT, 328–29).

Two: Derrida unhands or disarms the distinction between the thematic and the "operative," as he calls it, or between literal and figurative. This occurs pervasively, but is in more than one place explicitly signaled. One place comes after a complex discussion of the way Nancy's use of the word *touch* seems at first to be "manner of speaking: a trope of some kind. Just try to find someone who has literally 'touched' a denial [*dénégation*]" (OT, 268, trans. modified; LT, 303). Gradually, however, Derrida coaxes his discussion of Nancy toward a recognition that the literal and figurative "invade" one another.

> Why say "touch" [as I myself have done in this chapter, from the title on] for "to speak of," "to concern," "to aim," "to relate to" [*se rapporter à*] in general, and so forth? Is it because touch, as Aristotle said, is not a "unique sense"?
>
> Yet Nancy plays this game more and more, the most serious one there is. It consists in using, as if there were not the slightest problem [*comme si de rien n'était*], this common and ancestral figure of tactile language in order to draw attention to "'the' touch"—which is not [*qu'il n'y a pas*]. He invests this very invasion that, little by little, prevents us from distinguishing between thematic sense and operative function, between the proper or literal sense and all its tropic turnings [*ses tournures tropiques*]. (OT, 268, trans. modified; LT, 303).

Two pages later, Derrida says, "His [Nancy's] discourse here extends to all registers of an *operative* or *thematic* sort [*de façon* opératoire *ou* thématique]—if at the least we still distinguish, for convenience, where the dissociation between these two modes is no longer, in all rigor, *pertinent*)" (OT, 271, trans. modified; LT, 306). "Operative" was one of the terms Austin first thought of using to name what he decided to call a "performative," that is, a form of words that does something rather than naming something.[30] In Derrida's analysis here, "thematic" corresponds to "literal," and "operative function" corresponds to "figurative." (I note in passing that they are not the same. A figure of speech is not necessarily performative.) The oppositions break down, for Derrida, because there is no "the" touch and because, therefore, all touch words, literal or figurative, thematic or operative, are, strictly speaking, performative catachreses for what cannot be adequately named either in literal or in figurative language. It is as if Derrida were saying, in effect, "I arbitrarily, and in sovereign irresponsible and unjustified decision, call this nameless something 'touch.'" The word *catachresis*, so far as I remember, does not appear in *Le toucher*, but an elegant formulation of the catachrestic situation in our relation to touch does appear almost at the beginning of the book: "And," says Derrida, "to announce questions that will come back to us like boomerangs, what is the way to organize together the following four concepts or philosophemes: *extension, partes extra partes, to touch*, and *to touch oneself?* Their association and dissociation will soon enough compel us, in the closure of a combinatory play around a vacant center [*dans la clôture d'une combinatoire au centre vacant*], into a vertiginous wandering" (OT, 16, trans. modified; LT, 28). "The closure of a combinatory play around a vacant center" is a splendid formulation of the catachrestic situation in relation to the heart of touch in which Derrida (and Nancy before and after him) find themselves. They are forced to take a ceaseless detouring or digressive walk from metonymy to metonymy with nowhere a proper, literal word, nowhere a way to name "the" touch as such.

Three: Derrida manifests this breakdown of the distinction between conceptual and figurative in ostentatiously and exuberantly inventive passages of thematic/figurative overkill, passages that could only have been written, these days, by Derrida himself. This procedure involves an exasperating but clearly deliberate procedure of using in his own language some punning version of the theme or figure he is putting in question. In discussing Nancy's term *partage*, which means, as I have said, both "sharing" and "shearing," for example, Derrida speaks of "a partitioning that departs anew [*une partition qui départage*]" (OT, 218, trans modified; LT, 247). The most tangible evidence of this stylistic feature is the constant wordplay, throughout the book, on words that mean "touch," in all their semantic and idiomatic variation: *tact, tactile, contact, contingent, tangent, tangential, pertinent,* and so on. Why all this play on touch words? Derrida does this in order to demonstrate, out in the open, where the reader can hardly miss it, that he too is caught in the double bind of not having any proper language to use. He too must use metonymies, language that is at once conceptual and figurative, since all conceptual words are figurative, as their etymologies show. Here is another extravagant example, of which I cite only part:

In order to respond to his [Nancy's] invitation, or even injunction, if not to his question ("a very long detour should be made here. What of the sharing/dividing of the senses?" [the citation is from Nancy's "Laughter, Presence"; see OT, 340, n. 3]), I shall merely—timidly, gropingly [*à tâtons*]— sketch the ellipsis of such a detour. This would be a brief, tangential excursion, along margins, marches [*marches*; the word means a region out at the frontier, as in George Eliot's oxymoron *Middlemarch*], and frontiers, via the "modernity" of this "European" question of touch in the history of philosophy, as a sampler [*échantillon*], and *done by hand* [*et* à la main; it could also mean "and *made by hand*"], between France and Germany. Done by hand: it won't be more than a sampler, more or less well sewn [*cousu*], following, like a guiding thread, the contour of the hand and especially of the finger. (OT, 138, trans. modified; LT, 159)

And so on, with more extension of the figurative embroidered sampler, sample of larger pieces of cloth to come, as the paragraph continues, but you get the idea. Derrida wants continually to show that he cannot get on with his reading without using and extending the figures that Nancy uses. He cannot, even by the most extraordinary turns of phrase, turn Nancy's figures (by some "detour") into any literal conceptual formulation. I shall return to the question of why Derrida singles out especially the hand in this sampler of the tangential excursion into the exchanges between France and Germany in modern philosophies of touch.

Four: Derrida has a habit of putting everything in question, drawing himself up, taking nothing for granted, even the most idiomatic and banal of everyday phrases, as in the following, addressed by himself to himself: "—You exert yourself? [*Tu t'efforces?*] What does that mean?" (OT, 139; LT, 160). Or, early in the book, he uses the ordinary idiom "take place" (*prendre lieu* in French), and then pauses to make that phrase problematic, obscure: "everything is taking *place*, that is to say, is extended [*a lieu, c'est-à-dire est étendu(e)*], 'in places that divide themselves . . . ,' 'between these places, these locations . . . '" (OT, 15, trans. modified ; LT, 27). The interpolated citations are from "Psyche," Nancy's original short commentary on Freud's aphorism.[31]

Five: Derrida sets, with a cunning hand, mantraps of handy lists that look like synonyms but aren't. Here are some examples, out of almost innumerable possible ones, from the first three pages of *Le toucher*:

What is contact if it always *intervenes between* two *x*'s? A hidden, sealed, concealed [*scellée, celée*], signed, squeezed, compressed, and repressed, interruption? Or the *continual* interruption of an interruption, the sublating negation [an ironic antithetical reference to the Hegelian *Aufhebung* or dialectical sublation] of the interval, the death of the *between*. (OT, 2, trans. modified; LT, 12)

Is there still room, place, space [*de la place, du lieu, de l'espace*] or interval, *khōra*, for the day's phenomenality and its diaphanous visibility? (OT, 3, trans. modified; LT, 13)

But it [the heart] is also not something else; it is not a figure inherited (from the Bible, for example) to refer to the center, life, *psyche*, *pneuma*, spirit, interiority, feeling, love. It is the body, it is the heart insofar as it is mine belonging to you [*m'appartient à toi*], this heart, the heart of the other, there where the "spiritual" figure, the inherited metonymy, touches this heart here, my body, in my body, and can no longer be distinguished from it. (OT, 283, trans. modified; LT, 319)

I have often invoked the "technical" dimension (prosthesis, transplant [*greffe*], metonymic substitute, and so forth). [The words in apposition here are themselves prosthetic metonymies.] (OT, 286, trans. modified; LT, 322)

A pertinence does not fail to touch the object, which is at the same time risky and cocky [*suffisant*] ("I know what I'm talking about!"), arrogant, impolite, impertinent. (OT, 302, trans. modified; LT, 339)

What can this "selfsame" [*même*] mean about the heart's heart? The heart proper, the essence of the heart, of the sovereign heart, of the heart in itself, of the heart with itself nearest to itself (*ipse, ipsemet, metipse, meisme, même*)? (OT, 305, trans. modified; LT, 342)

What is the effect, or purpose, or function, of these extravagant lists? Their ubiquity certainly contributes to the immense density of Derrida's style in *Le toucher*. The reader, the careful reader, has to slow down, pause, and interrupt the flow of her reading to ask herself just what each of the terms on the list means and just why Derrida needed so many. What is the difference in meaning between one item in a given list and the next in the series, between "the heart proper" and "the essence of the heart," or between a "prosthesis" and a "transplant"? Are the items in each list synonyms, just proof that Derrida could think of a lot of ways to say the same thing, or a progression that gets somewhere as the list progresses, by "method as detour," perhaps from one thing to its apparent opposite, or just a random list of variants that just happened to come into Derrida's mind? Nancy is also the master of the list, as in a great example Derrida cites, from the concluding paragraph of *Corpus*. This is Nancy's list of parts of the body offered as a "whole corpus of images stretched from body to body." (I have already discussed this list in this chapter and will discuss it again in Chapter 12.) Derrida may in his own lists be playing his inveterate game of one-upsmanship or upping the ante. Derrida overbids what Nancy bids by showing that whatever Nancy does he can do better, that he has higher cards in his hand. (This figure is used by Derrida himself about Nancy by way of the word *surenchère*, an overbid; OT, 307; LT, 346.)

The lists call attention to the contingency of words, to the way a slightly different form of saying anything always exists, therefore no single right way can be found. The lists call attention, also, to the way a given word is part of an immense network of connected words in a given lexicon, French, English, Greek, or Latin, and to the relations among those lexicons. Most of all, the lists indicate that Derrida is trying to say something that cannot be said except in approximate catachreses that bend ordinary language in the service of trying (always unsuccessfully) to say what is at the limit of the sayable. He needs to try this word and then that word and then another word or phrase, but can never quite get it right. The lists are therefore potentially interminable, as is *Le toucher* itself. Derrida often laments the way he is not getting anywhere with Nancy. He feels he is continually starting over again from the beginning, without having ever really touched Nancy on touching. This chapter records my similar experience in trying to touch Derrida or to touch Derrida's book about touch.

Just what was it that Derrida found so difficult to say clearly and succinctly, in so many words? No careful reader can doubt that the answer is that it was touch itself, the heart of the book, that was so impossible to say clearly and that led Derrida to invent such baroque lists. All my examples, by a no doubt not quite accidental serendipity, exemplify this difficulty. "The" "central thesis" of *Le toucher*, if I may put it that way, which Derrida explicitly forbids me to do, is the untouchability of the heart of touch, the impossibility both of touching itself and of talking/writing directly about touch. You cannot touch touch, or touch on touch. An interval, interruption, or spacing that cannot itself be touched, any more than can the object of touch or the limit of touch, always intervenes between my finger and what I reach out to touch, as in the old telephone advertisement "Reach out and touch someone." What is contact if it always intervenes between x and x? That is the theme of all these lists. Also, in their implicit interminability, which could go on and on, these lists constitute in themselves the uncrossable interval between reaching out and actually touching someone or something.

Six: Derrida handles in a masterly and deliberate way a technique of micrological reading that is itself thematized as the only way to go, the only way to have any hope, a hope without hope, of getting where he is going or wants to go, that is, touching Nancy on touching. Speaking of the proper way to get a handle on what Husserl says about the hand, for example, Derrida says it is irresponsible to stand back and try to make generalizations about Husserl's doctrine of the hand. He says:

> before posing the questions seemingly raised by the *reasoning* or the *argument* to which this network of phenomenological evidence gives rise [*donne lieu*], before interrogating the demonstrative procedures or theses that, in truth, seem to parasitize or contaminate in advance the alleged description, it would be better to remain closer to the text and to its letter [*au plus près du texte et de sa lettre*]. (OT, 174, trans. modified; LT, 199)

Derrida means that in Husserl's phenomenology the terminology used to pose a question already begs the question of the answer. The means of definition contaminates the definition. Derrida certainly keeps close "to the text and to its letter" in all sections of *Le toucher*. He makes careful, mostly short, citations and then teases out their meaning, often in commentaries that greatly exceed the length of the citations he has made. Derrida, in the passage I have cited, distinguishes between, on the one hand, "the text and . . . its letter," that is, in this case, the actual German words that Husserl used in his phenomenological "descriptions" of the role of the hand in touching and self-touching and, on the other hand, the reasoning or argument that Husserl makes, the theses he proposes about one hand touching the other hand, etc. These theses might be summarized without citation and in any language: "Husserl asserts so and so." This close attention to the letter of the text is absolutely necessary for the accomplishment of Derrida's goal, which is to show that Husserl's vaunted objective, unbiased description of the facts themselves, as they are given through the phenomenological reduction, are "in fact" contaminated beforehand or parasitized by the general arguments or theses he wants to sustain. The descriptions are not objective at all. They are just imported into the "facts" he allegedly describes objectively. The conclusions Husserl wants to reach contaminate the evidence he adduces. Only a micrological reading that sticks tenaciously to the letter of the text can show that this is actually the case.

Seven: Derrida habitually postpones a full taking in hand of a given topic or passage in the name of a potentially (or actually) interminable reading. He constantly employs a rhetoric of postponement or of deferral, saying things like: this "would call for an interminable analysis" (OT, 14; LT, 26); "One could never mediate on [these lines] enough" (OT, 307, trans. modified; LT, 346); "unable to follow here this great text here step by step and word by word, as one nevertheless should" (OT, 295, trans. modified; LT, 332); "*The Experience of Freedom*, a book far too rich and novel [*trop riche et neuf*] for me to dare touch on it here" (OT, 304, trans. modified; LT, 341); or "let me say a word about what I would have liked to do but shall not do" (OT, 297; LT, 333).

One reason for this habitual gesture of postponement I have already identified. A micrological reading of, say, Husserl's *Ideas II* would be more or less interminable, so it is better, more responsible, to keep one's nose close to the letter of the text and try to say something verifiable about a few short passages. The result is a sense of perpetual, frustrating, incompleteness.

Derrida says repeatedly that he has not even gotten started yet. An example is a passage late in the book in which he formulates once more the project of his book and despairs, once more, of ever even beginning his enterprise, much less bring it to a conclusion. After a substantial citation from Nancy's *Corpus* about touching, Derrida apparently paraphrases Nancy:

> To touch, so one believes [*croit-on*: One believes? Who is this "one"? Nancy? People in general? Those in that long Western philosophical tradition of thinking about touch? Derrida himself? How can "one" decide?], amounts, therefore, to letting oneself be touched by what one touches. This is, then, to touch, with pertinence, upon touch, in a manner that is at once touching and touched. Nancy will have said and thus thought this *like* others before him but also *otherwise*. In what way does he say something other than the tradition up until Merleau-Ponty or Henri Maldiney, for example? That is where it would now be necessary to start or start over again. (OT, 276–77, trans. modified; LT, 312)

That is the question, all right, the basic question of the whole book. How does Nancy say something other than the tradition about touch? Surely by page 276 in the English translation Derrida must, the reader thinks, have made at least a start in answering that question. But no, as the following paragraph attests, he has not even got started yet. He despairs of ever getting started, much less ending, of ever getting in touch with Nancy on touch, just as I despair of ever getting in touch with Derrida on Nancy on touching in such a relatively short chapter as this. I have the feeling that things are continually getting out of hand, that I am continually flying off at a tangent, not touching the truth of what Derrida says, just as Derrida's book is mostly made of a series of digressions away from Nancy to discussions of Husserl, Maine de Biran, Chrétien, and so on, digressions that Derrida calls "Tangents."

Just after the citation made above, Derrida says, in what he calls a "parenthesis within square brackets":

> Pretend to be re-commencing, rather, since I have the feeling, as I realize and have never ceased to avow, of never arriving at it, at the truth, of never touching the point of departure, even less the end. I dare to content myself with telling, out of order [*sans ordre*], the story of what I would have liked to write in order to reach him, precisely, in an appropriate, *fitting* [*apte*] way. No, not even the story, then, but certain stories, more or less anecdotal, of what touched me while I was trying to write "Le toucher." (OT, 277, trans. modified; LT, 312)

Then follows a story about how Derrida missed a planned meeting with Nancy at an airport on the way to a conference. It was "the contretemps at the rendezvous, probably [*sans doute*] in 1992" (OT, 277, trans. modified; LT, 312). Probably? He's not even sure in what year it occurred.

It is an interesting story, but what good is it in answering the fundamental question about what Nancy adds to the tradition about touching? I suppose the answer is that the little anecdote is an allegory of how Derrida can never touch Nancy. He missed the planned airport rendezvous. That missed encounter, in turn, is a manifestation of Derrida's fundamental argument in this book against the idea that touching, even touching oneself in self-touching, ever takes place as an immediate presence, "in the flesh," so to speak. Touch, for Derrida, is always nontouch. It is divided, distanced, *partagé*, mediated by some technical prosthetics, for example, by the hand that manipulates the pen or types on the computer keyboard.

Does Nancy say just this, that is, the same thing that Derrida wants to say? Probably not quite, or not even. There are three othernesses here, in this triangular power struggle or hand-to-hand combat. These are: (1) the philosophical tradition, in all its diversity; (2) Nancy; and (3) Derrida himself. Derrida always plays hardball. He wants to put the other two in their places, that is, make them submit to Derrida's "reading." He always wants to have the last word. I shall return to this in Chapter 12, in a discussion of the way *Le toucher* is a strange work of mourning, a mourning for someone who is not yet dead and an oblique mourning for Derrida himself, who is of course also not yet dead when he writes the book.

The length of *Le toucher*, not to speak of Derrida's claim that he has never really gotten started with his project, indicates that Derrida finds putting Nancy in his place not all that easy to do, for more than one reason. This is analogous to the way Derrida's interminable return to Heidegger in his seminars over the years indicates not only respect for Heidegger but also a sense of the passive resistance Heidegger puts up, like a judo master who uses your own moves to defeat you, to being floored by deconstruction. With Heidegger, or with Nancy, for that matter, Derrida has to move carefully, warily, since either is likely to have been there already and to be prepared with a masterly parry. The would-be floorer may be floored.

In the paragraph in italics at the end of part 1, just before he begins the long detour, the five "Tangents," attempting to get in touch with modern phenomenologists (Husserl, Merleau-Ponty, et al.), Derrida admits ruefully, *"I've not taken a step that he hasn't already run ahead of me."* He accounts for the baroque stylistic excesses of his book by saying that they are a response to the impossibility of ever touching Nancy on touch or of ever touching touch: *"I would like to think of the story of the baroque composition, and the flaunted taste* [le goût affiché] *for delirious profusion, as a response—calculated but embarrassed, playful and elusive—to the aporias of tact"* (OT, 131, trans modified; LT, 151).

Eight: Derrida manhandles or manipulates the notions of aporia, paradox, and the contradictory. He does this to undo any satisfactory and univocal concept of touch in any of the many authors whom he reads, from Aristotle and the Gospels to Nancy. The theme of aporia appears early in *Le toucher* apropos of Aristotle's use of the word in *On the Soul* (*Peri psuchēs*; in Latin known as *De Anima*). Derrida lists a series of "aporetic elements" Aristotle finds in the sense of touch and that make touch obscure (*adēlon*). Touch is only potential, not actual. It therefore does not sense itself. It does not have a single, sensible object, like the other senses, etc. Derrida says that this obscurity and these aporias will govern his whole book. They will be rediscovered in all the philosophers of touch he discusses, down to Nancy himself, for all his "exactitude." Here is one explanation for the obscurity I find in both Derrida and Nancy when they touch on touch. "To this day," says Derrida, "these aporematic [*aporématique*] elements have not stopped telling tales [*de faire des histoires*], if one can say so, in the history of this interminable aporia. This will be borne out at every step we take" (OT, 6, trans. modified; LT, 16). This obscurity, a darkness on which no light can by any means be shown, also explains why Derrida's book is so unwieldy, shapeless, doomed to failure, reduced to anecdotes and storytelling. I mean "storytelling" both in the sense of proffering narratives and in the sense of telling lies, whoppers:

For, with this history of touch, one gropes along [*on tâtonne*], no longer knowing how to set out or what to set forth, and above all no longer able to see it clearly. An epigraph [*Exergue*] out of breath from the word go, then, to what I have renounced writing, for a thousand reasons that will soon become apparent. For, to admit the inadmissible, I shall have to content myself, not concealing failure and renunciation, with *storytelling* [raconter]. (OT, 6–7, trans. modified; LT, 16)

The whole of *Le toucher*, Derrida is saying, is no more than an extended epigraph to the book that he wanted to write but that he finds it impossible to write. Pretty long epigraph!

To return now to trait number one: In what sense does Derrida take away with one hand what he gives with the other? The aim of *Le toucher, Jean-Luc Nancy*, no careful reader can doubt, is the "deconstruction" (whatever, exactly, *that* means) of the Western concepts of touching from Aristotle and the Gospels through Husserl down even to Nancy himself. Derrida wants to show that all these concepts are riven by one sort or another of aporia, so that: (1) there is no "the" touch; and (2) the commonsense intuition of an immediacy and intimacy of touch never happens, not even when I touch myself touching myself. Touch is always mediated, distanced, divided, parted, translated, transplanted, grafted, prosthetic, like Nancy's transplanted heart, a constant theme or figure, theme/figure, in *Le toucher*.

What Derrida gives with one hand is his grateful praise and admiration for all the many writers on touch he reads, including even the Christian ones like the Gospel texts and Chrétien's quite recent and quite assertively Christian book about touch. Chrétien, for example, sees the Son as the Hand of the Father touching man's heart. For the writings of his friend Nancy, Derrida has seemingly unqualified, hyperbolic praise. He constantly calls it "this immense work," "this great work," etc. Derrida often uses Nancy's pronouncements about the preoriginary division of touch (along with the primordial division of everything else), about the way there is no "the" touch, and so on, as a means to dismantle, as at a catastrophic juncture, previous philosophers of touch and the body.

Nevertheless, at certain crucial, equally catastrophic (in the etymological sense of suddenly reversing) moments, Derrida parts ways with Nancy. He takes back with the left hand what he has given with the right, no doubt more subtly than when he takes issue with Aristotle, Maine de Biran, Husserl, or Levinas. Just because of that offhand subtlety, he takes back in an even more devastating way, a way more catastrophic for Nancy's thought. He says something like, "Well, I wouldn't have had the courage to put it that way myself," ironically praising Nancy for formulations that he, Derrida, would not dare to make. The issue between him and Nancy is always a matter of the way things are put, that is, it is always a matter of language. Of course, that makes it always more than just a matter of language. Derrida finds disabling vestiges of ontotheological, even outright Christian terminology in Nancy's conceptual lexicon, despite his announced aim to "deconstruct Christianity." Derrida, as I have said, more than once declares that goal to be unattainable. Our culture and our languages are Christian, as in the everyday notions of the "materiality of the body" and its unequivocal tangibility, its vulnerability to violent touches, as these notions are often used, without perhaps enough reflection, by those in feminist cultural studies today. I shall return to the question of language later on.

The most striking example of giving the back of his hand to Nancy, or of taking back with one hand what he has given with the other, is a wonderfully ironic, intimate, friendly, but nonetheless devastating paragraph of apostrophic prosopopoeia addressed directly to Nancy himself, after an opening in which Derrida addresses himself, in a self-apostrophe cleaving himself in two, with one part scarcely touching the other, if at all. The *se toucher*, self-touching the untouchable self, becomes *toucher l'autre*, touching the untouchable other. The paragraph appears once (OT, 107; LT, 125), and then is repeated almost word for word later in the book, in a different context. I quote the second version. It is a splendid example of Derrida's inimitable ironic, self-reflexive exuberance, his "hand" at its most recognizable, as a kind of password or signature: "Derrida was here," or even, almost, "Derrida *is* here. You can touch him here." The passage also shows Derrida's penchant for dividing himself, or being divided, into several incompatible selves, and then talking to himself in a strange, solitary dialogue that the reader has the sense of just accidentally overhearing. The passage is also a splendid, exemplary case of taking back with one hand what has been given with the other. Derrida takes Nancy sternly in hand and, so to speak, verbally spanks him, as one spanks a disobedient child, or he tries to touch him with an admonitory finger:

> —And in an aside you [*tu*] tell yourself: what a funny, admiring, and grateful salutation [*salut*] you're addressing to him, to Jean-Luc Nancy, a curious way of pretending to touch him while acting *altogether as if* you wanted to put his lexicon about touch again in the service of a tradition, or worse, a filiation. Or reminding us that this lexicon should always already have been related to its usages, that is to say, to an ageless usury [I shall return to this word below], even if we like that—touching—anew, precisely

when it's impossible-prohibited, and we even like to call that loving—abstaining oneself. What a funny present, indeed, what an offering! Altogether as if at the moment of summoning others to become ecstatic before this great work and this immense philosophical treatise on touch, you whispered in his ear: Now, Jean-Luc, that's quite enough, give this word back, it's prohibited, you hear, leave it to the ancestors, don't compromise with it, don't let yourself be contaminated by this *megalovirus*, and once and for all stop using this incredible vocabulary, this concept nothing can really vouch for, these figures without figure and therefore without credit. Don't keep pretending, as they do, to believe, stop acting as if you wanted to make us believe that there is something one could call touch [*le toucher*], a thing about which we could pretend to understand one another [*s'entendre*], and say something new, just where, touching upon the untouchable, this thing remains untouchable. Touch is finitude, period. Haven't you yourself said "there is no 'the' touch"? Knowing you, I don't think this objection will stop you—I tell myself.

—Nor you [he means himself, Derrida]. Would you like to touch him, as you say, in the way in which one touches, in a fencing match, with the point of a buttoned tip? *Touché*, Americans also say in French, with a funny accent, when a point is scored.

—On the contrary, it is his singularity, his "being singular plural," that matters to me here above all, even when I speak to others of others [*aux autres des autres*]. It's this absolute singularity of his signature that I exert myself to attain.

—You exert yourself? What does that mean? (OT, 138–39, trans. modified; LT, 160)

What is going on in this quite amazing passage? It is amazing not least in its comedy and in its touching, intimate tone, as well as in its use of apostrophe, direct address, to himself as well as to Nancy, something not often found in a philosophical treatise. Derrida comments in one place on the exclusion of apostrophe as "an essential displacement in the gesture of the thinking." (Note the relation of the word *apostrophe* to the word *catastrophe*. Both words involve the notion of a "turn," a "turn toward" in "apostrophe," a "turn down" in "catastrophe.") "To convince oneself of this," says Derrida, "though it certainly does not suffice, it is good to underscore to what degree, like 'thou' and even 'you' [*le 'tu' ou même le 'vous'*], this strophic turn of the apostrophe is excluded from philosophical discourse , one might even say prohibited, from Aristotle to Kant, from Descartes to Hegel and to Heidegger. As to many others, even today" (OT, 23, trans. modified; LT, 36). Using an apostrophe is a catastrophe for the supposed objectivity and impersonality of philosophical reasoning. The philosopher speaks as no one to no one, as the disembodied voice of reason. (I might note parenthetically, tangentially, another prohibition. Philosophers—Heidegger, for example—do not say "I." They say "we." Derrida often follows Heidegger and the philosophical tradition generally in saying "we," though not always. In *Le toucher* Derrida often says "I," in defiance of philosophical convention.)

Derrida's "tone" in *Le toucher* is an intimacy both of Derrida's self with himself and also of Derrida's self with the self of his great friend Nancy. This is a miming of Nancy's phrase *se toucher toi*, to touch oneself touching the other, discussed at length by Derrida. Derrida divides himself into two Derridas in touching converse with one another, though not quite touching. The failure of touching ever quite to happen, contrary to what the philosophical tradition avers, is, as I have said, the central thesis of *Le toucher*, tirelessly argued in defiance of every philosopher from Aristotle down even to Nancy, when the latter does not watch what he is saying.

Here is exactly what Derrida says about the division of the self "at the moment when the 'I' 'makes its entrance'" (OT, 34, trans. modified; LT, 47). This entrance "signs . . . the possibility or the necessity for the said 'I,' as soon as it touches itself, to address itself, to speak of itself, to treat itself, in a soliloquy interrupted in advance, *as an other*" (OT, 34, trans. modified; LT, 47). This touching oneself, *se toucher*, however, as Derrida goes on to say, fails to make contact. It is a touching without touching: "But I touches itself in spacing itself, in losing contact with itself, precisely at touching itself. In order to touch itself, it breaks off contact [*il coupe le contact*], it abstains from touching" (OT, 34, trans. modified; LT, 47).

This paradoxical formulation is *Le toucher* in a nutshell. If you understand it thoroughly, dear reader, you need not go on reading. You could have written the book yourself. Certainly the two Derridas in the passage I have cited above seem to speak to one another at cross-purposes, in contretemps, or in misunderstanding and disagreement.

Derrida then goes on to add an important corollary to this law of self-touching without touching. Self-touching is the necessary condition of being touched by the other, that is, by another person, either through being addressed by that other or by addressing the other "oneself," that is, by addressing one or another of the multiple "I's": "*Il se touche* means . . . that he is touched, touchable (by any other whatsoever). *Il se tutoie* signifies that he is saying 'thou' to himself [*qu'il se tutoie lui-même*] or that he is being addressed in this way—he is *tutoyable*, addressable with *tu* by any other whatsoever" (OT, 34, trans. modified; LT, 47). Sure enough, in the funny passage I have cited and am trying to understand, as soon as Derrida has divided into two Derridas, or perhaps more,[32] then one of those Derridas (the first to speak) imagines himself addressing an earnest reproach to Nancy: "Now, Jean-Luc, that's quite enough, give this word back, it's prohibited, you hear," though one of his "I's" admits that he does not think his injunction will have any effect.

Stop what at once? The passage is clear on that. You can't touch pitch without being defiled. Though you, Jean-Luc, think you can with impunity use words from the age-old philosophical lexicon (words such as *being*, *touch*, *body*, *hand*, etc.), and twist them to say something other than the traditional *doxa* about "'the' touch," "'the' body," and so on, you cannot use these words without being contaminated. You will inevitably catch the megalovirus that will vitiate everything you say, make it repeat, in spite of yourself, just what you want to avoid saying. These words are counterfeit coin, without credit, incredible. When he says these words are "figures without figure," I suppose he means that they are like coins that have been worn away so that their inscriptions are no longer legible. He means that conceptual words lose their metaphorical force through centuries of use and become abstract, empty counters, which should not pass as current. Derrida, for example, in "White Mythology" ("La mythologie blanche"), characteristically connects "usury" with the idea of being used up, devalued (Me, 209; Mfr, 249). *Usure* in French means both "usury" and "worn away." You cannot invest these old, used-up words or buy anything with them. Derrida's reproach to Nancy for trying to do this takes away with one hand what he has just given with the other when he spoke of wanting to summon "others so that they will become ecstatic before this great work and this immense philosophical treatise on touch." He doth protest too much? A touch of irony always contaminates Derrida's hyperbolic praise of Nancy, as of the other great philosophers he discusses.

A hilarious version of that irony is part of the extended discussion of Freud's note. Derrida, in a comic making concrete of a metaphor (psyche, the soul, as Psyche the mythological personage) imagines all the great European philosophers as doctors gathered around Psyche's extended body, neither alive nor dead, trying to figure out what it means to say, as Freud, did, "Psyche ist ausgedehnt, weiss nicht davon":

> There, around Psyche (*peri psuchēs*) [this is the title, in Greek, of Aristotle's
> *On the Soul*, but *peri* can be taken to mean "around"], which is to say,
> around the great question of a "pure" self-touching and a pre-empirical
> auto-affection, the doctors Kant, Husserl, Freud, Heidegger, Merleau-
> Ponty, and so many others living closer to us, whom we will interrogate

later, hold what is called a consultation. No doubt they will call upon their ancestor Aristotle. They ought to, in any case. Either to follow him or to have done with him. (OT, 46, trans. modified; LT, 61)

I shall return in Chapter 12 to this wonderful scene of anxious consultation. *Le toucher* as a whole sets itself the task of reading carefully just what all these physicians of the psyche had to say about what Derrida calls "our guiding thread [*notre fil conducteur*]" (he means "*my* guiding thread"), namely, the possibility of "a kind of sensibility touching nothing," "or a kind of touch without empirical contact, a self-touching or being touched without touching anything" (OT, 45; LT, 59). Since Nancy did not do that careful reading (he barely mentions Aristotle on touch, for example), Derrida's book is, among many other things, a mild and veiled, but distinct and iterated, reproach to Nancy for not having done what he ought to have done, for not having done that careful reading. These "doctors" were "immense," a priceless heritage, but they were also wrong, deluded, unthinking repeaters of one aspect of "white mythology," that is, the ideological error of thinking touch is immediate.

The long passage I cited above, implying that Nancy is among those deluded ones, makes Derrida's book "a funny present." It is a funny "offering," in the sense that we speak of "funny money" as a term for counterfeit currency. It is not a "sublime offering," as in the title of a chapter by Nancy, "The Sublime Offering" ("L'offrande sublime") in *A Finite Thinking*.[33] Derrida's reproach to Nancy for using viral terms surfaces here and there throughout this book and in other comments on Nancy. "But how can he say that one is 'properly exposed' to an origin that is not 'appropriable'? I'll have to ask him this. Just as I ask myself why I would never have dared write that" (OT, 116, trans. modified; LT, 133). The rest of the paragraph, which should be read word by word and line by line, explains why. To put it briefly and inadequately, Derrida finds in Nancy's phrasing a lingering nostalgia for immediate touching, so Nancy makes "an affirmation that is possible for him, and not for me" (OT, 11, trans. modified; LT, 134). In an important passage in *A Taste for the Secret*, Derrida explains what he means by saying "I am not one of the family" (TS, 27). I have discussed the passage in detail in Chapter 8 of this book. Derrida praises Nancy's *The Inoperative Community* (*La communauté désoeuvrée*) and Blanchot's *The Unavowable Community* (*La communauté inavouable*),[34] but then demurs: "I have no qualms about these communities; my only question is, why call them communities? If I have always hesitated to use this word, it is because too often the word 'community' resounds with the 'common' [*commun*], the as-one [*comme un*]" (TS, 25).

If Nancy's "unworked [*désoeuvrée*] community" (I prefer that neologism to "inoperative") is a congeries of people who have nothing in common but the fact that they have nothing in common, why risk using the word *community* to describe this assembly? The word buys into, or invests in, just what Nancy is trying to put in question. In an early passage in *Le toucher*, Derrida lists a series of "big" words that are "incredible" and therefore fathomless mysteries to him. *Le toucher*, he says, is no more than the "memoirs" of a short treatise he had long dreamed of writing and dedicating to Nancy. It would have been about Aristotle's *On the Soul*, "a murky, baroque essay, overloaded with stories (wanting to tell tales [*envie de faire des histoires*]), an unimaginable scene that to a friend would resemble what has always been my relation to incredible words like *soul*, *mind*, *spirit*, *body*, *sense*, *world*, and other similar things [*choses*]" (OT, 7, trans. modified; LT, 17). "Things"? A little later Derrida "timidly" takes issue with Nancy's use, in *The Experience of Freedom* (*L'expérience de la liberté*),[35] of the words *generosity* and *fraternity*:

> Doesn't my timid, reticent inquietude about the *word generosity* (it is the word I worry about and not necessarily the concept at work in it) pertain to the very reserve that the *sympathetic* [sympathique] motif and the *good movement* of "fraternity" always inspire in me? . . . Briefly, what embarrasses me [*me gêne*: an oddly apt word: Derrida would be ashamed or embarrassed to be caught using such words] in the word *generosity*, as in the word *fraternity*, finally amounts to the same thing. In both cases, one salutes some genealogy, some filiation, a principle having to do with "birth," whether or not it is as it is often thought to be, "natural." And above all, one privileges some "virility." A brother, even if he is an orphan, is a son and therefore a man. If one wanted to include here, for example, the sister or the woman or the daughter, it would perhaps be necessary to change words. Generously—and then change, while one is at it, the word *generosity* itself. (OT, 22, trans. modified; LT, 35–36)

Derrida goes on to make clear that his objection is to the implication in the word *generosity* that one has something to give: "Indeed, if one gives or offers because one is naturally, genially, congenitally, or ontologically *generous*, at birth. . . . then does one offer, does one still give?" (OT, 22–23; LT, 36). No, says Derrida, because true giving is of what one does not have. "Giving is possible only when it remains *im-possible*, and not even im-possible *as such* [since the "as such" would be a return to ontology and essence]" (OT, 23; LT, 36). Derrida's extended seminars and published writings on the gift (for example, *Given Time*), therefore, in order to avoid

the "genital" ontologizing implicit in "generosity," always say "the gift, if
there is any [*s'il y en a*]." There is no "'the' gift," no "is" for the gift.

Derrida's taking back, with his left hand, his praise of Nancy, like his
praise of Aristotle, Maine de Biran, Husserl, Merleau-Ponty, and others,
is always a matter of words, of the lexicon of the old philosophical words:
"it is the word I worry about [*je dis bien le mot*] and not necessarily the
concept at work in it" (OT, 22; LT, 35). What an odd distinction! "Not
necessarily"? Does that mean sometimes yes and sometimes no? In any
case, what would a concept be without a word for it? I thought the word
was the concept, the *Begriff*. Do you not change the concept when you
change the word?

As Derrida acknowledges in a place already cited, however, "I gotta use
words when I talk to yuh," so as soon as you open your mouth and speak
you are infected, as by a megalovirus, with the ideology, the "white mythology," that is inextricably embedded or incarnated in those words. Derrida himself is not exempt from this inescapable fate, nor am I. I think,
however, that Derrida is perhaps more aware of this impasse and more
prone either not to use certain words at all, to use them only ironically, or
to invent new words (as indeed also does Nancy), words like *différance*, in
order to try to say something that has never been said before. That includes the word *deconstruction* itself. In any case, this complex, double-
handed, or sometimes even underhanded movement of giving and taking
away in the same gesture is a fundamental characteristic of *Le toucher*, both
on the local scale of "the letter of the text" and on the large scale of the
advancing and retreating movement of the book as a whole.

Hands in Derrida (and Nancy)

It is high time to fulfill my promise to follow the thread in the sampler
outlining Derrida's treatment of "'the' hand" as a leitmotif in Western
philosophy. I choose this motif because it is a good metonymy for the way
Derrida handles the entire question of touch in the Western philosophical
tradition. The hand is crucial to Western white mythology or ingrained
ideology of the haptic. Just why?

The background, a ground without ground or, one might dare to say,
the unsaturatable "context" for Derrida's manipulation of the hand motif
in *Le toucher* is his magnificent essay of 1984–85, "Heidegger's Hand
(*Geschlecht* II)." I have already mentioned this essay earlier in this chapter.
It was presented, in John P. Leavey, Jr.'s translation, at a conference at

Loyola University in Chicago in March 1985. That essay was drawn from the much longer texts of Derrida's seminars of that time, for example, a hundred-page-long analysis of Heidegger's essay on Georg Trakl. The essay was, of course, written in French, though with awareness that it was to be presented in English. It refers constantly to Heidegger's original German, as well as to both French and English translations of Heidegger. Some Greek philosophical terms are also cited. In a way, it is an essay on the problems of translation. Anything in any language can be translated into any other language, but puzzling, indeed insoluble problems always arise, as, for example, Derrida notes, in trying to translate French reflexives into English (OT, 34; LT, 47). The focus of Derrida's essay is on the untranslatability of the German word *Geschlecht*. It can, says Derrida, "be translated by 'sex,' 'race,' 'species,' 'genus,' 'gender' [*genre*], 'stock' [*souche*], 'family,' 'generation' or 'genealogy,' or 'community'" (PIIe, 28, and see also GII, 162; P, 416. I cite here and below the translation as revised for PIIe by Elizabeth Rottenberg). None of those words, nor their French equivalents, carries over the derivation from *schlagen*, a word meaning "to strike," as a coin is "struck" with the effigy and inscribed words that it then carries as an indication of its worth in a system of exchange. These inscriptions make a coin of authentic value as a member of the family of coins passing current in a given community, in a given nation. *Geschlecht* is essential in its untranslatability for Heidegger's thinking about thinking. The differences among the four languages (English, French, German, Greek) in their sets of idioms using "hand," *main*, *Hand*, and *cheir* are also made salient in Derrida's essay.

"*Geschlecht* II" interrogates passages from Heidegger's Trakl essay, from his *What Is Called Thinking*, and from his *Parmenides* to show that Heidegger repeats in his own way the Western millennial tradition of claiming that only the *Geschlecht* of *Menschheit*, *Menschlichkeit*, mankind has hands, or, rather, "Man does not 'have' hands, but the hand holds, in order to have it in hand [*pour en disposer*], the essence of man. (*Der Mensch 'hat' nicht Hände, sondern die Hand hat das Wesen des Menschen inne*)" (PIIe, 50, trans. modified; see also GII, 182; Pf, 438). All other animals, even apes, are handless. This means that only man is capable of thinking and speaking. Man thinks with his hands, so to speak. This explains the high value Heidegger places on handwriting as the putting on paper of thinking and speaking. Writing with a pen is a tool-using craft like carpentry or joinery. Heidegger's hand ideology explains his extreme distaste for the typewriter. He saw it as a submission to the thought-destroying dominance of technology. Derrida viewed these assumptions as dogmatic and extremely problematic, the product of "a greatly muddled analysis [*analyse fort embar-rassé*]" (GII, 195; Pf, 429):

> What Heidegger says of the ape deprived of hand—and thus, as we are going to see, deprived of thought, of language, of gift—is not only dog-matic in its form because Heidegger knows nothing about it and does not want to know anything about it here [, has no doubt studied neither the zoologists (even were it to criticize them) nor the apes of the Black Forest]. [The section in brackets was in Leavey's original translation for the oral delivery, but was eliminated from the French version.] It is serious because it traces a system of limits within which everything he says about man's hand takes on meaning and value. From the moment such a delimitation is problematic, the name of man, his *Geschlecht*, itself becomes problematic. For it names that which has the hand, and thus thought, speech or lan-guage, and opening to the gift. . . . Thus one sees organizing themselves around the hand and speech, with great coherence, all the traits whose incessant recurrence I have elsewhere recalled under the names logocen-trism and phonocentrism. (PIIe, 41, 48, trans. modified; see also GII, 174, 181; Pf, 429, 437)

Derrida's overall project, as is well known, was to "deconstruct" logo-centrism and phonocentrism. In his later work, this is often done by put-ting in question all the age-old Western definitions of man that are said to distinguish him from animals: only man has speech, only man is tool-using, only man can think, only man creates a "world" for himself, only man has hands, and so on. What *Le toucher* has to say about the Western ideology of the hand is a part of that deconstructive effort.

A passage early in *Le toucher*, a digression, characteristic of this book, away from Nancy, apropos of Kant, puts the cards in Derrida's hand on the table, or, as Austin wittily puts it in *How to Do Things with Words*, "lets some of [his] cats on the table."[36] The entire Western philosophical tradition, says Derrida, asserts the primacy of touch. It is premier among the senses just because it is the most immediate. The hand, with its palpat-ing fingers, is, in turn, the premier organ of touch. The possession of a prehensile hand, a hand that can feel things all around and identify their form and texture, a hand that can grasp things and make other things out of them, distinguishes man from all other living beings. Not only can men (!) alone make things with their hands. The uniquely human possession of hands also means human beings can make themselves: "if it is nature that has provided the hand, so to speak, she has given it to man only; and by thus making man, she has then allowed him freely to make himself [*de se faire ensuite librement*]" (OT, 41, trans. modified; LT, 55). Derrida is referring here to Kant's *Anthropology from a Pragmatic Point of View*. All animals of a given species, Kant believed, are the same, behave the same, and have the same ways of living together (a dogmatic and ignorant assumption). Only human beings, because they have hands, make themselves. "Piece the world together, boys, but not with your hands," says Wallace Stevens.[37] For Kant, it is precisely hands that piece the human world together. Therefore human beings can make themselves differently in different communities. As a result, we need anthropology in the modern sense to study these differences. Kant is, by the way, wrong in assuming that all members of the same animal species are the same. Different flocks of the same species of birds develop, for example, different calls, as ornithologists have found.

All Kant says seems so intuitively correct that it is extremely difficult to stand back and say it is wrong, as I just have and as Derrida does. His aim is to show that every expression of this ideology from Aristotle on, different as they are from one another, in one way or another betrays the error of these assumptions by coming up against some paradox or aporia or contradictory bit of empirical evidence. It requires close reading, word by word, line by line, and page by page, of these learned doctors gathered around Psyche to see where they encounter aporias. This is what Derrida does. Derrida's goal in this "close reading" is to persuade the reader that the tradition is wrong, wrong, wrong, on its own terms, admirable though it is.

Much of the long middle part of *Le toucher*, the sections called "Tangents," is devoted to showing in detail the various permutations and combinations of this error through the ages. The apparently coherent and univocal affirmations of this doctrine always betray their incoherence in some aporia, paradox, or contradiction. A fundamental part of Derrida's strategy is a patient recapitulation, with lots of citations, and just a touch of insolent irony, of what these estimable philosophers actually wrote about hands. That is the thread Derrida follows in the hand-sewn embroidery of the Western tradition. Often doing that is enough to show the contradictions and loopholes in the arguments of Maine de Biran, Ravaisson, Husserl, Merleau-Ponty, Heidegger, Franck, Henri Maldiney, and Chrétien.

Derrida's five "Tangents" (five like the putative five senses and the five fingers, as Derrida observes; OT, 182; LT, 208) are extremely complex and reticulated. "Things are subtle enough," says Derrida, "and the stakes [*les enjeux*] are serious enough to call here for prudence and meticulousness, sticking very close to the text" (OT, 164, trans. modified; LT, 189). The five "Tangents" make up all of *Le toucher*'s part 2. To try to summarize them or to reduce them to detachable themes is to falsify them, and, no doubt, to fail to touch on them in any pertinent way. I can only recommend that my readers read and re-read *Le toucher*, as I have done. Nevertheless, in order ever to finish this chapter, I must handpick Derrida's argument by following his example and focusing on as careful a reading as I can make of some important passages in *Le toucher*. I claim, perhaps fallaciously (how could I prove I am right?), that these are synecdochic samples (*échantillons*) of the whole, and that the part is *like* the whole. Several elements that Derrida finds in his own close readings recur. Each is intertwined with all the others, even though they are also spaced out.

The primacy of touch and of the human hand as the primary organ of touch in the Western philosophical tradition, from Aristotle down to Husserl and Heidegger, by way of Aquinas, Kant, Maine de Biran, and others, is so strong and so consistent that Derrida can speak of this tradition as a *humainisme*, a "humanualism," as the English translation renders it, trying for an echo of the play on *main*, "hand," in the French neologism (OT, 152; LT, 176). The uniformity of this humanualism holds even though, as Derrida says, "There is a Kantian hand, and there will be a Husserlian hand, and a Heideggerian hand, and so forth. They have traits in common but do not overlap. And there is also a Biranian hand [une main de Maine de Biran]" (OT, 149, trans. modified; LT, 172).

Here is one passage, among many, about the hand, in this case from "Tangent II," the analysis of hands in Husserl. I focus on what Derrida says about Husserl because Husserl is the patriarch of the phenomenological tradition. Husserl's writings, in the "Tangents," interest Derrida in their complex relation to Nancy's thought. I especially take Husserl in hand because Derrida's "deconstruction," if I may dare to call it that, of Husserl on touch, hand, and fingers establishes the program for the deconstructions of Merleau-Ponty, of Franck, and, in a different way, of Chrétien, in the remaining three of the five "tangents."

> In the chapter [in Husserl's *Ideas II*] immediately preceding the one from which we have been citing this "for example . . . my . . . hand," Husserl has abundantly multiplied illustrations of touch, each time describing digital manipulations. As if the only way one could ever touch were with the hand and as if the hand were made of nothing but fingers. And this unsurprisingly occurs at a point where the phenomenologist credits touch with an absolute, unparalleled , and foundational preeminence.

We are going to identify the signs of this excellence of touch among the senses, of the hand among the parts or organs of the tactile body proper, and of the fingers at the tip of the hand. But can't we already interpret these signs as so many testimonies to the primacy conferred upon the thing as "object"? First on the external object, and then on this other original "object" that remains as the subjective and phenomenological experience of the body proper?

... the external object is at issue, and very soon the possibility of touching with a finger lays bare the complication that will make for a difference between digital touching and seeing: knowing that fingers can also touch *each other* [se *toucher*: as eyes, for Husserl, cannot], "fingers touching the finger": "double apprehension" (*Doppelauffassung*), "double sensations" (*Doppelempfindungen*). (OT, 162, trans. modified; LT, 186–87)

Why is the hand so important? Well, for one thing, if touch is the most important sense, the one without which no animate body would be alive, whereas a body can live on without sight, hearing, smell, or taste, then the hand, as the primary organ of touch, is what, according to these philosophers, distinguishes "man" (!) from the other animals. Only "man" has a hand, with its five tactile and prehensile fingers, a hand that can reach out, touch, and grasp another body, or an inanimate object, or, for example when I touch or hold one finger with another, myself. Touching something, somebody else, or myself with the fingers of my hand is the essential model of immediate experience, of immediacy, of the presence of the present. These three forms of touching are the quite different uses of the hand among which Husserl distinguishes. Sight, which is often assumed to be the primary sense in these days of the dominance of the visual is secondary because my eyes may always be deceiving me. I may be seeing a mere reflection or simulacrum, whereas touch is harder to fool. This is true even though blind Isaac was fooled into blessing Jacob under the false impression that he was touching Esau's hairy hand, for Esau was "a hairy man," while Jacob was "a smooth man" (Gen. 27:8–27). (*Esau* means "hairy.") I always know there is *some* external object or other there by palpating it. Isaac ought to have been able to figure out by touch that he was fingering the skins of "the kids of the goats," not Esau's hands and neck. I know there is another person there by touching him or her with my hand or finger, as in what doubting Thomas wanted to do with the risen Christ. I know that I am I, that my soul permeates my "body proper" by touching myself, for example, touching one hand with the other. In the latter case, each hand becomes both toucher and touched, a quite ordinary but nevertheless somewhat weird experience, if you think about it.

Does that make the hand just a figure for immediate experience, or is it something paradigmatically literal, that is, essential to immediate experience of any sort? Derrida asks whether touch is figurative or literal again and again (e.g., as early as OT, 109; LT, 127). Belief that such a thing as immediate experience exists is the ground of all phenomenologies from Aristotle on. This is what Husserl calls "originary presenting intuition [*intuition donatrice originaire*, in Derrida's French rendition]" (OT, 164; LT, 189). If you can "deconstruct" this confidence in intuitionism, continuity, immediacy, presence, figuratively or literally present in the self-touching of my right hand touching my left hand, the whole stately edifice will come tumbling down, as at a Samsonlike touch, or like that statue in the *New Yorker* cartoon I mentioned earlier. Doing that is Derrida's goal in this book. In this he professes to be following Nancy, but he also reproaches Nancy, as I have shown, for being at times too "phenomenological," too prone to use the old words, too given still to speak of touching as though it is something that might happen and does actually happen.

One final, crucial element in Derrida's characterization of this primacy of touch from Aristotle to Levinas is his stress on its Christian heritage. This is worked out in detail in the discussion of Chrétien, an explicitly Christian phenomenologist, in "Tangent V." Chrétien asserts, for example, that the primary, most literal hand of all is the Hand of God, that is, Christ the Son, as God manipulates the world through Christ as the immanent presence of God in the world. All human hands are figures of that originary and originating hand. This Christian heritage of the doctrine of the touching hand is already asserted, however, at the end of the discussion of Husserl in "Tangent II":

> And so we [who is this "we"?] at our own pace [a pretty leisurely pace], approach [*nous nous approchons*] the places of a resemblance that we can already guess at [well, *I* had not guessed at it]: a hand and especially a hand of "flesh," a *hand of man*, has always begun to resemble a *man's hand*. And thus already a father's hand. Sometimes, more "originarily," the hand of the merciful Father, which is to say, his Son, the hand that the Son is, according to the Logos or Word [*le Verbe*] of the Incarnation. As we shall see, all these values touch one another by virtue of a "spiritual touch": *infinite, mutual, and immediate.* The last of our five *Tangents* (five, like the fingers of one hand, five like the five senses) will perhaps unfurl the indisputable consequence of this. (OT, 182, trans. modified; LT, 208)

Well, what's wrong with this doctrine of the three touches of the fingered hand, the touch of an object, the touch of another person, and the touch of oneself, the latter two what Derrida calls, following Nancy, *se toucher toi*? What is wrong with the idea that these three touches are the primary and most irrefutable forms of immediate experience, self-evident intuition? What's even wrong with acknowledging the Christian lineage of the touching hand, even in nominally secular texts like Husserl's *Ideas II*? Derrida himself discusses, both earlier in *Le toucher* and in a section of *Memoirs of the Blind* (*Mémoires d'aveugle*; MB, 6–12; MA, 15–19) on graphic representations of Christ's healing the blind, many examples of Jesus' heal-ing touch with his hand or fingers in the Gospels, the stories of Christ's being touched or not touched, down to the two great episodes of touch that are only in John's Gospel, the story of Thomas Didymus, "doubting Thomas," and the story of the risen Christ's "Touch me not," *Noli me tangere*, said to Mary Magdalene. (I shall return in the conclusion of this chapter to *Noli me tangere*.) Derrida also discusses at length the emphasis in Nancy's *Corpus* on Christ's *Hoc est enim corpus meum*, "This is truly my body," said at the Last Supper. Both Derrida and Nancy, correctly, see this sentence as a founding text for body theory in Western culture. Our body theory may be called essentially a theory of incarnation and commu-nion, for which the Christian Eucharist is the archetype. As for God's hand or finger, one thinks of the great Michelangelo fresco in the Sistine Chapel, the one that shows God's forefinger giving life to Adam by reach-ing out and touching Adam's forefinger, while Adam's male member, a rather small one, given the heroic size of his body, hangs limply, as if waiting to be made potent by Jehovah's touch.

Husserl's argument seems watertight, something that anyone can ac-cept, something almost impossible to put in question. It seems the handi-est way to explain how I know my body and know it is me, how I know objects, and how I know other people. Of course I can touch my left hand with my right hand. Of course I can explore an object by touching it. Of course I can empathize with another person by touching him or her, for example, by a caress or a kiss, both discussed at length in *Le toucher*. The caress comes up apropos of Levinas's theory of the caress. The kiss appears by way of Novalis's claim that the first kiss is the beginning of philosophy and by way of a touching anecdote about the way Derrida kissed Nancy on the cheeks for the first time when he visited Nancy in the hospital after the latter had survived a heart transplant. "As after a resurrection," says Derrida. "And not only his" (OT, 302; LT, 339).[38] How can Derrida pre-sume to "deconstruct" what Husserl says, and, if he has the temerity or perversity to try, how does he go about doing it?

Derrida employs three strategies of Samsonlike demolition. I bring Samson back in because I think these strategies are ultimately self-destructive as well as deconstructive, and that Derrida knows this, as my last chapter will obliquely try to show.

One strategy is the simple act of citation. Citation, as the exact repetition of what the other has said or written, always carries an element of ironic insolence, along with solemn respect for the literality of exactly what the other has put down on paper. This accompanies the respect for the procedure of close reading that goes along with the need for citation. "Things are subtle enough," you will remember I have cited Derrida as saying, "and the stakes are serious enough to call here for prudence and meticulousness, sticking very close to the text" (OT, 164, trans. modified; LT, 189). Citation, including my own quotations of Derrida, always carries, along with the respectful "Let me show you the admirable eloquence of exactly what he or she wrote," another, almost indistinguishable, note: "You won't believe he or she actually said this unless I cite it. It's unbelievable. I wouldn't believe it myself if I hadn't seen it with my own eyes." Citation, followed by exact paraphrase, undermines as well as celebrates. An example is the extremely disquieting experience of reading a student paper or examination that quotes exactly what you have said in class but somehow makes it sound perverse and stupid, in any case entirely unpersuasive. "Did I really say that? Yes, I guess I did." Derrida is a master of citation as tactful and hard-to-detect insolence. He can always say, "Well, I was just quoting exactly what Husserl says. You can look it up." As for paraphrase, Derrida mocks Husserl's restriction of phenomenological intuition to human beings by pointing out that what he says implies that "we 'phenomenologists' . . . alone can have an immediate, full, and originary intuition of what we are talking about" (OT, 165; LT, 189).

Another such "pulling the rug out from under" strategy is the apparently casual but explicit putting in question of something the analysand has said, often something that seems plausible enough at first glance, that is, until you begin to think about it and ask questions, often what seem like naïvely dumb questions. A good example is Derrida's questioning of the primacy Husserl gives to the experience of touching one of my hands with the other hand, or finger touching finger. After a substantial citation from Husserl, he says:

> One might be tempted to think that the privilege granted to the hand or the finger in this analysis of touch has to do in the first place with what the sentence [3 in the citation just made] specifies, that is, the case in which

"one or another bodily part [*partie du corps propre*] as a physical object" can touch one or another part of the same body—or be touched by it. Certainly. And it is also true that this cannot be said of every external part of the body. But why only the hand and the finger? And why not my foot and toes? Can they not touch another part of my body and touch one another? What about the lips, especially? All of the lips on the lips? And the tongue on the lips? And the tongue on the palate or on many other parts of "my body"? How could one *speak* without this (a question with which I merely point toward some of the most obvious issues at stake in these choices)? And the eyelids in the blink of an eye? And, if we take sexual differences into account, the sides of the anal or genital opening? (OT, 163–64, trans. modified; LT, 188)

The passage rises to a climax of almost delirious absurdity. Who would think of proving "I am I" by touching one big toe with the other big toe, or by pressing my lips together, or by tightening my gluteal muscles so that the two sides of my anal opening touch, or, for a woman, proving that "she is she" by pressing together the two sides of her vulva? What a sad limitation, Derrida implies, it is for a man not to have that female *Geschlecht*'s means of self-touching affirmation of self! The effect of these questions is to suggest that arguing I can prove "I am that I am" by touching my left hand with my right hand is both as arbitrary and as absurd as the other examples Derrida gives, in a deliberate crescendo of indecency, the *ob-scène*.

In another place, Derrida asks, speaking of Husserl's claim that we can always tell the difference between touching ourselves and touching another's body, "Who exactly is this 'we' of whom Husserl says, *Aber wir merken sofort den Unterschied*, 'But we immediately sense [*remarquons*] the difference'? . . . But we ask [*Mais demandons-nous*] turning back to Husserl: what difference exactly [*au juste*]? What difference would we be led to notice and remark without delay?" (OT, 170, trans. modified; LT, 195). The implication is that Husserl really has no way of answering these questions, or at any rate does not answer them in anything he says. In a sardonic footnote, Derrida accuses Merleau-Ponty of being ignorant of cultural difference and of not taking into account variations of the kiss, the caress, and the handshake (which might seem universal, natural rather than cultural) by citing a description of the Maori custom of "Hongi," which "consists in *touching* the other's nose, with a double or triple pressure, with one's own nose [touchez *le nez de l'autre, d'une double ou triple pression, avec son propre nez*] while sometimes also shaking hands, both hands at once, sometimes weeping and collecting the shared tears" (OT, 352, trans. modified; LT, 216). Try that in Grand Central Station! Whereas it is perfectly all right to exchange Western-style kisses there. A similar reaction of distaste and disbelief might, however, be generated in Maoris who saw Westerners kissing for the first time. Public kissing as a greeting among friends is quite uncommon, indeed almost nonexistent, in China, at least in my experience.

Another ironic and ultimately self-destructive form of undermining is Derrida's constant play on the key words he is analyzing in the authors he discusses. I have already mentioned this irrepressible and pervasive stylistic habit, the deliberate contamination of the analysis by what it analyzes. Here is one example among a great many in the "Tangents." Derrida has been touching on the way Merleau-Ponty traduces Husserl by making him say the exact opposite of what he does say:

> One can imagine [*On imagine*] Husserl's spontaneous resistances, justified or not, to this "translation," to this discourse [Merleau-Ponty's], at its every step and every turn [*à chacun de ses pas et de ses tours*: in the sense of a path of thought, and in the sense of turn as trope, figure of speech, as well as turn in that path]. But this displacement of the letter, in which one [Merleau-Ponty] says again, nevertheless, "taking literally" [*prendre à la lettre*; in the sense that Merleau-Ponty claims he is echoing what Husserl "literally," in the letters on the page, says, whereas he has reversed what Husserl says], signs Merleau-Ponty's whole design in *Signs* [*signe tout le dessein . . . de* Signes; ha!] and *The Visible and the Invisible*. (OT, 188, trans. modified; LT, 215)

Such plays on words (e.g., "signs the whole design in *Signs*") are mockingly funny. They suggest that Merleau-Ponty cannot write a sentence without getting himself tangled up in the contradictions of "the language, the linguistic and cultural ensemble of a traditional semantic" (OT, 170, trans. modified; LT, 194). These tangles make him always say something other than he apparently thinks he means to say.

A somewhat dismaying accompanying implication, however, is that Derrida himself cannot extricate himself from the same tangles. He can only, somewhat ruefully and comically, highlight them, holding them at arm's length or suspending them with the clothespins of quotation marks, while admitting that they inevitably enter into his own language. It is all very well to accuse Nancy of being contaminated by using outworn words, but Derrida himself is, necessarily, guilty of the same crime. If he says, "Stop it at once, Jean-Luc!" he could also say, and does implicitly say in passages such as the one I have just quoted above, "Stop it at once, Jacques!" No pure language, language free of tropes and wordplay, exists. Knowing that, moreover, does not protect anyone from using impure words, such as the words *literal* and *signs*. This means that Derrida is parasitized by what he would exclude in order to remain pure and safe, in a process that Derrida calls, in "Faith and Knowledge" and elsewhere, a political and psychological appropriation, as a figure of a figure, of the fatal physiological autoimmune response (FK, 80–82, 87–88; FS, 59–62, 68–69). In this response, the body's antibodies turn against its own tissues to destroy them, mistaking those tissues for foreign invaders, as in the autoimmune pancreatic cancer that, "literally," killed Derrida. I have discussed Derrida's figure of autoimmunity in detail in Chapters 6 and 10.

A final example of such putting in question asserts explicitly that any serious interrogation of what, for example, Husserl says makes Husserl's whole argumentative structure extremely fragile or reveals its fragility, its shakiness. It is likely that this structure will collapse at a finger's touch or at a more vigorous pull of the hands, like the force blind Samson applied, "with all his might," to the pillars of the Philistine house, one with his right hand, the other with his left (Judges 17:21–30). "For if one questions," says Derrida, "this absolute *simultaneity* of the touching and the touched, of the active and the passive in immediate and direct intuition, this whole argument risks becoming fragile. Coincidence, intuitive plenitude, direct immediacy, that is what, according to Husserl, characterizes the experience of the touching-touched" (OT, 172, trans. modified; LT, 197). All it takes is a respectful questioning, in this case on the basis of the syncope or infinitesimal time lag in any experience of touching, and down comes the building.

Derrida's final and most important strategy of deconstruction is to show from the analysand's own words, in this case Husserl's, that he contradicts himself in ways that are devastating for the argument he is trying to make. This strategy is a form of close reading as the demonstration of necessary and at first unsuspected contradictions in the formulations. In the case of Husserl, this demolition takes place by way of the basic contradiction or fissure in all of Husserl's thought between, on the one hand, his commitment to the phenomenological principle of principles, intuitive immediacy, and, on the other, the way this commitment to the facts themselves leads him to recognize that our knowledge of the other ego is always a matter of indirect, analogical, appresentation, never of direct, intuitive, immediate apprehension. Derrida's deconstruction of Husserl, or demonstration that he deconstructs himself by way of "the demonstrative procedures or theses that, in truth, seem to parasitize or contaminate in advance the alleged description [*la prétendue description*]" (OT, 174, trans. modified; LT, 199), takes place over several pages of intricate argumentation at the end of "Tangent II" (OT, 174–82; LT, 199–208). You should read these pages for yourself, dear reader.

What Derrida does to Husserl, or shows that Husserl does to himself, turns on the identification of several parasites or contaminants that get in the way of the immediacy Husserl wants to claim for touch. They get in the way within Husserl's own language, not by way of something that Derrida brings in from the outside. These parasites mean that an interval, spacing, syncopated time delay, prosthesis, or material, visible skin always intervenes between toucher and touched, whether it is my hand touching my other hand, my hand touching an object, or my hand touching the body of another I, an alter ego. Derrida, I should note, admits in one place that extending this spacing to my right hand touching my left hand "would strictly be neither Husserlian nor Merleau-Pontyian" (OT, 193; LT, 219). Nevertheless, Derrida dares

> to extend rather than reduce the field of appresentation [i.e., indirect access as named by Husserl] and to recognize the irreducible gap [*écart*] even in the said touching-touched of my "own proper" hand, my own body proper as a human *ego* . . . . Even between me and me, if I may put it this way, between my body and my body, there is no such "original" contemporaneity, this "confusion" that Merleau-Ponty believes he can recognize, claiming [*prétendant*] to follow Husserl, between the other's body and mine. (OT, 192–93, trans. modified; LT, 219)

Derrida is implicitly claiming that Husserl cannot without contradiction claim, on the one hand, that I cannot directly know the other while claiming, on the other hand, that my left hand always knows what my right hand is doing when one hand touches the other. The betrayal of this interval or interruption takes several forms in Husserl's discourse.

One form is discourse itself, the idiomatic language, German in this case, that Husserl uses. This undermines, prima facie, Husserl's claim that the immediacy he talks about, "the universalizable intuition of the things themselves," comes "before all discourse and all linguistic experience, before any mark, before any other difference, before any language and any culture" (OT, 170, trans. modified; LT, 195). No such "before" ever exists for man. Words, marks of some kind, always come between touching-touched and touching-touched.

A second contaminant of immediacy is that some form of materiality, like a sort of intervening skin or membrane, always comes between the two touchers and touched, even when I touch myself. This materiality is the concomitant of four other forms of interruption that Derrida names:

1. Some form of contaminating distancing by seeing enters into Husserl's phenomenological descriptions of even the closest and most intimate touching.

2. Some form of extension or spacing always separates toucher and touched, even at the moment of tangent or contact, or even especially in that moment.

3. Temporality, in Husserl's own descriptions, establishes a time-lag, a syncopation or syncope, like a momentarily held-in breath or like a missed heartbeat, which forbids the simultaneity of touching that Husserl needs to assert in order to be faithful to his phenomenological principle of principles. Derrida argues that Husserl's "principle of principles, the principle of intuition, finds itself threatened. . . . by the experience of temporalization" (OT, 192; LT, 219), as it is described by Husserl himself. "Syncope," says Derrida, paraphrasing Nancy, "is this parting and sharing out of spacing [*partage d'espacement*]: it separates and interrupts at the heart of contact" (OT, 195, trans. modified; LT, 221).

4. The solipsistic impossibility, already named, of direct apprehension of the other. All that is possible is an analogical appresentation that assumes, without any possibility of verification, that this other body must be inhabited by a "soul" like my own. "If," says Derrida, "there is some introjection [a Freudian word interjected there] and thus some analogical appresentation at the threshold of the touching-touched, then the latter cannot be accessible for an originary, immediate, and full intuition, any more than the *alter ego*" (OT, 176, trans. modified; LT, 202).

Most of the forms of distancing I have named tend to appear together in all Derrida's formulations of Husserl's plight or, to borrow Paul de Man's frequently used word, his "predicament." Here is one somewhat extended example:

> No matter how subtle, furtive, and elusive, this detour by way of the foreign outside is at the same time what allows us to speak of a "double" apprehension (without which there would be only one: only some touching or only some touched) and what allows me, through the test of this singular experience, to distinguish between the I and the non-I, to say "this is my body" or, quoting Husserl himself, to draw the "consequence that I, the 'subject of the Body,' can say that what belongs to [*concerne*] the material thing is its, not mine [*la concerne, elle, et non moi*]." For that, it is necessary that the space of the material thing, like a difference, like the heterogeneity of a

spacing, slip between the touching and the touched. For the two neither must nor can coincide if, indeed, there is to be a double apprehension. (OT, 175, trans. modified; LT, 200)

Perhaps the most dramatic expression of this contamination of immediacy by some form or other of separation, spacing, discontinuity, disconnect, or delay uses the figure of the parasitical ghost within the domestic enclosure. With this figure I shall conclude my demonstration of the way Derrida unhands Husserl's doctrine of hands, his humanualism:

> We ask ourselves whether there is any pure auto-affection of the touching or the touched, and therefore a pure, immediate experience of the purely proper body, the body proper that is living, purely living. Or if, on the contrary, this experience is at least not already *haunted*, but *constitutively* haunted, by some hetero-affection related to spacing and then to visible spatiality—where an intruder [*l'intrus*] may come through, the guest, a guest [*hôte*: this word in French can mean both "guest" and "host"] wished or unwished for, a saving other or a parasite to be rejected, a *pharmakon* that, already having at its disposal a dwelling in the place, inhabits as a ghost [*en revenant*] every interior enclosure [*tout for intérieur*]. (OT, 179–80, trans. modified; LT, 205)

Final Touch on the Failure to Touch: Brief Coda or Grasp of a Prehensile Tail

Tiens!

This is a common imperative exclamation in French, hard to translate. It is also hard, for someone not a native speaker, to know in just what circumstances it is correct to say *Tiens!* The word is the second person singular imperative of the verb *tenir*, "to hold." Literally, *Tiens* means "Hold," that is, "You (thou) hold onto this," "Take this." I use the word in allusion to a characteristically exuberant, even a little wild paragraph in *Le toucher* in which Derrida relates the exclamation to tactful touching without touching. Here is part of that paragraph:

> "Tiens!" [There! Hold on to this! Take it! Have it!—Trans.]. What is one saying, what is one giving to understand when one says "Tiens!"? Is what is wanting here the virtual shadow, at least, of a hand gesture ("Tiens!": "Take this!"), a touching hand or a giving one [*main . . . donnante*], a hand given to touch the other, a hand held out to or extending something to the other? "Tiens!" Take this! [*prends!*] But tact commands neither to tender

nor to grasp ourselves and each other without trembling, without some
relinquishment at the heart of the seizing [*dessaisissement au coeur de la sai-
sie*]. Tact enjoins not to touch, not to take what one takes, or rather, not to
be taken in by what one takes. Tact beyond contact. Which does not necessarily mean to say a *neutralization* of touching. (OT, 76, trans. modified;
LT, 91)

This kind of reflection on the nuances of everyday language would perhaps
be most likely to be made by someone like Derrida (an Algerian) or Joyce
(an Irishman), who was both inside the language in question and at the
same time distanced from it as the language of the imperial occupier of
one's native land. If *Finnegans Wake* might be described as Joyce's revenge
on the English language, Derrida's work, for example, *Glas* or *Le toucher*
itself, in spite of his often-expressed self-identification as a writer in
French, could be described as the deconstruction of French, leaving it
never quite the same again.[39]

Do I think I have succeeded in tactfully touching Jacques Derrida, or
in putting my finger on his singularity? Have I earned the right to say
Tiens! to him? As the reader will perhaps remember, touching him was
what I began by saying I wanted to do, especially by way of what he says
about hands. To tell the truth, I do not feel that I have laid a hand on him.
I have not "kept in touch" with him, as when we say to a friend or an
acquaintance: "Please keep in touch." Derrida has eluded my grasp, like
an animal's tail that slips through my fingers when I try to seize it, though
I think I have said some things that are true about his way of writing, his
"hand," in his in many ways outrageous book, *Le toucher, Jean-Luc Nancy.*
I do not believe, nevertheless, *pace* Tennyson, that you can ever reach out
and touch a person through what he or she has written. So my work is all
to begin again, even though it is high time to stop.

Coda means "tail," from Latin *cauda.* That reminds me again that one
reproach Derrida makes to Husserl and to the whole haptic tradition from
Aristotle on is their exclusion of animals. They perform this exclusion by
way of the claim that only "man" has hands, even though they begin their
analysis of touch by saying it applies to all "animals," that is, all animate
creatures. Derrida's passing reference to this is a characteristic putting in
question. It ties in with all he was to say later, in his two final years of
seminars entitled "The Beast and the Sovereign," about the animal's
claimed lack of human qualities in assertions by Western philosophers
from Aristotle to Heidegger and Lacan. Derrida says:

And concerning life, where touch is in question . . . , it is practically a
question only of man, and especially the fingers of the human hand, never

seriously the "animal," which is nevertheless a living being; it is not even a question of the body proper of those which, among animals, have members or organs that resemble hands! Even with fingers! And what about opportunities, for so many handless animals, to touch and be touched in countless ways!" (OT, 168, trans. modified; LT, 192–93)

Derrida presumably has in mind the hands of monkeys and apes, but he might also have mentioned the prehensile tales so many long-tailed animals, not just monkeys, have, or that wonderful organ of touch, the elephant's trunk, or, had he known about her, even the way our cat Daisy kisses us with her nose and rests with her paws crossed, the left paw touching the right paw. How could we know whether or not that leads to a confirmation, for her, that "she is she," touching herself touching herself?

Here is my own prehensile tail or coda: Derrida's *Le toucher, Jean-Luc Nancy*, as I said at this chapter's beginning, was originally published in 2000, four years before Derrida's death, though parts had been written much earlier, in 1992, then extensively revised and augmented during the intervening eight years. Derrida often, in the book itself, ruefully complains that not only does he need to read Nancy's earlier books over and over in order to understand them fully, but that Nancy has published so many new books during the decade of the nineties that he (Derrida) has great difficulty keeping up. The English translation of *Le toucher* was published in 2004, just after Derrida's death. It includes a moving memorial statement by Nancy, written two days after Derrida's death, "*Salut* to you, *salut* to the blind we become" (OT, 313–14). Nancy, however, had published in 2003, while Derrida was still alive, though ill, a wonderful short book entitled *Noli me tangere*. This is a book about paintings, primarily Renaissance paintings, which represent the moving episode in John's Gospel of Mary Magdalene's encounter with the risen Christ. Derrida had already discussed this episode in *Le toucher*. Mary Magdalene does not recognize Jesus. She thinks he is the gardener, until he calls her by name. She then turns back and addresses him as "Rabboni!" which means "Master," as the King James Bible says. This is one of the few places in the New Testament where the actual vernacular word a person would then have spoken is given, another being Christ's words on the Cross. Mary reaches out to touch Jesus, who says, in the King James version, "Touch me not [*Noli me tangere* in Latin; *Mē haptou mou* in Greek]; for I am not yet ascended to my Father" (John 20:17).

Nancy's book is both explicitly and implicitly a response to Derrida's book about him. Nancy gets the last word, after all. I say explicitly because one footnote respectfully but with gentle irony refers directly to one point against Nancy that Derrida's book makes. Implicitly, however, Nancy's whole book is a reply to Derrida. A chapter, for example, is called "Hands" ("Mains"). It analyzes in detail the admirable play of reaching, touching, refraining, and pointing hands, both those of Mary and those of Jesus, in paintings by Titian, Pontormo, Bronzino, and others. Mary reaches out to touch Jesus or his garments, but he draws back, sometimes touching, or almost touching, Mary on the head or breast, in a gesture that is both affectionate and resisting. His other hand, in many paintings, points toward heaven, where his Father waits. It is as though Nancy were saying, "You want hands? Let me show you a thing or two about hands!"

No home should be without this superb book. It observes how odd Jesus' words are, as anyone who thinks about them may also do. What is the force of Jesus' "for"? Why is it that, because he has not yet ascended to his father, he forbids Mary to touch him? It doesn't quite make sense. Is it because the risen Christ is an insubstantial ghost who may not be touched in any case? Mary's hand would go right through the apparition. This hardly seems compatible with the doctrines of the Incarnation and Resurrection. Should we read *Noli me tangere*, as some translations do, as meaning "Hold me not," meaning "Don't hold me back, for I am about to ascend to my Father"? The gestures in several of the paintings Nancy discusses would suggest that. Or should we read *Noli*, as would be good Latin, as saying "Do not wish to touch me" or even "Don't you dare touch me, for I am in that intermediate state of resurrection, between death and ascension. Touching me might keep me too long in that state." Jesus might then become like Kafka's Hunter Gracchus, who got caught forever on the stairway between this world and the other,[40] or like Nancy after his heart transplant, whose survival Derrida calls a "resurrection." Jesus has to be free from human touching, however much he loves Mary Magdalene, so he can ascend to his Father. Mary must turn away from him to bring the good news of his resurrection to the disciples: "go to my brethren," says Jesus to Mary, "and say unto them, I ascend unto my Father, and your Father; and to my God, and your God" (John 20:17).

Nancy's direct reference to *Le toucher* in *Noli me tangere* comes in a footnote to a formulation about touching without touching that echoes Derrida. The text proper seems to acquiesce gracefully to Derrida's reproaches to him about being too prone, in spite of all his care, still to want to believe that touching actually takes place. "This sensitive point," says Nancy in the main text, ". . . is precisely the point where touching does not touch [*le toucher ne touche pas*] and where it must not touch in order to carry out its touch (its art, its tact, its grace): the point or the space without dimension that separates what touching gathers together [*rassemble*], the line that separates the touching from the touched and thus the touch from itself."[41] This sounds like something Derrida himself might have written. So far so good.

The footnote, however, is not quite so meek. After having said that what he has just written about the "problematic of touch" "evidently owes much [*est évidemment redevable*] to Derrida's work in *Le toucher, Jean-Luc Nancy*" and after having acknowledged that Derrida discusses Christ's *Noli me tangere* in that book, Nancy goes on to give the back of his hand to Derrida in a remark that may have touched him to the quick, or that at any rate is hardly kind. What really annoyed Nancy about Derrida's book, it appears, is Derrida's resistance to Nancy's project of "the deconstruction of Christianity." "Just you try to do it," in effect says Derrida. "It is impossible. Christianity cannot be deconstructed."[42] This, among other things, implies that Nancy's work is still deeply and inevitably Christian. Nancy replies to this by accusing Derrida of being "rabbinical," that is, of being unable to detach himself from his Judaic roots. The "evocation" of all those examples of touching in the Jesus story by Derrida, says Nancy, is "inscribed in the question that I have called 'the deconstruction of Christianity,' a question on which Derrida intends to touch with a skeptical or rabbinical distance, one that I do not despair of having reduced here just a little [he means in his book *Noli me tangere*]."[43] That's it! I had not thought of that analogy, though of course many scholars have commented on Derrida's relation to Judaic traditions. Derrida was a Jew, therefore, such comments tend to assume, there must be something Jewish about his interpretative procedures.

Derrida's extremely complex relation to his Jewishness is formulated in "Abraham, the Other." I have already discussed this essay in Chapter 7, but need to mention it again in this new context of Nancy's comment. "Abraham, the Other" was presented as a lecture for a conference entitled *Judéités: Questions pour Jacques Derrida*, held in the Jewish Community Center in Paris in December 2000. The question of Derrida's Jewishness was the matter at hand, so to speak. The essay is confessional. Its more or less evident background is Derrida's resistance, best articulated in *A Taste for the Secret* and discussed in my Chapter 6, to being a member of any family, group, community, sect, clique, *Geschlecht*, "herd," or *gregge*, to give the word for "herd" that appears in the original Italian version of *A Taste for the Secret*. To summarize inadequately an intricate argument that would merit lengthy, perhaps interminable, analysis, Derrida in "Abraham, the Other," says repeatedly that he is proud of being a Jew, while putting this "election" under the ambiguous shelter of what Kafka in one of his parables says about the "other Abrahams" he could imagine. This includes the Abraham who perhaps only mistakenly thought he was called by God to sacrifice his beloved only son, Isaac. How could he be sure? How can Derrida be sure of his Jewishness, his Judeity, whatever, exactly, those two rather different words mean? Derrida repeatedly puts his uncertainty under the aegis of Kafka's troublingly comic analogy for one of those other Abrahams. I cite again a passage already cited, in a different context, in Chapter 7:

> An Abraham who should come unsummoned [*ungerufen*]! It is as if, at the end of the year, when the best student was solemnly about to receive a prize, the worst student rose in the expectant stillness and came forward from his dirty desk in the last row because he had made a mistake of hearing, and the whole class burst out laughing [*losplatzt*]. And perhaps he had made no mistake at all, his name really was called, it having been the teacher's intention to make the rewarding of the best student at the same time a punishment for the worst one.[44]

In spite of Derrida's "vertiginous" (his word) reservations about what it means to say "I am a Jew," discussed in Chapter 7, Nancy's term "rabbinical" puts its finger on something essential about Derrida's interpretative procedures, his inimitable "hand" as a reader. "Rabbinical" is a good analogy for Derrida's demonstration that, for him at least, *Methode ist Unweg*. Derrida's *Le toucher*, in its baroque complexity, in its endless, nit-picking questions and endless suspensions or syncopes, forbidding firm conclusions, its interminable digressions, each flying off at a different tangent, is something like rabbinical Midrash. The interpretative techniques of Midrash can get endless, undecidable meanings out of a simple story or a brief biblical phrase, or could get, in this case, such meanings out of what Nancy says about touching.[45] Derrida himself once told me that his friend Levinas, himself not a little rabbinical, once looked him in the eye and said, "Do you know what you remind me of, Jacques? You remind me of a heretical Cabbalist of the Middle Ages." "Heretical" is important here. With that borrowed formulation and with help from Nancy, I may have perhaps finally touched Derrida and put him in his place. I wish I could be sure of that. Happily, or, rather, unhappily, Derrida is no longer around to answer back. I am sure he would have a lot more to say, to put me in my place in what I say about him.

However, to say a final final word, or to give Derrida the last word, one must be extremely careful about pushing the analogy with Midrash too far, or even very far at all. Derrida more than once somewhat ruefully confessed to his more or less complete ignorance of Judaic commentary on the Torah. A good example is what he says in "Others Are Secret Because They Are Other" ("Autrui est secret parce qu'il est autre"), an interview by Antoine Spire for *Le Monde de l'éducation*, collected in *Paper Machine*:

> On the Jewish [*judaïque*] reference, my "belonging" to Judaism, to put it like that, much has been written, as you probably know, for years now, and this always leaves me puzzled. First, because I think that patient, vigilant, micrological, interminable reading is not exclusive to the Jewish tradition. Also, I must confess that my familiarity with the Jewish culture you mention is, alas, very weak and indirect. I regret this, of course; it's too late. If what I do reminds people of Jewish annotation [*une glose juive*], that is not the result of a choice, or a desire, or even of a memory or cultural formation. (PMe, 141; PMf, 373)

Such denials forbid one to think of Derrida of an afternoon deep in reading Midrash. The Christian Bible was probably more pertinent for him than the Torah, as his many references to it suggest, and St. Augustine or Kierkegaard much more important than Midrash, as, for example, *The Gift of Death* and "Circumfession" attest, as well as some admirable sessions of the unpublished seminars. I remember hearing one that expounded St. Augustine in the most intimate and sympathetic way. How strange, thought I to myself, to hear this supposed atheist, destroyer of Western civilization, speak with such affectionate warmth and insight about his fellow North African, Augustine! In *A Taste for the Secret*, Derrida pays homage not to Midrash as the source of his ways of reading but, with characteristically complex reservations, to the French tradition of commentary on canonical philosophical texts. This was represented, for him, by one of his teachers at the École normale supérieure, Martial Guéroult, "about whom hardly anyone now talks" (TS, 44): "Whatever the doubts I may have about it now, this model wielded great authority over me, even if at a certain point I contested it; still, it was the contestation of someone who recognized the great value of what he was contesting" (TS, 45).

With this last, hesitant pertinent/impertinent touch without touching, I leave *Le toucher, Jean-Luc Nancy*, for the moment at least.

CHAPTER 12

Absolute Mourning: It Is Jacques You Mourn For

In memory of Rosie, a cat

In the previous chapter I asserted that Derrida's *Le toucher, Jean-Luc Nancy* is an extremely odd or exceptional work of mourning. It mourns someone who is not yet dead, since Nancy survived his heart transplant operation to persist in what might be called a posthumous life. This has lasted down to the day I am writing this. For this I rejoice. Nancy has survived Derrida's death to write more about Derrida. As I showed, he is having the last word about matters on which they did not quite agree, now that Derrida cannot answer back.

This chapter will explore, as the previous chapter did not do, the word or concept of mourning (*deuil*), especially the enigmatic phrase "absolute mourning [*deuil absolu*]" in *Le toucher*. This necessarily means coming back from a different angle or way of access to the central notions in *Le toucher* of metonymy, ecotechnics, prosthesis, the body, the impossibility of touch, and so on, already discussed from a different perspective in Chapter 11. This will be a little like coming back to the same crossroads by different access roads. *Le toucher* is not so much a sequential argument as many nodes of metonymic variations on a single set of intertwined themes, inexhaustibly reinvestigated, as if in an always unsuccessful attempt to "get it right" in a final satisfactory formulation of all these motifs in their interconnection. This is "method is detour" with a vengeance. "Mourning" keeps coming back as a leitmotif in these detours and intersections.

Derrida, in *Le toucher*, as I noted in the previous chapter, defines Nancy's survival, his "living on," as a death and resurrection, Derrida's as well as Nancy's. Derrida says that when he visited Nancy in the hospital after the heart-transplant operation, he kissed him on the cheeks for the first time ever and felt "as after a resurrection—and not only his" (OT, 302; LT, 339). Derrida too is henceforth a survivor and writes as such, from this exceptional position, beyond life and death.

This gives another meaning, perhaps, to Derrida's solemn assertions, both to me in conversation and in an interview with Gianni Vattimo in *A Taste for the Secret*, that he thought about death every day (TS, 88). I have cited and analyzed these assertions already in Chapter 5. For Derrida, it appears, to live is to be a survivor. It is to be a survivor not so much of the deaths of others as of one's own death. Already in 1967, one epigraph to *Speech and Phenomena* (*La voix et le phénomène*) (SP, 1; VP1, [v]) cites Poe's M. Valdemar's extraordinary statement: "*I am dead.*" (Mar: Mort? Valdemar: Val de mort? Valley of death? Valiant before death or because of death? Poe's name seems to hide some reference to death.) In any case, to live, for Derrida, is to think about death all the time, to analyze death all the time. And he does this in the face of an apparent conviction that no afterlife exists, no survival after death, even though the first word in his assertion of this of contains a demurrer: "insofar as I do not believe that one lives on post mortem" (TS, 88). How far does that "insofar" go?

Le toucher, as I have shown in the previous chapter, has a lot to say about the prosthetic and about technicity as prosthesis. The writing of *Le toucher* more or less coincides with Derrida's adoption of the laptop computer as his writing instrument. It is one of the first great works written on the computer whose form depends on that mode of writing, for example, in the way Derrida could go on for eight years adding, interpolating, revising, deleting (mostly adding), without any traces remaining of that process. This can be done with a pen or typewriter too, of course, but it is immensely easier on the computer. That *Le toucher* was written on the computer explains why it was so easy for it to remain unfinished and impossible to finish. It could always be so easily augmented or revised, as I am augmenting this essay right at this moment. (I leave it to the reader to decide on the referent of "right at this moment.") The writing of *Le toucher* coincides also with Derrida's survival of Nancy's virtual death and resurrection and with his quasi-mourning for a death that did not occur. Writing this book, it almost seems, needed to go on as long as Derrida and Nancy remained alive, though Derrida survived its publication by four years. It appears that this virtually endless revision and extension were necessary because Nancy, precisely, was not dead. He was going on living and writing more and more quasi-posthumous books. As Derrida ruefully observes more than once in *Le toucher*, he could never catch up with what Nancy was writing and publishing in the 1990s. How can you successfully mourn someone who is not yet dead? Writing *Le toucher*, however, was perhaps a way to try to hold off death, I mean Derrida's own death.

The writing of *Le toucher* registers the extremely odd relation to oneself and to another person that Nancy, and Derrida at length after him, calls *se toucher toi*, "touching oneself touching the other." This relation keeps me from death, in a kind of extended detour away from death or in a syncope suspending death, as Derrida in one place eloquently asserts. He says it in the form of a performative apostrophe, a beseeching. This imploring is addressed not just to Nancy's heart but to that of any reader, to the heart of any and every other person, and even to Derrida's own heart as the other within himself. The apostrophe arises in the context of a discussion of the heart, Nancy's transplanted heart of the other beating in his own breast, but any "my heart" as the locus of an inside that exceeds any interiority and that is the death I carry always within me:

> This other heart self-touches you [*toi*] only to be exposed to death. We are here at the heart of a *finite thinking*. [*A Finite Thinking (Une pensée finie)* is the title of a book by Nancy, footnoted in Chapter 11.] The heart is always of a finite thinking. It thinks, for the heart is the place of thinking and not only the place of feeling, love, desire. In it a finite thinking is thought. You are/is also my death. [*Toi es(t) aussi ma mort.*] You keep it for me, you keep me from it always a little, isn't that so, from death. Keep me from it still a little longer, if you please, just a little longer, keep me from it as much as possible, as well as possible, the longest time possible. (OT, 289, trans. modified; LT, 325)

The French uses the second personal singular, as if to emphasize the intimacy of this imploring conjuration: "Toi es(t) aussi ma mort. Toi, tu me la gardes, tu m'en gardes toujours un peu, n'est-ce pas, de la mort. Garde-m'en encore un peu, s'il te plait, juste encore un peu, mais garde-m'en le plus possible, le mieux possible, le plus longtemps possible" (LT, 325). The reader will see the play here on *garde*, both as "keep sequestered in you my death" and "keep me, guard me, from death." This play is elegantly carried over in the play on "keep" in the translation. The *en* in *tu m'en gardes* and *garde-m'en encore un peu* is a little harder to transfer into

English. "You keep it for me" and "you guard me from it" are expressed in the same idiomatic phrases.

Mourning is a conspicuous but enigmatic thread that runs all through *Le toucher*, as well as through Derrida's work *in toto*. What does he mean by "mourning"? More precisely, I want to identify what Derrida means by "absolute mourning." I have already, in Chapter 5, identified Derrida's double motive for writing so many memorial essays and books for dead friends or associates, almost before their bodies were cold. He wanted both to give them decent burial and to put them in their places, in the sense of passing final judgment on their works.

The theme of mourning appears frequently, almost obsessively, in Derrida's work all along, not only in those memorial writings but also in such works as *The Politics of Friendship* (*Politiques de l'amitié*). There he notes that friendship is defined by the way one friend is almost certain to outlive the other. "Circumfession" is a work of mourning for Derrida's mother's death. Mourning is a central theme in *Memoirs of the Blind, Glas, Specters of Marx, The Gift of Death*, and "Rams." From one Derrida work to the next, mourning appears in one way or another as an essential theme.[1] A careful reading of what Derrida says about "absolute mourning" in *Le toucher* may help make sense of this strange phrase. "Absolute mourning": What can that possibly mean? At the end of the *Avant-propos* of *Chaque fois unique, la fin du monde* (not in the English version, *The Work of Mourning*), Derrida mentions the line from a poem by Celan that is the focus of "Rams": "Die Welt ist fort, ich muss dich tragen." He says that the line has been haunting him for years and that he would recommend a reading of his commentary on it in "Rams" as a "veritable introduction" to *Chaque fois unique* (CFU, 11).

Mourning for Derrida almost always involves an implicit reference to Freud's essay "Mourning and Melancholia."[2] An example is a sentence in *Memoires for Paul de Man*: "Memory and interiorization: since Freud, this is how the 'normal' 'work of mourning' [*travail du deuil*] is often described. It entails a movement in which an interiorizing idealization takes in itself or upon itself the body and voice of the other, the other's visage and person, ideally *and* quasi-literally [*quasi littréralement*] devouring them" (MPdMe, 34; MPdMf, 54). Just what a "quasi-literal devouring" literally means is a little obscure to me. I suppose he is referring to sacrificial cannibalistic ingestion of the dead, but as transferred to a symbolic substitute, as in the bread and wine of the Eucharist. As for "interiorizing idealization," Derrida reports that after Barthes' death he succumbed to "a certain mimetism" of Barthes, even though that was "at once a duty . . . and the worst of temptations" (WM, 38; CFU, 64).

For Freud, then, mourning goes with introjection, the taking into oneself idealized features of the dead person as part of the work of mourning, as Derrida explains. That process is finished when one outlives, through a working through, the pain of the other's death. It is healthy for that to happen. Melancholy, however, goes with incorporation, the sudden transfer of the dead person to being a haunting specter within the self. The dead friend, beloved, or relative becomes a ghost within myself that cannot be laid. That may prolong the melancholic suffering indefinitely, in a way that is psychologically unhealthy. Who would want to be perpetually melancholy, for the rest of one's life? Nicolas Abraham and Maria Torok forcefully argue for this pairing, following Freud and Ferenzi, in "Introject-incorporate: Mourning *or* Melancholy" ("Introjecter-incorporer: deuil *ou* mélancolie").[3] Derrida discusses the joining of mourning with introjection and melancholy with incorporation, while putting in question these distinctions, in his essay on Abraham and Torok, "Fors: The Anglish Words of Nicolas Abraham and Maria Torok" ("Fors: Les mots anglés de Nicolas Abraham et Maria Torok"). "Rather than . . . the partitions themselves and the spaces they divide," says Derrida, "one could be tempted to see a simple polarity, a polarized system (introjection/incorporation) rather than the intractable, untreatable rigor [*la rigueur intraitable*] of their distinction" (Fe, xviii; Ff, 19). A lot hangs, as I shall show, on Derrida's claim that it is impossible to keep mourning and melancholy separate, that one shades into the other.

My presupposition here, as in all these chapters "for Derrida," as I have said before, is that the only way to talk sensibly about Derrida is to eschew big generalizations about *différance*, "grammatology," "Derrida's politics," or whatever and to read him micrologically, line by line, word by word, and letter by letter, in order to try to figure out what he actually says about a given topic, in this case "absolute mourning." I also presuppose that Derrida may turn out to be saying something rather different from what many people think he says. This is perhaps because our resistance to what he is actually saying, or our congenital gift for plain misreading, is so great. "We," it may be, are a community of bad readers, though we do not all read badly in the same way. I do not exempt myself from membership in that community.

What in the world could "absolute mourning" be? The term, along with *impossible mourning, pre-originary mourning*, and just the word *mourning*, appears and disappears, at irregular, arhythmic intervals, in *Le toucher*, like a red thread woven into a complex tapestry. Let me try to follow that thread as best I can. The reappearances of references to mourning or absolute mourning are not just repetitions. The earlier surfacings of the red thread are extremely compressed and enigmatic, like tips of an iceberg. What, for example, is "exappropriation"? What does mourning have to do with prosthesis and with "ecotechnicity"? Just what is "ecotechnicity," anyway? The string of references to mourning gradually elucidates the system of figures or concepts, figure-concepts, circling around what Derrida calls "absolute mourning." The series of references to mourning, one might say, is like one of those films that returns again and again to the same scene, in this case a scene of mourning, until finally the viewer is perhaps able to figure out what was going on in it, but "invisibly," the first time she saw it.

The word *mourning* appears first in *Le toucher* in the early sequence about Nancy's little essay "Psyche."[4] "Mourning," as I have said, is *deuil* in French, echoed in the English words *dole* and *doleful*. The Indo-European root was *del-*, meaning "to split, carve, cut," as, I suppose, when we say, "I am cut up by his or her death." Derrida's pages about "Psyche" are an exuberant commentary on Nancy's exuberant little essay on Freud's enigmatic late aphorism "Psyche ist ausgedehnt, weiss nicht davon." The story from late antiquity of Cupid and Psyche is taken to be an allegory of the soul, since *psyche*, after all, means "soul." At one point, in a passage already mentioned in Chapter 11, though not with attention to what it says about mourning, Derrida imagines an amusing scene in which all the philosophers from Aristotle down to Freud and Merleau-Ponty are standing anxiously around Psyche's bedside like consulting doctors or like participants in an academic conference entitled The Soul. More likely today the conference would be entitled The Body, but in the end this would come to the same thing. I shall soon show why.

These learned persons are trying to decide whether Psyche is asleep or dead. She must be one or the other because she is "extended," both in the sense that she is stretched out in inanimate motionlessness, exposed to their voyeuristic looking, in repetition of Cupid's, and in the sense that, at the allegorical level of meaning, the soul, the psyche, is divided into separate parts that are not connected. The parts of the soul are, in Nancy's phrase, *partes extra partes*, parts outside of parts. That is why the soul knows nothing about it, is in a state of unknowing, *weiss nicht davon*. One part doesn't know what the other parts are doing, thinking, or feeling. That means Psyche must be unconscious or dead. In fact, she is dead, about to be entombed: "Nancy's Psyche sees herself treated as a dead woman" (OT, 19; LT, 31).

The soul is always already dead, at least when looked at from the outside, by the learned doctor-philosophers. That is why they are in mourning. They are in mourning, Derrida says, because Psyche, the soul, is an absence, a black hole, something that cannot be named directly, only named in perpetually displacing, sideways moving, metonymies, what Derrida calls, in a phrase commented on in Chapter 11, "the closure of a combinatory play around a vacant center" (OT, 16, trans. modified; LT, 28):

> They [the learned philosophers, no doubt all male] are there *subject* to her [or "because of her": *à son sujet*]. They now *hold* onto her subject. They *hold* a session [*séance*], a council, a conference on her as subject [*à son sujet*]. Just as they take up their places *around* this locus where nothing takes place but place, that is, extension, one can also sense that they *take the place of*—but of whom? Of what? [*de qui de quoi?*] What then does this metonymy announce? For whom and for what [*De qui de quoi*] is it in mourning, if every metonymy remains a sign of mourning?
>
> (A metonymy is in mourning, at least, for a proper sense or a proper name.) (OT 17, trans. modified; LT, 29)

Mourning, as Derrida here defines it, is grief for an absence that cannot be introjected, much less incorporated. It is just total loss, absence, lack of a proper sense or name, here figured (but is it really a figure?) in Psyche's extended body, asleep or dead. We are always in mourning for the absent or dead. It is the human condition. To be human is to be in mourning, or, rather, mourning is melancholic, since you can never get over it, never put aside your black crape. To be human is to be perpetually in mourning for one's own death, as in Derrida's solemn assertion to me: "I think about it *every* day."

Mourning returns on the next page, in confirmation of what I have just said: "In any case, it was time to start with a tableau of mourning. Not mourning for someone, male or female, some determined living being, some singularity or other, but mourning life itself, and what in life is the very living thing, the living spring, the breath of life. Psyche is also a common proper name, designating the principle of life, breath, the soul, the animation of the animal" (OT, 18; LT, 30).

I have said that an academic conference entitled The Soul would be the same as an academic conference entitled The Body, of which there are so many these days. That is confirmed by a compressed passage on the next page that introduces Derrida's enigmatic versions of prosthesis, technicity, and autoimmunity, in their interlaced complexity. After having said that Nancy's Psyche sees herself [sees herself? I thought she was asleep or dead] as a dead woman, Derrida goes on to say that this would have "some consequences" for our current discourses about "'the living body' [*corps vivant*] (*Leib*), whether as "body proper" or as "flesh [*chair*]." What would those consequences be? Derrida's answer is to say that: "The principle or drive to expropriation introduced there [he means in "the body," such as Psyche's extended body] forthwith by death or even the other or time [*sans attendre la mort, voire l'autre ou le temps*], is certainly hard to tolerate, but, as we shall see, less resistant to thought than what complicates an *incarnation* even more, which is to say, the prosthesis, the metonymic substitute, the process of autoimmunity, and *technical* survival" (OT, 19, trans. modified; LT, 31). Derrida goes on immediately after this, in a separate paragraph, to add yet more terms to this metonymic series: "Among the names that Nancy bestows on these are, for example, the *technē of bodies, ecotechnics*, or the intrusion of *L'intrus*" (OT, 19, trans. modifed; LT, 31). "These" refers to "the prosthesis, the metonymic substitute," etc. in the previous sentence. "The Intruder" (*L'intrus*) is a book by Nancy that is, in part at least, about the "intrusion" into his body of the transplanted heart of another person, a person now dead, naturally, and a person who may have been either male or female.[5] This sequence says a mouthful, as we say, since it brings in so many new and, in the immediate context, somewhat inscrutable terms.

Just what does the passage mean? "The living body," Derrida is saying, is not a self-enclosed unity. It is always already inhabited by death. Death installs within the body a drive to "expropriation," by which Derrida means that the body is never a "body proper" but is always put beside itself or outside itself, or made improper, "expropriated." The body is taken possession of or is hollowed out by death, the other, or time.

Why these three terms? Are they equivalents, or just sideways metonymies? All three are metonymies or catachreses for the unnamable something, in the closure of a combinatory play around a vacant center. "Death," as Paul de Man said, "is a displaced name for a linguistic predicament."[6] Nobody ever saw death face to face or touched it; therefore it is not open to referential naming. The other person is similar to death in his or her absence, according to Derrida's formula that *tout autre est tout autre*, "every other is wholly other." Temporality, as later passages on mourning in *Le toucher* make clear, in its anti-Heideggerian *différance*, going forward into the future in order to come back to the past, with never a present

present as such, is one phenomenological form the experience of the "vacant center" takes.

To say "I think about death every day, every moment of every day," is to define the moment to moment sequence of times for a given consciousness as a thinking about what eludes thinking, namely, death. That is "hard to tolerate," says Derrida, but even more resistant to thought is the way *incarnation*, by which I suppose Derrida means the inhabitation of the body by a soul, is "complicated" by "the prosthesis, the metonymic substitute, the process of autoimmunity, and *technical* survival." To this series of metonymic displacements Derrida then adds Nancy's terms: "the *technē* of bodies, ecotechnics, and the intrusion of *L'intrus*." All these words describe the way the body may be supplemented by prosthetic limbs or by transplanted organs—the heart, for example—in a way that reveals that "the" body is always expropriated by something foreign to it. The conjoined body and soul can survive "technically," as after a heart transplant, but this means that it was always a survivor, since its body parts are replaceable. We just happen to have the heart that we do happen to have, plugged into our body. The body is always a technical apparatus, hence the term "ecotechnics." There is no "the" body in the sense of an organic whole, Nancy says, and Derrida repeats this after him. How many organs would have to be replaced before the "soul" would be different?

One evidence for "*technical* survival" is the process of autoimmunity, which Derrida takes in "Faith and Knowledge" to be a powerful figure for the auto-destructive drive of any community, society, or nation, as it destroys itself through its very effort to keep itself safe, immune, by way of immense efforts to achieve "homeland security." At the level of "literal" incarnation, the autoimmune process defines not the immune system's tendency to "reject" transplanted organs as foreign invaders but, more disturbingly, the immune system's unhappy propensity, in certain cases, to reject its own organs as foreign invaders, in an ecotechnical disaster. The warriors of the immune system are not clever enough to tell the difference between the body's "own" or "proper" organs and foreign organs transplanted into the body, perhaps because, in the end, these two kinds are in some ways similar. That may be because the body is always a technical apparatus and always lives on through *technical* survival. Some scientists think that certain cancers, such as the pancreatic cancer that killed Derrida, are autoimmune disorders. What all these metonymic displacements have to do with mourning is not yet entirely clear. I agree, however, that one resists the line of thinking Derrida calls "ecotechnics." It is pretty weird.

We learn, from the serio-comic erotico-philosophic scene of all those doctors consulting about Psyche, that mourning has something to do with the impossibility of naming the psyche. The psyche is an absence from the word go. It is a place where nothing takes place but place. (The last phrase is a citation from Mallarmé's *Un coup de dés* [*A Throw of the Dice*]). Therefore, what mourning mourns for is not some particular dead person but "life itself," that is, the principle of life and animation that "psyche" names. This proposition is reaffirmed in a somewhat later page in *Le toucher*:

> There where the taking-place of the event doesn't find its place, a gaping locus, indeed, a mouth, except in *replacement*, where it doesn't find room [*sa place*] except in replacement, isn't that the trace of metonymy or of the technical prosthesis, and the place for the phantasm as well, that is to say, the ghostly revenant (*phantasma*)? The phantasm at the heart of (self) feeling? Thus the revenant, between life and death, dictates an impossible mourning, an endless mourning, life itself. Barely visible scene of this mourning. It pertains to a *spacing* that is irreducible or even heterogeneous to the stretching out of an *extensio* from which, however, one should not dissociate it. (OT, 35, trans. modified; LT, 48)

A technical prosthesis, this passage affirms, is a kind of metonymy. It is a sideways displacement or replacement for something that is not there to be given a literal or proper name. That something is a gaping locus, a mouth, a void, around which the learned doctors gather when they inspect Psyche. Metonymies and technical prostheses, moreover, are revenants, ghosts, hovering between life and death, undecidably. Metonymies and prostheses are like phantasms both in the sense that they are like specters and in the sense that they are like fictions, imaginary images, signs without any identifiable referent.

These phantasms "dictate" an impossible mourning, in an irresistible command. We have no choice in the matter. This mourning is impossible because we can never have done with it or get over it, as is supposed to happen in "normal" mourning for the death of a friend, a beloved, or a relative. For Derrida, life itself is mourning. To live is to be in mourning, to mourn for life itself, for my own life. It is Jacques Jacques mourns for.[7] We mourn for psyche because she/it is gone, inaccessible in her/its extension, *partes extra partes*.

A footnote to the passage just cited is a sort of technical prosthesis, as footnotes in general are. This footnote is perhaps a metonymy/prosthesis/ phantasm added late in the composition of *Le toucher*. It supplements or glosses, speaking in a spectral voice from outside, the formulation in the passage proper about "a *spacing* that is irreducible or even heterogeneous in relation to the stretching out of an *extensio* from which, however, one should not dissociate it." Derrida in the footnote says the spacing he has in mind is not wholly compatible (it is associated and not associated) with Descartes' *extensio* or even with Freud's *Ausdehnung*, as when Freud says Psyche is extended (*ausgedehnt*). What Derrida means by spacing, he says, is to be identified with what he has called *différance* as a feature of the trace. It is closer, he says, to Heidegger's *Gespanntheit*, distancing, than to Descartes or Freud. It is a tension or stretching out "which is as spatial as it is temporal, 'before' the opposition space/time" (OT, 321; LT, 48). Is Derrida's "impossible mourning" in this passage the same as "absolute mourning"? The latter phrase has not yet appeared.

The next place where the red thread I am following appears again on the surface of the immense tapestry of words that makes up *Le toucher* does not even yet use the term "absolute mourning." It speaks rather of "pre-originary mourning," whatever that may be. Prior to what origin? And is "pre-originary" (*pré-originaire* in the French; LT, 218) to be taken as just a neutral temporal location prior to the origin, or is pre-originary mourning somehow performatively necessary as a preliminary to whatever it is that originates at some point after pre-originary mourning? What is the difference between "pre-originary mourning" and "originary mourning"? The latter term appears in *Aporias*: "One can also . . . take into consideration a sort of originary mourning [*deuil originaire*], something that it seems to me neither Heidegger, Freud, nor Levinas does" (Ae, 39; Af, 75). The phrase appears again in *Learning to Live Finally*. Derrida says that the concept of the trace or of the spectral, as related to "surviving," an "originary dimension," "is not derived from either living or dying. No more than what I call 'originary mourning' [*deuil originaire*], that is, a mourning that does not wait for the so-called 'actual' [*effective*] death" (LLF, 26; AV, 26). I think the two phrases "originary mourning" and "pre-originary mourning" mean more or less the same thing, that is, a mourning that is always already there, before anything else has begun, either living or dying. Nevertheless, calling it "pre-originary" does make a difference. It does add an important nuance. The passage in *Le toucher* must be read in detail and put in its context.

The context of the phrase "pre-originary mourning" in *Le toucher* is Derrida's put-down of Merleau-Ponty in comparison to Husserl on the question of my access to the interiority of the other person. Derrida has been showing that Merleau-Ponty falsifies Husserl on a crucial point.

Though Merleau-Ponty claims to be following Husserl literally, even putting in German words and phrases from Husserl to support that illusion, nevertheless, says Derrida, "he takes Husserl's text literally in a diametrically opposite way, not to say in an erroneous interpretation [*il prend littéralement à contre-pied, pour ne pas dire à contresens le text de Husserl*]" (OT, 190, trans. modified; LT, 217).

This sentence is not at all easy to translate, or even to paraphrase approximately. The reader or translator is in danger of doing to Derrida what Derrida says Merleau-Ponty did to Husserl. Derrida plays here on the way *contresens* echoes *contre-pied*, just as a passage discussed in the previous chapter turns on the way *voire en ob-scène* echoes *mise-en-scène*. The first meaning of *contre-pied* given in my *Petit Robert* French dictionary is "false track followed by the dogs." The second meaning is "that which is diametrically opposed to (an opinion, a behavior)." The closest English idiom I can think of is "getting off on the wrong foot," but that phrase has different connotations. *Contresens* means "interpretation contrary to the verifiable signification," "bad interpretation," "error." Merleau-Ponty, Derrida seems to be saying, has followed a false track, a diametrically opposed track, through Husserl's words and has made a false interpretation.

Just what does Derrida mean by "literally" in the phrase *littéralement à contre-pied?* I suppose he means that Merleau-Ponty literally, by way of the letters on the page, follows a false track in Husserl's language, but "false track" is, after all, a metaphor. The reader needs to step carefully to distinguish literal and figurative in Derrida's language. Perhaps it might be better to say that this distinction breaks down in the way he uses words. *À contre-pied* is both literal and figurative at once. Derrida, it may be, is accusing Merleau-Ponty of the aboriginal error of misreading figurative language, taking a figure literally or making a metaphorical reading of words that should be taken literally. This combination of the figure of steps taken on a path of language and the way the turns in that path can be thought of as figures or tropes (*trope* means turn) had appeared two pages earlier in a passage already cited in Chapter 11. One can imagine, says Derrida, Husserl's "spontaneous resistances" to Merleau-Ponty's "translation" of his, Husserl's, words, "at its every step and every turn [*à chacun de ses pas et de ses tours*]." *Pas*, "steps," suggests a path of language, but it also has a negative sense, as in *pas de tout*, "not at all," whereas *tours* means turns in the steps taken on that path, but can also mean "turns" in the sense of figures of speech, tropes. A lot is at stake in Merleau-Ponty's misreading of Husserl, since he ascribes to Husserl a literal intuition of the other person's thoughts and feelings, whereas Husserl says, in passages that are crucial for Derrida, that my access to the other person's interiority is always metaphorical, indirect, a matter of "analogical perception," that is, a figurative transfer of my sense of myself to my sense of the other.

Merleau-Ponty claims that when I touch another person's hand it is just like touching my own hand. I have immediate perception ("*we have here neither comparison, nor analogy, nor projection or 'introjection' [ohne Introjektion]*" [OT, 190; LT, 216], says Merleau-Ponty, citing a phrase from Husserl's German) of the other's "being there," his or her *Dasein*: "If, when I shake the hand of the other man [writes Merleau-Ponty] I have evidence of his being-there [*de son être-là*], it is that his hand substitutes itself [*se substitue*] for my left hand" (OT, 190, trans. modified; LT, 216).

That is a pretty strange idea, if you think about it. The weasel word here is "substitutes." In a metaphor one figuratively used term substitutes for a literal one, as when we say, "The ship *ploughs* the waves." How can the hand of another person "substitute" for my own hand, in an odd prosthesis? Such an immediate intuition of the other person is, says Derrida, just what Husserl never allows, even though what he is forced to testify to goes against the basic phenomenological principle of immediate intuition. "Husserl in the name of phenomenology, and phenomenological faithfulness, prefers to betray phenomenology (the intuitionism of his principle of principles) rather than transform indirect appresentation into direct presentation, which it can never be [*qu'elle ne saurait jamais être*]—which would reappropriate the alterity of the *alter ego* within 'my Ego's' own properness" (OT, 192, trans. modified; LT, 219). For Husserl, the other is always, *always*, "present for me only indirectly and by way of analogical 'introjection': appresented, as this passage well says it [*dit bien ce passage*]" (OT, 191; LT, 217). An unbridgeable abyss always intervenes between my subjectivity and the other person's subjectivity. "It is necessary to watch over the other's alterity: it will always remain inaccessible to an originally presentive [*donatrice*] intuition, an immediate and direct presentation of the *here*" (OT, 191; LT, 218).

Paradoxically, Derrida holds, this inaccessibility is what makes it possible for me to "make contact" with the other as other. "It is necessary to emphasize that without this unbridgeable abyss there would be no handshake, nor blow or caress, nor, in general, any experience of the other's body as such" (OT, 191; LT, 217). Moreover, as Derrida has already argued in the discussion of Heidegger in "Tangent II" of *Le toucher*, in a passage discussed in Chapter 11, I do not even have direct contact with myself. If I can only ever have indirect, analogical appresentation of the interiority of the other person, I also cannot, against all appearances, according to Derrida, though not according to either Husserl or Merleau-Ponty, even get "in contact" with myself, as when my right hand touches my left hand (OT, 192–93; LT, 219).

Here time as syncope, syncopation, noncoincidence, *différance* (though Derrida does not use that word here) enters the formulation:

> I do know or feel that there is *another* here, certainly, and since this is our theme, the other here of a touching-touched (another who is also put at a distance from himself or herself, up to and including in the presentation of his or her present, by the timing of his or her experience and the simple gap, the syncopated non-coincidence of his or her self-relation), but this other "here" presents itself as that which will never be mine, this non-mine-ness being part of the sense of this presentation, which, like my own, itself suffers already from the "same" expropriation. Without possible substitution; and the most surprising logic of the substitution, wherever it is necessarily at work, presupposes the substitution of nonsubstitutables, of unique and other ones [*des uniques et des autres*], of uniquely others. (OT, 191–2, trans. modified; LT, 218)

Derrida here gives a succinct reason for the inappropriateness of Merleau-Ponty's word "substitutes." Since substitution is another name for "metonymy," Derrida's intransigent formulation about the uniqueness of the other disqualifies the apparent relation of substitutability among those strings of terms cited earlier here, in that circle of terms in combinatorial sequence around an absent center, like the learned doctors in mourning around Psyche, asleep or dead.

The powerful formulations about pre-originary mourning follow immediately after the put-down of Merleau-Ponty I have been citing. They are grounded on the double assertion of an irreducible gap between me and the other ego and between me and myself. "If I have often spoken of pre-originary mourning on this subject," says Derrida, "tying this motif to that of an *ex-appropriation*, it has been in order to mark that interiorization, in this mourning before death, and even introjection, which we often take for granted in normal mourning, cannot and must not [*ne peut pas et ne doit pas*] be achieved. Mourning as im-possible mourning. And moreover, ahuman, more than human, prehuman, different from the human 'in' the human of humanualism" (OT, 192, trans. modified; LT, 218).

"Humanualism" (*humainisme* in French) is Derrida's term, discussed here in Chapter 11, for the ideology of the Western philosophical tradition that assumes in one way or another that having and using hands is distinctively human. An example is Merleau-Ponty's expression of confidence in a direct intersubjectivity, which he falsely ascribes to Husserl by saying that, when I shake hands with another person, it is as if I were shaking hands with myself, touching one hand with the other hand. For Derrida, as for Husserl, on the contrary, such a making contact by touching hands never happens, however many hands I may shake and however reassuring touching my left hand with my right hand to be sure "I am here" may be. This play on "human" and "hand" in "humanualism" is clearer in the French, which presents a series of words in which the French word for "human," *humain*, contains within itself the French word for "hand," *main*: "Et d'ailleurs an-humain, plus qu'humain, pré-humain, autre que l'humain 'dans' l'humain de l'humainisme" (LT, 218). *Humainisme* is a portmanteau word. It combines the French word for "humanism" (*humanisme*) with the French word for "hand" (*main*). I never make direct contact with the other, and I never even make direct contact with myself, as the Western tradition of "humanualism" falsely assumes.

Mourning, for example, in Freud's "Mourning and Melancholia," always presupposes the interiorization or introjection of the other. I take the other into myself and work through the loss of a loved one who was, until he or she died, directly accessible and present to me, as present as me to myself. For Derrida, as a result of the "unbridgeable abysses" between me and the other and between me and myself that I have just sketched out, this common-sense Freudian paradigm is quite wrong. Interiorization of the dead other in introjection cannot and should not take place. The force of "should not" in Derrida's formulation is a little obscure. If it *cannot* take place, there would appear to be no need to say it *should* not. I suppose Derrida means that even if introjection could take place, it would be a bad thing, since it would betray the absolute otherness of the other.

In the place of interiorization or introjection, Derrida puts "pre-originary mourning," a mourning that has always already begun. The nonavailability of the other and of myself to myself means both the other and myself are in a sense always already dead, like Psyche in Nancy's tableau. I am always already in an impossible mourning for the death of the other and for my own death. "It is Jacques you mourn for," one might say to Derrida, who pretends to mourn for a Nancy who did not even die when he had his heart-transplant operation. That prosthesis embodied Nancy's death, his ex-appropriation, in the sense of actualizing "in the flesh" his syncopated distance from himself. Or rather, our common-sense assumption that both Jacques and Jean-Luc are subjectivities that may have direct intuition of themselves and of other human beings is a post-originary illusion grounded in what ungrounds it, the pre-originary ahuman, the more than human, the prehuman, something different from the human in the human of humanualism.

These terms, the ahuman, the more than human, and the prehuman, are yet more nonequivalent metonymies for the vacant place at the center whose inaccessibility leads to a pre-originary mourning that is "before death." It is before death in the sense, as I understand it, that it is the universal death before the mourning-originating death of any particular person, including the "I" of Derrida, Nancy, or I as writer of this chapter. Pre-originary mourning is mourning for the death that inhabits me, unreachably, at every moment of my always already posthumous "life": "I think about it *every* day."

The red thread of mourning reappears once more in an extraordinary several pages analyzing Nancy's strange locution *se toucher toi* (OT, 288ff.; LT, 324ff.). The context is a commentary on the last words of Nancy's *Corpus*, already cited in the previous chapter. I approach that passage now from another direction, that is, as a way to understand absolute mourning. What Derrida is saying touching Nancy's *se toucher toi* is hard to touch, hard to think and say. These pages are, to some degree, about Nancy's heart transplant, *l'intrus*, the intruder. The transplant meant that Nancy had within his own body part of the body of another, another person now dead but resurrected, at least the other's heart, to go on beating in Nancy's chest. Perhaps it is a woman's heart, Derrida speculates. The phrase *se toucher toi*, however, names not just Nancy's relation to that strange heart beating in his breast but also my relation to another person by way of our bodies. This is an essentially sexual or sexed relation. "These offerings," says Derrida, in commentary on the passage that ends *Corpus*, "anything and everything whatsoever being offered [*de l'offrande*], these bodies, these pieces of a body not in pieces, this world, these shared-out [*en partage*] worlds do nothing but feign empirical accumulation. Apparently, it is a headlong contagious abandoned thrust, a general contamination. But everything remains exactly calculated" (OT, 289, trans. modified; LT, 325).

A footnote connects the word *contamination* in this passage to autoimmunity, to AIDS, and to anti-autoimmunization drugs, like those necessary to keep the body from rejecting a transplanted organ, for example, the heart of another. This is another surfacing of the themes of prosthesis and ecotechnicity that are such important features of Derrida's thinking concerning mourning. It is only because I can, apparently, self-touch that I can, apparently, touch you, as Derrida says. But the *toi* in *se toucher toi*, "touching myself touching you," breaks the narcissistic circuit of self-touching, I relating directly to me. At the same time this *toi* destroys, by way of the detour through prosthetic technicity, any hope of immediacy, any hope of self-presence. Any "I" is always inhabited by a prosthetic "you."

As Derrida observes elsewhere in *Le toucher*, this circuit of pre-originary mourning, leading from death to death and hanging at every minute over the abyss of death, is like the first kiss for Novalis or like suicide. The kiss is the origin and suicide is the end in a circular coinciding of apparent opposites. The first kiss is, for Novalis, the beginning of philosophy, while suicide, for Novalis, is the only proper conclusion of philosophical reflection. These pages leading up to the first appearance of the phrase "absolute mourning" are an extreme version of Derrida's characteristic Blanchotian formulations about a possible that is at the same time impossible. Since self-touching is death, only my openness to the other keeps me alive, holds off death. This is expressed in the paragraph already cited in which Derrida says "this other heart self-touches you only to be exposed to death," and beseeches the other to keep him *from*, and, at the same time, *in*, death. "You are/is also my death. . . . Keep me from it still a little longer, if you please, just a little longer" (OT, 289; LT, 325).

"Absolute mourning" appears at last as the key term in the paragraph that just follows this:

> Isn't what the "heart" names, at bottom, the ultimate place of absolute mourning [*deuil absolu*]? The sanctuary of what one keeps [*garde*] when one can no longer keep anything? Keep inside oneself, as one often says, to name what infinitely exceeds the inside? The sensible but invisible and untouchable place for what one not only keeps committed to memory, not only in oneself, but in yourself in myself [*mais en toi en moi*: note the intimacy of the second person singular, *toi*, used throughout the passage, not *vous*], when you are greater still, a heart in me greater than my heart [*une coeur en moi plus grand que mon coeur*], more alive than I, more singular and more other than what I can anticipate, know, imagine, represent, remember? When "my" heart is first of all the heart of the other, and therefore, yes, greater than my heart in my heart? (OT, 290, trans, modified; LT, 325)

The reader will note how all these sentences are questions. This makes them in effect, like "rhetorical questions" in general, performative demands asking for the reader's assent. Derrida demands from the reader a "yes," a "yea verily." The reader will also see that all the terms associated with mourning in earlier passages in *Le toucher* here converge, or encircle, or are held in uneasy combinatory displacement around an absent center: the prosthetic, ecotechnicity, expropriation, temporalizing spaces, and so on. The absent center, death, is here figured in Nancy's prosthetic heart, the heart of another that beats in his breast. This heart is both accessible and inaccessible to him, in an experience of exappropriation. This exappropriated heart is the place where he keeps his most intimate memories, as when I say, "I shall keep it in my heart." These memories, are kept "in yourself in myself." At the same time, they are something that is absolutely beyond me, something impossible to reach or know. This heart of the other beating in my breast is a kind of capacious reservoir of singular otherness within me but at the same time exceeding the inside. It is something that I can never see or touch, "greater than my heart in my heart."

These formulations are like a strange version or perversion of Augustine's appeal to God as more interior and more intimate to me than myself. The difference from Augustine is that this part of myself that infinitely exceeds me while being the most intimate part is, in Derrida's version, wholly impersonal, wholly other, and wholly inaccessible, as inaccessible as the other's subjectivity is for me in Husserl's or in Derrida's thought. Augustine's conversion, on the contrary, when he hears God command *tolle, lege,* "take up and read," leads to the hope of Heaven, the place of universal communion and intuitive knowledge.

Derrida's recognition that *tout autre est tout autre,* when reformulated here as my inability to reach the other within myself, leads to what he calls "absolute mourning." This mourning is "absolute" in the sense that it is absolutely general. It is identified with life itself. This mourning is "untied" (the etymological meaning of "absolute"), unmoored from any particular death in an endless mournful or doleful drifting like that of the Flying Dutchman, Blanchot's impossibility of dying, or Kafka's Hunter Gracchus, to return to an analogy invoked in Chapter 11, though Derrida's version lacks the references to the "hereafter" that Kafka makes. I cite Kafka again here. The Hunter Gracchus has died without having quite died. He is dead and, as he says, "in a sense I'm alive at the same time."[8] His death barge drifts perpetually back and forth on the staircase that leads up to the hereafter:

> My death barge went off course, a wrong turn of the tiller, the momentary inattentiveness of the boatman. . . . On this infinitely wide and open stairway [the one leading up to the hereafter] I drift, now toward the top, now toward the bottom, now to the right, now to the left, always in motion. . . . My barge has no tiller, it is driven by the wind that blows in the nethermost regions of death.[9]

The last appearance of my red thread confirms the reading I have been making of what Derrida means by "absolute mourning." Once more the formulations are made by way of reflections about that inaccessible "heart's heart," and once more Derrida's reflections are made in the guise of glosses on phrases from Nancy. I have cited this passage in Chapter 11 as an example of Derrida's stylistic habit of concocting long sequences of phrases in apposition. Now I add the way this series culminates in a formulation about absolute mourning:

> What can this "selfsame itself" [*même*; Nancy's phrase] mean about the heart's heart? The heart proper, the essence of the heart, of the sovereign heart, of the heart by itself, of the heart with itself nearest to itself [*avec soi-même au plus près de soi-même*] (*ipse, ipsemet, metipse, meisme, même*)? Nancy knows that the *selfsame* heart *itself*, in every possible sense of the self and the same, is the place where the selfsame itself exappropriates itself [*le même lui-même s'exapproprie*], at the same instant when I am invisibly touched by the other, without any possible reappropriation. Which is what I earlier termed absolute mourning. But also the locus of possible transplants [*du greffon possible*], possibly from "another sex." It is quite possible, as I have heard it said, that women's hearts lend themselves better to transplantations and have a better survival rate. (OT, 305, trans. modified; LT, 342)

Absolute mourning, the reader can see, is a consequence of a double division, the division of the selfsame, of me, *ipse, ipsemet*, etc., within "myself" as self-same and of me from you, in the double "exappropriation" that Derrida, in a characteristic taking with one hand what he gives with the other, calls simultaneously a "touching" by the other and a splitting that makes that touching "invisible," therefore impossible to be taken possession of, to be reappropriated.

Mourning, for Derrida, is not just sorrow for the death of another, though that may trigger an act of mourning. Mourning is a universal condition of human existence. What Derrida calls "absolute mourning" is generated by my perpetual "enisled" isolation, my inability to touch the other or be touched by him or her. I am in perpetual mourning for the impossibility of "appropriating" the other or myself, of making the other my "property," properly mine, or of appropriating myself in an act of self-possession, as in the Cartesian *Cogito ergo sum*. This means that the other is already dead, from my perspective (and I have no other perspective). That in turn means that *I* am already dead, enclosed in the coffin of my windowless monad. Derrida, in *A Taste for the Secret*, as I have shown in Chapter 6, borrows Leibniz's figure of the windowless monad to define his own sense of the human situation, though he says his position is "a Leibnizianism without God." For Leibniz, God guarantees the monads' harmony. Derrida, however, adds, in a significant qualification, that this "means that, *nevertheless*, in these monads, in this hypersolipsism, the appeal of God finds place" (TS, 71). This formulation is quite different from Nancy's idea of an aboriginal *partage*, which is a sharing as well as a shearing, a parting of the ways and a taking part. For Derrida no sharing or taking part exists.

The admirably rigorous passage I cited above from *Le toucher* says this by way of the figure of the heart, with Nancy's transplanted heart in mind and with allusions to passages in Nancy's work, in this case from *The Experience of Freedom*. The paragraph makes an odd shift at the end to what seems a different key or register, that is, to the question of whether the heart Nancy received in his heart transplant was possibly that of a woman. The idea is dramatic enough, since we assume that sexual difference permeates the whole body. The idea of a male body with a woman's heart seems somehow scandalous. Women's hearts are indeed different from men's hearts. They tend to beat slower, for one thing, and to be stronger for the sake of childbearing. This may explain why they survive better when transplanted. The "materiality" of an actual heart transplant, however, seems to have little to do with all Derrida's language about "the heart's heart" and "absolute mourning." Central in Derrida, however, as I have shown in Chapter 11, is a breakdown of the distinction between the "material body" and the body as the incarnation of what Derrida calls a "quasi-transcendence." This is the situation in which I am "invisibly touched by the other, without any possible reappropriation, which I earlier termed absolute mourning." Nancy's experience, which Derrida can only guess at, of having the heart of another person (now dead, but in a sense still living) beating in his own breast, perhaps a woman's heart, is not a figure for absolute mourning. It *is* absolute mourning, self-same, *même*, *ipse*, the thing itself. Each of us has always been in a state of perpetual mourning, in the end mourning for our own deaths. "I think about it *every* day." It is Jacques Jacques mourns for.

I claim to have provided a reading of what Derrida means by "absolute mourning," *deuil absolu*, as it is generated by the combinatory displacements of those various nonmetonymical metonymies—prosthesis, death, expropriation, ecotechnics, temporalization, and so on—around a vacant place. They are "nonmetonymic metonymies" because a true metonymy is a sideways displacement from a literal, referential term. Such a term is, for Derrida, lacking. Does this exposition help at all in understanding what

Derrida meant by saying that the death of another is *chaque fois unique*, wholly different each time, and yet at the same time *la fin du monde*, the end of the world, the whole world, not just the unique world of that other who has died?

If I myself am my relation to the other, in that strange relation Derrida, following Nancy, calls *se toucher toi*, touching myself touching you, that relation is maintained at one and the same time to all the others, including all animals and all divine beings (that's what he says!), in an immense system of exappropriations, relations without relation, that forms a whole, the whole world, in fact. The death of one other in that immense system obviously means the end of the world in the sense that its systematic wholeness depends on the co-presence of all the unique others that constituted it. The "world" is the product of their collective "worlding," to use an English neologism modeled on Heidegger's *Welten*. Heidegger, in *The Fundamental Concepts of Metaphysics*,[10] defines human beings as *weltbilden*, world building, though he denies that animals are world building. For Derrida (and me), contra Heidegger, dogs and cats and ants, as well as whatever divinities there be, are also world building. When one world-builder vanishes, the whole "world" vanishes too, to be reconstituted anew, but as different. The world is re-created, instantly, by those who are left, the survivors. The survivors' work of world building (and we are all survivors) is augmented by all the newborns that are constantly appearing and contributing their part to the continuous creation of the world(s). One must never forget, however, that, for Derrida, this world-system is constructed over absence. It is a system that is not a system, a system that is not systematic. It is hollowed out in all directions by the impossibility of touching or knowing any one of those others, though each, in an enormous multitude, is "in yourself in myself." Each, however, is veiled from me by that "sensible but invisible and untouchable place" that comes between us, as well as between me and myself, one (non)metonymic name for which is "death."

That is my last word, at least for now. It is the end of what I have to say "for Derrida," in the double sense of "in memory of Derrida, dedicated to Derrida," and "on behalf of Derrida." As though he needs my defense! Are these chapters "works of mourning"? Probably, though they have also been my way of discovering that Derrida was right when he said that mourning is "impossible," "absolute," "endless," and, in the end, only with difficulty to be distinguished from melancholy. If these essays are works of mourning, they haven't worked.

NOTES

PREFACE

1. A play on Walter Benjamin's title "The Work of Art in the Age of Mechanical Reproduction," in *Illuminations*, trans. Harry Zohn, ed. Hannah Arendt (New York: Schocken Books, 1969), 217–51; "Das Kunstwerk im Zeitalter seiner technischen Reproduzierbarkeit," in *Illuminationen*, ed. Siegfried Unseld (Frankfurt am Main: Suhrkamp, 1969), 148–84. Benjamin did not live to see the appearance of the personal computer connected to the Internet, but his essay is one of the first great reflections on the epochal changes in individual and social life being brought about by new communications technologies.

2. Geoffrey Bennington and Jacques Derrida, *Jacques Derrida*, trans. Geoffrey Bennington (Chicago: University of Chicago Press, 1993), 1; *Jacques Derrida* (Paris: Seuil, 1991), 3.

3. Marcel Proust, "Journées de pélerinage" ("Days of Pilgrimage"), in *Mélanges*, in *Contre Sainte-Beuve: Précédé de pastiches et mélanges, et suivi de essais et articles*, ed. Pierre Clarac and Yves Sandre (Paris: Gallimard, 1971), 76: "Thus I have tried to empower the reader as if with an improvised memory [*comme d'une mémoire improvisée*] in which I have deposited memories [*souvenirs*] of other books by Ruskin—a sort of resonance box [*caisse de resonance*], where the words of *The Bible at Amiens* can take on a certain repercussive vibration [*retentissement*] by way of awakening fraternal echoes" (my trans.).

4. Leland de la Durantaye, *The Idea of Work: Giorgio Agamben's Philosophy of Potentiality* (forthcoming). My epigraph from Benjamin also comes from a citation in this book. *Method* derives from the Greek *hodos*, meaning "road," "way," or "path." To say *Methode ist Umweg* is to say that the best way to reach the goal is by detours and digressions.

5. In "Dialogue and Dialogism," a brief essay on Mikhail Bakhtin, de Man said, "since I ignore the Russian language, it [an "attentive and critical reading of Bakhtin's work"] is not an enterprise in which I can responsibly hope to take part" (Paul de Man, *The Resistance to Theory* [Minneapolis: University of Minnesota Press, 1986], 107).

6. "Notes Toward a Supreme Fiction," in Wallace Stevens, *The Collected Poems* (New York: Vintage, 1990), 389.

CHAPTER I. A PROFESSION OF FAITH

1. This is the only chapter in this book written before Derrida's death and therefore the only one read by Derrida himself. He was, as always, courteous and generous in his response. It was initially published, in French translation, in a celebratory volume for Derrida in *L'Herne*. I have somewhat revised the essay and have interpolated references forward to chapters in this book written since then, after Derrida's death.

2. J. L. Austin, *How to Do Things with Words*, 2d ed., ed. J. O. Urmson and Marina Sbisà (Oxford: Oxford University Press, 1980), 154.

3. Maurice Blanchot, "Literature and the Right to Death," in *The Gaze of Orpheus*, trans. Lydia Davis (Barrytown, N.Y.: Station Hill Press, 1981), 21–62; "Littérature et le droit à la mort," in *La part du feu* (Paris: Gallimard, 1949), 291–331.

4. E. M. Forster, *Howards End* (New York: Vintage, 1989), 30–31. The passage is cited in Chapter 6, n. 28, of this book.

5. Gerard Manley Hopkins, "Pied Beauty," l. 7, *Poems*, 3d ed., ed. W. H. Gardner (New York: Oxford University Press. 1948), 74.

CHAPTER 2. WHO OR WHAT DECIDES, FOR DERRIDA

1. This chapter is based on work for my seminars of 2000 and 2001 at the University of California at Irvine. The seminars were on concepts of decision in philosophy and critical theory from Aristotle down to Heidegger and Derrida, and on the representation of moments of decision in nineteenth- and twentieth-century novels.

2. J. L. Austin, *How to Do Things with Words*, 2d ed., ed. J. O. Urmson and Marina Sbisà (Oxford: Oxford University Press, 1980), 10, and see the preceding sentences.

3. Anthony Trollope, *Phineas Finn* (London: Oxford University Press, 1962), 2:268.

4. Henry James, *The Portrait of a Lady*, vols. 3–4 of *The Novels and Tales*, 26 vols., rpt. of the New York Edition (Fairfield, N. J.: Augustus M. Kelley, 1971), 3:318.

5. Austin, *How to Do Things with Words*, 154.

6. Lewis Carroll, *Through the Looking-Glass*, in *Alice in Wonderland*, ed. Donald J. Gray (New York: W. W. Norton, 1971), 150.

7. See my discussion of James's novel in "The Story of a Kiss: Isabel's Decisions in *The Portrait of a Lady*," in *Literature as Conduct: Speech Acts in Henry James* (New York: Fordham University Press, 2005), 30–83.

CHAPTER 3. DERRIDA'S *DESTINERRANCE*

1. John P. Leavey, Jr., "Destinerrance: The Apotropocalyptics of Translation," in *Deconstruction and Philosophy: The Texts of Jacques Derrida*, ed. John

Sallis (Chicago: University of Chicago Press, 1987), 33–43. Leavey's essay is the best discussion I know of Derrida's *destinerrance*. I am grateful for his help and for help from Julian Wolfreys in tracking down Derrida's uses of the word or, sometimes, the figurative idea without the word.

2. Derrida's paraphrase in *Aporias* of Diderot's comment on Seneca's "De brevitate vitae" (Ae, 2; Af, 17). It appears elsewhere in Derrida's writing, for example, in the last seminars, "The Beast and the Sovereign (Two)." The last example is cited in Chapter 4 of this book.

3. Jacques Lacan, "Seminar on 'The Purloined Letter,'" *Yale French Studies* 48 (1972): 72; *Écrits* (Paris: Seuil, 1966), 41.

4. This is a reference to Mr. Dick, in Dickens's *David Copperfield*. Whatever Mr. Dick started talking about, sooner or later the decapitation of Charles I came up.

5. "My Chances" was presented in October 1982 as the Weigert Lecture before the Forum on Psychiatry and the Humanities of the Washington School of Psychiatry.

6. I discuss this passage again in later chapters.

7. J. Hillis Miller, "Thomas Hardy, Jacques Derrida, and the 'Dislocation of Souls,'" in *Taking Chances: Derrida, Psychoanalysis, and Literature*, ed. Joseph H. Smith and William Kerrigan (Baltimore: Johns Hopkins University Press, 1984), 135–36.

8. Franz Kafka, *Letters to Milena*, ed. W. Haas, trans. T. and J. Stern (New York: Schocken, 1954), 299; *Briefe an Milena*, ed. W. Haas (New York: Schocken, 1952), 259–60.

9. Maurice Blanchot, *De Kafka à Kafka* (Paris: Gallimard, 1981), 155–70.

10. I have explored "Telepathy" from a different perspective in *The Medium is the Maker: Browning, Freud, Derrida and the New Telepathic Ecotechnologies*, forthcoming in September 2009 from Sussex Academic Press.

11. Franz Kafka, *The Great Wall of China: Stories and Reflections*, trans. Willa and Edwin Muir (New York: Schocken, 1946), 283; for the German, see http://www.kafka.org/index.php?aphorismen.

12. Since the original French is not yet in print, I give it here: "Heidegger a beau se moquer souvent de ceux qui cherchent le sécurité du sauf-conduit ou du fondement, du sol fondateur et du chemin sûr, il ne veut pas, lui non plus, se perdre, c'est un penseur de l'errance qui ne veut pas errer quand il philosophe, quand il pense, écrit ou surtout enseigne (car ceci est un séminaire), et il veut non seulement l'ordre et la carte, mais la sortie, l'issue (*Ausweg*). Il veut la bonne orientation et la bonne direction pour échapper à l'enfermement ou à l'insularité circulaire."

13. Freud's *Fort/Da* plays a big role in the "Envois," in *The Post Card*, of which "Telepathy," as I have said, was a destinerred, disinterred remnant (*restance*). See Sigmund Freud, "Beyond the Pleasure Principle," in *The Standard*

Edition of the Complete Psychological Works of Sigmund Freud, ed. James Strachey (London: Hogarth Press, 1955), 18:14–15: "This good little boy, however, had an occasional disturbing habit of taking any small objects he could get hold of and throwing them away from him into a corner, under the bed, and so on, so that hunting for his toys and picking them up was often quite a business. As he did this he gave vent to a loud, long-drawn-out 'o-o-o-o,' accompanied by an expression of interest and satisfaction. His mother and the writer of the present account were agreed in thinking that this was not a mere interjection but represented the German word 'fort' ["gone"]. I eventually realized that it was a game and that the only use he made of any of his toys was to play 'gone' with them. One day I made an observation which confirmed my view. The child had a wooden reel with a piece of string tied around it. It never occurred to him to pull it along the floor behind him, for instance, and play at its being a carriage. What he did was to hold the reel by the string and very skillfully throw it over the edge of his curtained cot, so that it disappeared into it, at the same time uttering his expressive 'o-o-o-o.' He then pulled the reel again by the string and hailed its reappearance with a joyful 'da' ["there"]. This, then, was the complete game of disappearance and return. As a rule one only witnessed its first act, which was repeated untiringly as a game in itself, though there is no doubt that the greater pleasure was attached to the second act. The interpretation of the game then became obvious. It was related to the child's great cultural achievement—the instinctual renunciation (that is, the renunciation of instinctual satisfaction) which he had made in allowing his mother to go away without protesting." The "little boy" was Freud's grandson Ernst.

14. "Notes Toward a Supreme Fiction," in Wallace Stevens, *The Collected Poems* (New York: Vintage, 1990), 406.

15. From a speech by "Earth" in *Prometheus Unbound*: "Ere Babylon was dust, / The Magus Zoroaster, my dead child, / Met his own image walking in the garden," I:191–93, in Percy Bysshe Shelley, *Poetical Works*, ed. Thomas Hutchinson and G. M. Matthews (London: Oxford University Press, 1973), 212.

16. I possess, tucked into my copy of *La carte postale*, a precious copy of this postcard, sent to me not by Derrida but by Cynthia Chase. It is dated June 9, 1977, with a quite lengthy message in tiny handwriting telling me that Derrida had been there the week before to lecture in Jonathan Culler's seminar. Derrida, wrote Cynthia, "spoke about parasitage and the more amusing features of his lengthy response to Searle in a forthcoming *Glyph*," that is, "Limited Inc a b c. . . ." It was Cynthia Chase who, along with Jonathan Culler, showed these postcards to Derrida, where they were on sale at the Bodleian, I assume during this visit of his to Oxford. That initiated part, at least, of *The Post Card*.

17. I steal this fine phrase from somewhere in Geoffrey Hartman's writings. Hartman, I daresay, takes it by *destinerrance* as a distant echo of Shakespeare's *Hamlet*. Horatio says to the ghost: "Stay! Speak, speak! I charge thee speak!" (*Hamlet*, 1.1.51).

CHAPTER 4. THE LATE DERRIDA

1. Thomas Hardy, "Old Furniture," ll. 11–14, in Hardy, *The Complete Poems*, ed. James Gibson (New York: Macmillan, 1978), 486.

2. Percy Bysshe Shelley, "Death," ll. 1–2, in Shelley, *Poetical Works*, ed. Thomas Hutchinson and G. M. Matthews (London: Oxford University Press, 1973), 622. Cleanth Brooks and Robert Penn Warren, in *Understanding Poetry* (New York: Henry Holt, 1945), 219–20, take this poem as an example of how not to do it. They see it as an example of a misfit between form, in this case meter and rhyme, and subject matter. I had taken their word for it for sixty years, but now I am not so sure. The "jigging rhythm," as they call it, of the poem can be taken to match the triviality and ubiquity of death. Death is all around us. It is the most commonplace, everyday event imaginable, until we start thinking about our own death. Death is certainly everywhere as a motif in Derrida's work from the beginning, and therefore we are likely to become inured to his obsession with it.

3. Daniel Defoe, *Robinson Crusoe*, introd. Virginia Woolf (New York: Modern Library, 2001), 142ff. This is the edition Derrida used.

4. Ibid., 145–46.

5. Here is the original French, cited with permission. I append the original here since these seminars will not be in print until Fall 2009, with an English translation eventually to follow:

Enfin, alors qu'il vient de poser sa Bible et de se réconforter par la prière, voilà qu'il se demande où il est, en quel lieu, quel aura été son chemin. Il se demande avec encore plus d'anxiété si cette empreinte de pied nu n'est pas celle de son propre pied? De son propre pied sur un chemin qu'il aurait déjà parcouru. Au fond, il n'arrive pas à décider si cette trace est ou non la sienne, une trace laissée sur un chemin dont il ne sait pas trop s'il l'a déjà foulé, frayé ou passé— ou non. Il n'en sait trop rien. Est-ce moi? Est-ce ma trace? Est-ce mon chemin? Est-ce le spectre de mon empreinte, l'empreinte de mon spectre? Suis-je en train de revenir? Suis-je ou ne suis-je pas revenant? un revenant de moi-même que je croise sur mon chemin comme la trace de l'autre, sur un chemin qui est déjà un chemin de retour et de revenance, etc.? J'en sais trop rien, ou je n'en sais trop rien de la possibilité de ce double *uncanny, unheimlich.* . . .

Il se fait peur. Il devient la peur qu'il est et qu'il se fait. Et toutes ces pages, parmi les plus extraordinaires du livre, celles qui le montrent, où il se montre en train de méditer, dans la terreur, sur cette trace de pied nu, ces pages devraient être lues pas à pas, et par exemple en parallèle avec la *Gradiva* de Freud, avec tous les *fantasmata*, à savoir les fantasmes et les fantômes qui reviennent sur l'empreinte d'un pas, ou d'un pied nu, *the print of a naked Foot*.

6. Georges Poulet, *Études sur le temps humain* (Paris: Plon, 1962).

7. From a speech by Earth in *Prometheus Unbound*: "Ere Babylon was dust, / The Magus Zoroaster, my dead child, / Met his own image walking in the garden" (1:191–93, in Shelley, *Poetical Works*, 212).

8. Here is the French original:

Il se sent suivi par une trace, en somme, chassé ou traqué par une trace. Voire par sa propre trace. Peut-être persécuté par lui-même et par sa propre reven-ance. Comme s'il vivait tout au passé de son propre passé comme avenir terrifi-ant. Il croit qu'il va bientôt mourir, qu'il court après sa mort ou que la mort lui court après, que la vie aura été si courte, et donc, comme s'il était déjà mort, à cause de cette course de vitesse avec sa revenance, tout ce qui lui arrive lui arrive non comme nouveau, neuf ou à venir mais comme (peut-être, il n'en sait trop rien) déjà passé, déjà vu, à venir comme hier et non comme demain.

9. Ll. 3–4 of John Donne's "Holy Sonnets, I," in Donne, *Poems of John Donne*, ed. E. K. Chambers, 1 (London: Lawrence & Bullen, 1896), 157. I have retained the capitalization Derrida uses, though it does not exactly corre-spond to the Chambers text. See also, for an online version: http://www .luminarium.org/sevenlit/donne/holysonnet1.php/

10. Here is the French:

Je cours vers la mort, je me précipite vers la mort et la mort vient à ma rencon-tre tout aussi vite. (Je cours sus à la mort, je cours à mort (*I run to Death*) et mort me vient dessus, mort de rencontre me saisit, m'attrape ou me rattrappe aussi vite, me rattrappe à la même vitesse, aussi tôt.)

Et tous mes plaisirs sont comme hier, *like Yesterday*, comme l'hier, comme venus d'hier, mes plaisirs sont déjà d'hier, mes plaisirs sont l'hier même, d'a-vance ils sont datés — et d'hier. D'avance ils ont passé, ils sont passés, déjà passés dépassé, déjà des mémoires de jouissance révolue ou des revenances de plaisir. Mes plaisir présents sont au présent (*are*) des présents d'hier, ils sont hier. Non pas: ils ont été ou ils furent hier, mais ils sont présentement hier. Leur être présent est hier, l'hier.

11. Here is the French:

Non seulement ce dont je jouis est hier mais peut-être, c'est peut-être *mon* hier ou peut-être l'hier, déjà, aujourd'hui, d'*un autre*, et de toute façon d'un autre, même si c'est déjà, même si ce fut déjà un autre moi-même. Mon plaisir est dès hier, par hier altéré, venu de l'autre, la venue de l'autre.

Et l'autre me dirait, ou je me dirais à l'autre: comme je cours à mort toujours après hier, hier sera toujours à venir: non pas demain, au futur, mais à venir, au-devant, là devant, avant hier.

12. See also Martin Heidegger, *The Fundamental Concepts of Metaphysics: World, Finitude, Solitude*, trans. William McNeill and Nicholas Walker (Bloomington: Indiana University Press, 1995), 267; *Die Grundbegriffe der Metaphysik: Welt—Endlichkeit—Einsamkeit* (Frankfurt am Main: Vittorio Klostermann, 1983), 388.

13. Martin Heidegger, *Being and Time*, trans. John Macquarrie and Edward Robinson (London: SCM Press Ltd, 1962), 154–55; *Sein und Zeit* (Tübingen: Max Niemeyer, 1967), 118.

14. Lewis Carroll, *Alice in Wonderland*, ed. Donald J. Gray (New York: W. W. Norton, 1972), 7.

15. Derrida's formulations, both for and against Gadamer's description of hermeneutics as a "processus infini" (Bf, 38), about the inexhaustibility of interpretation and its uncertainty are the theoretical expression of this as a principle of responsible reading, reading as a response to the otherness of the text:

> This formal analysis [that Gadamer exemplifies] can be taken very far. It must, in fact. But it hardly seems risky. It belongs to the order of calculable guarantees [*assurance*] and decidable evidence. It is not the same [*Il n'en va plus de même*] for the hermeneutical response to the *Anspruch* of the poem or in the interior dialogue of the reader or counter-signatory. This response, this responsibility, can be pursued to infinity, in uninterrupted fashion, going from meaning to meaning, from truth to truth, with no calculable law other than that which the letter and the formal arrangement of the poem assign to it. But even though overseen by the same law, forever subjected to it, every bit as responsible, the experience that I call disseminal undergoes and takes on, in and through the hermeneutic moment itself, even in the hermeneutic moment [*à même l'herméneutique*], the test of an interruption, of a caesura or of an ellipsis, of an inaugural cut or opening. Such a gaping [*béance*] belongs neither to the meaning, nor to the phenomenon, nor to the truth, but, by making these possible in their remaining [*restance*], it marks in the poem the hiatus of a wound whose lips will never close, will never draw together. (R, 152–53, trans. modified; B, 54)

CHAPTER 5. DERRIDA'S REMAINS

1. Dylan Thomas, "Do not go gentle into that good night," *The Collected Poems* (New York: New Directions, 1953), 128.

2. For a commentary on "The Time of a Thesis," see my "Derrida and Literature," in *Jacques Derrida and the Humanities*, ed. Tom Cohen (Cambridge: Cambridge University Press, 2001), 58–81.

3. See the fascinating essays on the Estonia Internet event by Joshua Davis, John Robb, and Ralph Peters, "Web War One," *Wired* (September 2007),

162–69, 182, 184. John Robb, in his sidebar, imagines that China might insti-
gate a full-scale "distributed denial of service [DDoS] attack." The choice is
not accidental. It is a sign of the Sinophobia that the media generates and
inflames these days. The imagined attack would be launched using "rented
botnets," that is, networks of private computers that have been secretly turned
into robots that can be manipulated by hackers. These would send out hun-
dreds of thousands or even millions of messages, flooding and making inoperative the target countries' Web sites. "A full-scale assault lasting days or
weeks," writes Robb, "could bring an entire modern information economy to
its knees. . . . A full-scale DDoS attack meant as an act of war might target
military and governmental servers, civilian email, banks, and phone companies" (166, 167).

4. De Man's essay on Derrida is reprinted in Paul de Man, *Blindness and
Insight*, 2d ed., introd. Wlad Godzich (Minneapolis: University of Minnesota
Press, 1983), 102–41.

CHAPTER 6. DERRIDA ENISLED

1. Walter Benjamin, "On Language as Such and on the Language of
Man," in *Selected Writings*, vol. 1, *1913–1926*, ed. Marcus Bullock and Michael
W. Jennings (Cambridge: Harvard University Press, 1999), 64.

2. Ibid., 65.

3. Ibid., 66.

4. Ibid.

5. Ibid., 67.

6. Raymond Williams, "Enclosures, Commons and Communities" and
"Knowable Communities," in *The Country and the City* (1973; New York: Oxford University Press, 1975), 96–107; 165–81; Raymond Williams, "Community," in *Keywords: A Vocabulary of Culture and Society*, rev. ed. (1983; New
York: Oxford University Press, 1985), 75–76.

7. Karl Marx and Frederick Engels, *The German Ideology*, ed. Roy Pascal
(New York: International Publishers, 1969), 74. Scholars think the words are
probably Marx's.

8. Jean-Luc Nancy, *The Inoperative Community*, ed. Peter Connor, trans.
Peter Connor, Lisa Garbus, Michael Holland, and Simona Sawhney (Minne-
apolis: University of Minnesota Press, 1991); *La communauté désoeuvrée* (Paris:
Christian Bourgois, 1986); Jean-Luc Nancy, *Being Singular Plural*, trans. Rob-
ert D. Richardson and Anne E. O'Byrne (Stanford, Calif.: Stanford University
Press, 2000); *Être singulier pluriel* (Paris: Galilée, 1996); Georges Bataille,
*L'Apprenti Sorcier du cercle communiste démocratique à Acéphale: Textes, lettres et
documents (1932–1939)*, ed. Marina Galletti, notes trans. Natália Vital (Paris:

Éditions de la Différence, 1999); Maurice Blanchot, *The Inavowable Community*, trans. Pierre Joris (Barrytown, N.Y.: Station Hill Press, 1988); *La communauté inavouable* (Paris: Minuit, 1983); Giorgio Agamben, *The Coming Community*, trans. Michael Hardt (Minneapolis: University of Minnesota Press, 1993); *La comunità che viene* (Turin: Einaudi, 1990); Alphonso Lingis, *The Community of Those Who Have Nothing in Common* (Bloomington: Indiana University Press, 1994). See later notes for Heidegger, Levinas, and Lacan references.

    9. Edmund Husserl, "Fifth Meditation: Uncovering the Sphere of Transcendental Being as Monadological Intersubjectivity," in *Cartesian Meditations: An Introduction to Phenomenology*, trans. Dorion Cairns (The Hague: Martinus Nijhoff, 1960), 89–151. See esp. paragraph 50, "The mediate intentionality of experiencing someone else, as 'appresentation' (analogical apperception)" (108–11).

    10. Ibid., 129.

    11. Martin Heidegger, *Being and Time*, trans. John Macquarrie and Edward Robinson (London: SCM Press, 1962), 154–55; *Sein und Zeit* (Tübingen: Max Niemeyer, 1967), 118. Page numbers will appear in the text hereafter.

    12. Ibid., 334; 288.

    13. Ibid.

    14. Williams, *The Country and the City*, 105.

    15. Martin Heidegger, *The Fundamental Concepts of Metaphysics: World, Finitude, Solitude*, trans. William McNeill and Nicholas Walker (Bloomington: Indiana University Press, 1995), 207; *Die Grundbegriffe der Metaphysik: Welt—Endlichkeit—Einsamkeit* (Frankfurt am Main: Vittorio Klostermann, 1983), 304.

    16. Derrida had already discussed this aspect of Heidegger's thought, in the context of his ideas about *Geist*, "spirit," in OS.

    17. Here is the original: "H. lui-même est en train de faire son chemin, de frayer son propre chemin quand, prétendant traduire l'intuition géniale quoique confuse et insuffisamment expliquée d'A. [Aristotle], H. nous explique, lui, que les mots naissent de cet accord essentiel (*jener wesenhaften Übereinkunft*) des hommes entre eux dans leur *Miteinandersein*, en tant qu'ils sont ensemble, dans leur *Miteinandersein*, dans leur être-l'un-pour-l'autre, les uns-avec-les-autres, ouverts à l'étant qui les entoure, à l'étant comme tel. C'est cette transcendance partagée dans le Mitsein, dans l'ouverture commune à l'étant, qui est le fondement (*Grund*) de leur accord originel et qui rend ensuite la parole, le discours (*Rede*) possible. Donc c'est toujours *umgekehrt*: ce n'est pas la convention qui vient s'ajouter au son naturel, voire animal, pour rendre ensuite le langage humain possible, puis la société humaine possibles. Au contraire, à l'inverse, *umgekehrt*, c'est la transcendance, l'ouverture à l'étant

comme tel et en totalité (au monde), transcendance qui, originellement com-
mune, partagée dans le *Miteinandersein,* permet l'accord, le langage, la convention, etc. Et on ne peut pas séparer la transcendance du *Miteinandersein.* La
transcendance, le mouvement qui porte, qui rapporte à l'étant comme tel, elle
est d'entrée de jeu un mouvement social, si vous voulez, un être-l'un-avec-
l'autre, un *Mitsein.* Le *Mitsein* est originaire et non dérivé, et la transcendance
est un *Mitsein.* Il n'y aurait pas de transcendance sans ce *Miteinandersein.* La
solitude elle-même, qui est l'un des thèmes majeurs de ce séminaire, dès lors
qu'elle suppose transcendance et langage, elle suppose aussi, comme solitude
en tant que telle, comme robinsonophilie, robinsonocratie, robinsonocen-
trisme, si vous voulez, [la solitude suppose] le *Mitsein* et le *Miteinandersein.*"

18. Ludwig Wittgenstein, *Philosophical Investigations,* trans. G. E. M. Ans-
combe (Oxford: Basil Blackwell, 1968), 3ᵉ.

19. In Paul de Man, *The Resistance to Theory,* Foreword by Wlad Godzich
(Minneapolis: University of Minnesota Press, 1986), 73–105; Walter Benjamin, "The Task of the Translator," trans. Harry Zohn, in *Selected Writings,*
vol. 1, 253–63; "*Die Aufgabe des Übersetzers,*" in *Illuminationen* (Frankfurt am
Main: Suhrkamp, 1969), 56–69.

20. Benjamin, "The Task of the Translator," de Man's translation, in *The
Resistance to Theory,* 79, *Illuminationen,* 69.

21. De Man, *The Resistance to Theory,* 79–80.

22. Benjamin, "The Task of the Translator," 259; 64.

23. Benjamin, "The Task of the Translator," 262; 69.

24. Judith Butler, in recent discussion of Levinas, especially his *Otherwise
than Being, or Beyond Essence,* in *Giving an Account of Oneself* (New York: Fordham University Press, 2005), 84–101, stresses what is coercive, even "persecutory," in Levinas's thinking about the demands the other makes on me. The
"I" is created in the responsibility forced on me by the other. "A formation in
passivity, then," writes Butler, "constitutes the prehistory of the subject, ins-
tating an ego as object, acted on by others, prior to any possibility of its own
acting. This scene is persecutory because it is unwilled and unchosen" (87).

25. Emmanuel Levinas, "Is Ontology Fundamental?" in *Entre Nous: On
Thinking-of-the-Other,* trans. Michael B. Smith and Barbara Harshav (New
York: Columbia University Press, 1998), 6; "L'ontologie est-elle fondamen-
tal?" in *Entre nous: Essais sur le penser-à-l'autre* (Paris: Grasset, 1991), 17.

26. Ibid., 7; 19.

27. The original reads: "L'éthique, ici, ne vient pas en supplément à une
base existentielle préalable. . . . Être humain, cela signifie: vivre comme si l'on
n'était pas un être parmi les êtres," back cover of Emmanuel Levinas, *Autrement qu'être ou au-delà de l'essence* (Paris: Le Livre de poche, n.d).

28. Levinas is being somewhat unfair to Heidegger in repeatedly asserting
that the whole story, for Heidegger, of my responsibility to other *Daseins* is to

"let them be." In a passage in *Being and Time* about *Mitsein* later than the one I have already cited, Heidegger asserts, pace Levinas, that a *Dasein* that has achieved its own ownmost possibilities of being can go beyond passive letting other *Daseins* be (which Levinas associates with knowledge [*connaissance*] of the other as a form of being) to helping those others actively through "solicitude" (*Fürsorge*) to achieve their own ownmost possibilities of being and through becoming the conscience of others: "Dasein's resoluteness towards itself is what first makes it possible to let the Others who are with it 'be' in their ownmost potentiality-for-being, and to co-disclose this potentiality in the solicitude which leaps forth and liberates. When Dasein is resolute, it can become the 'conscience' of Others. Only by authentically Being-their-Selves in resoluteness can people authentically be with one another—not by ambiguous and jealous stipulations and talkative fraternizing in the 'they' and in what 'they' want to undertake" (344–45); "Die Entschlossenheit zu sich selbst bringt das Dasein erst in die Möglichkeit, die mitseienden Anderen 'sein' zu lassen in ihrem eigensten Seinkönnen und dieses in der vorspringend-befreienden Fürsorge mitzuerschließen. Das entschlossene Dasein kann zum 'Gewissen' der Anderen werden. Aus dem eigentlichen Selbstsein der Entschlossenheit entspringt allererst das eigentliche Miteinander, nicht aber aus de zweideutigen und eifersüchtigen Verabredungen und den redseligen Verbrüderungen im Man und dem, was man unternehmen will" (298). I cite the German original because the play on other Heideggerian words in *-schloss* ("enclosure," as in Kafka's title *Das Schloss* [*The Castle*]) is lost in translating *Entschlossenheit* as "resoluteness," though it is a perfectly accurate translation. *Beschlossenheit* is Heidegger's negative word for the closed minds of *das Man*, the "they." *Schließen* means "shut, close, lock." *Entschließen* means "make up one's mind, come to a decision, decide." *Beschließen* means "resolve, determine on, decide." But what a difference between *ent* and *be*! *Entschlossenheit* is a good thing. *Beschlossenheit* is a bad thing. Compare English "besotted." Ah, the wonders of the German language, at least as manipulated by Heidegger! For "Heidegger's Hand," see my discussion of Derrida's essay of that title in Chapter 11 of this book.

29. Levinas, *Entre Nous*, 6; 17.

30. Ibid., 7, 8; 19.

31. Henry James, "The Aspern Papers," in *The Novels and Tales*, 26 vols., a reprint of the New York Edition (Fairfield, N.J.: Augustus M. Kelley, 1971–79), 12:42.

32. Levinas, *Entre Nous*, 7; 19.

33. Ibid. 220; 228.

34. Ibid., 221; 229.

35. Ibid., 217; 214.

36. Ibid., xii, trans. modified; 10.

37. Ibid., 7; 18.

38. Ibid., 10; 22.

39. Ibid, 11; 22.

40. GD, 78–79; DM, 110–11. Further important references to Levinas appear in GD, 83–84; DM, 166–67. I shall discuss the latter passage later in this chapter.

41. Martin Heidegger, *An Introduction to Metaphysics*, trans. Ralph Manheim (New Haven, Conn.: Yale University Press, 1959), 50; *Einführung in die Metaphysik* (Tübingen: Max Niemeyer, 1966), 38.

42. Ibid., 49; 37–38.

43. Martin Heidegger, *Elucidations of Hölderlin's Poetry*, trans. Keith Hoeller (New York: Humanity Books, 2000), 48; *Erläuterungen zu Hölderlins Dichtung*, ed. Friedrich-Wilhelm von Herrmann (Frankfurt am Main: Vittorio Klostermann, 1981), 30.

44. Jennifer Bajorek, "The Offices of Homeland Security, or Hölderlin's Terrorism," *Critical Inquiry* 31, no. 4 (Summer 2005): 874–902. In opposition to Heidegger's positive reading of Hölderlin's "Heimkunft / An die Verwandten," Bajorek says, "on the contrary, . . . it [Hölderlin's poem] inscribes a movement of *infinite return*, or of *returning without return*, at the beginning of every homecoming, as its very condition of possibility and as its falling ground" (893). Paul de Man had already defined Heidegger's radical misreading in words he italicized in "Heidegger's Exegeses of Hölderlin," trans. Wlad Godzich: "*it is the fact that Hölderlin says exactly the opposite of what Heidegger makes him say*" (*Blindness and Insight*, 2d ed., introd. Wlad Godzich [Minneapolis: University of Minnesota Press, 1983], 254–55). The original French version, "Les exégèses de Hölderlin par Martin Heidegger," was published in *Critique*, nos. 100–1 (September-October 1955): 800–19.

45. Martin Heidegger, *Hölderlin's Hymn "The Ister,"* trans. William McNeill and Julia Davis (Bloomington: Indiana University Press, 1966); *Hölderlins Hymne "Der Ister"* (Frankfurt am Main: Vittorio Klostermann, 1984).

46. I may perhaps be permitted to cite a passage from my essay on E. M. Forster's *Howards End*: "*Howards End* dramatizes and puts in question the ideological assumption that nationality determines personal identity not only in many remarks by the characters but, more centrally, in the way the two chief protagonists, Margaret Schlegel and her sister Helen, are defined as products of a marriage between nationalities. Their father was German, their mother English. The narrator remarks that being half English and half German 'was a unique education for the little girls' (30). Their mixed national heritage means that as children they have been exposed to English people, like their Aunt Julia, who think God has appointed England to govern the world,

and to German people, like their cousins who visit their father in England, who think God has appointed Germany to lead the world. The precocious Margaret, aged thirteen, causes embarrassment all around when she says, 'To me one of two things is very clear: either God does not know his own mind about England and Germany, or else these do not know the mind of God' (31). The narrator comments: 'A hateful little girl, but at thirteen she had grasped a dilemma that most people travel through life without perceiving' (ibid.). The dangerous absurdity of these assumptions is evident, but how many of us can say we are entirely free of such ideas about fixed national identity and its God-given mission, as well as its ability to define my identity as 'American' or 'German,' or whatever? Which of us does not have some ignoble hankering to live in a country where everyone speaks the same language, shares the same 'values,' reads the same books, and inhabits the same culture? Do not some Americans still think that God has appointed the United States to govern the world?" ("Just Reading *Howards End*," in *Others* [Princeton: Princeton University Press, 2001], 193–94, citation slightly altered and augmented). The citations are from E. M. Forster, *Howards End* (New York: Vintage International, 1989).

47. Jacques Lacan, "Seminar on 'The Purloined Letter,'" trans. Jeffrey Mehlman, *Yale French Studies* 48 (1972), 44; *Écrits* (Paris: Seuil, 1966), 15.

48. Ibid., 44; 15.

49. Ibid., 44–45; 16.

50. Ibid., 72; 41.

51. Nancy, *Being Singular Plural*, 61–62, 63, note on 201; 83–84, 85.

52. Here is the original: "ni les animaux d'espèce différente, ni les hommes de culture différente, ni aucun individu animal ou humain n'habite le même monde qu'un autre, si proche et si semblable ces individus vivants soient-ils (humains ou animaux), et la différence d'un monde à l'autre restera toujours infranchissable, la communauté du monde étant toujours construite, simulée par un ensemble de dispositifs stabilisants, plus ou moins stables, donc et jamais naturels, le langage au sens large, les codes de traces étant destinés, chez tous les vivants, à construire une unité du monde toujours déconstructible et nulle part et jamais donnée dans la nature. Entre mon monde, le 'mon monde'; ce que j'appelle 'mon monde' et il n'y en a d'autre pour moi, tout autre monde en faisant partie, entre mon monde et tout autre monde, il y a d'abord l'espace et le temps d'un différence infinie, d'une interruption incommensurable à toutes les tentatives de passage, de pont, d'isthme, de communication, de traduction, de trope et de transfert que le désir de monde ou le mal du monde, l'être en mal de monde tentera de poser, d'imposer, de proposer, de stabiliser. Il n'y a pas de monde, il n'y a que des îles. C'est là une des milles directions dans lesquelles je serai [incliner?] d'interpréter le dernier vers d'un court et

grand poème de Celan: *Die Welt ist fort, ich muss dich tragen,* poème de deuil ou de naissance."

53. In W. J. T. Mitchell, "Picturing Terror: Derrida's Autoimmunity," in special issue "The Late Derrida," ed. W. J. T. Mitchell and Arnold I. Davidson, *Critical Inquiry* 33, no. 2 (Winter 2007): 277–90, esp. 282. As Kir Kuiken, in a superb, unpublished reading of Shelley's *Defense of Poetry*, has taught me, the name for this figure is "metalepsis." Kuiken cites Chris Baldick, in *The Concise Oxford Dictionary of Literary Terms* (Oxford: Oxford University Press, 2001), 152: "In rhetoric, the precise sense of metalepsis is uncertain, but it refers to various kinds of figure and trope that are figurative to the second and third degree; that is, they involve a figure that either refers us to yet another figure or requires a further imaginative leap to establish its reference, usually by process of metonymy."

54. For a recent lucid description of what has happened, with focus on Citigroup, see Thomas Friedman, "All Fall Down," *New York Times,* November 26, 2008 (http://www.nytimes.com/2008/11/26/opinion/26friedman .html?th&emc = th)

55. In GD, 64–65; DM, 92–93, Derrida cites and eloquently comments on the version of this in Luke 14:26: "If any one comes to me and does not hate his own father and mother and his wife and children and brothers and sisters, yes, and even his own life, he cannot be my disciple."

56. The word is, of course, related to English *gregarious,* which means "happy to be with others, to herd with them." Arnold Davidson tells me that *gregge* means not only "herd" in the sense of "a herd of sheep" but also has a special modern meaning as the name for the team of cyclists who help the star rider win a given segment of the race.

CHAPTER 7. DERRIDA'S SPECIAL THEORY OF PERFORMATIVITY

1. www.wikipedia.org/.

2. http://en.wikipedia.org/wiki/Performativity.

3. http://en.wikipedia.org/wiki/Performance studies.

4. http://en.wikipedia.org/wiki/Judith Butler.

5. Judith Butler, *Gender Trouble: Feminism and the Subversion of Identity* (New York: Routledge, 2006), 3. Subsequent citations are given parenthetically by page number in the text.

6. Butler discusses Austin explicitly and in some detail in an essay of 2003 written as an afterword to a new edition with a new title of the English translation of Shoshana Felman's *Le scandale du corps parlant* (Paris: Seuil, 1980): *The Scandal of the Speaking Body* (Stanford, Calif.: Stanford University Press, 2003). The afterword uses the term *performativity* and explicitly mentions performance studies as having been influenced by Austin's speech act theory as inflected by Derrida and Felman. Butler's focus remains on the way all speech

acts are bodily acts, though she sees that relation as paradoxical. Lacanian psychoanalysis is invoked as the way to confront that paradox. Butler's essay distinguishes Felman's speech act theory from those of Austin and Derrida. See Judith Butler, "Afterword to *The Scandal of the Speaking Body*," in *The Claims of Literature: A Shoshana Felman Reader*, ed. Emily Sun, Eyal Peretz, and Ulrich Baer (New York: Fordham University Press, 2007), 142–51. Performance studies are mentioned on p. 143. The same page speaks of "Eve Sedgwick's reading of the performativity of the marriage ceremony."

7. For a collection of essays primarily on de Man's concepts of materiality, see Tom Cohen, Barbara Cohen, J. Hillis Miller, and Andrzej Warminski, eds., *Material Events: Paul de Man and the Afterlife of Theory* (Minneapolis: University of Minnesota Press, 2001). This volume contains Judith Butler's essay on the relation of the body to language by way of a discussion of Descartes's *Meditations*, "How Can I Deny That These Hands and This Body Are Mine" (254–73), as well as Jacques Derrida's essay on, among other things, de Man's "materiality without matter," "Typewriter Ribbon: Limited Ink (2) ('within such limits')" (TR, 277–360). Both essays would merit extensive discussion, especially when they are set side by side. "The Body" is, of course, a major topic in recent feminist studies and in cultural studies. A search on December 21, 2008, of the keywords "body, politics" in melvyl.worldcat.org turned up about 5,385 books and articles, with titles like *Body Politics in Paradise Lost* or *The Female Body and the Law*, in inexhaustible permutations. A book by Butler subsequent to *Gender Trouble*, *Bodies That Matter: On the Discursive Limits of "Sex"* (New York: Routledge, 1993), focuses on the problematic of the body's materiality in relation to the performativity of gender. Chapter 11 of the present book returns to Derrida's take on the body by way of his major late book *Le toucher, Jean-Luc Nancy*.

8. See Jean-François Lyotard, *The Postmodern Condition: A Report on Knowledge*, trans. Geoff Bennington and Brian Massumi (Minneapolis: University of Minnesota Press, 1984), 9–11. Subsequent citations are given parenthetically by page number in the text.

9. For a discussion of the latter, see my "The Aftermath of Victorian Humanism: Oscar in *The Tragic Muse*," *Renaissance Humanism—Modern Humanisms(s): Festszchrift for Claus Uhlig*, ed. Walter Göbel and Bianca Ross (Heidelberg: C. Winter, 2001), 231–39; reprinted as "Oscar in *The Tragic Muse*," in *The Importance of Being Misunderstood*, ed. Giovanna Franci and Giovanna Silvani (Bologna: Pàtron Editore, 2003), 49–61.

10. Lewis Carroll, *Through the Looking-Glass*, chap. 6, in *Alice in Wonderland*, ed. Donald J. Gray (New York: Norton, 1971), 163.

11. J. L. Austin, *How to Do Things with Words*, 2d ed., ed. J. O. Urmson and Marina Sbisà (Oxford: Oxford University Press, 1980), 12. Subsequent

citations are given parenthetically by page number in the text. I have read
Austin's great book in more detail and from a different perspective in *Speech
Acts in Literature* (Stanford, Calif.: Stanford University Press, 2001), 6–62.

12. Judith Butler, *Giving an Account of Oneself* (New York: Fordham University Press, 2005).

13. An earlier version of this discussion of *Daniel Deronda* was given as a
lecture in Bergen, Norway, at a workshop entitled "Text, Action, Space,"
sponsored by Lars Saetre, on June 25–26, 2007.

14. George Eliot, *Daniel Deronda*, ed. Barbara Hardy (Harmondsworth,
Middlesex: Penguin, 1986), 79. Further citations are given parenthetically by
page number from this edition.

15. Cynthia Chase, "The Decomposition of the Elephants: Double-Reading *Daniel Deronda*," in *Decomposing Figures: Rhetorical Readings in the Romantic
Tradition* (Baltimore: The Johns Hopkins University Press, 1986), 157–74.
Page numbers from this essay are indicated parenthetically in the text.

16. Steven Marcus, *Representations: Essays on Literature and Society* (New
York: Random, 1976), 212, note. As Chase observes (224), Mary Wilson Carpenter, in "The Apocalypse of the Old Testament: *Daniel Deronda* and the
Interpretation of Interpretation," *PMLA* 99 (January 1984): 56–71, argues
that "the plot [of *Daniel Deronda*] is in fact richly informed by Eliot's use of
contemporary theological interpretation of the Feast of the Circumcision."
Deronda's encounter with Gwendolen to urge her to penitence takes place on
New Year's Day, the Feast of the Circumcision. The circumcision in question
is, of course, that of the infant Jesus. Victorian Protestant theologians read
that event as inaugurating the union of the two "churches," Judaic and
Christian.

17. Paul de Man, *Allegories of Reading: Figural Language in Rousseau, Nietzsche, Rilke, and Proust* (New Haven, Conn.: Yale University Press, 1979).

18. For a full discussion of Paul de Man's theory of speech acts, see chapter
3 of my *Speech Acts in Literature* (Stanford, Calif.: Stanford University Press,
2001).

19. Charles Dickens, *Pickwick Papers*, ed. Robert L. Patten (Harmondsworth, Middlesex: Penguin, 1972), 562.

20. Hélène Cixous, *Portrait of Jacques Derrida as a Young Jewish Saint*, trans.
Beverley Bie Brahic (New York: Columbia University Press, 2004); *Portrait de
Jacques Derrida en Jeune Saint Juif* (Paris: Galilée, 2001).

21. That conference was held at the Jewish Community Center in Paris,
December 3–5, 2000. "Abraham, the Other" was first given as a lecture at that
conference.

22. Gérard Bensussan's fine essay "The Last, The Remnant . . . (Derrida
and Rosenzweig)" ("Le dernier, le reste . . . [Derrida et Rosenzweig]"), which

comes just after Derrida's "Abraham, the Other" in *Judeities*, makes just this connection. See *Judeities: Questions for Jacques Derrida*, ed. Bettina Bergo, Joseph Cohen, and Raphael Zagury-Orly, trans. Bettina Bergo and Michael B. Smith (New York: Fordham University Press, 2007), 36–51; *Judéités: Questions pour Jacques Derrida*, ed. Joseph Cohen and Raphael Zagury-Orly (Paris: Galilée, 2003), 43–58.

23. Franz Kafka, "Abraham," trans. Clement Greenberg, in *Parables and Paradoxes*, bilingual ed. (New York: Schocken Books, 1969), 44, 45.

CHAPTER 8. "DON'T COUNT ME IN": DERRIDA'S REFRAINING

1. Simon Morgan Wortham, *Counter-institutions: Jacques Derrida and the Question of the University* (New York: Fordham University Press, 2006).

2. Martin Heidegger, *The Fundamental Concepts of Metaphysics: World, Finitude, Solitude*, trans. William McNeill and Nicholas Walker (Bloomington: Indiana University Press, 1995); *Die Grundbegriffe der Metaphysik: Welt—Endlichkeit—Einsamkeit* (Frankfurt am Main: Vittorio Klostermann, 1983).

3. Here is the original: "Entre mon monde, le 'mon monde'; ce que j'appelle 'mon monde' et il n'y en a d'autre pour moi, tout autre monde en faisant partie, entre mon monde et tout autre monde, il y a d'abord l'espace et le temps d'un différence infinie, d'une interruption incommensurable à toutes les tentatives de passage, de pont, d'isthme, de communication, de traduction, de trope et de transfert que le désir de monde ou le mal du monde, l'être en mal de monde tentera de poser, d'imposer, de proposer, de stabiliser. Il n'y a pas de monde, il n'y a que des îles."

4. If it is true that a translation totally changes the text, and I suppose, "so to speak," it is true, that makes me wish all the more that I could see the original French of the interviews in *A Taste for the Secret*. The Italian version is already a translation, which, no doubt, "totally changes the text," as does the English version I have been citing, *faut de mieux*.

CHAPTER 9. DERRIDA'S ETHICS OF IRRESPONSIBILIZATION; OR, HOW TO GET IRRESPONSIBLE, IN TWO EASY LESSONS

1. Matthew Arnold, *Friendship's Garland*, in *The Complete Prose Works of Matthew Arnold*, vol. 5, *Culture and Anarchy, with Friendship's Garland and Some Literary Essays*, ed. R. H. Super (Ann Arbor: University of Michigan Press. 1965), 42. The context of Arminius's adjuration explains what he means by *Geist* (37–42). Here is a bit of what he says: "We North-Germans have worked for 'Geist' in our way, by loving knowledge, by having the best-educated middle and lower class in the world. . . . Where have you [English] got it?—got it as a force, I mean, and not only in a few scattered individuals. Your common people is barbarous; in your middle class 'Ungeist' is rampant; and as for your

aristocracy, you know 'Geist' is forbidden by nature to flourish in an aristocracy" (41).

2. J. Hillis Miller, "The Poetics of Cyberspace: Two Ways to Get a Life," in *Contemporary Poetics*, ed. Louis Armand (Evanston, Ill.: Northwestern University Press, 2007), 256–78. Part of this paper, in a somewhat different form, was published in a special issue on automobility of *The Sociological Review* (2006): 193–207.

3. "[M]y attempt to marry by saying 'I will' is abortive if the woman says 'I will not'" (J. L. Austin, *How to Do Things with Words*, ed. J. O. Urmson and Marina Sbisà, 2d ed. [Oxford: Oxford University Press, 1980], 37). Earlier, on p. 5, Austin had the bridegroom saying "I do." A footnote by one of the editors, J. O. Urmson, observes that Austin made a mistake. The correct words, says Urmson, are "I will," but, says Urmson, "it is philosophically unimportant that it is a mistake" (5). I am not so sure about that. A slight difference in performative force exists between "I will" and "I do." The first is oriented toward the future, while the second is a promise oriented toward the present. One might even argue that the entire philosophical problematic of speech acts, especially of that paradigmatic speech act, the promise to marry, turns on the difference between "I do" and "I will." To commit another speech act: I'll bet I could do that arguing persuasively. Moreover, Austin and Urmson were wrong. Marriage ceremonies differ quite a bit, but a common one does use "I do" for both bride and bridegroom. Is that mistake about a putative mistake "philosophically unimportant"? I answer that details of language are always important for philosophy as well as for literary theory and literary criticism.

4. See J. Hillis Miller, *The Practice of Public Prayer* (New York: Columbia University Press, 1934). This J. Hillis Miller is the present author's father.

5. *http://www.english.udel.edu/dean/cangrand.html*. This gives Dante's Latin, with and English translation by James Marchand. All following quotations from this source will be taken from this site.

6. Marcel Proust, *Remembrance of Things Past*, trans. C. K. Scott Moncrieff, Terence Kilmartin, and Andreas Major (New York: Vintage, 1982), 3:180–86; *À la recherche du temps perdu*, ed. Jean-Yves Tadié, Antoine Campagnon, and Pierre-Edmond Robert (Paris: Gallimard, 1988–89), 3:687–93.

7. Patočka, "along with Vaclav Havel and Jiri Hajek, was one of three spokesmen for the Charta 77 human rights declaration of 1977. He died of a brain hemorrhage after eleven hours of police interrogation on 13 March 1977" (David Wills's preface, GD, vii). One must bear witness to this perfidy again and again. It would be irresponsible not to do so.

8. These page numbers refer to the French edition of Patočka's *Heretical Essays on the Philosophy of History*, which apparently includes some Czech words. I have not been able to consult this book.

9. Plato, *Phaedo*, trans. Harold North Fowler (Cambridge: Harvard University Press, 1966), 211. "Make music" translates *mousikon poiei*" (210).

10. The page number refers to the English translation David Wills used: Søren Kierkegaard, *Fear and Trembling, and Repetition*, vol. 6 of *Kierkegaard's Writings*, ed. and trans. Howard V. Hong and Edna H. Hong (Princeton, N.J.: Princeton University Press, 1983).

11. Franz Kafka, "A Little Fable," in *The Great Wall of China: Stories and Reflections*, trans. Willa and Edwin Muir (New York: Schocken, 1946), 260.

CHAPTER 10. DERRIDA'S POLITICS OF AUTOIMMUNITY

1. Linda J. Bilmes and Joseph E. Stiglitz, "The $10 Trillion Hangover: Paying the Price for Eight Years of Bush," *Harper's* 318, no. 1904 (January 2009): 31–35.

2. The French adds: "et cela fait partie de la folie dont nous parlions à l'instant [and that is part of the madness we have just talked about]." Derrida means the discussion a couple of pages earlier of the "madness of decision," in Kierkegaard's phrase, the fact that no rational justification can be given for a true decision.

3. *Destinerrance*, discussed in detail in Chapter 3 of this book, returns often in political contexts in Derrida's later work, for example, in analyses of the aporetic structure of the "apocalypse without apocalypse," the "Come!" that is never answered with a definitive unveiling or revelation, in "Of an Apocalyptic Tone Recently Adopted in Philosophy" (AT; TA).

4. The title was "I Am at War with Myself."

CHAPTER 11. TOUCHING DERRIDA TOUCHING NANCY

1. In the Foreword, Derrida calls Nancy's writings "one of the immense philosophic works of our time" (OT, x; LT, 10). I call Derrida's book on Nancy "immense and complex," not just in ironic echo of what Derrida says about Nancy's work, but as a confession that I have found *Le toucher*, in French and in English, immensely difficult. It has taken me several word by word, line by line, and page by page readings, in both languages, even to begin to think I may have a handle on this book. I shall return to Derrida's recommendation, in *Le toucher*, of such a procedure of reading as the only way to go.

2. Double or triple tangents exist, but Derrida in his pervasive use of the tangent motif does not, so far as I remember, take explicit account of that possibility. See http://en.wikipedia.org/wiki/Tangent:

> In plane geometry, a straight line is tangent to a curve, at some point, if both line and curve pass through the point with the same direction. Such a line is called the tangent line (or tangent). The tangent line is the best straight-line approximation to the curve at that point. The curve, at point P, has the same

slope as a tangent line passing through *P*. The slope of a tangent line can be approximated by a secant line. It is a mistake to think of tangents as lines which intersect a curve at only one single point. There are tangents which intersect curves at several points . . . , and there are non-tangential lines which intersect curves at only one single point. (Note that in the important case of a conic section, such as a circle, the tangent line will intersect the curve at only one point.) It is also possible for a line to be a *double* tangent, when it is tangent to the same curve at two distinct points. Higher numbers of tangent points are possible as well.

3. For Peggy Kamuf's translation of the title, see Jacques Derrida, *"Le toucher:* Touch / To Touch Him," trans. Peggy Kamuf, in *On the Work of Jean-Luc Nancy,* ed. Peggy Kamuf, *Paragraph* 16, no. 2 (July 1993): 122–57.

4. Alfred Lord Tennyson, "In Memoriam," XCV, ll. 33–40, in *The Poems of Tennyson,* ed. Christopher Ricks, 3 vols. (Berkeley: University of California Press, 1987), 2:413.

5. Jean-Luc Nancy, *Noli me tangere: On the Raising of the* Body, trans. Sarah Clift, Pascale-Anne Brault, and Michael Naas (New York: Fordham University Press, 2008), 31; *Noli me tangere: Essai sur la levée du corps* (Paris: Bayard, 2003), 55.

6. James Thurber, "The Car We Had to Push," *The Thurber Carnival* (New York: Harper & Brothers, n.d.), 182.

7. Thomas Hardy, *The Life and Death of the Mayor of Casterbridge: A Story of a Man of Character* (New York: Harper & Brothers, n.d.), 32. (This is vol. 5 of the Anniversary Edition of *The Writings of Thomas Hardy in Prose and Verse.* It is a reprint of the original Wessex Edition, with the same texts and pagination.)

8. James Joyce, *Ulysses* (New York: Modern Library, 1934), 145.

9. See J. Hillis Miller, *Literature as Conduct* (New York: Fordham University Press, 2005), 36–39.

10. Jean-Luc Nancy, *The Discourse of the Syncope: Logodaedalus,* trans. Saul Anton (Stanford, Calif.: Stanford University Press, 2008); Le *discours de la syncope: I. Logodaedalus* (Paris: Aubier-Flammarion, 1976).

11. See 36–38 in chap. 2, "The Story of a Kiss: Isabel's Decisions in *The Portrait of a Lady,"* in my *Literature as Conduct.*

12. Jean-Luc Nancy, *The Inoperative Community,* trans. Peter Conner, Lisa Garbus, Michael Holland, and Simona Sawhney (Minneapolis: University of Minnesota Press, 2001; *La communauté désoeuvrée* (Paris: Christian Bourgois, 2004); *La communauté affrontée* (Paris: Galilée, 2001).

13. Jean-Luc Nancy, *Being Singular Plural,* trans. Robert D. Richardson and Anne E. O'Byrne (Stanford, Calif.: Stanford University Press, 2000); *Être singulier pluriel* (Paris: Galilée, 1996).

14. In *The Conflagration of Community*, in progress.
15. Jean-Luc Nancy, *Corpus*, trans. Richard A. Rand (New York: Fordham University Press, 2008), 119, trans. modified; *Corpus*, 2d ed. (Paris: Métailié, 2006), 104.
16. In Jean-Luc Nancy, *A Finite Thinking*, ed. Simon Sparks, trans. Edward Bullard, Jonathan Derbyshire, and Simon Sparks (Stanford, Calif.: Stanford University Press, 2003), 25, 24 (Christine Irizarry has modified the translation); *Une pensée finie* (Paris: Galilée, 1990), 45, 44.
17. Martin Heidegger, "The Question Concerning Technology," in *The Question Concerning Technology and Other Essays*, trans. William Lovitt (New York: Harper & Row, 1977), 3–35; "Die Frage nach der Technik," in *Vorträge und Aufsätze* (Pfullingen: Günther Neske, 1954), 13–44.
18. Wallace Stevens, *The Collected Poems* (New York: Vintage, 1990), 10.
19. Ibid., 203.
20. Nancy, *Corpus*, 121; 105.
21. Ibid., 121, 104–5. The essay entitled "Corpus," trans. Claudette Sartiliot, in *The Birth to Presence*, trans. Brian Holmes et. al. (Stanford, Calif.: Stanford University Press, 1993), 207, has a quite different version of this final sentence. This essay is a short early draft of what became the book *Corpus*.
22. This is the title Nancy gave a collection of essays he assembled for translation into English. See note 21.
23. Jean-Luc Nancy, *Dis-Enclosure: The Deconstruction of Christianity*, trans. Bettina Bergo, Gabriel Malenfant, and Michael B. Smith (New York: Fordham University Press, 2008; *La Déclosion: (Déconstruction du christianisme, 1)* (Paris: Galilée, 2005).
24. I have, in an as yet unpublished essay, discussed the way feminist appeals to "the materiality of the body" may sometimes entrap their authors once more in the sexist patriarchal traditions they are trying to contest. An example is the resistance Judith Butler reports, in *Bodies That Matter: On the Discursive Limits of Sex* (New York: Routledge, 1993), ix, to her theory of the body. Women in her audiences often asked, "But what about the materiality of the body, *Judy*?" This assumes, contra Nancy, that such a thing as "the" body exists. Examples of more careful interrogations of "the" body by feminists include, in addition to Butler's book, Deleuzian books and essays such as Elizabeth Grosz, *Volatile Bodies: Towards a Corporeal Feminism* (Bloomington: University of Indiana Press, 1994); Rosi Braidotti, "Toward a New Nomadism: Feminist Deleuzian Tracks; or Metaphysics and Metabolism," in *Gilles Deleuze and the Theater of Philosophy*, ed. Constantine V. Boundas and Dorothea Olkowski (New York: Routledge, 1994); and ibid., *Nomadic Subjects: Embodiment and Sexual Difference in Contemporary Feminist Theory* (New York: Columbia University Press, 1994). For a sympathetic critique of these, see

chap. 2, "Towards a Feminist Philosophy of Mind," in Eleanor Kaufman's forthcoming book, *Gilles Deleuze: Dialectic, Structure, and Being.* No feminist books or essays that I have encountered, however, confront either Derrida's *Le toucher* or Nancy's work on the body and its (non)touchability, for example, his *Corpus.*

25. Animals (all animals?), argues Heidegger in a lengthy development in *The Fundamental Concepts of Metaphysics: World, Finitude, Solitude,* trans. William McNeill and Nicholas Walker (Bloomington: Indiana University Press, 1995); *Die Grundbegriffe der Metaphysik. Welt—Endlichkeit—Einsamkeit* (Frankfurt am Main: Vittorio Klostermann, 1992), are *weltarm* (poor in world), while man is *weltbilden* (world making). The stone is *weltlos,* worldless. In *Of Spirit: Heidegger and the Question,* Derrida had already discussed Heidegger's distinctions at length.

26. Jason Smith, "The 'pure materiality of the Fact': Studies in Literature and Politics (Husserl, Derrida, Nancy)," Ph.D. dissertation in Comparative Literature, University of California at Irvine, March 2006.

27. David Crystal, *Language and the Internet* (Cambridge: Cambridge University Press, 2001): "It is possible to do calculus homework and have tinysex at the same time, if you type fast enough" (187).

28. Derrida's fantasy has an uncanny analogy with the motive behind the invention of a big stainless-steel machine shown on television in December 2007. Playing on the knowledge people have that an erased hard drive is not really erased, that the information stored on it may be retrieved, this machine was designed to pulverize old computers, along with their hard drives. Big letters on the side of this machine say DECONSTRUCTION. This is a new proof that Derrida invented a word the world needs, even if common usage, as in this case, is foreign to what Derrida meant by the word.

29. Jean-Luc Nancy, *Le poids d'une pensée* (Sainte-Foy, Québec: Le Griffon d'argile and Les Presses Universitaires de Grenoble, 1991); the preface, "The Weight of a Thought," is translated in *The Gravity of Thought,* trans. François Raffoul and Gregory Recco (Atlantic Highlands, N.J.: Humanities Press, 1997), 75–84.

30. J. L. Austin, *How to Do Things with Words,* ed. J. O. Urmson and Marina Sbisà, 2d ed. (Oxford: Oxford University Press, 1980), 7.

31. Jean-Luc Nancy, "Psyche," trans. Emily McVarish, in Nancy, *The Birth to Presence,* trans. Brian Holmes and others (Stanford, Calif.: Stanford University Press, 1993), 393; "Psyche," *Première Livraisson,* no. 16, 1978.

32. As also happens systematically in the "Restitutions" section of *The Truth in Painting (La vérité en peinture)* (TP, 255–382; VP2, 291–436). I remember how difficult it was to follow the change in speakers when Derrida presented this part of the book orally in seminar form at Yale. The preliminary

note to the printed version does not help much. Derrida calls the essay a "'polylogue' (for n + 1—female—voices)" (TP, 256; VP, 292). One would like to know how many is n.

33. *A Finite Thinking*, 211–44; 147–95.

34. Maurice Blanchot, *The Unavowable Community*, trans. Pierre Joris (Barrytown, N.Y.: Station Hill Press, 1988); *La communauté inavouable* (Paris: Minuit, 1983).

35. Jean-Luc Nancy, *The Experience of Freedom*, trans. Bridget McDonald (Stanford, Calif.: Stanford University Press, 1993); *L'expérience de la liberté* (Paris: Galilée, 1988).

36. Austin, *How to Do Things with Words*, 20.

37. Wallace Stevens, "Parochial Theme," in *Collected Poems*, 192.

38. See n. 11, above.

39. For recent commentary on Derrida's aspiration "to leave traces in the history of the French language" (LLF, 37), see Michael Naas, *Derrida From Now On* (New York: Fordham University Press, 2008), 3–6.

40. Franz Kafka, "The Hunter Gracchus [Two Fragments]," trans. Stanley Corngold, in *Kafka's Selected Stories* (New York: Norton, 2007), 109–13.

41. Nancy, *Noli me tangere*, 13; 25.

42. Here are Derrida's exact words, the words that apparently nettled Nancy and seemed to him impertinent, so impertinent that he needed to believe he might persuade Derrida that Christianity is deconstructible and that he, Nancy, has done that: "What Nancy announces today under the title of 'deconstruction of Christianity' will no doubt be the test of a dechristianizing of the world: no doubt as necessary, and fatal, as it is impossible. Almost by definition, one can only acknowledge this [*qu'en prendre acte*]. Only Christianity can do this work, that is, undo it while doing it. Heidegger, too, Heidegger already, has only succeeded in failing at this. Dechristianization will be a Christian victory" (OT, 54, trans. modified; LT, 68). Well, if the great Heidegger cannot do it, it is unlikely that Nancy can do it either, "immense" as his work is.

43. Nancy, *Noli me tangere*, 110, trans. modified; 25–26.

44. Franz Kafka, "Abraham," in Kafka, *Parables and Paradoxes*, bilingual ed. (New York: Schocken Books, 1969), 44, 45.

45. Here is part of what Wikipedia says about Midrash: "Many different exegetical methods are employed to derive deeper meaning from text. This is not limited to the traditional thirteen textual tools attributed to the Tanna Rabbi Ishmael, which are used in the interpretation of *halakha* (Jewish law). Presence of superfluous words or letters, chronology of events, parallel narratives or other textual anomalies are often a springboard for interpretation of segments of Biblical text. In many cases, a dialogue is expanded manifold:

handfuls of lines in the Biblical narrative may become long philosophical discussions. It is unclear whether the Midrash assumes these dialogues took place in reality or if this refers only to subtext or religious implication" (*http://en .wikipedia.org/wiki/Midrash*). This makes Midrash sound like Derrida's procedures in *Le toucher*, all right.

CHAPTER 12. ABSOLUTE MOURNING: IT IS JACQUES YOU MOURN FOR

1. Mourning in Derrida has also, not surprisingly, received a good bit of attention from Derrida scholars. See, for one admirable example, David Farrell Krell, *The Purest of Bastards: Works of Mourning, Art, and Affirmation in the Thought of Jacques Derrida* (University Park: Pennsylvania State University Press, 2000).

2. See Sigmund Freud, "Mourning and Melancholia" (1917), trans. Joan Riviere, *Collected Papers*, 4 vols., ed. Joan Riviere (New York: Basic Books, 1959), 4:152–70, and the revised translation in Sigmund Freud, *The Standard Edition of the Complete Psychological Works*, ed. James Strachey, with Anna Freud, Alix Strachey, and Alan Tyson (London: Vintage; The Hogarth Press and the Institute of Psychoanalysis, 2001), 14:243–58.

3. Nicolas Abraham and Maria Torok, "Introjecter-incorporer: deuil *ou* mélancolie," *Nouvelle Revue de Psychanalyse* 6 (Autumn 1972).

4. Jean-Luc Nancy, "Psyche," trans. Emily McVarish, in *The Birth to Presence*, trans. Brian Holmes and others (Stanford, Calif.: Stanford University Press, 1993), 393. The French original first appeared, as "Psyche" (without accent), in *Première Livraisson*, no. 16 (Paris: 1978).

5. Jean-Luc Nancy, "The Intruder" in Nancy, *Corpus*, trans. Richard Rand (New York: Fordham University Press, 2008), 161–70; *L'intrus* (Paris: Galilée, 2000).

6. Paul de Man, "Autobiography as De-Facement," in *The Rhetoric of Romanticism* (New York: Columbia University Press, 1984), 81.

7. I am echoing here Gerard Manley Hopkins's "Spring and Fall: To a Young Child," *Poems*, ed. W. H. Gardner and N. H. MacKenzie, 4th ed. (London: Oxford University Press, 1967), 88–89. The first two lines are: "Márgarét, áre you grieving / Over Goldengrove unleaving?" The last line is "It is Margaret you mourn for." I retain Hopkins's diacritical marks in the first line. That Jacques Derrida's widow is named Marguerite is a dissonant accident. I hope this will not forbid my using a variant of Hopkins's formulation to express the way mourning for something or someone outside oneself is really mourning for oneself.

8. Franz Kafka, "The Hunter Gracchus [Two Fragments]," trans. Stanley Corngold, in *Kafka's Selected Stories* (New York: Norton, 2007), 111.

9. Ibid., 111, 112.

10. See footnote 25 of Chapter 11 in this book.

Index